GREENBOOK®

Guide To

The Enesco

PRECIOUS MOMENTS®

Collection

Ninth Edition

The Most Respected Guides to Popular Collectibles & Their After Market Values

Old Coach at Main, Box 515
East Setauket, New York 11733
516.689.8466
FAX 516.689.8177

This paper is recycled, can be recycled, and is made from a renewable resource.

ISBN 0-923628-19-3

GREENBOOK TRUMARKET PRICES published in *The GREENBOOK Guide To The Enesco PRECIOUS MOMENTS Collection*, *The GREENBOOK Guide To DEPARTMENT 56*, *The GREENBOOK Guide To HALLMARK Collectibles*, and *The GREENBOOK Guide To ENESCO Collectibles* are obtained from retailers and collectors. Enesco Corporation, Department 56, and Hallmark Cards, Inc. verify factual information only and are not consulted or involved in any way in determining GREENBOOK TRUMARKET PRICES.

The GREENBOOK would like to thank -

SAM BUTCHER, for the use of his copyrighted line drawings.

ENESCO, for assisting in the compilation of the factual information contained in this Guide.

THE PRECIOUS MOMENTS CHAPEL, for assisting in the compilation of the factual information contained in this Guide.

The DEALERS and COLLECTORS across the country who supply us with information including secondary market status and prices.

NOTE FROM THE PUBLISHER

Finally - a redhead in the Collection!

Period. The end. Just kidding ...

CHANGES - SOME IN RESPONSE TO YOUR INPUT

My husband says I'm spoiled. I've worked for myself for so long I basically always get my own way. Except this time. We've added Line Art to the GREENBOOK Listings. We did it with me kicking and screaming. I like the at-a-glance format. Given the opportunity to do my spiel at shows or events, I always go to extremes and say "If you wanted to know all the Retired figurines that begin with the letter 'B' you can find the answer in seconds." That's the advantage of the heavily cross-referenced GREENBOOK format. Of course, that's assuming you understand how to use the Guide. So, in a world where VCRs are blinking "12:00," I've made this concession. There are some tradeoffs however - the size of the Line Art is directly proportional to the length of time a piece is/has been available. The Guide must remain a *portable* source of all the facts!

Because of our publication date, combined with a price change the following year, we missed tracking interim increases in Suggested Retail Price in 1987. Thank you to Lori Holle for 1) alerting us to this, and, 2) the hours of research she invested to supply us with the correct information.

Another change we've made is one we've tossed around for quite some time; that is using the cost of membership dues as the base price for the Symbols of Membership. So now the Suggested Retail Price column for these pieces will reflect the cost of joining the Clubs that year. But if a piece is currently available, we will use the "comparable value" suggested by Enesco for GREENBOOK TRUMARKET PRICE.

A WALLET SIZE WOULD HAVE BEEN APPROPRIATE

Many collectors are questioning the acquisition of the "Sammy's Circus" vignette with a $200.00 price tag. Retailers tell me it's a hard sell. And I can see why. It's the same reason you don't send an 11" x 14" size of your child's school picture to family and friends.

With the pieces named after Mr. Butcher's grandchildren, they're just cute figurines competing with zillions of other cute figurines on the market. Inspirational titles would have made them a) Precious Moments, and, b) every grandparent's grandchildren. Think about it - what grandparent thinks someone else's grandchildren - even Sam Butcher's - are cuter than their own. I was going to say, "In my opinion," but actually I think it's pretty much fact, people purchase Precious Moments for the titles. That's the magic. The magic is missing from "Sammy's Circus." (and Noah's Ark and Sugar Town)

I MAY BE REPETITIOUS BUT AT LEAST I'M CONSISTENT

Apparently I'm not the only person who sailed through Logic 101. For all of us out there, can someone please explain why Sam is counted four times in the "13 + 1" population of Sugar Town?

AN ENTERTAINING WAY TO BE INFORMED

We've added a new feature by GREENBOOK Precious Moments Historian, Sheryl J. Williams - a PM Glossary including terms you've probably used hoping someone wouldn't ask you to explain exactly what they meant. Sheryl has a way with words and uses expressions that tickle me. Occasionally I pick one up and try it out a time or two. For example, rather than say someone is upset or perturbed, Sheryl will say they "have their undies in a major knot." I knew my 5 year-old lost something in the translation when I heard her telling Grandma Daddy was mad and had a knot in his undies.

In addition to her status as noted collector and author, Sheryl makes a mean chocolate chip cookie. As a matter of fact, they are often the currency of her bribes. Around here it usually works as none of us have a reputation as great chefs. Not naming names, let me just say one of us once made blueberry muffins with Concord grapes - realizing the error when the batter crunched.

OLD BUSINESS

The minute the ink hits the paper, there's something in the Guide that could be revised. In an effort to keep the Guide up-to-the-minute we produce an update bookmark when anything of major significance happens. Depending on when you purchased your Guide, an update may or may not be slipped inside the front cover. In any case, to receive an update, free of charge, send us a stamped, self-addressed business size envelope with "PM update" written in the lower left-hand corner.

IN CLOSING

Fifteen years and it seems like yesterday. Twenty-one dime store variety bisque figurines changed collecting, retailing, my life, and, if you're reading this, possibly yours, forever. Quite frankly, Precious Moments has enabled me to make a very nice living doing something I love. Although GREENBOOK has gone on to do four additional guides, the Precious Moment Guide is the flagship book. Sometimes I look around at a sports stadium filled with fans and think this many people own and use the Guide. For someone still trying to decide what to do when they grow up, it's overwhelming. But I'm also selfish enough to want it to continue. That's why I voice concern over things like Sammy's Circus and Sugar Town. Or would urge collectors who care about secondary market performance to campaign for "drop-dead" retirements. (Check out the TRUMARKET PRICES on "Faith Is A Victory" or " I'm So Glad You Fluttered Into My Life.")

Next year GREENBOOK will celebrate 10 years with a surprise and a very special 10th Anniversary Edition of this Guide.

Who would have ever guessed?

Louise Patterson Langenfeld
Editor & Publisher

TABLE OF CONTENTS

INTRODUCTION

The GREENBOOK provides information about The Enesco PRECIOUS MOMENTS Collection in the form of GREENBOOK TRUMARKET PRICES™ plus factual information describing each piece. The factual information includes:

- Inspirational Title
- Descriptive Title
- Type of Product
- Enesco Item Number
- Year of Issue
- Edition Size
- Issue Price when first issued as well as each year the Annual Production Symbol is/was changed
- Size
- Certification
- Is it individually numbered?
- Is it part of a set or series?
- Annual Production Symbol

The factual information is compiled by the GREENBOOK with assistance from Enesco. It appears in the Guide in many different forms making it possible for a new collector as well as the experienced collector to identify the pieces in their collection or the pieces they wish to buy or sell. The inclusion of GREENBOOK TRUMARKET PRICES, as reported by retailers and collectors, make it possible to determine the value of each piece.

Market prices are important for insurance purposes as well as buying and selling.

The GREENBOOK also affords collectors an opportunity to become familiar with the entire PRECIOUS MOMENTS Collection - not just the pieces that are currently available at Suggested Retail and displayed in stores. Current, Retired, Suspended, Discontinued, Annuals, Two-Year Collectibles, Limited Editions, and earlier issue figurines, plates, bells, musicals, ornaments, etc. are included.

The GREENBOOK's exclusive **ARTCHART**™ contains authorized reproductions of 707 line drawings. In addition, it lists the Enesco Item Number for the figurine, plate, bell, musical, ornament, doll, thimble, frame, candle climber, box, night light, egg, plaque, wreath, medallion, stocking hanger, tree topper, and wall hanging derived from each drawing. It is noted, also, if each piece is a Dated Annual, an Annual that is not dated, a Two-Year Collectible, a Limited Edition, Retired, Suspended, has a special Inspirational Title or is derived from only a portion of the line drawing.

The ARTCHART is designed to provide a graphic illustration of how individual pieces relate to each other and to the entire Collection as well as add to the fun of collecting PRECIOUS MOMENTS.

The GREENBOOK **ALPHA-LOG** lists PRECIOUS MOMENTS Titles alphabetically. The titles are cross-referenced with the GREENBOOK ARTCHART Number and the

Enesco Item Number for each piece by product type. In addition, the ALPHA-LOG notes if each piece is a Dated Annual, an Annual, a Two-Year Collectible, a Limited Edition, Retired, or Suspended.

Many times certain pieces become important as part of a group. PRECIOUS MOMENTS groups that have become important are included in the **QUIKREFERENCE™ SECTION**: The Chapel Exclusives, The "Original 21," Limited Editions, Retired pieces, Suspended pieces, Re-introduced pieces, pieces that have moved from the Suspended list to the Retired list, Dated Annuals, Annuals that are not dated, Two-Year Collectibles, The Enesco PRECIOUS MOMENTS Birthday Club pieces, and The Enesco PRECIOUS MOMENTS Collectors' Club pieces.

In addition, the OUTLINE OF ANNUALS Section groups annual collectibles by series and product type. The OUTLINE OF THE SERIES Section itemizes the individual pieces that comprise each series. There's a **QUIKREFERENCE CALENDAR** as well. It's a summary, by year, of Retired, Suspended, and Annual pieces.

The **GREENBOOK LISTINGS™** are where specific factual information as well as GREENBOOK TRUMARKET PRICES for each collectible can be found. GREENBOOK Listings are in Enesco Item Number order. Enesco Item Numbers can be found on the understamp of most pieces produced from 1982 to the present. If you don't know the Enesco Item Number, but you do know the Inspirational Title, use the ALPHA-LOG to obtain the Enesco Item Number. If you don't know the Enesco Item Number or the Inspirational Title, use the ARTCHART to obtain the Enesco Item Number.

Since mid-1981 Enesco has indicated when PRECIOUS MOMENTS collectibles were produced by including an Annual Production Symbol as part of the understamp. Pieces crafted prior to 1981 have no Annual Production Symbol and have become known as "No Marks."

The GREENBOOK lists the year of issue, issue price (suggested retail) and a GREENBOOK TRUMARKET PRICE for each change in Annual Production Symbol.

Knowing issue prices for each PRECIOUS MOMENTS collectible when it was first produced as well as the current issue price or suggested retail can also be important when investment performance is evaluated. Many PRECIOUS MOMENTS collectibles have been produced for years and collectors who purchased earlier production pieces are enjoying an increase in value even though the piece is still current.

A very common error made by collectors is to mistake the copyright date for the year of issue because the copyright date appears on the understamp written out as ©19XX. In order to determine what year your piece was produced, you must refer to the Annual Production Symbol, not the © date.

In addition to indicating when pieces were produced by an Annual Production Symbol on the understamp, Enesco periodically retires and suspends individual pieces. As a result, the GREENBOOK contains nine different classifications of availability or Market Status.

continued ...

They are:

PRIMARY Piece available from retailers at issue price.

SECONDARY Piece *not* generally available from retailers at issue price.

RETIRED/PRIMARY Piece with specific Enesco Item Number will never be produced again. Piece still available from retailers at issue price.

RETIRED/SECONDARY Piece with specific Enesco Item Number will never be produced again. Piece *not* generally available from retailers at issue price.

SUSPENDED/PRIMARY Piece with specific Enesco Item Number not currently being produced but may be re-sculptured and re-introduced in the future. Piece available from retailers at issue price.

SUSPENDED/SECONDARY Piece with specific Enesco Item Number not currently being produced but may be re-sculptured and re-introduced in the future. Piece *not* generally available from retailers at issue price.

SUSPENDED/RETIRED/SECONDARY Piece with specific Enesco Item Number was suspended, re-sculptured and re-introduced, and subsequently retired. Piece *not* generally available from retailers at issue price.

DISCONTINUED/PRIMARY Production ceased on piece with specific Enesco Item Number. Piece still available from retailers at issue price.

DISCONTINUED/SECONDARY Production ceased on piece with specific Enesco Item Number. Piece *not* generally available from retailers at issue price.

The nine Market Status classifications have a major effect on the value of PRECIOUS MOMENTS collectibles. This is reflected in the GREENBOOK TRUMARKET PRICE.

Factors other than current availability that affect secondary market prices include rarity, year of issue, condition, and general appeal.

Because there are so many factors based on individual judgements, and because prices can vary from one section of the country to another, GREENBOOK TRUMARKET PRICES **are never an absolute number**. Use them as a benchmark. Three questions that come up frequently in regard to their effect on GREENBOOK TRUMARKET PRICES are 1) boxes, 2) Sam Butcher's signature on the piece, and 3) variations:

1) GREENBOOK TRUMARKET Prices are for pieces "Mint in Box." In general, the newer the piece the more important it is to have the box. On hard-to-find, scarce, older pieces, not having a box usually does not subtract significantly from the GREENBOOK TRUMARKET PRICE. On the other hand, pieces that are easier to come by are a tough sell without the box, because one with a box can always be found.

2) In the past we've said Sam Butcher signing a piece does not add appreciably to its GREENBOOK TRUMARKET PRICE, but that it does vary with the rarity of the piece. In our experience many collectors expect that a Sam Butcher signature will add hundreds or even thousands to the value of a piece. To date, a Sam Butcher signature has added in the range of $25 to $75 to the market price, depending on the piece.

3) As with all things made by human hands, PRECIOUS MOMENTS porcelains exist with variations. Some differences occur naturally as a result of firing and painting. There are also pieces with variations caused by production changes or human error. Again, an error must be highly visible or be an announced production change before secondary market prices are affected appreciably.

The **GREENBOOK GIFT GIVER'S GUIDE™** contains currently available pieces that are appropriate as gifts for special people and special occasions. Items in bold are 1994 annuals and historically have only been readily available at issue price that calendar year.

Because they are "Collections within a Collection," **SUGAR TOWN, TWO BY TWO,** and **SAMMY'S CIRCUS** have been done as "Guides within a Guide."

INSURING YOUR PRECIOUS MOMENTS COLLECTIBLES is a brief overview of the topic. By no means should it substitute for discussing the subject with your agent, rather it empowers you with a little bit of knowledge helping you to ask the right questions of your insurance professional.

GLOSSARY

by GREENBOOK Precious Moments Historian, Sheryl J. Williams

DSR -

A DSR is a "Distinguished Service Retailer." DSR status is the highest level which a Precious Moments retailer can achieve. The DSR program replaced what was once known as the "Collectors' Center." DSR stores are the only stores which can redeem Members Only coupons for members of the Enesco Precious Moments Collectors' Club or the Enesco Precious Moments Birthday Club. In addition to handling these special orders, these stores have access to the entire Precious Moments porcelain bisque collection. DSR stores also participate in special events during the year.

Special Event -

Each year, DSR stores are invited to participate in a Special Events Program. Retailers choosing to participate in this program can hold their event at any time during the year although the bulk of the Precious Moments Retail Events weekends are held in the Spring. At these events, a special piece is made available to collectors. These pieces are limited to the year of introduction.

In the Fall, a special ornament weekend event is also held. At these events, a special ornament is made available to collectors. These ornaments are limited to the year of introduction.

Chapel Exclusive -

A very special collection within the Enesco Precious Moments Collection is a group of figurines and ornaments created by special agreement between Sam Butcher and Enesco. This special group of pieces is sold only through the Precious Moments Chapel in Carthage, Missouri. With the exception of the Christmas pieces, all the figurines in this little collection are unique, in that they depict particular works of Precious Moments art which can only be seen at the Chapel. For example, the first piece released was the Chapel figurine itself, which features the Chapel with "Timmy" the angel standing beside it. When the "Chapel Exclusive" figurines were first introduced, they could only be purchased by actually visiting the Chapel and buying the piece in the Gift Shop. However, because many people wanted the Chapel pieces, but couldn't necessarily travel to the Chapel each time a new piece came out, the policy was changed, and the "Chapel Exclusive" figurines and ornaments can now be ordered through the Chapel's mail order department (1-800-543-7975). The Precious Moment Chapel Gift Shops carry a complete line of porcelains, but the Chapel Exclusives are the only ones which can be accessed by mail order. This was done in order that the relationship between the collectors and their local retailers be preserved.

Spring Catalog Exclusive -

Beginning in 1993, Enesco introduced a new program featuring a figurine exclusively for retailers who purchased and distributed the spring Enesco advertising catalog for the Enesco Precious Moments Collection. Allocations of these figurines were determined by the number of catalogs a store purchased. "Happiness Is At Our Fingertips" was the first piece introduced as a "Spring Catalog Exclusive."

... continued on page 86

GREENBOOK ARTCHART™

The GREENBOOK ARTCHART contains authorized reproductions of 707 line drawings. In addition, it lists the Enesco Item Number for the figurine, plate, bell, musical, ornament, doll, thimble, frame, candle climber, box, night light, egg, plaque, wreath, medallion, stocking hanger, tree topper, and wall hanging derived from each drawing. It is noted, also, if each piece is a Dated Annual, an Annual that is not dated, a Two-Year Collectible, a Limited Edition, Retired, Suspended, has a special Inspirational Title, or is derived from only a portion of the line drawing.

The ARTCHART is designed to provide a graphic illustration of how individual pieces relate to each other and to the entire Collection as well as add to the fun of collecting PRECIOUS MOMENTS.

#	DESCRIPTION	FIG	PLT	BELL	MUSC	ORN	DOLL	THMBL	FRAME	CNDL CLMB	BOX	OTHER
1	Boy with Teddy	E-1372B E-9278	**E-9275**	**E-5208**		**E-5631***			**E-7170**		**E-9280**	
2	Girl with Bunny	E-1372G E-9279 *104531*	**E-9276**	**E-5209**		**E-5632***			**E-7171**		**E-9281**	
3	Boy with Black Eye	E-1373B										
4	Girl with Doll & Candle	E-1373G										
5	Girl with Goose	E-1374G *520322*	*E-7174*			522910						528617 Egg
6	Boy & Girl on Seesaw	E-1375A										
7	Boy & Girl with Bluebirds	**E-1375B**										
8	Boy & Girl Sitting/Stump	E-1376	*E-5215*			522929						
9	Boy Leading Lamb	**E-1377A**										
10	Boy Helping Lamb	**E-1377B**										
11	Boy with Turtle	**E-1379A**										
12	Boy with Report Card	**E-1379B**		E-5211								
13	Indian Boy	E-1380B										
14	Indian Girl	E-1380G										
15	Boy Patching World	**E-1381** (Also see ART CHART NUMBER 611)										
16	Boy Holding Lamb	**E-2010**		**E-5620**		E-6120						
17	Boy & Girl Playing Angels	**E-2012**			**E-2809**							
18	Boy & Girl Reading Book	**E-2013**			**E-2808**							
19	Boy with Dog	E-1374B										
20	Girl with Puppies	E-1378										

BOLD = Suspended *Italics* = Limited Edition Shaded Area = Retired ◆ = Two-Year Collectible

Boxed = Dated Annual Rounded Box = Annual * = Special Inspirational Title <u>or</u> piece derived from a portion of the drawing

1
Jesus Loves Me
* Baby's First Christmas
2
Jesus Loves Me
*Baby's First Christmas
3
Smile, God Loves You
4
Jesus Is The Light
5
Make A Joyful Noise
6
Love Lifted Me
7
Prayer Changes Things
8
Love One Another
9
He Leadeth Me
10
He Careth For You
11
Love Is Kind
12
REPORT CARD
God Understands
13
O, How I Love Jesus
14
His Burden Is Light
15
Jesus Is The Answer
16
We Have Seen His Star
17
Jesus Is Born
18
Unto Us A Child Is Born
19
Praise The Lord Anyhow
20
God Loveth
A Cheerful Giver

#	DESCRIPTION	FIG	PLT	BELL	MUSC	ORN	DOLL	THMBL	FRAME	CNDL CLMB	BOX	OTHER
21	Boy with Manger Baby	E-2011										
22	Nativity Set	E-2800 E-2395 also includes a camel, donkey, and Three Kings	*E-5646*		**E-2810***	**E-5633***						
23	Angels in Chariot	**E-2801**										
24	Boy Giving Toy Lamb	**E-2802**			E-2806							
25	Boy Kneel Manger/Crown	**E-2803**			**E-2807**							
26	Boy on Globe with Teddy	**E-2804**										
27	Boy in Santa Cap with Dog	E-2805										
28	Rocking Cradle	**E-3104**				E-0518 E-5392			**E-0521**			
29	Boy with Bible/Crutches	**E-3105**										
30	Mother Needlepointing	E-3106	*E-5217*	**E-7181**	E-7182	E-0514	E-2850	13293	**E-7241**			
31	Boy Holding Cat/Dog	E-3107										
32	Girl Rocking Cradle	**E-3108**	*E-9256*		E-5204							
33	Grandma in Rocker	E-3109	*E-7173*	**E-7183**	**E-7184**	E-0516		13307	**E-7242**			
34	Boy Sharing with Puppy	E-3110B										
35	Girl Sharing with Puppy	E-3110G										
36	Girl Helper	E-3111										
37	Boy Writing in Sand/Girl	E-3113										
38	Bride and Groom	E-3114	**E-5216**	**E-7179**	E-7180	**E-2385***			**E-7166**		**E-7167**	
39	Boy/Girl Angels on Cloud	E-3115 E-0001									Plaques } Night Light }	E-0102 E-0202 **E-5207***
40	Boy Carving/Tree for Girl	E-3116										

BOLD = Suspended *Italics* = Limited Edition Shaded Area = Retired ◆ = Two-Year Collectible

Boxed = Dated Annual Rounded Box = Annual * = Special Inspirational Title or piece derived from a portion of the drawing

21
Come Let Us Adore Him
22
Come Let Us Adore Him
*4 main pieces
23
Jesus Is Born
24
Christmas Is A
Time To Share
25
Crown Him Lord Of All
26
Peace On Earth
27
Wishing You A Season
Filled With Joy
28
Blessed Are The
Pure In Heart
29
He Watches Over Us All
30
Mother Sew Dear
31
Blessed Are
The Peacemakers
32
The Hand That
Rocks The Future
33
The Purr-fect Grandma
34
Loving Is Sharing
35
Loving Is Sharing
36
Be Not Weary
In Well Doing
37
Thou Art Mine
38
The Lord Bless You
And Keep You
*Our First Christmas Together
39
But Love Goes On Forever
*My Guardian Angel
40
Thee I Love

#	DESCRIPTION	FIG	PLT	BELL	MUSC	ORN	DOLL	THMBL	FRAME	CNDL CLMB	BOX	OTHER
41	Boy Pulling Wagon w/Girl	E-3117										
42	Boy with Books	**E-3119**										
43	Girl with Box of Kittens	**E-3120**				E-0534						
44	Boy Jogging with Dog	E-3112										
45	Girl with Fry Pan	E-3118										
46	Boy Graduate	**E-4720**		**E-7175**					**E-7177**			
47	Girl Graduate	E-4721		**E-7176**					**E-7178**			
48	Girl with Piggy Bank	**E-4722**										
49	Boy Reading Holy Bible	**E-4723**										
50	Christening	E-4724	**E-7172**									
51	Choir Boys w/Bandages	**E-4725**			**E-4726**							
52	Sad Boy with Teddy	**E-5200**										
53	Boy Helping Friend	**E-5201**										
54	Lemonade Stand	**E-5202**										
55	Boy with Dog on Stairs	**E-5203**										
56	Boy Angel on Cloud				**E-5205**	**E-5627***				**E-6118*** (set)	Plaque}	**E-6901****
57	Girl Angel on Cloud				**E-5206**	**E-5628***						
58	Girl Praying in Field	**E-7155***		**E-5210**								
59	Boy in Dad's Duds/Dog	E-5212				**E-0515***						
60	Girl with Goose in Lap	**E-5213**										

BOLD = Suspended *Italics* = Limited Edition Shaded Area = Retired ◆ = Two-Year Collectible

Boxed = Dated Annual Rounded Box = Annual * = Special Inspirational Title or piece derived from a portion of the drawing

41
Walking By Faith
42
It's What's Inside
That Counts
43
To Thee With Love
44
God's Speed
45
Eggs Over Easy
46
The Lord Bless You
And Keep You
47
The Lord Bless You
And Keep You
48
Love Cannot Break
A True Friendship
49
Peace Amid The Storm
50
Rejoicing With You
51
Peace On Earth
52
Bear Ye
One Another's Burdens
53
Love Lifted Me
54
Thank You For Coming
To My Ade
55
Let Not The Sun Go
Down Upon Your Wrath
56
My Guardian Angel
*But Love Goes On Forever
**Collection Plaque
57
My Guardian Angel
*But Love Goes On Forever
58
Prayer Changes Things
*Thanking Him For You
59
To A Special Dad
*w/o dog
60
God Is Love

#	DESCRIPTION	FIG	PLT	BELL	MUSC	ORN	DOLL	THMBL	FRAME	CNDL CLMB	BOX	OTHER
61	Boy & Girl/Praying/Table	**E-5214**										
62	Manger with Child	**E-5619**										
63	Donkey	E-5621										
64	Shepherd			**E-5623**		**E-5630***						
65	Three Kings on Camels	E-5624 108243										
66	Three Kings	E-5635	*E-0538*		**E-0520**	**E-5634**						
67	Angel with Trumpet	E-5636 520268			E-5645	113980						
68	Angel with Flashlight	E-5637										
69	Cow with Bell	E-5638										
70	Boy Angel Praying w/Harp	**E-5639**										
71	Girl Angel Praying w/Harp	**E-5640**										
72	Follow Me Angel w/3 Kings	**E-5641**										
73	Boy Angel and Knight				**E-5642**							
74	Two Section Wall	E-5644										
75	Mikey						**E-6214B**					
76	Debbie						**E-6214G**					
77	Praying Angel			E-5622		E-5629						
78	Boy on Telephone	PM-811										
79	Boy Angel Playing Trumpet					**E-2343**				**E-2344** (pair)		
80	Boy in Pajamas w/Teddy	**E-2345**										

BOLD = Suspended *Italics* = Limited Edition Shaded Area = Retired ◆ = Two-Year Collectible

Boxed = Dated Annual Rounded Box = Annual * = Special Inspirational Title or piece derived from a portion of the drawing

61 Prayer Changes Things
62 O Come Let Us Adore Him
63 Donkey
64 Jesus Is Born *Unto Us A Child Is Born
65 They Followed The Star
66 Wee Three Kings
67 Rejoice O Earth
Rejoice
68 The Heavenly Light
69 Cow
70 Isn't He Wonderful
71 Isn't He Wonderful
72 They Followed The Star
Follow Me
73 Silent Knight
74 Two Section Wall
75 Mikey
76 Debbie
77 Let The Heavens Rejoice
78 Hello Lord, It's Me Again
Dear Jon
79 Joy To The World
80 May Your Christmas Be Cozy

#	DESCRIPTION	FIG	PLT	BELL	MUSC	ORN	DOLL	THMBL	FRAME	CNDL CLMB	BOX	OTHER
81	Angel w/Friends Caroling		*E-2347*		**E-2346**	E-0532*						
82	Boy Next/Potbellied Stove	**E-2348**										
83	Girl w/Doll/Reading Book	**E-2349**	15237			**E-0533***						
84	Boy Ice Skater/Santa Cap	**E-2350**				E-2369						
85	Two Angels with Candles	E-2351										
86	Boy Carolling next to Lamp Post	E-2353			**E-2352**	**E-0531***						
87	Drummer Boy with Manger	**E-2356** E-2360* E-5384*	E-2357	E-2358*	**E-2355**	E-2359*						
88	Girl with Stocking	**E-2361**										
89	Baby in Christmas Stocking					**E-2362**						
90	Camel	E-2363										
91	Goat	**E-2364**										
92	Boy Angel with Candle	**E-2365**				**E-2367**						
93	Angel Praying	**E-2366**				E-2368						
94	Unicorn					E-2371						
95	Boy Holding Block					**E-2372**						
96	Girl with Presents	E-2374				525057						
97	Girl with Pie	E-2375				E-2376*						
98	Girl Knitting Tie for Boy	**E-2377**	**E-2378**									
99	Mouse with Cheese					**E-2381**						
100	Camel, Donkey, Cow					**E-2386**						

BOLD = Suspended *Italics* = Limited Edition Shaded Area = Retired ◆ = Two-Year Collectible

Boxed = Dated Annual Rounded Box = Annual * = Special Inspirational Title or piece derived from a portion of the drawing

81
Let Heaven
And Nature Sing
*without animals
82
May Your Christmas
Be Warm
83
Tell Me The Story Of Jesus
*without tree & gifts
84
Dropping In For Christmas
85
Holy Smokes
86
O Come All Ye Faithful
*without lamp post
87
I'll Play My Drum For Him
*without manger
88
Christmas Joy
From Head To Toe
89
Baby's First Christmas
90
Camel
91
Goat
92
The First Noel
93
The First Noel
94
Unicorn
95
Baby's First Christmas
96
Bundles of Joy
97
Dropping Over For Christmas
*without dog
98
Our First Christmas
Together
99
Mouse With Cheese
100
Camel, Donkey, Cow

#	DESCRIPTION	FIG	PLT	BELL	MUSC	ORN	DOLL	THMBL	FRAME	CNDL CLMB	BOX	OTHER
101	Mini Houses w/Palm Tree	E-2387										
102	Boy Holding Heart	**E-7153**							**12017***			
103	Girl Holding Heart	**E-7154**						**100625**	**12025***			
104	Girl with Shopping Bag	E-0005 E-0105										
105	Boy Holding Chick	**E-7156**	*E-9257* (Also see ART CHART Number 374)									
106	Waitress Carrying Food	E-7157										
107	Nurse Giving Shot to Bear	E-7158										
108	Bandaged Boy by Sign	**E-7159**										
109	Grandpa in Rocking Chair	**E-7160**				**E-0517***						
110	Shepherd Painting Lamb	**E-7161**										
111	Girl at School Desk	**E-7162**			E-7185							
112	Boy with Ice Bag on Head	**E-7163**										
113	Boy/Girl Paint'g Dog House	**E-7164**										
114	Boy/Girl Baptism Bucket	**E-7165**			**E-7186**							
115	Groom Doll						*E-7267B*					
116	Bride Doll						*E-7267G*					
117	Girl with Curlers	PM-821										
118	Boy Pushing Girl on Sled	**E-0501**			E-0519							
119	Boy w/Candle & Mouse	**E-0502**				**E-0537***						
120	Girl/Snow Look'g Birdhouse	**E-0503**	523860*									

BOLD = Suspended *Italics* = Limited Edition Shaded Area = Retired ◆ = Two-Year Collectible

Boxed = Dated Annual Rounded Box = Annual * = Special Inspirational Title or piece derived from a portion of the drawing

101
House And Palm Tree
102
God Is Love, Dear Valentine
*Loving You
103
God Is Love, Dear Valentine
*Loving You
104
Seek And Ye Shall Find
105
I Believe In Miracles
106
There Is Joy In Serving Jesus
107
Love Beareth All Things
108
Lord Give Me Patience
109
The Perfect Grandpa
*without dog
110
His Sheep Am I
111
Love Is Sharing
112
God Is Watching Over You
113
Bless This House
114
Let The Whole World Know
115
Cubby
116
Tammy
117
Smile, God Loves You
118
Sharing Our
Season Together
119
Jesus Is The
Light That Shines
*without mouse
120
Blessings From My House To Yours
*Blessings From Me To Thee

#	DESCRIPTION	FIG	PLT	BELL	MUSC	ORN	DOLL	THMBL	FRAME	CNDL CLMB	BOX	OTHER
121	Boy Giving Teddy/Poor Boy	E-0504	E-0505									
122	Boy with Wreath	E-0506		E-0522		E-0513*						
123	Girl Looking into Manger	**E-0507**										
124	Boy/Girl Preparing Manger	**E-0508**										
125	Girl Angel Push Jesus/Cart	**E-0509**										
126	Rooster & Bird on Pig	**E-0511** 525278*										
127	Boy Angel/Red Cross Bag	**E-0512** 525286*				**102415***						
128	Knight in Armor	E-0523										
129	Boy & Dog Running Away	E-0525										
130	Angel Catch Falling Skater	**E-0526**										
131	Girl with Bird in Hand	E-0530										
132	Boy with Slate					**E-0535**						
133	Girl with Slate					**E-0536**						
134	Baby Collector's Doll						**E-0539**					
135	Boy Hold Board/Girl/Chalk	**E-9251**										
136	Boy & Girl with Bandage	**E-9252**										
137	Boy with Dog Rip'g Pants	**E-9253**										
138	Girl at Typewriter	E-9254										
139	Groom Carrying Bride	E-9255										
140	Bonnet Girl with Butterfly	E-9258 *523879*										525960 Egg

BOLD = Suspended *Italics* = Limited Edition Shaded Area = Retired ◆ = Two-Year Collectible

Boxed = Dated Annual Rounded Box = Annual * = Special Inspirational Title or piece derived from a portion of the drawing

121 Christmastime Is For Sharing

122 Surrounded With Joy
*Surround Us With Joy

123 God Sent His Son

124 Prepare Ye The
Way Of The Lord

125 Bringing God's
Blessing To You

126 Tubby's First Christmas
*no bird

127 It's A Perfect Boy
*without manger

128 Onward Christian Soldiers

129 You Can't Run
Away From God

130 He Upholdeth
Those Who Call

131 His Eye Is On The Sparrow

132 Love Is Patient

133 Love Is Patient

134 Katie Lynne

135 Love Is Patient

136 Forgiving Is Forgetting

137 The End Is In Sight

138 Praise The Lord Anyhow

139 Bless You Two

140 We Are God's Workmanship

#	DESCRIPTION	FIG	PLT	BELL	MUSC	ORN	DOLL	THMBL	FRAME	CNDL CLMB	BOX	OTHER
141	Boy with Piggy	**E-9259**										
142	Boy Angel Wind'g Rainbow	**E-9260**										
143	Boy Graduate with Scroll	**E-9261**										
144	Girl Graduate with Scroll	**E-9262**										
145	Boy & Girl/Horse Costume	**E-9263**										
146	Girl Ironing Clothes	E-9265										
147	Animals	**E-9267** (Also see ART CHART Numbers 407, 408, 409, 412, 413 & 414)										
148	Boy with Dunce Cap	E-9268										
149	Girl with Chicks in Umbrella	E-9273										
150	Girl Angel Making Food	E-9274										
151	Pig	**E-9282** **E-9282B**										
152	Bunny	**E-9282** **E-9282A**										
153	Lamb	**E-9282** **E-9282C**										
154	Boy at Pulpit	**E-9285**										
155	Girl with Lion & Lamb	**E-9287**										
156	Girl Angel w/Sprinkl'g Can	**E-9288**										
157	Boy Angel /Flying Lessons	**E-9289**										
158	Club Meeting	E-0103 E-0303										
159	Boy Clown Holding Mask	PM-822										
160	Girl Covering Kitten	PM-831										

BOLD = Suspended *Italics* = Limited Edition Shaded Area = Retired ◆ = Two-Year Collectible

Boxed = Dated Annual Rounded Box = Annual * = Special Inspirational Title or piece derived from a portion of the drawing

141
We're In It Together
142
God's Promises Are Sure
143
Seek Ye The Lord
144
Seek Ye The Lord
145
How Can Two Walk
Together Except They Agree
146
Press On
147
Animal Collection
148
DUNCE
Nobody's Perfect
149
Let Love Reign
150
Taste And See
That The Lord Is Good
151
You're Worth Your
Weight In Gold
152
To Somebunny Special
153
Especially For Ewe
154
If God Be For Us,
Who Can Be Against Us
155
Peace On Earth
156
Sending You A Rainbow
157
Trust In The Lord
158
Let Us Call
The Club To Order
159
Put On A Happy Face
160
Dawn's Early Light

#	DESCRIPTION	FIG	PLT	BELL	MUSC	ORN	DOLL	THMBL	FRAME	CNDL CLMB	BOX	OTHER
161	Girl with String of Hearts	E-2821 *523283* 527661			112577 422282◆	112356	427527◆					
162	Girl Polishing Table	E-2822										
163	Boy Holding Picture Frame	**E-2823**										
164	Girl with Floppy Hat	E-2824										
165	Girl Put'g Bows/Sister's Hair	E-2825										
166	Girl at Table with Dolls	**E-2826**										
167	Girl with Bucket on Head	**E-2827**										
168	Girl/Trunk/Wedding Gown	E-2828										
169	Girl Mailing Snowball	E-2829	101834		112402	**112372**						
170	Bridesmaid	E-2831										
171	Bride with Flower Girl	E-2832										
172	Groomsman with Frog	E-2836										
173	Angel Helping Baby	**E-2840**										
174	Baby's First Photo	E-2841										
175	Boy & Girl on Swing		*E-2847*									
176	Mother Wrapping Bread		*E-2848*									
177	Baby Collector Doll						**E-2851**					
178	Baby Figurines	E-2852 (Also see ART CHART Numbers 401-406)										
179	Happy Anniversary	E-2853										
180	1st Anniversary	E-2854										

BOLD = Suspended *Italics* = Limited Edition Shaded Area = Retired ◆ = Two-Year Collectible

Boxed = Dated Annual Rounded Box = Annual * = Special Inspirational Title or piece derived from a portion of the drawing

161
You Have Touched
So Many Hearts
162
This Is Your Day To Shine
163
To God Be The Glory
164
To A Very Special Mom
165
To A Very Special Sister
166
May Your Birthday
Be A Blessing
167
I Get A Kick Out Of You
168
Precious Memories
169
I'm Sending You
A White Christmas
170
Bridesmaid
171
God Bless The Bride
172
Groomsman
173
Baby's First Step
174
Baby's First Picture
175
Love Is Kind
176
Loving Thy Neighbor
177
Kristy
178
Baby Figurines
179
God Blessed Our Years Together
With So Much Love & Happiness
180
God Blessed Our Year Together
With So Much Love & Happiness

#	DESCRIPTION	FIG	PLT	BELL	MUSC	ORN	DOLL	THMBL	FRAME	CNDL CLMB	BOX	OTHER
181	5th Anniversary	E-2855										
182	10th Anniversary	E-2856										
183	25th Anniversary	E-2857										
184	40th Anniversary	E-2859										
185	50th Anniversary	E-2860										
186	Girl w/Long Hair & Bible	E-**5376**										
187	Girl with Mouse	E-5377										
188	Boy with Harp	E-**5378**				E-5388						
189	Girl with Broom	E-5379 **522988**										
190	Boy w/Butterfly at Manger	E-**5380**										
191	Boys at Manger	E-**5381**										
192	Deluxe 4-Piece Nativity	E-**5382**										
193	"1984" Girl in Choir	E-5383		E-5393		E-5387						
194	Boy Angel with Candle	E-**5385**										
195	Girl Angel Praying	E-**5386**										
196	Boy in Choir					E-**5389**						
197	Girl in Scarf & Cap					E-**5390**						
198	Girl with Gift					E-**5391**						
199	Angel Behind Rainbow											**16020** Night Light
200	Carollers with Puppy				E-**5394**							

BOLD = Suspended *Italics* = Limited Edition Shaded Area = Retired ◆ = Two-Year Collectible

Boxed = Dated Annual Rounded Box = Annual * = Special Inspirational Title or piece derived from a portion of the drawing

181 God Blessed Our Years Together With So Much Love & Happiness

182 God Blessed Our Years Together With So Much Love & Happiness

183 God Blessed Our Years Together With So Much Love & Happiness

184 God Blessed Our Years Together With So Much Love & Happiness

185 God Blessed Our Years Together With So Much Love & Happiness

186 May Your Christmas Be Blessed

187 Love Is Kind

188 Joy To The World

189 Isn't He Precious

190 A Monarch Is Born

191 His Name Is Jesus

192 For God So Loved The World

193 Wishing You A Merry Christmas

194 Oh Worship The Lord

195 Oh Worship The Lord

196 Peace On Earth

197 May God Bless You With A Perfect Holiday Season

198 Love Is Kind

199 God Bless You With Rainbows

200 Wishing You A Merry Christmas

#	DESCRIPTION	FIG	PLT	BELL	MUSC	ORN	DOLL	THMBL	FRAME	CNDL CLMB	BOX	OTHER
201	Nativity Scene		*E-5395*									
202	Boy Pull Sled w/Girl & Tree		E-5396									
203	Boy Jogger						**E-5397**					
204	Girl with Present & Kitten	**E-6613**										
205	Girl with Dues Bank	E-0104 E-0404										
206	Boy Angel with Flashlight	PM-841										
207	Boy with Racing Cup	PM-842										
208	Ringbearer	E-2833										
209	Flower Girl	E-2835										
210	Junior Bridesmaid	E-2845										
211	Boy Sitting with Teddy	**100021**										
212	Boy/Bow & Arrow/Cloud	**100056**										
213	Girl Kneel/Church Window	100064										
214	Two Girls with Flowers	100072				113956						
215	Baseball Player with Bat	100110										
216	Ballerina	100129				102423*						
217	Mother with Babies	100137										
218	Tennis Girl	**100161**				**102458***						
219	Kids in Boat	100250				522937						
220	Girl in Old Bath Tub	100277				112380						

BOLD = Suspended *Italics* = Limited Edition Shaded Area = Retired ◆ = Two-Year Collectible

Boxed = Dated Annual Rounded Box = Annual * = Special Inspirational Title or piece derived from a portion of the drawing

201 Unto Us A Child Is Born
202 The Wonder Of Christmas
203 Timmy
204 God Sends The Gift Of His Love
205 Join In On The Blessings
206 God's Ray Of Mercy
207 Trust In The Lord To The Finish
208 Ringbearer
209 Flower Girl
210 Junior Bridesmaid
211 To My Favorite Paw
212 Sending My Love
213 Worship The Lord
214 To My Forever Friend
215 Lord I'm Coming Home
216 Lord, Keep Me On My Toes *without bar
217 The Joy Of The Lord Is My Strength
218 Serving The Lord *Serve With A Smile
219 Friends Never Drift Apart
220 He Cleansed My Soul

#	DESCRIPTION	FIG	PLT	BELL	MUSC	ORN	DOLL	THMBL	FRAME	CNDL CLMB	BOX	OTHER
221	Baby w/Bunny & Turtle	520934			**100285**							
222	Tennis Boy	**100293**				**102431***						
223	Boy Kneel/Church Window	102229										
224	Girl Holding Cross	103632				**522953**						523534* Egg
225	Girl Making Heart Quilt	**12009**						**12254**				
226	Girl by Fence	12068	12106		408735◆		408786◆					
227	Girl with Crossed Arms	12076	12114		408743◆		408794◆	100641				
228	Girl with Hands behind Her	12084	12122		408751◆		408808◆					
229	Girl w/Scarf & Hat/Birds	12092	12130		408778◆		408816◆					
230	Angel Boy in Devil's Suit	**12149**										
231	Boy Playing Piano				**12165**							
232	Girl Playing Triangle	**12173**										
233	Nun	**12203**										
234	Angel Cutting Baby's Hair	**12211**										
235	Mini Clowns	12238 (Also see ART CHART Numbers 416-419)										
	*Girl Clown w/Balloon					**15822***		**100668** (Set of the two with balls)				
	**Boy Clown w/Cap & Ball					**15830****						
236	Clown Holding Balloons	12262										
237	Policeman Writing Ticket	**12297**				102377*						
238	Teacher w/Report Card	12300										
239	Boy & Girl/Sandcastle	12319										
240	Mary Knitting Booties	**12343**										

BOLD = Suspended *Italics* = Limited Edition Shaded Area = Retired ◆ = Two-Year Collectible

Boxed = Dated Annual Rounded Box = Annual * = Special Inspirational Title or piece derived from a portion of the drawing

221
Heaven Bless You
222
Serving The Lord
*Serve With A Smile
223
Worship The Lord
224
I Believe In The Old Rugged Cross
*I Will Cherish The Old Rugged Cross
225
Love Covers All
226
The Voice Of Spring
227
Summer's Joy
228
Autumn's Praise
229
Winter's Song
230
Part Of Me
Wants To Be Good
231
Lord, Keep My Life In Tune
232
There's A Song In My Heart
233
Get Into The Habit Of Prayer
234
Baby's First Haircut
235
Clown Figurines
*May Your Christmas Be Happy
**Happiness Is The Lord
236
I Get A Bang Out Of You
237
It Is Better To Give Than To Receive
*Trust And Obey
238
Love Never Fails
239
God Bless Our Home
240
Jesus Is Coming Soon

#	DESCRIPTION	FIG	PLT	BELL	MUSC	ORN	DOLL	THMBL	FRAME	CNDL CLMB	BOX	OTHER
241	Angels Make Snowman	**12351**										
242	Boy Playing Banjo	**12378**										
243	Girl Playing Harmonica	**12386**										
244	Boy Playing Trumpet/Dog	**12394**										
245	Two Angels Sawing Star				**12408**							
246	Boy in Airplane					12416						
247	Boy Angel						**12424**					
248	Girl Angel						**12432**					
249	5th Anniversary Piece	12440										
250	Girl Clown w/Bskt/Goose	12459				112364						
251	Clown with Dog on Mud	12467										
252	Baby Boy						**12475**					
253	Baby Girl						**12483**					
254	Boy Tangled in Christmas Lights	**15482**				**15849**						
255	Mother Goose/Bonnet/ Babes	15490				**15857***						
256	Boy Clown Holding Jack-in-the-Box				15504	**113972**						
257	Baby Boy Holding Bottle	15539				15903						
258	Baby Girl Holding Bottle	15547				15911						
259	Angel with Holly Wreath	15881		15873		15768		15865				
260	Mother with Cookie Sheet	**15776**										

BOLD = Suspended *Italics* = Limited Edition Shaded Area = Retired ◆ = Two-Year Collectible

Boxed = Dated Annual Rounded Box = Annual * = Special Inspirational Title or piece derived from a portion of the drawing

241
Halo, And Merry Christmas
242
Happiness Is The Lord
243
Lord Give Me A Song
244
He Is My Song
245
We Saw A Star
246
Have A Heavenly Christmas
247
Aaron
248
Bethany
249
God Bless Our Years Together
250
Waddle I Do Without You
251
The Lord Will Carry You Through
252
P.D.
253
Trish
254
May Your Christmas Be Delightful
255
Honk If You Love Jesus
*without babies
256
God Sent You Just In Time
257
Baby's First Christmas
258
Baby's First Christmas
259
1985
God Sent His Love
260
May You Have The Sweetest Christmas

#	DESCRIPTION	FIG	PLT	BELL	MUSC	ORN	DOLL	THMBL	FRAME	CNDL CLMB	BOX	OTHER
261	Father Reading Bible	**15784**										
262	Boy Sitting Listen to Story	**15792**										
263	Girl with Ornament	**15806**										
264	Christmas Tree				**15814**							
265	Boy Angel								**E-7168**			
266	Girl Angel								**E-7169**			
267	Angel Pushing Buggy	**16012**										
268	Bridesmaid with Kitten	**E-2834**										
269	Groom	E-2837										
270	Clown Sitting on Ball	12270										
271	Boy Angel on Cloud	**12335**										
272	Mom & Dad w/Girl/ Adoption	**100145**										
273	Mom & Dad w/Boy/ Adoption	**100153**										
274	Boy with Football	100188				**111120**						
275	Boy Standing in Ink Spot	100269										
276	Pilgrim & Indian w/Turkey	**100544**										
277	Boy and Girl in Box				101702	102350 112399 520233						
278	Angel with Black Lamb	102261				**102288**						
279	Three Mini Animals	**102296**										
280	Girl with Muff	102342		102318		102326		102334				

BOLD = Suspended *Italics* = Limited Edition Shaded Area = Retired ◆ = Two-Year Collectible

Boxed = Dated Annual Rounded Box = Annual * = Special Inspirational Title or piece derived from a portion of the drawing

261
The Story of God's Love
262
Tell Me A Story
263
God Gave His Best
264
Silent Night
265
My Guardian Angel
266
My Guardian Angel
267
Baby's First Trip
268
Sharing Our Joy Together
269
Groom
270
Lord Keep Me On The Ball
271
You Can Fly
272
God Bless The Day
We Found You
273
God Bless The Day
We Found You
274
I'm A Possibility
275
Help Lord, I'm In A Spot
276
Brotherly Love
277
Our First Christmas Together
278
Shepherd Of Love
279
Mini Animal Figurines
280
Wishing You A
Cozy Christmas

#	DESCRIPTION	FIG	PLT	BELL	MUSC	ORN	DOLL	THMBL	FRAME	CNDL CLMB	BOX	OTHER
281	Fireman Holding Puppy	102393				102385						
282	Nurse with Potted Plant	102482				102407						
283	Rocking Horse					**102474**						
284	Husband/Wife/Puppy/ and Cookies	**102490**										
285	Baby Girl w/Candy Cane					102504						
286	Baby Boy w/Candy Cane					102512						
287	Clown on Elephant				102520							
288	Boy Angel w/B'day Cake	**102962**										
289	Boy Clown						*100455*					
290	Girl Clown						*100463*					
291	Doll with Stand						*102253*					
292	Uncle Sam Holding Bible with Dog	102938										
293	Girl Holding Lamb	PM-851										
294	Boy with Lamb and Book	PM-852										
295	Girl with Embroidery Hoop/ Bird	E-0006 E-0106				PM-864						
296	Teddy/Caboose - For Baby	15938										
297	Lamb - Age 1	15946										
298	Seal - Age 2	15962										
299	Pig - Age 3	15954										
300	Elephant - Age 4	15970										

BOLD = Suspended *Italics* = Limited Edition Shaded Area = Retired ◆ = Two-Year Collectible

Boxed = Dated Annual Rounded Box = Annual * = Special Inspirational Title or piece derived from a portion of the drawing

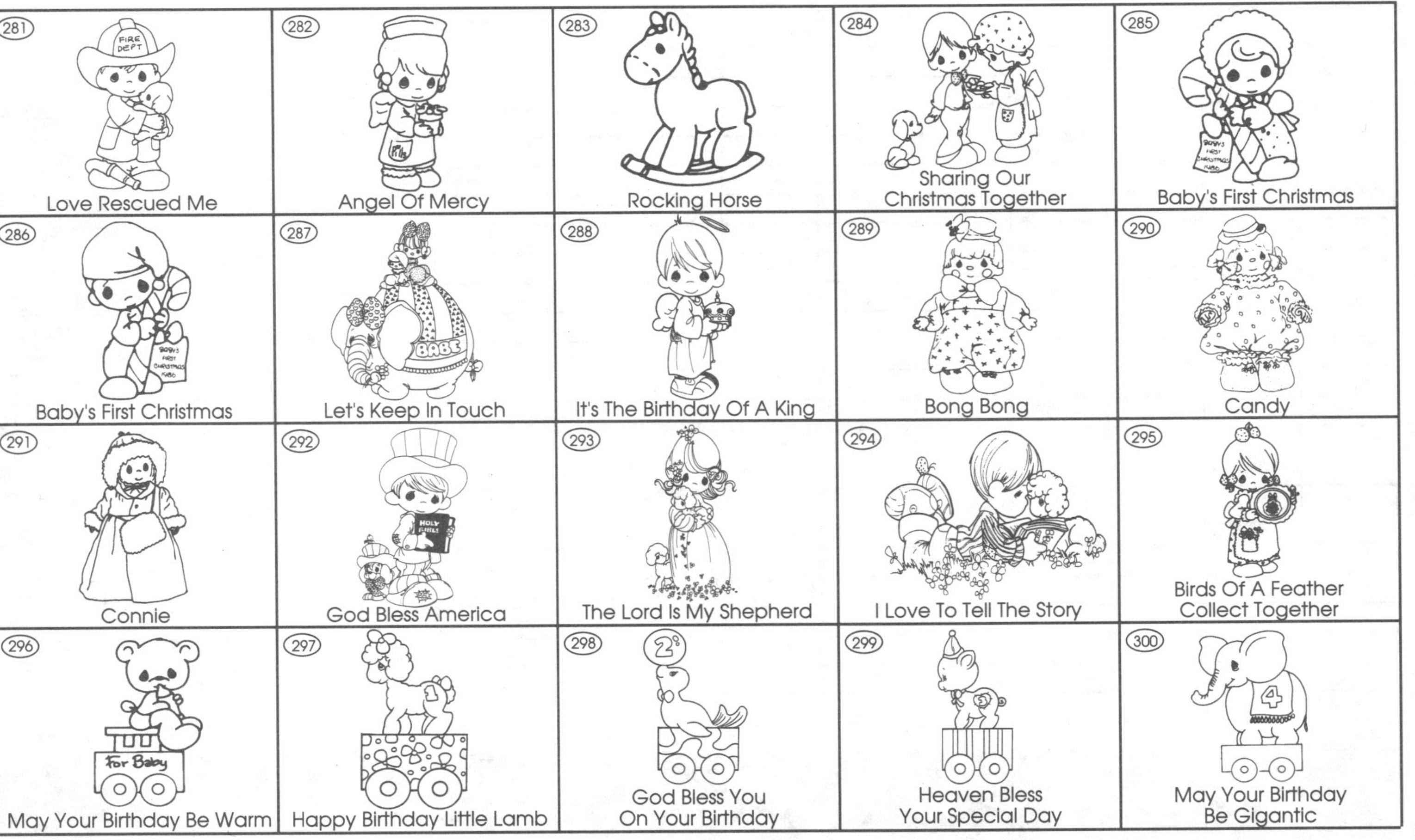
281 Love Rescued Me
FIRE DEPT
282 Angel Of Mercy
283 Rocking Horse
284 Sharing Our Christmas Together
285 Baby's First Christmas
286 Baby's First Christmas
287 Let's Keep In Touch
BABE
288 It's The Birthday Of A King
289 Bong Bong
290 Candy
291 Connie
292 God Bless America
HOLY BIBLE
293 The Lord Is My Shepherd
294 I Love To Tell The Story
295 Birds Of A Feather Collect Together
296 May Your Birthday Be Warm
For Baby
297 Happy Birthday Little Lamb
298 God Bless You On Your Birthday
299 Heaven Bless Your Special Day
300 May Your Birthday Be Gigantic

#	DESCRIPTION	FIG	PLT	BELL	MUSC	ORN	DOLL	THMBL	FRAME	CNDL CLMB	BOX	OTHER
301	Lion - Age 5	15989										
302	Giraffe - Age 6	15997										
303	Clown with Pull Rope	16004										
304	Clown with Drum	B-0001										
305	Praying Grandma	PM-861										
306	1986 Dated Reindeer					102466						
307	Nativity Set with Cassette	104000										
308	Lamb and Bunny Lamb and Skunk										**E-9266**	
309	Dog (A) Cat (B)										**E-9283**	
310	Baby Boy								**12033**			
311	Baby Girl								**12041**			
312	Complete Wedding Party	E-2838										
313	Bride	E-2846						**100633***				
314	Birthday Boy	**12157**										
315	Girl with Piano				**12580**							
316	Girl with Flowers & Deer	100048										
317	Girl/Boy Bandaging Heart	100080										
318	Girl Graduate	106208										
319	Girl/Crutches/Bible	107999										
320	Boy in Car	PM-862										

BOLD = Suspended *Italics* = Limited Edition Shaded Area = Retired ◆ = Two-Year Collectible

Boxed = Dated Annual Rounded Box = Annual * = Special Inspirational Title or piece derived from a portion of the drawing

301
This Day Is
Something To Roar About
302
Keep Looking Up
303
Bless The Days Of Our Youth
304
Our Club Can't Be Beat
305
Grandma's Prayer
306
Reindeer
307
Come Let Us Adore Him
308
I'm Falling For Somebunny,
Our Love Is Heaven Scent
309
Forever Friends
310
God's Precious Gift
311
God's Precious Gift
312
This Is The Day Which
The Lord Hath Made
313
Bride
*The Lord Bless You
And Keep You
314
This Is The Day Which
The Lord Has Made
315
Lord, Keep My Life In Tune
316
To My Deer Friend
317
He's The Healer
Of Broken Hearts
318
Congratulations, Princess
319
He Walks With Me
320
I'm Following Jesus

#	DESCRIPTION	FIG	PLT	BELL	MUSC	ORN	DOLL	THMBL	FRAME	CNDL CLMB	BOX	OTHER
321	Boy Painting Valentine	PM-873										
322	Girl w/Crayon/Valentine	PM-874										
323	Girl with Sick Bear	100102										
324	Girl on Scale	100196										
325	Parents of the Groom	100498										
326	Parents of the Bride	100501										
327	Girl with Skunk	100528										
328	Boy w/Gardening Mother	100536										
329	Girl at Gate to Heaven	101826										
330	Clown Balancing	101842				**113964***						
331	Clowns on Unicycle	101850										
332	Bridal Arch	**102369**										
333	Boy with Hat & Fish	103497				**114006**						
334	Boy Graduate	106194										
335	Raccoon Holding Fish	BC-861										
336	Girl Sending Package to Friend	E-0007 E-0107										
337	Nativity w/Backdrop/Video	104523										
338	Shepherd and Lambs	103004										
339	Nurse Doll						*12491*					
340	Girl/Cat/Bird Cage	100226										

BOLD = Suspended　*Italics* = Limited Edition　Shaded Area = Retired　◆ = Two-Year Collectible

Boxed = Dated Annual　Rounded Box = Annual　* = Special Inspirational Title or piece derived from a portion of the drawing

321 Loving You Dear Valentine
322 Loving You Dear Valentine
323 Make Me A Blessing
324 The Spirit Is Willing But The Flesh Is Weak
325 God Bless Our Family
326 God Bless Our Family
327 Scent From Above
328 I Picked A Very Special Mom
329 No Tears Past The Gate
330 Smile Along The Way *without base & ball
331 Lord, Help Us Keep Our Act Together
332 Wedding Arch
333 My Love Will Never Let You Go
334 God Bless You Graduate
335 Fishing For Friends
336 Sharing Is Universal
337 Dealer's Only Nativity
338 We Belong To The Lord
339 Angie, The Angel Of Mercy
340 The Lord Giveth & The Lord Taketh Away

#	DESCRIPTION	FIG	PLT	BELL	MUSC	ORN	DOLL	THMBL	FRAME	CNDL CLMB	BOX	OTHER
341	Kids w/Pup, Kitten, Bird		102954		**109746*/****	523062*						
342	Baby Boy/Tub	102970										
343	Boy Giving Girl Ring	104019										
344	Boy Mending Hobby Horse	**104027**										
345	Girl Cheerleader	104035				**113999**						
346	Girl Clown with Books	**104396**										
347	Bear on a Sled					104515						
348	Baby Boy/Wood Tub	104817										
349	Girl Angel on Stool	**104825**										
350	Boy Reading Scroll	**105635** **528137**										
351	Dentist/Patient/Pull Tooth	**105813**										
352	Elephant Showering Mouse	105945										
353	Boy with Donkey	**106151**										
354	Schoolboy Clown	**106216**										
355	Baby Boy/Dog	109231										
356	Baby Girl/Rocking Horse					109401						
357	Baby Boy/Rocking Horse					109428						
358	Girl with Ice Cream	**109754**	523801*									
359	Family Thanksgiving Set	109762										
360	Girl with Present	110930		109835		109770		109843				

BOLD = Suspended *Italics* = Limited Edition Shaded Area = Retired ◆ = Two-Year Collectible

Boxed = Dated Annual Rounded Box = Annual * = Special Inspirational Title or piece derived from a portion of the drawing

341
My Peace I Give Unto Thee
*Peace On Earth
** no lamp post
342
I Would Be Sunk Without You
343
With This Ring I...
344
Love Is The Glue That Mends
345
Cheers To The Leader
346
Happy Days Are Here Again
347
Bear The Good
News Of Christmas
348
A Tub Full Of Love
349
Sitting Pretty
350
Have I Got News For You
351
To Tell The Tooth
You're Special
352
Showers Of Blessings
353
We're Pulling For You
354
Lord Help Me
Make The Grade
355
The Greatest Gift Is A Friend
356
Baby's First Christmas
357
Baby's First Christmas
358
Wishing You A Yummy Christmas
*with a boy
359
We Gather Together To Ask
The Lord's Blessing
360
Love Is The Best Gift Of All

#	DESCRIPTION	FIG	PLT	BELL	MUSC	ORN	DOLL	THMBL	FRAME	CNDL CLMB	BOX	OTHER
361	Grandma on a Sled	109819										
362	4 Piece Large Nativity	**111333**										
363	Baby Girl/Wood Tub	112313										
364	Clown with Cymbals	B-0102 B-0002										
365	'84 Giveaway Medallion											12246 Medallion
366	Girl Feeding Lamb	PM-871										
367	Girl/Doll/Sleigh	109983				**521574***						
368	Girl/Plant in Snow	109991										
369	Girl with Kite	110019										
370	Girl with Umbrella	110027										
371	Girl with Potted Plant	110035										
372	Girl/Dress Up as Bride	110043										
373	Girl With Pearl	102903										
374	Boy Holding Bluebird	E-7156R	(Also see ART CHART Number 105)									
375	Boy Waiting /Seed/Grow	PM-872										
376	Brass Filigree Giveaway Ornament/Kids					PM-009						
377	Cowboy/Fence/Guitar	105821										
378	Groom/Trunk/Bride	106755				522945* 528870*						
379	Couple on Couch with Wedding Album	106763										
380	Anniversary Couple w/Dog	106798										

BOLD = Suspended　　*Italics* = Limited Edition　　Shaded Area = Retired　　◆ = Two-Year Collectible

Boxed = Dated Annual　　Rounded Box = Annual　　* = Special Inspirational Title or piece derived from a portion of the drawing

361 Oh What Fun It Is To Ride	362 O Come Let Us Adore Him	363 A Tub Full Of Love	364 A Smile's The Cymbal Of Joy	365 Precious Moments Last Forever
366 Feed My Sheep	367 January Girl *Dashing Through The Snow	368 February Girl	369 March Girl	370 April Girl
371 May Girl	372 June Girl	373 We Are All Precious In His Sight	374 I Believe In Miracles	375 In His Time
376 Sharing Season Ornament	377 Hallelujah Country	378 Heaven Bless Your Togetherness *Our First Christmas Together	379 Precious Memories	380 Puppy Love Is From Above

#	DESCRIPTION	FIG	PLT	BELL	MUSC	ORN	DOLL	THMBL	FRAME	CNDL CLMB	BOX	OTHER
381	Girl Holding Poppy Plant	**106836**										
382	Girl Sewing Boy's Pants	106844										
383	Boy with Barbells	**109487**										
384	Clown Angel with Flowers	109584										
385	Boy/Basket/Chick	109924										
386	Girl with Hearts in Cloud	109967										
387	Boy with Flower	109975										
388	Girl Holding Bunny	109886										
389	Girl with Plunger	111155										
390	Girl with Flower	112143										
391	Boy with Broken Heart	114014										
392	Couple w/Dog & Puppies	(114022)										
393	Leopard - Age 7	109479										
394	Ostrich - Age 8	109460										
395	Skunk & Mouse	**105953**										
396	Boy with Braces & Dog	(115479)										
397	Girl/Balloons/Satchel	(115231)										
398	Mouse in Sugar Bowl	BC-871										
399	Girl/Flowerpot/Sunflower	E-0108 E-0008				520349						
400	Kitten Hanging on Wreath					[520292]						

BOLD = Suspended *Italics* = Limited Edition Shaded Area = Retired ◆ = Two-Year Collectible

[Boxed] = Dated Annual (Rounded Box) = Annual * = Special Inspirational Title or piece derived from a portion of the drawing

381 Happy Birthday Poppy
382 Sew In Love
383 Believe The Impossible
384 Happiness Divine
385 Wishing You A Basket Full Of Blessings
386 Sending You My Love
AIR MAIL
387 Mommy, I Love You
388 Wishing You A Happy Easter
389 Faith Takes The Plunge
390 Mommy, I Love You
391 This Too Shall Pass
392 The Good Lord Has Blessed Us Tenfold
393 Wishing You Grrr-eatness
7
394 Isn't Eight Just Great
8
395 Brighten Someone's Day
396 Blessed Are They That Overcome
397 You Are My Main Event
You are my Main Event!
398 Hi Sugar!
SUGAR
399 A Growing Love
400 Hang On For The Holly Days

#	DESCRIPTION	FIG	PLT	BELL	MUSC	ORN	DOLL	THMBL	FRAME	CNDL CLMB	BOX	OTHER
401	Baby Boy Standing	E-2852A										
402	Baby Girl/Bow Hair	E-2852B										
403	Baby Boy Sitting	E-2852C	(Also see ART CHART Number 178)									
404	Baby Girl Clapping Hands	E-2852D										
405	Baby Boy Crawling	E-2852E										
406	Baby Girl Lying Down	E-2852F										
407	Dog with Slippers	**E-9267B**										
408	Bunny with Carrot	**E-9267C**	(Also see ART CHART Number 147)									
409	Lamb with Bird on Back	**E-9267E**										
410	Christmas Wreath											111465 Wreath
411	Kids on Cloud under Dome	E-7350										
412	Pig with Patches	**E-9267F**										
413	Cat with Bow Tie	**E-9267D**	(Also see ART CHART Number 147)									
414	Teddy Bear	**E-9267A**										
415	Retailer's Wreath Bell			112348								
416	Boy Balancing Ball	12238A										
417	Girl Holding Balloon	12238B	(Also see ART CHART Number 235)									
418	Boy Bending over Ball	12238C										
419	Girl with Flower Pot	12238D										
420	Rhino with Bird	**104418**										

BOLD = Suspended   *Italics* = Limited Edition   Shaded Area = Retired   ◆ = Two-Year Collectible

Boxed = Dated Annual   Rounded Box = Annual   * = Special Inspirational Title or piece derived from a portion of the drawing

401
Baby Figurine
402
Baby Figurine
403
Baby Figurine
404
Baby Figurine
405
Baby Figurine
406
Baby Figurine
407
408
409
412
413
414
Animal Collection
410
Retailer's Wreath
411
Retailer's Dome
415
THE ENESCO
COLLECTION
Retailer's Wreath Bell
416
Clown Figurine
417
Clown Figurine
418
Clown Figurine
419
Clown Figurine
420
Friends To The End

#	DESCRIPTION	FIG	PLT	BELL	MUSC	ORN	DOLL	THMBL	FRAME	CNDL CLMB	BOX	OTHER
421	Girl Holding Doll with Dog	**105643**										
422	Wreath Contestant Orn.					PM-008						
423	Girl with Kitten	109800										
424	Girl with Puppy in Basket	110051										
425	Girl in Swimming Pool	110078										
426	Girl Balancing Books	110086										
427	Girl with Pumpkins	110094										
428	Girl in Pilgrim Suit	110108										
429	Girl with Christmas Candle	110116				527211*						
430	Girl Adding Seasoning	111163										
431	Bunnies	115274 **522996***										
432	Baby Boy in Sleigh					115282 523194						
433	Couple with Gifts	**115290**										
434	Girl with Calendar & Clock	115339		115304		115320		115312				
435	Baby Girl in Sleigh					520241 523208						
436	Puppy in Stocking					520276						
437	Angel w/Newspaper/Dog	**520357**										
438	Girl Decorating Reindeer	522317	520284									
439	Girl Painting Butterfly	PM-881										
440	Pippin Popping out of a Birthday Cake	B-0003 B-0103										

BOLD = Suspended *Italics* = Limited Edition Shaded Area = Retired ◆ = Two-Year Collectible

Boxed = Dated Annual Rounded Box = Annual * = Special Inspirational Title or piece derived from a portion of the drawing

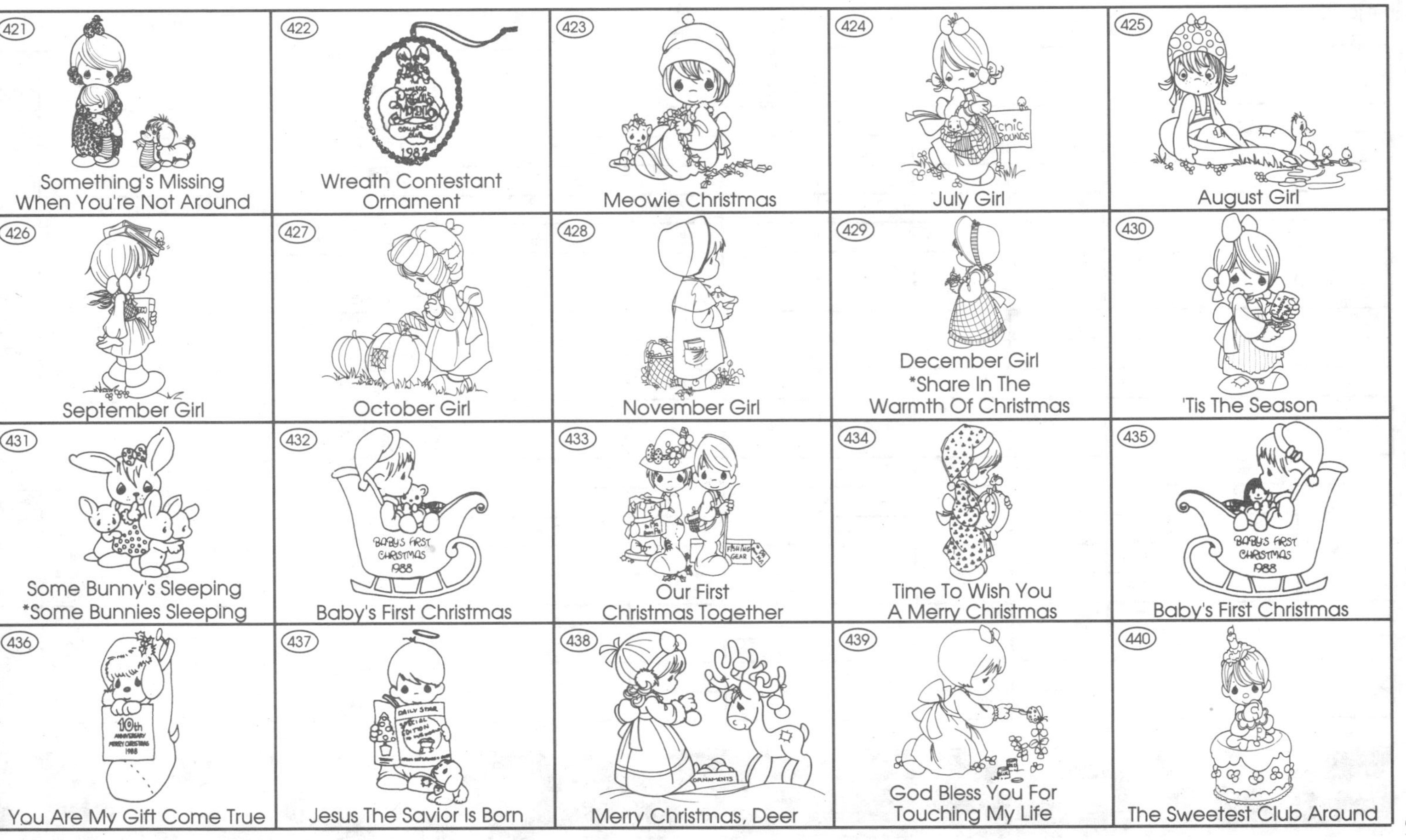
421
Something's Missing
When You're Not Around
422
1987
Wreath Contestant
Ornament
423
Meowie Christmas
424
July Girl
425
August Girl
426
September Girl
427
October Girl
428
November Girl
429
December Girl
*Share In The
Warmth Of Christmas
430
'Tis The Season
431
Some Bunny's Sleeping
*Some Bunnies Sleeping
432
BABY'S FIRST
CHRISTMAS
1988
Baby's First Christmas
433
FISHING
GEAR
Our First
Christmas Together
434
Time To Wish You
A Merry Christmas
435
BABY'S FIRST
CHRISTMAS
1988
Baby's First Christmas
436
10th
ANNIVERSARY
MERRY CHRISTMAS
1988
You Are My Gift Come True
437
DAILY STAR
Jesus The Savior Is Born
438
ORNAMENTS
Merry Christmas, Deer
439
God Bless You For
Touching My Life
440
The Sweetest Club Around

#	DESCRIPTION	FIG	PLT	BELL	MUSC	ORN	DOLL	THMBL	FRAME	CNDL CLMB	BOX	OTHER
441	Bunny with Stuffed Carrot	BC-881										
442	Boy/Dog/Trash Can	PM-882										
443	Girl with Lily	522376										
444	Girl/Puppies/Box	C-0109 C-0009				522961						
445	Boy Tangled in Lights											558125 Artplas Stock'g Hngr
446	Bride Holding Up Dress	520799										
447	Boy Angel w/Butterfly Net	520640										
448	Girl Holding Trophy	520829										
449	Mouse Wiping Clown's Tear	520632										
450	Boy with Newspaper over Head	520683										
451	Kangaroo/Baby in Pouch	521175										
452	Grandpa/Cane/Dog	**520810**										
453	Two Girls Having Tea Party	520748										
454	Boy Holding Girl up to Fountain	520675										
455	Girl with Hen & Easter Egg	520667										
456	Dog Pulling Boy's Fish'g Line	520721										
457	Indian Couple in Canoe	520772										
458	Nurse X-raying Boy's Heart	520624										
459	Boy Proposing to Girl	520845										
460	Bride & Groom in Car	520780				521558* 525324*						

BOLD = Suspended *Italics* = Limited Edition Shaded Area = Retired ◆ = Two-Year Collectible

Boxed = Dated Annual Rounded Box = Annual * = Special Inspirational Title or piece derived from a portion of the drawing

441
Somebunny Cares
442
You Just Cannot Chuck
A Good Friendship
443
His Love Will Shine On You
444
Always Room For One More
445
Stocking Hanger
446
Someday My Love
447
I'm So Glad You
Fluttered Into My Life
448
You Are My Number One
449
A Friend Is
Someone Who Cares
450
Sending You
Showers Of Blessings
451
Hello World!
452
We Need A Good Friend
Through The Ruff Times
453
Friendship Hits The Spot
454
Your Love Is So Uplifting
455
Eggspecially For You
456
Just A Line To Wish
You A Happy Day
457
Many Moons In Same
Canoe, Blessum You
458
My Heart Is
Exposed With Love
459
Wishing You
A Perfect Choice
460
Wishing You Roads Of Happiness
*Our First Christmas Together

#	DESCRIPTION	FIG	PLT	BELL	MUSC	ORN	DOLL	THMBL	FRAME	CNDL CLMB	BOX	OTHER
461	Boy w/Baby Feeding Dog	**520705**										
462	Girl w/Paint & Ladder	**520802**										
463	Orphan Girl	**520853**										
464	Boy at Crossroads	**520756**										
465	Two Puppies	520764										
466	Bridal Couple/Candle	520837										
467	Girl with Chalkboard	520861										
468	Angel w/ Baby Name Book	**523097**										
469	Teddy in Rocker	**522856**										
470	Puppy Resting on Elbow					520462						
471	Boy/Fallen Christmas Tree	522112				521590*						
472	Boy Dining with Turkey	**522031**										
473	Boy Playing Football/Dog	522023										
474	Boy & Girl on Motorcycle	522201										
475	Girl with Lamp Post				521507							
476	Girl on Telephone	521477										
477	Girl w/Snowball Tied with Ribbon					**521302**						
478	Boy/Pkg/Puppy & Bat	522120										
479	Family Christmas Scene		523003			523704						
480	Boy by Tree Stump	**521949**										

BOLD = Suspended *Italics* = Limited Edition Shaded Area = Retired ◆ = Two-Year Collectible

Boxed = Dated Annual Rounded Box = Annual * = Special Inspirational Title or piece derived from a portion of the drawing

461
Baby's First Pet
462
My Days Are
Blue Without You
463
ORPHAN
I Belong To The Lord
464
THIS WAY
NO THIS WAY
Jesus Is The Only Way
465
Puppy Love
466
The Lord Is Your Light
To Happiness
467
Sharing Begins In The Heart
468
NAMES for BABY
Jesus Is The Sweetest
Name I Know
469
Have A Beary
Merry Christmas
470
Christmas Is Ruff Without You
471
Don't Let The
Holidays Get You Down
*without axe
472
Thank You Lord
For Everything
473
RAM
May Your Life Be Blessed
With Touchdowns
474
Bon Voyage!
475
The Light Of The
World Is Jesus
476
Tell It To Jesus
477
May All Your
Christmases Be White
478
Wishing You A Very
Successful Season
479
1989
May Your Christmas
Be A Happy Home
480
Wishing You A Cozy Season

#	DESCRIPTION	FIG	PLT	BELL	MUSC	ORN	DOLL	THMBL	FRAME	CNDL CLMB	BOX	OTHER
481	Angel on Cloud w/Manger	**522252**										
482	Girl Playing Violin	522546		522821		522848		522554				
483	Angel Holding Commandments	**521868**										
484	Giraffe with Baby Bear	522260										
485	Girl with Ballot Box	PM-891										
486	Boy Pushing Lawn Mower	PM-892										
487	Teddy Bear with Balloon	B-0104 B-0004										
488	Teddy w/ Bee & Beehive	BC-891										
489	Girl at Table with Figurine	C-0110 C-0010				PM-904						
490	Girl with Fan	523526										
491	Angel outside Chapel	523011										
492	Girls with Flower	521817 525049										
493	Ballerina	520551										
494	Girl on Hobby Horse	**521205**				**523224***						
495	B&G Kiss'g under Mistletoe	523747										
496	Girl Wearing Boxing Gloves	521396										
497	Mom-To-Be w/Baby Book	523453				**527165**						
498	Boy with Kite	**521957**										
499	Girl on Roller Skates	**521280**				521566*						
500	Boy & Girl in Garden	522090										

BOLD = Suspended *Italics* = Limited Edition Shaded Area = Retired ◆ = Two-Year Collectible

Boxed = Dated Annual Rounded Box = Annual * = Special Inspirational Title or piece derived from a portion of the drawing

481 He Is The Star Of The Morning
482 Oh Holy Night
483 The Greatest Of These Is Love
484 To Be With You Is Uplifting
485 You Will Always Be My Choice
Ballot Box
486 Mow Power To Ya
487 Have A Beary Special Birthday
488 Can't Bee Hive Myself Without You
489 My Happiness
490 I'm A Precious Moments Fan
491 There's A Christian Welcome Here
492 Good Friends Are Forever
493 Lord, Turn My Life Around
494 Hope You're Up And On Trail Again
*Happy Trails Is Trusting Jesus
495 Blessings From Above
496 Faith Is A Victory
497 The Good Lord Always Delivers
498 High Hopes
499 Happy Trip
*Glide Through The Holidays
500 There Shall Be Showers Of Blessings

#	DESCRIPTION	FIG	PLT	BELL	MUSC	ORN	DOLL	THMBL	FRAME	CNDL CLMB	BOX	OTHER
501	Gorilla and Parrot	**521043**										
502	Girl Sweep Dust under Rug	521779										
503	Girl w/Account Bks & Glue	521450										
504	Kneeling Girl w/Bouquet	522287	531766									
505	Girl with Apple	**521310**										
506	Girl Holding Bible & Cross	523496			523682							
507	Girl/Sleep'g Chick in Egg	524522										
508	Boy Pull Wagon/Lily & Girl	521892										
509	Girl/Valentine behind Back	523518										
510	Boy Whispering to Girl	521841										
511	Girl w/Letters "Y" "O" "U"	521418										
512	Fireplace with Stockings	**524883**										
513	Teddy Bear in Package	**524875**										
514	Mouse on Cheese/Kitten	**524484**										
515	Girl and Melting Snowman	524913										
516	Baby Girl with Pie					523771						
517	Baby Boy with Pie					523798						
518	Nurse at Desk w/Clock	523739										
519	Girl with Book and Candle	523836		523828		523852		523844				
520	Crying Girls Hugging	521183										

BOLD = Suspended *Italics* = Limited Edition Shaded Area = Retired ◆ = Two-Year Collectible

Boxed = Dated Annual Rounded Box = Annual * = Special Inspirational Title or piece derived from a portion of the drawing

501
To My Favorite Fan
502
Sweep All Your Worries Away
503
Lord, Help Me Stick To My Job
504
Thinking Of You Is What I Really Like To Do
505
Yield Not To Temptation
506
This Day Has Been Made In Heaven
507
Always In His Care
508
Easter's On Its Way
509
God Is Love Dear Valentine
510
Love Is From Above
511
I'll Never Stop Loving You
512
Christmas Fireplace
513
Happy Birthday Dear Jesus
HAPPY BIRTHDAY Dear JESUS
514
Not A Creature Was Stirring
515
We're Going To Miss You
516
1990
Baby's First Christmas
517
1990
Baby's First Christmas
518
Time Heals
519
Once Upon A Holy Night
520
That's What Friends Are For

#	DESCRIPTION	FIG	PLT	BELL	MUSC	ORN	DOLL	THMBL	FRAME	CNDL CLMB	BOX	OTHER
521	Kitten with Ornament					520497						
522	Baby Boy on Pillow				**429570**							
523	Baby Girl on Pillow				**429589**							
524	Ballerina on Pointe	520543										
525	Ballerina at Barre				**520691**							
526	Girl and Boy Hugging	521299										
527	Girl/Bunny/Candle/Log	521485										
528	Girl Hammers Boy's Thumb	521698										
529	Girl Collecting Eggs/Frog	521906										
530	Boy/Bee/Flower Pot	521965										
531	Girl and Bird at Bird Bath	522279										529095 Egg
532	Stork Deliver'g Baby/Mom	523178										
533	Boy/Dog/Blocks/"Success"	**523763**										
534	Baby in Highchair w/Bowl	524077										
535	Girl Holding Flower	524263										
536	Girl w/Cake and Candles	524301										
537	Girl Holding Net/Butterfly	524425										
538	Bird on Cage Door/Kitten	524492										
539	Girl Helping Bird to Fly	527114										
540	Girl in Race Car	PM-901										

BOLD = Suspended *Italics* = Limited Edition Shaded Area = Retired ◆ = Two-Year Collectible

Boxed = Dated Annual Rounded Box = Annual * = Special Inspirational Title or piece derived from a portion of the drawing

521
Wishing You A
Purr-fect Holiday
522
The Eyes Of The
Lord Are Upon You
523
The Eyes Of The
Lord Are Upon You
524
In The Spotlight
Of His Grace
525
Lord, Keep My
Life In Balance
526
Hug One Another
527
There's A Light At
The End Of The Tunnel
528
Thumb-Body Loves You
529
Hoppy Easter Friend
530
To A Special Mum
531
A Reflection Of His Love
532
Joy On Arrival
533
I Can't Spell
Success Without You
534
Baby's First Meal
535
HE Loves Me
536
May Your
Birthday Be A Blessing
537
May Only Good
Things Come Your Way
538
Can't Be Without You
539
Sharing A Gift Of Love
540
Ten Years And
Still Going Strong

#	DESCRIPTION	FIG	PLT	BELL	MUSC	ORN	DOLL	THMBL	FRAME	CNDL CLMB	BOX	OTHER
541	Girl Sew'g Patch on Teddy	PM-902										
542	Chapel Stained Glass Window Replicas					PM-890 (Set of 7) (Also individually #'d PM-190, PM-290, PM-390, PM-490, PM-590, PM-690, PM-790)						
543	Clown/Puppy thru Drum	B-0105 B-0005										
544	Skunk with Flowers	BC-901										
545	Angel											617334 Tree Topper
546	Girl Holding Puppy	527122										
547	Squirrel/Mesh Bag/Nuts	BC-902										
548	Christmas Girl in Plaid Dress				417777◆		417785◆					
549	Rabbit on Skates					520438						
550	Boy on Rocking Horse	**521272**										
551	Girl Holding Picture Frame	**521434**										
552	Girl with Baby	521493										
553	Boy Decorating Globe	522082										
554	Girl Climbing Ladder	523615										
555	Girl in Snowsuit/Bunny	524123				524131						
556	Girl Holding Bird	524166		524182		524174 526940		524190				
557	Two Angels on Stool	524921										
558	Elephant/String/Tied/Trunk	526924										
559	Three Penguins	**526959**										
560	Boy with Drum					527084						

BOLD = Suspended   *Italics* = Limited Edition   Shaded Area = Retired   ◆ = Two-Year Collectible

Boxed = Dated Annual   Rounded Box = Annual   * = Special Inspirational Title or piece derived from a portion of the drawing

541 You Are A Blessing To Me
542 Beatitude Ornament Series
543 Our Club Is A Tough Act To Follow
544 Collecting Makes Good Scents
545 Rejoice, O Earth
546 You Can Always Bring A Friend
547 I'm Nuts Over My Collection
548 May You Have An Old Fashioned Christmas
549 Sno-Bunny Falls For You Like I Do
550 Take Heed When You Stand
551 To A Very Special Mom And Dad
552 A Special Delivery
553 May Your World Be Trimmed With Joy
554 Good News Is So Uplifting
555 Good Friends Are For Always
556 May Your Christmas Be Merry
557 Angels We Have Heard On High
558 How Can I Ever Forget You
559 We Have Come From Afar
560 Baby's First Christmas

#	DESCRIPTION	FIG	PLT	BELL	MUSC	ORN	DOLL	THMBL	FRAME	CNDL CLMB	BOX	OTHER
561	Girl with Drum					527092						
562	Girl at Mailbox/Newsletter	C-0011 C-0111				PM-037						
563	Sam Draws/Paints Animals	523038										
564	Child Tak'g First Steps/Mom	PM-911										
565	Indian Boy Hold'g Spinach	PM-912										
566	Baby Monkey w/Pacifier	BC-911										
567	Pup & Kitten Share Paint'g	BC-912										
568	Jester Jack-in-the-Box Playing Concertina	B-0106 B-0006										
569	Girl in Spacesuit Holding Space Helmet	C-0112 C-0012				PM-038						
570	Squirrel Decorat'g Tree/Log					520411						
571	Ballerina on Pointe	520535										
572	Ballerina on Pointe	520578										
573	Whale Riding Wave (10)	521825										
574	Curly Maned Pranc'g Pony	521833										
575	Hens Laugh/Egg on Pup	**522104**										
576	Boy Peek'g into Present				**522244**							
577	Girl Typing Message	523542										
578	Bird Watching Girl Swing	524085										
579	Girl Watering Seedling	524271										
580	Praying Girl/Globe	524352										

BOLD = Suspended *Italics* = Limited Edition Shaded Area = Retired ◆ = Two-Year Collectible

Boxed = Dated Annual Rounded Box = Annual * = Special Inspirational Title or piece derived from a portion of the drawing

561 Baby's First Christmas
562 Sharing The Good News Together
563 He Is My Inspiration
564 One Step At A Time
565 Lord, Keep Me In Teepee Top Shape
566 Love Pacifies
567 True Blue Friends
568 Jest To Let You Know You're Tops
569 The Club That's Out Of This World
570 I'm Nuts About You
1992
571 The Lord Turned My Life Around
572 You Deserve An Ovation
573 May Your Birthday Be Mammoth
574 Being Nine Is Just Divine
9
575 It's No Yolk When I Say I Love You
576 Do Not Open Till Christmas
577 You Are The Type I Love
578 My Warmest Thoughts Are You
579 Friendship Grows When You Plant A Seed
580 What The World Needs Now

#	DESCRIPTION	FIG	PLT	BELL	MUSC	ORN	DOLL	THMBL	FRAME	CNDL CLMB	BOX	OTHER
581	Girl on Skis Startl'd by Jump	524905				528846						
582	Ballerina on Pointe					525332						
583	Angels Ring'g Bell & Pray'g	525898										
584	Angel Tak'g Child/Heaven	525979										
585	Girl Cuddling Kitten	*526010* 524395										
586	Girl Checking Roadmap	526142										
587	Girl Holding Roses/Bluebird	(526185)										
588	Boy in Sailor Suit and Hat	**526568**										
589	Boy in Dress Uniform Salut'g	**526576**										
590	Boy in Dress Uniform/Duffel	**526584**										
591	Seated Child Sign'g Mes'g'	(527173)										
592	Baby Talking into Mike	527238										
593	Two Pups Hug Each Other	527270										
594	Girl Soldier in Dress Uniform	**527289**										
595	African-American Soldier	**527297**										
596	Girl Wades to Duck w/Eggs	(527319)										
597	B/Day Bird Blows Candle	527343										
598	Girl Puts Star on Boy's Head	527378										
599	Explorer/Animal Crew/Sail	527386										
600	Girl Sitting on Candy Cane					[527475]						

BOLD = Suspended *Italics* = Limited Edition Shaded Area = Retired ◆ = Two-Year Collectible

[Boxed] = Dated Annual (Rounded Box) = Annual * = Special Inspirational Title or piece derived from a portion of the drawing

581
It's So Uplifting To
Have A Friend Like You
582
Lord Keep Me On My Toes
583
Ring Those Christmas Bells
584
Going Home
585
You Are Such
A Purr-fect Friend
586
I Would Be Lost Without You
587
You Are My Happiness
588
Bless Those Who Serve
Their Country - Navy
589
Bless Those Who Serve
Their Country - Army
590
Bless Those Who Serve
Their Country - Air Force
591
A Universal Love
592
Baby's First Word
593
Let's Be Friends
594
Bless Those Who Serve
Their Country - Girl Soldier
595
Bless Those Who Serve
Their Country -
African-American Soldier
596
An Event Worth Wading For
597
Happy Birdie
598
You Are My Favorite Star
599
This Land Is Our Land
600
Baby's First Christmas - Girl

#	DESCRIPTION	FIG	PLT	BELL	MUSC	ORN	DOLL	THMBL	FRAME	CNDL CLMB	BOX	OTHER
601	Boy Sitting on Candy Cane					527483						
602	Boy/Full Dress at Attention	**527521**										
603	Mom/Wordless Book/Kids	527556	531359									
604	Uncle Sam Kneeling/Prayer	527564										
605	Boy Santa/Pup w/Whiskers	527629										
606	Girl Holding List to Santa	527688	527742	527726		527696 527734		527718				
607	Angel Holding Blanket	527750										
608	Explorer Hold'g Flag/Teddy	527777										
609	Girl Crying over Spilled Milk										Wall Hangings	523380
610	Princess Wash Servant Feet											523437
611	Boy/Stethoscope to World	E-1381R (Also see ART CHART NUMBER 15)										
612	Engineer Rid'g Locomotive	B-0107 B-0007										
613	Mr. Webb Build'g Birdhome	PM-921										
614	Girl Kneel'g by Grow'g Flwr	PM-922										
615	Beaver Building Home	BC-921										
616	Reindeer Turtle Carry'g Gift					520489						
617	Boy Swim'er/Oyster/Pearl	521000										
618	Girl Holding Bowl of Fruit	521213										
619	Monkey Rid'g/Camel's Back	521671										
620	Baby/Cloud/Angel Bird	521922										

BOLD = Suspended *Italics* = Limited Edition Shaded Area = Retired ◆ = Two-Year Collectible

Boxed = Dated Annual Rounded Box = Annual * = Special Inspirational Title or piece derived from a portion of the drawing

601
Baby's First Christmas - Boy
602
Bless Those Who Serve
Their Country - Marine
603
Bring The Little Ones To Jesus
604
God Bless The USA
605
Wishing You A Ho Ho Ho
606
But The Greatest
Of These Is Love
607
Wishing You A
Comfy Christmas
608
This Land Is Our Land
609
Blessed Are The
Ones Who Mourn
610
Blessed Are The Humble
611
Jesus Is The Answer
612
All Aboard For
Birthday Club Fun
613
Only Love Can
Make A Home
614
Sowing The Seeds Of Love
615
Every Man's House
Is His Castle
616
Slow Down And
Enjoy The Holidays
617
There Is No Greater
Treasure Than To Have
A Friend Like You
618
The Fruit Of The Spirit Is Love
619
Hope You're Over The Hump
620
Safe In The Arms Of Jesus

#	DESCRIPTION	FIG	PLT	BELL	MUSC	ORN	DOLL	THMBL	FRAME	CNDL CLMB	BOX	OTHER
621	Boy Carry'g Apple & Book	522015										
622	Girl w/Seeds for Flwrs/Birds	(523593)										
623	Girl Hold'g Kitten/Friend w/Milk	523623										
624	Baby by Cake w/1 Candle	524069										
625	Girl Blow'g Cake/Edge/Table	524298										
626	B/G Share Ice Cream Soda	524336										
627	Native American w/Fawn											Wall Hanging } (523313)
628	Bride/Groom Kiss over Mailbox	524441										
629	Boy in PJ's Ringing a Bell	524468										
630	Girl at Her First Communion	525316										
631	Girl Drop Coin/Wish'g Well				526916							
632	Nat. Amer. Girl Rais'g Hand	527335										
633	Pup Pull'g Ribbon/Tangled Girl	527580										
634	Boy on Sled/Turtle W/Gift	527599										
635	Octopus and Fish Hugging	527769										
636	Girl as Statue of Liberty	(528862)										
637	Girl Magician/Bunny/Top Hat					(529648)						
638	Girl Holds Bunnies in Apron	*529680*										
639	Girl Hold'g Doll Ring'g Bell	529966										
640	Girl Holding Trophy	(530026)										

BOLD = Suspended　*Italics* = Limited Edition　Shaded Area = Retired　◆ = Two-Year Collectible

Boxed = Dated Annual　(Rounded Box) = Annual　* = Special Inspirational Title or piece derived from a portion of the drawing

621 To The Apple Of God's Eye
622 The Lord Will Provide
623 I'm So Glad That God Blessed Me With A Friend Like You
624 Baby's First Birthday
625 May Your Every Wish Come True
626 Our Friendship Is Soda-Licious
627 Blessed Are The Meek
628 Sealed With A Kiss
629 A Special Chime For Jesus
630 May Your Future Be Blessed
631 Wishing You Were Here
632 Bless-um You
633 Tied Up For The Holidays
634 Bringing You A Merry Christmas
635 I Only Have Arms For You
636 America, You're Beautiful
637 The Magic Starts With You
638 Gather Your Dreams
639 Ring Out The Good News
640 You're My Number One Friend

#	DESCRIPTION	FIG	PLT	BELL	MUSC	ORN	DOLL	THMBL	FRAME	CNDL CLMB	BOX	OTHER
641	Girl Protect'g Puppy/Slicker	530158				529974						
642	Girl/G'ng'rbr'd Cooky for Santa	530166	530204	530174		530212 530190		530182				
643	Elephant Carrying Gift	530492										
644	Boy & Girl in Sleigh					530506						
645	Angel/Bluebird Choir/Bunnies	530786										
646	Angel w/Songbk & Blu'bird					530840						
647	Boy in PJ's Wrap'd in Rib'on					530859						
648	Girl in PJ's Wrap'd in Ribbon					530867						
649	Girl w/Butterfly	529931										
650	Girl at Crossroads	C-0113 C-0013				PM-040						
651	Pup Wearing Fleece	BC-922										
652	Girl Point'g to Sand Dollar	PM-931										
653	Girl Praying											523321
654	Girl by Prayer Plaque	530697										
655	Boy by Prayer Plaque	530700										
656	Girl by Gate Holds Flowers	523631										
657	Pig Holds Wrap'd Present	524506										
658	Boy Pluck'g Duck Feathers	526150										
659	Boy/Candy, Dog Lick Face	526487										
660	Girl Holds Open Oyster	531111										

BOLD = Suspended *Italics* = Limited Edition Shaded Area = Retired ◆ = Two-Year Collectible

Boxed = Dated Annual Rounded Box = Annual * = Special Inspirational Title or piece derived from a portion of the drawing

641
An Event For All Seasons
642
1993
Wishing You The
Sweetest Christmas
643
To Jesus
Happy Birthday Jesus
644
Our First Christmas Together 1993
Our First Christmas Together
645
15 Happy Years Together,
What A Tweet!
646
15 Years,
Tweet Music Together
647
Baby's First Christmas
648
Baby's First Christmas
649
Happiness Is
At Our Fingertips
650
Loving
Caring
Sharing
Loving, Caring And Sharing
Along The Way
651
I Got You Under My Skin
652
His Little Treasure
653
Blessed Are The
Ones Who Hunger
654
God grant me
The serenity
to accept the things
I cannot change
The courage to change
the things I can, and
The wisdom to know the
difference
Serenity Prayer Girl
655
God grant me
The serenity
to accept the things
I cannot change
The courage to change
the things I can, and
The wisdom to know the
difference
Serenity Prayer Boy
656
I Will Always Be
Thinking Of You
657
Oinky Birthday
658
Friends To The Very End
659
Sharing Sweet
Moments Together
660
It Is No Secret
What God Can Do

#	DESCRIPTION	FIG	PLT	BELL	MUSC	ORN	DOLL	THMBL	FRAME	CNDL CLMB	BOX	OTHER
661	Girl Holds Basket of Roses	*531243*										
662	Girl Chooses Club for Golf	526193										
663	Girl Kneels in Prayer	(524158)										
664	Girls w/Gifts of Kittens	528633										
665	Girl Holds Poppy	604208										
666	Girl Embroiders Phrase	531707										
667	Girl Points to Wedding Ring	530999										
668	Boy Points to Wedding Ring	531006										
669	African-Am Bride & Groom	532118										
670	African-Amer Girl Grad	532126										
671	African-Amer Boy Grad	532134										
672	Girl Wears Decorated Tree Outfit & Holds Star Aloft	[530425]	[530409]	[604216]		[530395 530387]						
673	Girl Hangs Orn on Tree	524476										
674	Boy & Puppies Carolling	521914										
675	Boy w/Candle & Book	522058										
676	Girl/Angel Jack-in-the-Box	523755										
677	Shepherd w/Lamb/Plaque	532916										
678	Angel in Egg Nog Cup	531952										
679	Santa Boy w/Bag of Toys					528226						
680	Soldier Boy					527327						

BOLD = Suspended *Italics* = Limited Edition Shaded Area = Retired ◆ = Two-Year Collectible

Boxed = Dated Annual Rounded Box = Annual * = Special Inspirational Title or piece derived from a portion of the drawing

661
You Are The Rose
Of His Creation
662
You Suit Me To A Tee
663
Lord, Teach Us To Pray
664
To A Very Special Sister
665
A Poppy For You
666
The Lord Is Counting On You
667
I Still Do
668
I Still Do
669
The Lord Bless You
And Keep You
670
The Lord Bless You
And Keep You
671
The Lord Bless You
And Keep You
672
1994
You're As Pretty
As A Christmas Tree
673
God Cared Enough
To Send His Best
674
Perfect Harmony
675
Now I Lay Me
Down To Sleep
676
Just Poppin' In To Say Hello!
677
Luke 2:10-11
678
Egg Nog
Dropping In For The Holidays
679
Bringing You A
Merry Christmas
680
Onward Christmas Soldiers

#	DESCRIPTION	FIG	PLT	BELL	MUSC	ORN	DOLL	THMBL	FRAME	CNDL CLMB	BOX	OTHER
681	Angel w/Bskt of Snowflakes					528218						
682	Teddy Rests on Heart					530972						
683	Chicken in Wagon w/Egg	528072										
684	B/G Sweethearts/Reindeer					529206						
685	Boy on Hobby Horse Deer					530263						
686	Girl on Hobby Horse Deer					530255						
687	Boy & Pup Fill Sandbag	603864										
688	Girl Blowing Bubbles	529982										
689	Girl Standing by Flower Pot	524379										
690	Pup in Santa Hat & Scarf					520470						
691	Angel atop Open Window											603171 Ornament Holder
692	Boy Bandaging Tree	531073										
693	Angel by Cave	527106										
694	Girl with Wreath	531677				531685						
695	Angel Looking over Lily	531928										
696	Baby Jesus in Manger	604151				532088						
697	Two Angels Guard'g Poem	603503										
698	Girl Giving Donation										Wall Hangings	523291
699	Girl with Butterfly on Hand											523399
700	Girl Hugs Teddy Bear	PM-931										

BOLD = Suspended *Italics* = Limited Edition Shaded Area = Retired ◆ = Two-Year Collectible

Boxed = Dated Annual Rounded Box = Annual * = Special Inspirational Title or piece derived from a portion of the drawing

681 Sending You A White Christmas

682 You Are Always In My Heart

683 Nativity Cart

684 Our First Christmas Together

685 Baby's First Christmas

686 Baby's First Christmas

687 Nothing Can Dampen The Spirit Of Caring

688 Memories Are Made Of This

689 So Glad I Picked You As A Friend

690 Take A Bow 'Cuz You're My Christmas Star

691 Bisque Ornament Holder

692 Money's Not The Only Green Thing Worth Saving

693 He Is Not Here For He Is Risen As He Said

694 Surrounded With Joy

695 Death Can't Keep Him In The Ground

696 A King Is Born

697 On The Hill Overlooking The Quiet Blue Stream ...

698 Blessed Are The Merciful

699 Blessed Are The Pure In Heart

700 Loving

#	DESCRIPTION	FIG	PLT	BELL	MUSC	ORN	DOLL	THMBL	FRAME	CNDL CLMB	BOX	OTHER
701	Mouse Naps on Turtle Shell	BC-941										
702	Girl Holds Peace Dove											523348 Wall Hanging
703	2 Owls Share Tree Branch	BC-932										
704	Kangaroo Boxer	BC-931										
705	Clown Carries Balloon	B-0108 B-0008										
706	Girl Sits in Pot of Gold	C-0114 C-0014										
707	Girl First Aid to Teddy	PM-941										

BOLD = Suspended *Italics* = Limited Edition Shaded Area = Retired ◆ = Two-Year Collectible

Boxed = Dated Annual Rounded Box = Annual * = Special Inspirational Title or piece derived from a portion of the drawing

701 God Bless Our Home	702 Blessed Are The Peacemakers	703 Owl Always Be Your Friend	704 Put A Little Punch In Your Birthday	705 Happiness Is Belonging
706 You Are The End Of My Rainbow	707 Caring			

GLOSSARY continued

National Day Of Prayer -

Each year, National Day Of Prayer is celebrated nationwide, and the White House has special activities, including a prayer breakfast that morning. Singer Pat Boone, who works closely with Mr. Freedman and Enesco on the Easter Seals program also works with National Day Of Prayer. Pat's friendship with Sam Butcher and Eugene Freedman led to the creation of the National Day Of Prayer figurines. The first figurine - "God Bless The USA," was created in a 9" size and presented by Sam Butcher to President George Bush during ceremonies at the White House in 1992.

Easter Seals -

For many years, Enesco has been a leading national corporate sponsor of the Easter Seals program, and in 1987, the first Precious Moments figurine, "He Walks With Me," was created, with part of the proceeds of the sale of the figurine going to the Easter Seals campaign. Each year since that time, a special figurine has been created for Easter Seals fund raising. With the exception of the 1988 figurine, "Blessed Are They That Overcome," each figurine has had the Easter Seals Lily included on the decal on the base of the figurine (this was forgotten on 1988 figurines).

In 1988, to enhance the fund raising efforts for Easter Seals, Enesco made a special 9" figurine available to retailers. To obtain one of these limited figurines, the retailer donated $500 to Easter Seals via Enesco. The figurine was shipped, along with a packet of raffle tickets, and the retailer was encouraged to sell the raffle tickets at $1 each to offset the cost of the figurine. Once all the tickets were sold, or at a date determined by the retailer, a drawing was held, and a lucky collector won the figurine. The program of 9" figurines has continued since 1988, and the cost to the retailer has remained at $500 per figurine (Enesco absorbs the shipping charges). Many retailers now simply obtain the figurines for their collectors who are willing to donate the $500 to Easter Seals. These special 9" figurines are among the most limited pieces in the Collection.

Damien Dutton Figurine -

The Damien Dutton figurine and matching Bible was the first fund raising effort which Sam Butcher and Enesco undertook by means of the Enesco Precious Moments Collection. This effort was handled differently than fund raising projects since that time. The Damien Dutton Figurine and Bible (optional) was introduced to collectors by means of a letter and order form mailed to them and an 800 number to call to place an order. Unfortunately, not all collectors in the Enesco Precious Moments Collectors Club received this mailing, so many collectors were unaware of this very limited figurine and Bible. Also, unlike any other fund raising figurine, this particular piece received a special understamp -- a diamond marking -- the only time this has been done in the history of the Collection. The Damien Dutton Society, operating from Long Island, New York, is a non-profit organization whose emphasis is research and treatment of those suffering from leprosy.

... continued on page 150

GREENBOOK ALPHA-LOG™

The GREENBOOK ALPHA-LOG lists PRECIOUS MOMENTS Titles alphabetically. The titles are cross-referenced with the GREENBOOK ARTCHART Number and the Enesco Item Number for each piece by product type. In addition, the ALPHA-LOG notes if each piece is a Dated Annual, an Annual, a Two-Year Collectible, a Limited Edition, Retired, or Suspended.

INSPIRATIONAL TITLE	DESCRIPTION	#	FIG	PLT	BELL	MUSC	ORN	DOLL	THMBL	FRAME	CNDL CLMB	BOX	OTHER
15 Happy Years Together, What A Tweet!	Bunnies Listen/Angel Leads Bluebird Choir	645	530786										
15 Years, Tweet Music Together	Angel w/Bird & S'ngbk	646					530840						
A Friend Is Someone Who Cares	Mouse Wiping Tears	449	520632										
A Growing Love	Girl/Flowerpot/Sunflwr	399	E-0108 E-0008				520349						
A King Is Born	Baby Jesus in Manger	696	604151				532088						
A Monarch Is Born	Boy/Butterfly/Manger	190	**E-5380**										
A Poppy For You	Girl Holds Poppy	665	604208										
A Reflection Of His Love	Girl/Bird/Bird Bath	552	522279										529095 Egg
A Smile's The Cymbal Of Joy	Clown with Cymbals	364	B-0102 B-0002										
A Special Chime For Jesus	Boy in PJ's/Bell	629	524468										
A Special Delivery	Girl with Baby	552	521493										
A Tub Full Of Love	Baby Girl/Wood Tub	363	112313										
A Tub Full Of Love	Baby Boy/Wood Tub	348	104817										
A Universal Love	Child Signing Message	591	527173										
Aaron	Boy Angel	247						**12424**					
All Aboard For Birthday Club Fun	Engineer Riding Locomotive	612	B-0107 B-0007										
Always In His Care	Girl/Chick in Egg	507	524522										
Always Room For One More	Girl/Box/Puppies	444	C-0009 C-0109				522961						
America, You're Beautiful	Girl as Stat. of Liberty	636	528862										
An Event For All Seasons	Girl in Slicker w/Puppy	641	530158				529974						
An Event Worth Wading For	Girl Wading to Ducks	596	527319										
Angel Of Mercy	Nurse w/Potted Plant	282	102482				102407						
Angels We Have Heard On High	Two Angels on Stool	557	524921										
Angie, The Angel Of Mercy	Nurse Doll	339						*12491*					
Animal Collection	Animals	147	**E-9267** (For A-F see ART CHART Numbers 407, 408, 409, 412, 413, & 414.)										
April Girl	Girl with Umbrella	370	110027										
August Girl	Girl in Swimming Pool	425	110078										
Autumn's Praise	Girl/Hands behind Her	228	12084	12122		408751 ◆		408808 ◆					

Baby Figurines	Baby Figurines	178	E-2852 (For A-F see ART CHART Numbers 401-406.)										
Baby's First Birthday	Baby/Cake w/1 Cndl	624	524069										
Baby's First Christmas	Baby Boy Hold Bottle	257	15539				15903						
Baby's First Christmas	Boy w/Candy Cane	286					102512						
Baby's First Christmas	Boy Holding Block	95					**E-2372**						
Baby's First Christmas	Baby Girl w/Bottle	258	15547				15911						
Baby's First Christmas	Baby/Chrstms Stock'g	89					**E-2362**						
Baby's First Christmas	Girl w/Candy Cane	285					102504						
Baby's First Christmas	Boy with Teddy	1					**E-5631**						
Baby's First Christmas	Girl with Bunny	2					**E-5632**						
Baby's First Christmas	Girl/Rocking Horse	356					109401						
Baby's First Christmas	Boy/Rocking Horse	357					109428						
Baby's First Christmas	Boy in Sleigh	432					115282 523194						
Baby's First Christmas	Girl in Sleigh	435					520241 523208						
Baby's First Christmas	Baby Girl with Pie	516					523771						
Baby's First Christmas	Baby Boy with Pie	517					523798						
Baby's First Christmas	Baby Boy with Drum	560					527084						
Baby's First Christmas	Baby Girl with Drum	561					527092						
Baby's First Christmas	Boy Sit/Candy Cane	601					527483						
Baby's First Christmas	Girl Sit/Candy Cane	600					527475						
Baby's First Christmas	Boy in PJ's/Ribbon	647					530859						
Baby's First Christmas	Girl in PJ's/Ribbon	648					530867						
Baby's First Christmas	Boy on Hobby Horse	685					530263						
Baby's First Christmas	Girl on Hobby Horse	686					530255						
Baby's First Haircut	Angel Cut Baby's Hair	234	**12211**										
Baby's First Meal	Baby/Highchair/Bowl	534	524077										
Baby's First Pet	Boy/Baby/Feed Dog	461	**520705**										
Baby's First Picture	Angel Tak'g Baby Pic	174	E-2841										
Baby's First Step	Angel Helping Baby	173	**E-2840**										
Baby's First Trip	Angel Pushing Buggy	267	**16012**										
Baby's First Word	Baby/Footed Sleepers	592	527238										
Be Not Weary In Well Doing	Girl Helper	36	E-3111										
Bear The Good News Of Christmas	Bear on Sled	347					104515						
Bear Ye One Another's Burdens	Sad Boy with Teddy	52	**E-5200**										

BOLD = Suspended *Italics* = Limited Edition Shaded Area = Retired Boxed = Dated Annual Rounded Box = Annual ◆ = Two Year Collectible

INSPIRATIONAL TITLE	DESCRIPTION	#	FIG	PLT	BELL	MUSC	ORN	DOLL	THMBL	FRAME	CNDL CLMB	BOX	OTHER
Beatitude Ornament Series	Chapel Stained Glass Window Replicas	542					PM-890 (Set of 7) (Also individually numbered PM-190 through PM-790.)						
Being Nine Is Just Divine	Prancing Pony	574	521833										
Believe The Impossible	Boy with Barbells	383	**109487**										
Bethany	Girl Angel	248						**12432**					
Birds Of A Feather Collect Together	Girl with Embroidery Hoop/Bird	295	E-0006 E-0106				PM-864						
Bisque Ornament Holder	Angel atop Window	691											603171 Ornament Holder
Bless The Days Of Our Youth	Clown with Pull Rope	303	16004										
Bless This House	B&G Paint Dog House	113	**E-7164**										
Bless Those Who Serve Their Country	African-American	595	**527297**										
	Air Force	590	**526584**										
	Army	589	**526576**										
	Girl Soldier	594	**527289**										
	Marine	602	**527521**										
	Navy	588	**526568**										
Bless You Two	Groom Carrying Bride	139	E-9255										
Bless-um You	Native American Girl	632	527335										
Blessed Are The Humble	Princess Washes Feet	610											523437
Blessed Are The Meek	Native Am. w/Fawn	627									Wall Hangings		523313
Blessed Are The Merciful	Girl Gives Donation	698											523291
Blessed Are The Ones Who Hunger	Girl Praying	653											523321
Blessed Are The Peacemakers	Boy Hold'g Cat & Dog	31	E-3107										
Blessed Are The Peacemakers	Girl Holds Peace Dove	702											523348
Blessed Are The Pure In Heart	Rocking Cradle	28	**E-3104**				E-0515 & E-5392				**E-0521**		
Blessed Are The Pure In Heart	Girl w/Butterfly	699										Wall Hangings	523399
Blessed Are The Ones Who Mourn	Girl Crying/Kitten/ Spilled Milk	609											523380
Blessed Are They That Overcome	Boy w/Braces & Dog	396	115479										
Blessings From Above	B&G Kissing/Mistletoe	495	523747										
Blessings From Me To Thee	Girl at Birdhouse	120		523860									
Blessings From My House To Yours	Girl at Birdhouse	120	**E-0503**										

Bon Voyage!	B&G on Motorcycle	474	522201										
Bong Bong	Boy Clown	289						*100455*					
Bride	Bride	313	E-2846										
Bridesmaid	Bridesmaid	170	E-2831										
Brighten Someone's Day	Skunk and Mouse	395	**105953**										
Bring The Little Ones To Jesus	Mom/Wordless Bk/Kids	603	527556	531359									
Bringing God's Blessing To You	Girl Angel Push'g Jesus	125	**E-0509**										
Bringing You A Merry Christmas	Boy on Sled/Turtle/Gift	634	527599										
Bringing You A Merry Christmas	Santa Boy/Bag of Toys	679					528226						
Brotherly Love	Pilgrim/Indian/Turkey	276	**100544**										
Bundles Of Joy	Girl with Presents	96	E-2374				525057						
But Love Goes On Forever	B/G Angels on Cloud	39	E-3115 E-0001									Plaques {	E-0102 E-0202
But Love Goes On Forever	Boy Angel on Cloud	56					**E-5627**				**E-6118**		
But Love Goes On Forever	Girl Angel on Cloud	57					**E-5628**						
But The Greatest Of These Is Love	Girl Holding Her List to Santa	606	527688	527742	527726		527696 527734		527718				
Camel	Camel	90	E-2363										
Camel, Donkey, Cow	Camel, Donkey, Cow	100					**E-2386**						
Candy	Girl Clown	290						*100463*					
Can't Be Without You	Kitty/open Cage/Bird	538	524492										
Can't Bee Hive Myself Without You	Teddy w/Bee & Hive	488	BC-891										
Caring	Girl/First Aid to Teddy	707	PM-941										
Cheers To The Leader	Girl Cheerleader	345	104035				**113999**						
Christmas Fireplace	Fireplace w/Stockings	512	**524883**										
Christmas Is A Time To Share	Boy Giving Toy Lamb	24	**E-2802**			E-2806							
Christmas Is Ruff Without You	Puppy Rest on Elbow	470					520462						
Christmas Joy From Head To Toe	Girl with Stocking	88	**E-2361**										
Christmastime Is For Sharing	Boy Giving Teddy	121	E-0504	E-0505									
Clown Figurines/Thimbles	Mini Clowns	235	12238(/A-D) (Also see ART CHART Numbers 416 - 419.)						**100668**				
Collecting Makes Good Scents	Skunk with Flowers	544	BC-901										
Collection Plaque	Boy Angel on Cloud	56										Plaque }	**E-6901**
Come Let Us Adore Him	Boy w/Manger Baby	21	E-2011										
Come Let Us Adore Him	Manger w/Child	62	**E-5619**										
Come Let Us Adore Him	Nativity Set/Cassette	307	104000										

BOLD = Suspended *Italics* = Limited Edition Shaded Area = Retired Boxed = Dated Annual Rounded Box = Annual ◆ = Two Year Collectible

INSPIRATIONAL TITLE	DESCRIPTION	#	FIG	PLT	BELL	MUSC	ORN	DOLL	THMBL	FRAME	CNDL CLMB	BOX	OTHER
Come Let Us Adore Him	Nativity	22	E-2800 E-2395	*E-5646*		**E-2810**	**E-5633**						
Congratulations, Princess	Girl Graduate	318	106208										
Connie	Doll with Stand	291						*102253*					
Cow	Cow with Bell	69	E-5638										
Crown Him Lord Of All	Boy/Manger/Crown	25	**E-2803**			**E-2807**							
Cubby	Groom Doll	115						*E-7267B*					
Dashing Through The Snow	Girl/Doll/Sleigh	367					**521574**						
Dawn's Early Light	Girl Covering Kitten	160	PM-831										
"Dealers Only" Nativity	Nativity w/Backdrop	337	104523										
Death Can't Keep Him In The Ground	Angel Look'g @ Lily	695	531928										
Debbie	Debbie Doll	76						**E-6214G**					
December Girl	Girl/Christmas Candle	429	110116										
Do Not Open Till Christmas	Boy Peeking into Pkg	576				**522244**							
Donkey	Donkey	63	E-5621										
Don't Let The Holidays Get You Down	Boy w/Christmas Tree	471	522112				521590						
Dropping In For Christmas	Boy Ice Skater/Cap	84	**E-2350**				E-2369						
Dropping In For The Holidays	Angel in Egg Nog Cup	678	531952										
Dropping Over For Christmas	Girl with Pie	97	E-2375				E-2376						
Easter's On Its Way	Boy/Wagon/Lily/Girl	508	521892										
Eggs Over Easy	Girl with Fry Pan	45	E-3118										
Eggspecially For You	Girl/Hen/Easter Egg	455	520667										
Especially For Ewe	Lamb	153	**E-9282 (/C)**										
Every Man's House Is His Castle	Beaver Building Home	615	BC-921										
Faith Is A Victory	Girl/Boxing Gloves	496	521396										
Faith Takes The Plunge	Girl with Plunger	389	111155										
February Girl	Girl/Plant in Snow	368	109991										
Feed My Sheep	Girl Feeding Lamb	366	PM-871										
Fishing For Friends	Raccoon Holding Fish	335	BC-861										
Flower Girl	Flower Girl	209	E-2835										

For God So Loved The World	Deluxe Nativity	192	**E-5382**										
Forever Friends	Dog and Cat (2)	309										**E-9283 (/A & /B)**	
Forgiving Is Forgetting	B&G with Bandage	136	**E-9252**										
Four Seasons	Four Seasons Thimbles	226	227 228 229						100641				
Friends Never Drift Apart	Kids in Boat	219	100250				522937						
Friends To The End	Rhino with Bird	420	**104418**										
Friends To The Very End	Boy Plucking Feathers	658	526150										
Friendship Grows When You Plant A Seed	Girl Watering Seedling	579	524271										
Friendship Hits The Spot	Two Girls/Tea Party	453	520748										

Gather Your Dreams	Girl w/Bunnies/Apron	638	*529680*										
Get Into The Habit Of Prayer	Nun	233	**12203**										
Glide Through The Holidays	Girl on Roller Skates	499					521566						
Goat	Goat	91	**E-2364**										
God Bless America	Uncle Sam/Bible/Dog	292	102938										
God Bless Our Family	Parents of the Groom	325	100498										
God Bless Our Family	Parents of the Bride	326	100501										
God Bless Our Home	B&G/Sandcastle	239	12319										
God Bless Our Home	Mouse on Turtle Shell	701	BC-941										
God Bless Our Years Together	Family/Birthday Cake	249	12440										
God Bless The Bride	Bride with Flower Girl	171	E-2832										
God Bless The Day We Found You	Mom/Dad/Girl w/Adoption	272	**100145**										
God Bless The Day We Found You	Mom/Dad/Boy w/Adoption	273	**100153**										
God Bless The USA	Uncle Sam Praying	604	527564										
God Bless You For Touching My Life	Girl Painting Butterfly	439	PM-881										
God Bless You Graduate	Boy Graduate	334	106194										
God Bless You On Your Birthday	Seal - Age 2	298	15962										
God Bless You With Rainbows	Angel/Rainbow	199										Night Light } **16020**	
God Blessed Our Year Together With So Much Love And Happiness	1st Anniversary	102	E-2854										

BOLD = Suspended *Italics* = Limited Edition Shaded Area = Retired Boxed = Dated Annual Rounded Box = Annual ◆ = Two Year Collectible

INSPIRATIONAL TITLE	DESCRIPTION	#	FIG	PLT	BELL	MUSC	ORN	DOLL	THMBL	FRAME	CNDL CLMB	BOX	OTHER
God Blessed Our Years Together With So Much Love And Happiness	Happy Anniversary	179	E-2853										
	5th Anniversary	181	E-2855										
	10th Anniversary	182	E-2856										
	25th Anniversary	183	E-2857										
	40th Anniversary	184	E-2859										
	50th Anniversary	185	E-2860										
God Cared Enough To Send His Best	Girl Hangs Ornament	673	524476										
God Gave His Best	Girl with Ornament	263	**15806**										
God Is Love	Girl w/Goose in Lap	60	**E-5213**										
God Is Love, Dear Valentine	Boy Holding Heart	102	**E-7153**										
God Is Love, Dear Valentine	Girl Holding Heart	103	**E-7154**						**100625**				
God Is Love Dear Valentine	Girl w/Valentine	509	523518										
God Is Watching Over You	Boy w/Ice Bag/Head	112	**E-7163**										
God Loveth A Cheerful Giver	Girl with Puppies	20	E-1378										
God Sends The Gift Of His Love	Girl/Present/Kitten	204	**E-6613**										
God Sent His Love	Angel w/Holly Wreath	259	15881		15873		15768		15865				
God Sent His Son	Girl Look'g in Manger	123	**E-0507**										
God Sent You Just In Time	Clown/Jack-in-Box	256				15504	**113972**						
God Understands	Boy w/Report Card	12	**E-1379B**		E-5211								
God's Precious Gift	Baby Boy	310								**12033**			
God's Precious Gift	Baby Girl	311								**12041**			
God's Promises Are Sure	Ang'l Wind'g Rainbow	142	**E-9260**										
God's Ray Of Mercy	Boy Angel/Flashlight	206	PM-841										
God's Speed	Boy Jogging w/Dog	44	E-3112										
Going Home	Angel/Child/Heaven	584	525979										
Good Friends Are For Always	Girl in Snowsuit/Bunny	555	524123				524131						
Good Friends Are Forever	Girls with Flower	492	521817 525049										
Good News Is So Uplifting	Girl on Ladder	554	523615										
Grandma's Prayer	Praying Grandma	305	PM-861										
Groom	Groom	269	E-2837										
Groomsman	Groomsman w/Frog	172	E-2836										
Hallelujah Country	Cowboy/Guitar	377	105821										
Halo, & Merry Christmas	Angels/Snowman	241	**12351**										

Hang On For The Holly Days	Kitten Hang/Wreath	400					520292						
Happiness Divine	Clown Angel/Flowers	384	109584										
Happiness Is At Our Fingertips	Girl Reach'g/Butterfly	649	529931										
Happiness Is Belonging	Clown Carries Balloon	705	B-0108 B-0008										
Happiness Is The Lord	Boy Playing Banjo	242	**12378**										
Happiness Is The Lord	Boy Clown w/Ball	235					**15830**						
Happy Birdie	Bird Blow/out Candle	597	527343										
Happy Birthday Dear Jesus	Teddy Bear in Pkg	513	**524875**										
Happy Birthday Jesus	Elephant Carrying Gift	643	530492										
Happy Birthday Little Lamb	Lamb - Age 1	297	15946										
Happy Birthday Poppy	Girl Holding Poppy	381	**106836**										
Happy Days Are Here Again	Girl Clown w/Books	346	**104396**										
Happy Trails Is Trusting Jesus	Girl on Hobby Horse	494					**523224**						
Happy Trip	Girl on Roller Skates	499	**521280**										
Have A Beary Merry Christmas	Teddy in Rocker	469	**522856**										
Have A Beary Special Birthday	Teddy Bear w/Balloon	487	B-0104 B-0004										
Have A Heavenly Christmas	Boy in Airplane	246					12416						
Have I Got News For You	Boy Reading Scroll	350	**105635** **528137**										
He Careth For You	Boy Helping Lamb	10	**E-1377B**										
He Cleansed My Soul	Girl in Old Bath Tub	220	100277				112380						
He Is My Inspiration	Sam Butcher as Artist	563	523038										
He Is My Song	Boy/Trumpet/Dog	244	**12394**										
He Is Not Here For He Is Risen As He Said	Angel by Cave	693	527106										
He Is The Star Of The Morning	Angel/Cloud/Manger	481	**522252**										
He Leadeth Me	Boy Leading Lamb	9	**E-1377A**										
HE Loves Me	Girl Holding Flower	535	524263										
He Upholdeth Those Who Call	Angel Catch'g Skater	130	**E-0526**										
He Walks With Me	Girl/Crutches/Bible	319	107999										
He Watches Over Us All	Boy/Bible/Crutches	29	**E-3105**										
Heaven Bless You	Baby w/Bunny/Turtle	221	520934			**100285**							
Heaven Bless Your Special Day	Pig - Age 3	299	15954										
Heaven Bless Your Togetherness	Groom/Trunk/Bride	378	106755										
Hello, Lord It's Me Again	Boy on Telephone	78	PM-811										
Hello World!	Kangaroo with Baby	451	521175										

INSPIRATIONAL TITLE	DESCRIPTION	#	FIG	PLT	BELL	MUSC	ORN	DOLL	THMBL	FRAME	CNDL CLMB	BOX	OTHER
Help Lord, I'm In A Spot	Boy Stand'g in Ink Spot	275	100269										
He's The Healer Of Broken Hearts	B/G Bandaging Heart	317	100080										
Hi Sugar!	Mouse in Sugar Bowl	398	BC-871										
High Hopes	Boy with Kite	498	**521957**										
His Burden Is Light	Indian Girl	14	E-1380G										
His Eye Is On The Sparrow	Girl w/Bird in Hand	131	E-0530										
His Little Treasure	Girl/Sand Dollar	652	PM-931										
His Love Will Shine On You	Girl with Lily	443	522376										
His Name Is Jesus	Boys at Manger	191	**E-5381**										
His Sheep Am I	Shepherd Paint Lamb	110	**E-7161**										
Holy Smokes	Two Angels/Candles	85	E-2351										
Honk If You Love Jesus	Mother Goose/Babes	255	15490				**15857**						
Hope You're Over The Hump	Monkey Rid'g Camel	619	521671										
Hope You're Up And On The Trail Again	Girl on Hobby Horse	494	**521205**										
Hoppy Easter Friend	Girl Collect Eggs/Frog	529	521906										
Houses And Palm Tree	Mini Houses w/Palms	101	E-2387										
How Can I Ever Forget You	Elephant/Knot in Trunk	558	526924										
How Can Two Walk Together Except They Agree	B/G Horse Costume	145	**E-9263**										
Hug One Another	B&G Hugging	526	521299										

INSPIRATIONAL TITLE	DESCRIPTION	#	FIG	PLT	BELL	MUSC	ORN	DOLL	THMBL	FRAME	CNDL CLMB	BOX	OTHER
I Believe In Miracles	Boy Holding Chick	105	**E-7156**	*E-9257*									
I Believe In Miracles	Boy Holding Bluebird	374	E-7156R										
I Believe In The Old Rugged Cross	Girl Holding Cross	224	103632				**522953**						
I Belong To The Lord	Orphan Girl	463	**520853**										
I Can't Spell Success Without You	Boy/Dog/Blocks	533	**523763**										
I Get A Bang Out Of You	Clown Hold'g Balloons	236	12262										
I Get A Kick Out Of You	Girl/Bucket on Head	167	**E-2827**										
I Got You Under My Skin	Pup/Sheep Fleece	651	BC-922										
I Love To Tell The Story	Boy w/Lamb & Book	294	PM-852										
I Only Have Arms For You	Octopus & Fish Hug'g	635	527769										
I Picked A (Very) Special Mom	Boy w/Garden'g Mom	328	100536										

I Still Do	Girl Points to Ring	667	530999										
I Still Do	Boy Points to Ring	668	531006										
I Will Always Be Thinking Of You	Girl Holds Flower	656	523631										
I Will Cherish The Old Rugged Cross	Girl Holding Cross	224											523534 Egg
I Would Be Lost Without You	Girl Check Roadmap	586	526142										
I Would Be Sunk Without You	Baby Boy/Tub	342	102970										
If God Be For Us, Who Can Be Against Us	Boy at Pulpit	154	**E-9285**										
I'll Never Stop Loving You	Girl/Letters "Y" "O" "U"	511	521418										
I'll Play My Drum For Him	Drummer Boy/Manger	87	**E-2356** E-2360 E-5384	E-2357	E-2358	**E-2355**	E-2359						
I'm A Possibility	Boy with Football	274	100188				**111120**						
I'm A PRECIOUS MOMENTS Fan	Girl with Fan	490	523526										
I'm Falling For Somebunny	Lamb and Bunny	308										**E-9266**	
I'm Following Jesus	Boy in Car	320	PM-862										
I'm Nuts About You	Squirrel Decorat'g Tree	570					520411						
I'm Nuts Over My Collection	Squirrel/Bag of Nuts	547	BC-902										
I'm Sending You A White Christmas	Girl Mailing Snowball	169	E-2829	101834		112402	**112372**						
I'm So Glad That God Blessed Me With A Friend Like You	Girl Holding Kitten Friend Offers Milk	623	523623										
I'm So Glad You Fluttered Into My Life	Boy Angel with Butterfly Net	447	520640										
In His Time	Boy Waiting for a Seed to Grow	375	PM-872										
In The Spotlight Of His Grace	Ballerina on Pointe	524	520543										
Isn't Eight Just Great	Ostrich - Age 8	394	109460										
Isn't He Precious?	Girl with Broom	189	E-5379 **522988**										
Isn't He Wonderful	Boy Angel Pray'g/Harp	70	**E-5639**										
Isn't He Wonderful	Girl Angel/Pray'g/Harp	71	**E-5640**										
It Is Better To Give Than To Receive	Policeman Writing Ticket	237	**12297**										
It Is No Secret What God Can Do	Girl Holds Oyster	660	531111										

BOLD = Suspended *Italics* = Limited Edition Shaded Area = Retired Boxed = Dated Annual Rounded Box = Annual ◆ = Two Year Collectible

INSPIRATIONAL TITLE	DESCRIPTION	#	FIG	PLT	BELL	MUSC	ORN	DOLL	THMBL	FRAME	CNDL CLMB	BOX	OTHER
It's A Perfect Boy	Boy Angel/Red Cross	127	**E-0512** 525286				**102415**						
It's No Yolk When I Say I Love You	Hens Laugh/Girl Drops Egg on Pup's Head	575	**522104**										
It's So Uplifting To Have A Friend Like You	Girl on Skis Startled by Ski Jump	581	524905				528846						
It's The Birthday Of A King	Boy Angel/B'day Cake	288	**102962**										
It's What's Inside That Counts	Boy with Books	42	**E-3119**										
January Girl	Girl/Doll/Sleigh	367	109983										
Jest To Let You Know You're Tops	Clown Pop'g out/Box	568	B-0106 B-0006										
Jesus Is Born	Angels in Chariot	23	**E-2801**										
Jesus Is Born	B&G Playing Angels	17	**E-2012**			**E-2809**							
Jesus Is Born	Shepherd	64			**E-5623**								
Jesus Is Coming Soon	Mary Knitting Booties	240	**12343**										
Jesus Is The Answer	Boy Patching World	15	**E-1381**										
Jesus Is The Answer	Boy/Steth'sc'pe/World	611	E-1381R										
Jesus Is The Light	Girl w/Doll & Candle	4	E-1373G										
Jesus Is The Light That Shines	Boy/Candle/Mouse	119	**E-0502**				**E-0537**						
Jesus Is The Only Way	Boy at Crossroads	464	**520756**										
Jesus Is The Sweetest Name I Know	Angel w/Baby Book	468	**523097**										
Jesus Loves Me	Boy with Teddy	1	E-1372B E-9278	**E-9275**	**E-5208**					**E-7170**		**E-9280**	
Jesus Loves Me	Girl with Bunny	2	E-1372G E-9279 *104531*	**E-9276**	**E-5209**					**E-7171**		**E-9281**	
Jesus The Savior Is Born	Angel/Newspaper	437	**520357**										
Join In On The Blessings	Girl w/Dues Bank	205	E-0104 E-0404										
Joy On Arrival	Stork Delivering Baby	532	523178										
Joy To The World	Boy Angel/Trumpet	79					**E-2343**				**E-2344**		
Joy To The World	Boy Playing Harp	188	**E-5378**				E-5388						
July Girl	Girl w/Puppy/Basket	424	110051										

June Girl	Girl Dress up/Bride	372	110043										
Junior Bridesmaid	Junior Bridesmaid	210	E-2845										
Just A Line To Wish You A Happy Day	Dog Pulling Boy's Fishing Line	456	520721										
Just Poppin' In To Say Halo!	Girl/Angel Jack in/Box	676	523755										
Katie Lynne	Baby Collector's Doll	134						**E-0539**					
Keep Looking Up	Giraffe - Age 6	302	15997										
Kristy	Baby Collector's Doll	177						**E-2851**					
Let Heaven And Nature Sing	Angel/Friends Carol'g	81		*E-2347*		**E-2346**	E-0532						
Let Love Reign	Girl/Chicks/Umbrella	149	E-9273										
Let Not The Sun Go Down Upon Your Wrath	Boy w/Dog on Stairs	270 525	**E-5203**										
Let The Heavens Rejoice	Praying Angel	77			E-5622		E-5629						
Let The Whole World Know	B/G Baptism Bucket	114	**E-7165**			**E-7186**							
Let Us Call The Club To Order	Club Meeting	158	E-0103 E-0303										
Let's Be Friends	Pups Hug Each Other	593	527270										
Let's Keep In Touch	Clown on Elephant	287				102520							
Lord Give Me A Song	Girl Play'g Harmonica	243	**12386**										
Lord Give Me Patience	Bandaged Boy/Sign	108	**E-7159**										
Lord, Help Me Make The Grade	Schoolboy Clown	354	**106216**										
Lord, Help Me Stick To My Job	Girl w/Account Books	503	521450										
Lord, Help Us Keep Our Act Together	Clowns on Unicycle	331	101850										
Lord I'm Coming Home	Baseball Player/Bat	215	100110										
Lord, Keep Me In Teepee Top Shape	Indian Boy with Can of Spinach	565	PM-912										
Lord Keep Me On My Toes	Ballerina	216	100129				102423						
Lord Keep Me On My Toes	Ballerina	582					525332						
Lord Keep Me On The Ball	Clown Sitting on Ball	270	12270										
Lord, Keep My Life In Balance	Ballerina at Barre	525				**520691**							
Lord, Keep My Life In Tune	Boy Playing Piano	231				**12165**							
Lord, Keep My Life In Tune	Girl with Piano	315				**12580**							
Lord, Teach Us To Pray	Girl Kneels in Prayer	663	524158										
Lord, Turn My Life Around	Ballerina	493	520551										

INSPIRATIONAL TITLE	DESCRIPTION	#	FIG	PLT	BELL	MUSC	ORN	DOLL	THMBL	FRAME	CNDL CLMB	BOX	OTHER
Love Beareth All Things	Nurse Give Shot/Bear	107	E-7158										
Love Cannot Break A True Friendship	Girl w/Piggy Bank	48	**E-4722**										
Love Covers All	Girl/Heart Quilt	225	**12009**						**12254**				
Love Is From Above	Boy Whisper'g to Girl	510	521841										
Love Is Kind	Boy w/Turtle	11	**E-1379A**										
Love Is Kind	Girl with Gift	198					**E-5391**						
Love Is Kind	Girl with Mouse	187	E-5377										
Love Is Kind	B/G on Swing	175		*E-2847*									
Love Is Patient	Teacher/Boy/Blkboard	135	**E-9251**										
Love Is Patient	Girl with Slate	133					**E-0536**						
Love Is Patient	Boy with Slate	132					**E-0535**						
Love Is Sharing	Girl at School Desk	111	**E-7162**			E-7185							
Love Is The Best Gift Of All	Girl with Present	360	110930		109835		109770		109843				
Love Is The Glue That Mends	Boy Mending Horse	344	**104027**										
Love Lifted Me	Boy Helping Friend	53	**E-5201**										
Love Lifted Me	B/G on Seesaw	6	E-1375A										
Love Never Fails	Teacher/Report Card	238	12300										
Love One Another	B/G Sitting on Stump	8	E-1376	*E-5215*			522929						
Love Pacifies	Monkey with Pacifier	566	BC-911										
Love Rescued Me	Fireman Hold Puppy	281	102393				102385						
Loving	Girl Hugs Teddy Bear	700	PM-931										
Loving, Caring And Sharing Along The Way	Girl at Crossroads	650	C-0113 C-0013				PM-040						
Loving Is Sharing	Boy Sharing w/Puppy	34	E-3110B										
Loving Is Sharing	Girl Sharing w/Puppy	35	E-3110G										
Loving Thy Neighbor	Mother Wrap Bread	176		*E-2848*									
Loving You	Boy Holding Heart	102								**12017**			
Loving You	Girl Holding Heart	103								**12025**			
Loving You Dear Valentine	Boy Paint'g Valentine	321	PM-873										
Loving You Dear Valentine	Girl/Valentine	322	PM-874										
Luke 2:10 - 11	Shepherd w/His Lamb	677	532916										

INSPIRATIONAL TITLE	DESCRIPTION	#	FIG	PLT	BELL	MUSC	ORN	DOLL	THMBL	FRAME	CNDL CLMB	BOX	OTHER
Make A Joyful Noise	Girl with Goose	5	E-1374G *520322*	*E-7174*			522910						528617 Egg
Make Me A Blessing	Girl with Sick Bear	323	100102										

Many Moons In Same Canoe, Blessum You	Indians in Canoe	(457)	520772										
March Girl	Girl with Kite	(369)	110019										
May All Your Christmases Be White	Girl/Snowball	(477)					**521302**						
May Girl	Girl/Potted Plant	(371)	110035										
May God Bless You With A Perfect Holiday Season	Girl in Scarf/Cap	(197)					**E-5390**						
May Only Good Things Come Your Way	Girl Holding Net for Butterfly	(537)	524425										
May You Have An Old Fashioned Christmas	Christmas Girl in Plaid Dress	(548)				417777◆		417785◆					
May You Have The Sweetest Christmas	Mother with Cookie Sheet	(260)	**15776**										
May Your Birthday Be A Blessing	Girl at Table with Dolls	(166)	**E-2826**										
May Your Birthday Be A Blessing	Girl with Cake with Candles	(536)	524301										
May Your Birthday Be Gigantic	Elephant - Age 4	(300)	15970										
May Your Birthday Be Mammoth	Whale - Age 10	(573)	521825										
May Your Birthday Be Warm	Teddy/Caboose	(296)	15938										
May Your Christmas Be A Happy Home	Family Christmas Scene	(479)		523003			523704						
May Your Christmas Be Blessed	Girl with Bible	(186)	**E-5376**										
May Your Christmas Be Cozy	Boy/PJ's/Teddy	(80)	**E-2345**										
May Your Christmas Be Delightful	Boy Tangled in Christmas Lights	(254)	**15482**				**15849**						
May Your Christmas Be Happy	Girl Clown/Balloon	(235)					**15822**						
May Your Christmas Be Merry	Girl Holding Bird	(56)	524166		524182		524174 526940		524190				
May Your Christmas Be Warm	Boy/Potbellied Stove	(82)	**E-2348**										
May Your Every Wish Come True	Girl/Cake/Table	(625)	524298										
May Your Future Be Blessed	Girl/First Communion	(630)	525316										
May Your Life Be Blessed With Touchdowns	Boy Playing Football	(473)	522023										
May Your World Be Trimmed With Joy	Boy Decorating Globe	(553)	522082										

BOLD = Suspended *Italics* = Limited Edition Shaded Area = Retired Boxed = Dated Annual (Rounded Box) = Annual ◆ = Two Year Collectible

INSPIRATIONAL TITLE	DESCRIPTION	#	FIG	PLT	BELL	MUSC	ORN	DOLL	THMBL	FRAME	CNDL CLMB	BOX	OTHER
Memories Are Made Of This	Girl Blowing Bubbles	688	529982										
Meowie Christmas	Girl with Kitten	423	109800										
Merry Christmas, Deer	Girl/Reindeer	438	522317	520284									
Mikey	Mikey	75						**E-6214B**					
Mini Animal Figurines	3 Mini Animals	279	**102296**										
Mommy, I Love You	Girl with Flower	390	112143										
Mommy, I Love You	Boy with Flower	387	109975										
Money's Not The Only Green Thing Worth Saving	Boy Bandaging Tree	692	531073										
Mother Sew Dear	Mother Needlepoint'g	30	E-3106	*E-5217*	**E-7181**	E-7182	E-0514	E-2850	13293	**E-7241**			
Mouse With Cheese	Mouse with Cheese	99					**E-2381**						
Mow Power To Ya	Boy Push Lawn Mower	486	PM-892										
My Days Are Blue Without You	Girl/Paint/Ladder	462	**520802**										
My Guardian Angel	Boy Angel on Cloud	56				**E-5205**							
My Guardian Angel	Girl Angel on Cloud	57				**E-5206**							
My Guardian Angel	Boy Angel	265								**E-7168**			
My Guardian Angel	Girl Angel	266								**E-7169**			
My Guardian Angels	B/G Angels/Cloud	39										Night Light}	**E-5207**
My Happiness	Girl at Table with Figurine	489	C-0110 C-0010				PM-904						
My Heart Is Exposed With Love	Nurse/Xray/Heart	458	520624										
My Love Will Never Let You Go	Boy w/Hat & Fish	333	103497				**114006**						
My Peace I Give Unto Thee	Kids/Lamp Post	341		102954									
My Warmest Thoughts Are You	Girl on Tree Swing	578	524085										
Nativity Cart	Chicken in Wagon	683	528072										
No Tears Past The Gate	Girl/Gate to Heaven	329	101826										
Nobody's Perfect!	Boy w/Dunce Cap	148	E-9268										
Not A Creature Was Stirring	Mouse/Cheese/Kitten	514	**524484**										
Nothing Can Dampen The Spirit Of Caring	Boy Fills Sandbag as Pup Holds Sack	687	603864										
November Girl	Girl in Pilgrim Suit	428	110108										
Now I Lay Me Down To Sleep	Boy Carries Candle	675	522058										
O Come All Ye Faithful	Boy Carolling	86	E-2353	**E-2352**	**E-0531**								

O Come Let Us Adore Him	4 Piece Nativity	362	**111333**										
O, How I Love Jesus	Indian Boy	13	E-1380B										
October Girl	Girl with Pumpkins	427	110094										
Oh Holy Night	Girl Playing Violin	482	522546		522821		522848		522554				
Oh What Fun It Is To Ride	Grandma on a Sled	361	109819										
Oh Worship The Lord	Boy Angel/Candle	194	**E-5385**										
Oh Worship The Lord	Girl Angel Praying	195	**E-5386**										
Oinky Birthday	Pig Holds Present	657	524506										
On The Hill Overlooking The Quiet Blue Stream ...	Two Angels/Poem	697	603503										
Once Upon A Holy Night	Girl w/Book & Candle	519	523836		523828		523852		523844				
One Step At A Time	Child Tak'g First Steps	564	PM-911										
Only Love Can Make A Home	Mr. Webb/Bird Home	613	PM-921										
Onward Christian Soldiers	Knight in Armor	128	E-0523										
Onward Christmas Soldiers	Soldier Boy	680					527327						
Our Club Can't Be Beat	Clown with Drum	304	B-0001										
Our Club Is A Tough Act To Follow	Clown/Puppy/Drum	543	B-0005 B-0105										
Our First Christmas Together	Boy and Girl in Box	277				101702	102350 112399 520233						
Our First Christmas Together	Girl Knitting Tie	98	**E-2377**	**E-2378**									
Our First Christmas Together	Bride and Groom	38					**E-2385**						
Our First Christmas Together	Couple with Gifts	433	**115290**										
Our First Christmas Together	Bride/Groom in Car	460					521558 525324						
Our First Christmas Together	Groom/Trunk/Bride	378					522945 528870						
Our First Christmas Together	Boy & Girl in Sleigh	644					530506						
Our First Christmas Together	B&G on Reindeer	684					529206						
Our Friendship Is Soda-Licious	G&B/Ice Cream Soda	626	524336										
Our Love Is Heaven Scent	Lamb and Skunk	308										**E-9266**	
Owl Always Be Your Friend	2 Owls Share Branch	703	BC-932										
P.D.	Baby Boy	252						**12475**					
Part Of Me Wants To Be Good	Boy Angel/Devil Suit	230	**12149**										
Peace Amid The Storm	Boy Reading Bible	49	**E-4723**										
Peace On Earth	Boy in Choir	196					**E-5389**						

BOLD = Suspended *Italics* = Limited Edition Shaded Area = Retired Boxed = Dated Annual Rounded Box = Annual ◆ = Two Year Collectible

INSPIRATIONAL TITLE	DESCRIPTION	#	FIG	PLT	BELL	MUSC	ORN	DOLL	THMBL	FRAME	CNDL CLMB	BOX	OTHER
Peace On Earth	Boy/Globe/Teddy	26	**E-2804**										
Peace On Earth	Choir Boys/Bandages	51	**E-4725**			**E-4726**							
Peace On Earth	Girl w/Lion & Lamb	155	**E-9287**										
Peace On Earth	Kids/Pup/Kitten/Bird	341				**109746**	523062						
Perfect Harmony	Boys & Pups Carolling	674	521914										
Praise The Lord Anyhow	Boy with Dog	19	E-1374B										
Praise The Lord Anyhow	Girl at Typewriter	138	E-9254										
Prayer Changes Things	B & G Praying @ Table	61	**E-5214**										
Prayer Changes Things	B & G with Bluebirds	7	**E-1375B**										
Prayer Changes Things	Girl Praying in Field	58			**E-5210**								
Precious Memories	Girl/Trunk/Wedding	168	E-2828										
Precious Memories	Couple/Album	379	106763										
Precious Moments Last Forever	Giveaway Medallion	365											12246 Medallion
Prepare Ye The Way Of The Lord	Angels Prep Manger	124	**E-0508**										
Press On	Girl Ironing Clothes	146	E-9265										
Puppy Love	Two Puppies	465	520764										
Puppy Love Is From Above	Anniversary Couple	380	106798										
Put A Little Punch In Your Birthday	Kangaroo Boxer	704	BC-931										
Put On A Happy Face	Boy Clown/Mask	159	PM-822										
Reindeer	Reindeer	306					102466						
Rejoice O Earth	Angel with Trumpet	382	E-5636 520268			E-5645	113980						
Rejoice, O Earth	Angel	545										Tree Topper }	617334
Rejoicing With You	Christening	50	E-4724	**E-7172**									
Retailer's Dome	Kids on Cloud/Dome	411	E-7350										
Retailer's Wreath	Wreath w/Ornaments	410										Wreath }	111465
Retailer's Wreath Bell	Retailer's Wreath Bell	415			112348								
Ring Out The Good News	Girl Hold'g Doll/Bell	639	529966										
Ring Those Christmas Bells	Angels Ring Bell/Pray	583	525898										
Ringbearer	Ringbearer	208	E-2833										
Rocking Horse	Rocking Horse	283					**102474**						
Safe In The Arms Of Jesus	Baby/Cloud/Ang'l Bird	620	521922										

Scent From Above	Girl with Skunk	327	100528										
Sealed With A Kiss	Bride/Groom/Kiss/Mlbx	628	524441										
Seek And Ye Shall Find	Girl/Shopping Bag	104	E-0005 E-0105										
Seek Ye The Lord	Boy Grad/Scroll	143	**E-9261**										
Seek Ye The Lord	Girl Grad/Scroll	144	**E-9262**										
Sending My Love	Boy/Bow and Arrow	212	**100056**										
Sending You A Rainbow	Girl Angel/Spr'kl'g Can	156	**E-9288**										
Sending You A White Christmas	Angel/Bskt Snowflakes	681					528218						
Sending You My Love	Girl w/Hearts/Cloud	386	109967										
Sending You Showers Of Blessings	Boy/Newspapers over Head	450	520683										
September Girl	Girl Balancing Books	426	110086										
Serenity Prayer Boy	Boy/Serenity Prayer	655	530700										
Serenity Prayer Girl	Girl/Serenity Prayer	654	530697										
Serve With A Smile	Tennis Boy	222					**102431**						
Serve With A Smile	Tennis Girl	218					**102458**						
Serving The Lord	Tennis Boy	222	**100293**										
Serving The Lord	Tennis Girl	218	**100161**										
Sew In Love	Girl Sewing Pants	382	106844										
Share In The Warmth Of Christmas	Girl with Christmas Candle	429					527211						
Sharing A Gift Of Love	Girl Help Bird to Fly	539	527114										
Sharing Begins In The Heart	Girl with Chalkboard	467	520861										
Sharing Is Universal	Girl/Package/Friend	336	E-0007 E-0107										
Sharing Our Christmas Together	Husband/Wife/Puppy	284	**102490**										
Sharing Our Joy Together	Bridesmaid w/Kitten	268	**E-2834**										
Sharing Our Season Together	Boy & Girl/Sled	118	**E-0501**			E-0519							
Sharing Season Ornament	Brass Filagree/Kids	376					PM-009						
Sharing Sweet Moments Together	Boy Eats Candy as Dog Licks His Face	659	526487										
Sharing The Good News Together	Girl at Mailbox with Club Newsletter	562	C-0011 C-0111				PM-037						
Shepherd Of Love	Angel w/Black Lamb	278	102261				**102288**						
Showers Of Blessings	Elephant /Mouse	352	105945										
Silent Knight	Boy Angel/Knight	73				**E-5642**							

BOLD = Suspended *Italics* = Limited Edition Shaded Area = Retired Boxed = Dated Annual Rounded Box = Annual ◆ = Two Year Collectible

INSPIRATIONAL TITLE	DESCRIPTION	#	FIG	PLT	BELL	MUSC	ORN	DOLL	THMBL	FRAME	CNDL CLMB	BOX	OTHER
Silent Night	Christmas Tree	264				**15814**							
Sitting Pretty	Girl Angel/Stool	349	**104825**										
Slow Down And Enjoy The Holidays	Reindeer Turtle Carrying Gift	616					520489						
Smile Along The Way	Clown Balancing	330	101842				**113964**						
Smile, God Loves You	Boy with Black Eye	3	E-1373B										
Smile, God Loves You	Girl with Curlers	117	PM-821										
Sno-Bunny Falls For You Like I Do	Rabbit on Skates	549					520438						
So Glad I Picked You As A Friend	Girl by Flowerpot	689	524379										
Some Bunnies Sleeping	Bunnies	431	**522996**										
Some Bunny's Sleeping	Bunnies	431	115274										
Somebunny Cares	Bunny/Stuffed Carrot	441	BC-881										
Someday My Love	Bride with Dress	446	520799										
Something's Missing When You're Not Around	Girl Holding Doll with Dog	421	**105643**										
Sowing The Seeds Of Love	Girl Pray'g/Flower	614	PM-922										
Stocking Hanger	Boy Tangled in Lights	445	558125										
Summer's Joy	Girl w/Crossed Arms	227	12076	12114		408743◆		408794◆					
Surround Us With Joy	Boy with Wreath	122					E-0513						
Surrounded With Joy	Boy with Wreath	122	E-0506		E-0522								
Surrounded With Joy	Girl with Wreath	694	531677				531685						
Sweep All Your Worries Away	Girl/Dust under Rug	502	521779										

INSPIRATIONAL TITLE	DESCRIPTION	#	FIG	PLT	BELL	MUSC	ORN	DOLL	THMBL	FRAME	CNDL CLMB	BOX	OTHER
Take A Bow 'Cuz You're My Christmas Star	Pup Carries Holly Sprig	690					520470						
Take Heed When You Stand	Boy on Rocking Horse	550	**521272**										
Tammy	Bride Doll	116						*E-7267G*					
Taste And See That The Lord Is Good	Girl Angel Making Food	150	E-9274										
Tell It To Jesus	Girl on Telephone	476	521477										
Tell Me A Story	Boy Sit Listen/Story	262	**15792**										
Tell Me The Story Of Jesus	Girl/Doll/Book	83	**E-2349**	15237			**E-0533**						
Ten Years And Still Going Strong	Girl in Race Car	540	PM-901										
Thank You For Coming To My Ade	Lemonade Stand	54	**E-5202**										

Thank You Lord For Everything	Boy/Turkey/Dine	472	**522031**										
Thanking Him For You	Girl Praying in Field	58	**E-7155**										
That's What Friends Are For	Crying Girls Hugging	520	521183										
The Club That's Out Of This World	Girl in Spacesuit	569	C-0112 C-0012				PM-038						
The End Is In Sight	Dog Rip'g Boy's Pants	137	**E-9253**										
The Eyes Of The Lord Are Upon You	Baby Girl on Pillow	523				**429589**							
The Eyes Of The Lord Are Upon You	Baby Boy on Pillow	522				**429570**							
The First Noel	Boy Angel/Candle	92	**E-2365**				**E-2367**						
The First Noel	Girl Angel Praying	93	**E-2366**				E-2368						
The Fruit Of The Spirit Is Love	Girl Holding Fruit	618	521213										
The Good Lord Always Delivers	Mom-To-Be/Baby Bk	497	523453				**527165**						
The Good Lord Has Blessed Us Ten Fold	Couple w/ Dog & Puppies	392	114022										
The Greatest Gift Is A Friend	Baby Boy/Dog	355	109231										
The Greatest Of These Is Love	Commandments	483	**521868**										
The Hand That Rocks The Future	Girl Rocking Cradle	32	**E-3108**	*E-9256*		E-5204							
The Heavenly Light	Angel with Flashlight	68	E-5637										
The Joy Of The Lord Is My Strength	Mother with Babies	217	100137										
The Light Of The World Is Jesus	Girl with Lamppost	475				521507							
The Lord Bless You & Keep You	Boy Graduate	46	**E-4720**		**E-7175**					**E-7177**			
The Lord Bless You & Keep You	Bride and Groom	38	E-3114	**E-5216**	**E-7179**	E-7180				**E-7166**		**E-7167**	
The Lord Bless You & Keep You	Girl Graduate	47	E-4721		**E-7176**					**E-7178**			
The Lord Bless You & Keep You	Bride	313							**100633**				
The Lord Bless You & Keep You	Bride & Groom	669	532118										
The Lord Bless You & Keep You	Girl Graduate	670	532126										
The Lord Bless You & Keep You	Boy Graduate	671	532134										
The Lord Giveth And The Lord Taketh Away	Girl with Cat and Birdcage	340	100226										
The Lord Is Counting On You	Girl Embroiders Phrase	666	531707										
The Lord Is My Shepherd	Girl Holding Lamb	293	PM-851										
The Lord Is Your Light To Happiness	Bridal Couple Lighting Candle	466	520837										
The Lord Turned My Life Around	Ballerina on Pointe	571	520535										
The Lord Will Carry You Through	Clown w/Dog/Mud	251	12467										

BOLD = Suspended *Italics* = Limited Edition Shaded Area = Retired Boxed = Dated Annual Rounded Box = Annual ◆ = Two Year Collectible

INSPIRATIONAL TITLE	DESCRIPTION	#	FIG	PLT	BELL	MUSC	ORN	DOLL	THMBL	FRAME	CNDL CLMB	BOX	OTHER
The Lord Will Provide	Girl/Seeds/Flwrs/Birds	622	523593										
The Magic Starts With You	Magician/Bunny/Hat	637					529648						
The Perfect Grandpa	Grandpa in Rocker	109	**E-7160**				**E-0517**						
The Purr-fect Grandma	Grandma in Rocker	33	E-3109	*E-7173*	**E-7183**	**E-7184**	E-0516		13307	**E-7242**			
The Spirit Is Willing But The Flesh Is Weak	Girl/Candy/Scale	324	100196										
The Story Of God's Love	Father Reading Bible	261	**15784**										
The Sweetest Club Around	Pippin/Pop/Cake	440	B-0003 B-0103										
The Voice Of Spring	Girl by Fence	226	12068	12106		408735◆		408786◆					
The Wonder Of Christmas	Boy/Sled/Girl/Tree	202		E-5396									
Thee I Love	Boy Carving Tree	40	E-3116										
There Is Joy In Serving Jesus	Waitress Carry'g Food	106	E-7157										
There Is No Greater Treasure Than To Have A Friend Like You	Boy Swimmer Holding Oyster with Pearl	617	521000										
There Shall Be Showers Of Blessings	Boy and Girl in Garden	500	522090										
There's A Christian Welcome Here	Angel outside Chapel	491	523011				528021						
There's A Light At The End Of The Tunnel	Girl Peek thru Log at Bunny with Candle	527	521485										
There's A Song In My Heart	Girl Playing Triangle	232	**12173**										
They Followed The Star	Angel/3 Kings	72	**E-5641**										
They Followed The Star	3 Kings/Camels	65	E-5624 108243										
Thinking Of You Is What I Really Like To Do	Kneel'g Girl/Bouquet	504	522287	531766									
This Day Has Been Made In Heaven	Girl/Bible/Cross	506	523496			523682							
This Day Is Something To Roar About	Lion - Age 5	301	15989										
This Is The Day Which The Lord Has Made	Birthday Boy	314	**12157**										
This Is The Day Which The Lord Hath Made	Complete Wedding Party	312	E-2838										

This Is Your Day To Shine	Girl Polishing Table	162	E-2822										
This Land Is Our Land	Explorer/Animal Crew	599	527386										
This Land Is Our Land	Explorer w/Flag/Teddy	608	527777										
This Too Shall Pass	Boy w/Broken Heart	391	114014										
Thou Art Mine	B/G Writing in Sand	37	E-3113										
Thumb-body Loves You	Girl Nails Boy's Thumb	528	521698										
Tied Up For The Holidays	Pup/Ribbon/Girl/Gift	633	527580										
Time Heals	Nurse at Desk w/Clock	518	523739										
Time To Wish You A Merry Christmas	Girl/Calendar/Clock/ Mouse	434	115339		115304		115320		115312				
Timmy	Boy Jogger	203						**E-5397**					
'Tis The Season	Girl Adding Seasoning	430	111163										
To A Special Dad	Boy in Dad's Duds	59	E-5212				**E-0515**						
To A Special Mum	Boy/Bee/Flower Pot	530	521965										
To A Very Special Mom	Girl with Floppy Hat	164	E-2824										
To A Very Special Mom & Dad	Girl Hold'g Picture Frm	551	**521434**										
To A Very Special Sister	Bows/Sister's Hair	165	E-2825										
To A Very Special Sister	Girls Exchange Kittens	664	528633										
To Be With You Is Uplifting	Giraffe/Baby Bear	484	522260										
To God Be The Glory	Boy Holding Frame	163	**E-2823**										
To My Deer Friend	Girl w/Flowers/Deer	316	100048										
To My Favorite Fan	Gorilla and Parrot	501	**521043**										
To My Favorite Paw	Boy Sitting w/Teddy	211	**100021**										
To My Forever Friend	Two Girls w/Flowers	214	100072				113956						
To Somebunny Special	Bunny	152	**E-9282 (/A)**										
To Tell The Tooth You're Special	Dentist/Patient Pulled Tooth	351	**105813**										
To The Apple Of God's Eye	Boy Carry'g Apple/Bk	621	522015										
To Thee With Love	Girl w/Box/Kittens	43	**E-3120**				E-0534						
Trish	Baby Girl	253						**12483**					
True Blue Friends	Pup/Kit'n Share Paint'g	567	BC-912										
Trust And Obey	Policeman Writing Tkt	237					102377						
Trust In The Lord	Angel/Fly Lessons	157	**E-9289**										
Trust In The Lord To The Finish	Boy w/Racing Cup	207	PM-842										
Tubby's First Christmas	Rooster & Bird on Pig	126	**E-0511** 525278										
Two Section Wall	Two Section Wall	74	E-5644										

BOLD = Suspended *Italics* = Limited Edition Shaded Area = Retired Boxed = Dated Annual Rounded Box = Annual ◆ = Two Year Collectible

INSPIRATIONAL TITLE	DESCRIPTION	#	FIG	PLT	BELL	MUSC	ORN	DOLL	THMBL	FRAME	CNDL CLMB	BOX	OTHER
Unicorn	Unicorn	94					E-2371						
Unto Us A Child Is Born	B/G Reading Book	18	**E-2013**			**E-2808**							
Unto Us A Child Is Born	Nativity Scene	201		*E-5395*									
Unto Us A Child Is Born	Shepherd	64					**E-5630**						
Waddle I Do Without You	Clown/Basket/Goose	250	12459				112364						
Walking By Faith	Boy Pull'g Wagon/Girl	41	E-3117										
We Are All Precious In His Sight	Girl with Pearl	373	102903										
We Are God's Workmanship	Bonnet Girl/Butterfly	140	E-9258 *523879*										525960 Egg
We Belong To The Lord	Boy with Staff/Lambs	338	103004										
We Gather Together To Ask The Lord's Blessing	Thanksgiving Set	359	109762										
We Have Come From Afar	Penguins	559	**526959**										
We Have Seen His Star	Boy Holding Lamb	16	**E-2010**		**E-5620**		E-6120						
We Need A Good Friend Through The Ruff Times	Grandpa/Cane/Dog	452	**520810**										
We Saw A Star	2 Angels Sawing Star	245				**12408**							
Wedding Arch	Bridal Arch	332	**102369**										
Wee Three Kings	Three Kings	66	E-5635	*E-0538*		**E-0520**	**E-5634**						
We're Going To Miss You	Girl/Melting Snowman	515	524913										
We're In It Together	Boy with Piggy	141	**E-9259**										
We're Pulling For You	Boy with Donkey	353	**106151**										
What The World Needs Now	Girl/Globe/Praying	580	524352										
Winter's Song	Girl Feeding Birds	229	12092	12130		408778◆		408816◆					
Wishing You A Basket Full Of Blessings	Boy/Basket/Chick	385	109924										
Wishing You A Comfy Christmas	Angel Hold'g Blanket	607	527750										
Wishing You A Cozy Christmas	Girl with Muff	280	102342		102318		102326		102334				
Wishing You A Cozy Season	Boy by Stump	480	**521949**										
Wishing You A Happy Easter	Girl Holding Bunny	388	109886										
Wishing You A Ho Ho Ho	Boy Santa/Pup/Whskrs	605	527629										
Wishing You A Merry Christmas	Carollers with Puppy	200				**E-5394**							
Wishing You A Merry Christmas	Girl in Choir	193	E-5383		E-5393		E-5387						

Wishing You A Perfect Choice	Boy Propose to Girl	459	520845										
Wishing You A Purr-fect Holiday	Kitten with Ornament	521					520497						
Wishing You A Season Filled With Joy	Boy/Santa Cap/Dog	27	E-2805										
Wishing You A Very Successful Season	Boy/Package/Puppy	478	522120										
Wishing You A Yummy Christmas	Girl w/Ice Cream/Boy	358	**109754**	523801									
Wishing You Grrr-eatness	Leopard - Age 7	393	109479										
Wishing You Roads Of Happiness	Bride & Groom in Car	460	520780										
Wishing You The Sweetest Christmas	Girl in PJ's Holding Gingerbread Cookie	642	530166	530204	530174		530212 530190		530182				
Wishing You Were Here	Girl/Coin/Wishing Well	631				526916							
With This Ring I...	Boy Giving Girl Ring	343	104019										
Worship The Lord	Boy Kneeling/Church	223	102229										
Worship The Lord	Girl Kneeling /Church	213	100064										
Wreath Contestant Ornament	Boy/Girl/Cloud/ w/PM Logo	422					PM-008						

Yield Not To Temptation	Girl with Apple	505	**521310**										
You Are A Blessing To Me	Girl/Patch Teddy Bear	541	PM-902										
You Are Always In My Heart	Teddy Bear on Heart	682					530972						
You Are My Favorite Star	Girl/Star/Boy's Head	598	527378										
You Are My Gift Come True	Puppy in Stocking	436					520276						
You Are My Happiness	Girl Hold'g Roses/Bird	587	526185										
You Are My Main Event	Girl/Balloons/Satchel	397	115231										
You Are My Number One	Girl Holding Trophy	448	520829										
You Are Such A Purr-fect Friend	Girl Cuddling Kitten	585	*526010* 524395										
You Are The End Of My Rainbow	Girl Sits in Pot of Gold	706	C-0114 C-0014										
You Are The Rose Of His Creation	Girl Holds Bskt/Roses	661	*531243*										
You Are The Type I Love	Girl Typing Message	577	523542										
You Can Always Bring A Friend	Girl Holding Puppy	546	527122										
You Can Fly	Boy Angel on Cloud	271	**12335**										
You Can't Run Away From God	Boy & Dog Run Away	129	E-0525										
You Deserve An Ovation	Ballerina on Toe-point	572	520578										

BOLD = Suspended *Italics* = Limited Edition Shaded Area = Retired Boxed = Dated Annual Rounded Box = Annual ◆ = Two Year Collectible

INSPIRATIONAL TITLE	DESCRIPTION	#	FIG	PLT	BELL	MUSC	ORN	DOLL	THMBL	FRAME	CNDL CLMB	BOX	OTHER
You Have Touched So Many Hearts	Girl with Hearts	161	E-2821 *523283* 527661			112577 422282◆	112356	427527◆					
You Just Cannot Chuck A Good Friendship	Boy/Dog/Trash	442	PM-882										
You Suit Me To A Tee	Girl Golfer	662	526193										
You Will Always Be My Choice	Girl with Ballot Box	485	PM-891										
Your Love Is So Uplifting	Boy Hold Girl/Fountain	454	520675										
You're As Pretty As A Christmas Tree	Girl in Tree Outfit	672	530425	530409	604216		530395 530387						
You're My Number One Friend	Girl Holding Trophy	640	530026										
You're Worth Your Weight In Gold	Pig	151	**E-9282 (/B)**										

BOLD = Suspended *Italics* = Limited Edition Shaded Area = Retired Boxed = Dated Annual Rounded Box = Annual ◆ = Two Year Collectible

NOTES

QUIKREFERENCE™ SECTION

Many times certain pieces become important as part of a group. PRECIOUS MOMENTS groups that have become important are included in this QUIKREFERENCE SECTION. Groups included are The Chapel Exclusives, The "Original 21," Limited Editions, Retired pieces, Suspended pieces, Re-introduced pieces, pieces that have moved from the Suspended List to the Retired List, Dated Annuals, Annuals that are not dated, Two-Year Collectibles, The Enesco PRECIOUS MOMENTS Birthday Club pieces, and The Enesco PRECIOUS MOMENTS Collectors' Club pieces.

In addition, the OUTLINE OF ANNUALS Section groups annual collectibles by series and product type. The OUTLINE OF THE SERIES Section itemizes the individual pieces that comprise each series.

There's a QUIKREFERENCE CALENDAR as well. It's a summary, by year, of Retired, Suspended, and Annual pieces.

CHAPEL EXCLUSIVES

FIGURINES:

1991	523038	He Is My Inspiration
1992	523011	There's A Christian Welcome Here
1993	527106	He Is Not Here For He Is Risen As He Said
1993	531677	Surrounded With Joy
1994	531928	Death Can't Keep Him In The Ground
1994	603503	On The Hill Overlooking The Quiet Blue Stream ...
1994	604151	A King Is Born

ORNAMENTS:

1992	528021	There's A Christian Welcome Here
1993	531685	Surrounded With Joy
1994	532088	A King Is Born

CHAPEL WINDOW BEATITUDE SERIES WALL HANGINGS:

1992	523437	Blessed Are The Humble
1992	523380	Blessed Are The Ones Who Mourn
1993	523313	Blessed Are The Meek
1993	523321	Blessed Are The Ones Who Hunger
1994	523291	Blessed Are The Merciful
1994	523348	Blessed Are The Peacemakers
1995	523399	Blessed Are The Pure In Heart

THE "ORIGINAL 21"

E-1372B .... Figurine ...... Jesus Loves Me
E-1372G ...... Figurine ...... Jesus Loves Me
E-1373B .... Figurine ...... Smile, God Loves You
E-1373G ...... Figurine ...... Jesus Is The Light
E-1374B .... Figurine ...... Praise The Lord Anyhow
E-1374G ...... Figurine ...... Make A Joyful Noise
E-1375A ...... Figurine ...... Love Lifted Me
E-1375B .... Figurine ...... Prayer Changes Things
E-1376 .... Figurine ...... Love One Another
E-1377A ...... Figurine ...... Love Leadeth Me
E-1377B .... Figurine ...... He Careth For You
E-1378 .... Figurine ...... God Loveth A Cheerful Giver
E-1379A ...... Figurine ...... Love Is Kind
E-1379B .... Figurine ...... God Understands
E-1380B .... Figurine ...... O, How I Love Jesus
E-1380G ...... Figurine ...... His Burden Is Light
E-1381 .... Figurine ...... Jesus Is The Answer
E-2010 .... Figurine ...... We Have Seen His Star
E-2011 .... Figurine ...... Come Let Us Adore Him
E-2012 .... Figurine ...... Jesus Is Born
E-2013 .... Figurine ...... Unto Us A Child Is Born

###############

LIMITED EDITIONS

E-0538 .... Plate .... 15,000 ...... Wee Three Kings
E-2347 .... Plate .... 15,000 ...... Let Heaven And Nature Sing
E-2847 .... Plate .... 15,000 ...... Love Is Kind
E-2848 .... Plate .... 15,000 ...... Loving Thy Neighbor
E-5215 .... Plate .... 15,000 ...... Love One Another
E-5217 .... Plate .... 15,000 ...... Mother Sew Dear
E-5395 .... Plate .... 15,000 ...... Unto Us A Child Is Born
E-5646 .... Plate .... 15,000 ...... Come Let Us Adore Him
E-7173 .... Plate .... 15,000 ...... The Purr-fect Grandma
E-7174 .... Plate .... 15,000 ...... Make A Joyful Noise
E-7267B ..... Doll .... 5,000 ...... Cubby
E-7267G .... Doll .... 5,000 ...... Tammy
E-9256 .... Plate .... 15,000 ...... The Hand That Rocks The Future
E-9257 .... Plate .... 15,000 ...... I Believe In Miracles
12491 .... Doll .... 12,500 ...... Angie, The Angel Of Mercy
100455 .... Doll .... 12,000 ...... Bong Bong
100463 .... Doll .... 12,000 ...... Candy
102253 .... Doll .... 7,500 ...... Connie

104531 .... Figurine .... 1,000 ...... Jesus Loves Me
520322 .... Figurine .... 1,500 ...... Make A Joyful Noise
523283 .... Figurine .... 2,000 ...... You Have Touched So Many Hearts
523879 .... Figurine .... 2,000 ...... We Are God's Workmanship
526010 .... Figurine .... 2,000 ...... You Are Such A Purr-fect Friend
529680 .... Figurine .... 2,000 ...... Gather Your Dreams
531243 .... Figurine .... 2,000 ...... You Are The Rose Of His Creation

Large Easter Seal Figurines are a sub-set of the Limited Editions.

###############

RETIRED –

"A figurine or collectible that has been permanently removed from production and the molds destroyed. It is regarded as an honor for a figurine to be chosen for Retired status. Pieces are Retired from time to time to make room in the Collection for new introductions." - ENESCO

E-0504 ..... Figurine .... 1990 .... Christmastime Is For Sharing
E-0506 ..... Figurine .... 1989 .... Surrounded With Joy
E-0519 ..... Musical .... 1986 .... Sharing Our Season Together
E-0525 ..... Figurine .... 1989 .... You Can't Run Away From God
E-0530 ..... Figurine .... 1987 .... His Eye Is On The Sparrow
E-0532 ..... Ornament .... 1986 .... Let Heaven And Nature Sing
E-0534 ..... Ornament .... 1989 .... To Thee With Love
E-1373B .. Figurine .... 1984 .... Smile God Loves You
E-1373G .. Figurine .... 1988 .... Jesus Is The Light
E-1374B .. Figurine .... 1982 .... Praise The Lord Anyhow
E-1375A .. Figurine .... 1993 .... Love Lifted Me
E-1378 ..... Figurine .... 1981 .... God Loveth A Cheerful Giver
E-1380G .. Figurine .... 1984 .... His Burden Is Light
E-1380B .. Figurine .... 1984 .... O, How I Love Jesus
E-2011 ..... Figurine .... 1981 .... Come Let Us Adore Him
E-2351 ..... Figurine .... 1987 .... Holy Smokes
E-2353 ..... Figurine .... 1986 .... O Come All Ye Faithful
E-2368 ..... Ornament .... 1984 .... The First Noel
E-2369 ..... Ornament .... 1986 .... Dropping In For Christmas
E-2371 ..... Ornament .... 1988 .... Unicorn
E-2374 ..... Figurine .... 1993 .... Bundles Of Joy
E-2375 ..... Figurine .... 1991 .... Dropping Over For Christmas
E-2376 ..... Ornament .... 1985 .... Dropping Over For Christmas
E-2805 ..... Figurine .... 1985 .... Wishing You A Season Filled With Joy
E-2806 ..... Musical .... 1984 .... Christmas Is A Time To Share
E-2822 ..... Figurine .... 1988 .... This Is Your Day To Shine
E-2841 ..... Figurine .... 1986 .... Baby's First Picture
E-2850 ..... Doll .... 1985 .... Mother Sew Dear
E-3107 ..... Figurine .... 1985 .... Blessed Are The Peacemakers
E-3110B .. Figurine .... 1993 .... Loving Is Sharing
E-3111 ..... Figurine .... 1985 .... Be Not Weary In Well Doing
E-3112 ..... Figurine .... 1983 .... God's Speed
E-3116 ..... Figurine .... 1994 .... Thee I Love
E-3118 ..... Figurine .... 1983 .... Eggs Over Easy
E-5211 ..... Bell .... 1984 .... God Understands
E-5377 ..... Figurine .... 1987 .... Love Is Kind
E-5388 ..... Ornament .... 1987 .... Joy To The World
E-5645 ..... Musical .... 1988 .... Rejoice O Earth
E-6120 ..... Ornament .... 1984 .... We Have Seen His Star
E-7156 ..... Figurine .... 1992 .... I Believe In Miracles
E-7156R .. Figurine .... 1992 .... I Believe In Miracles
E-7157 ..... Figurine .... 1986 .... There Is Joy In Serving Jesus
E-7185 ..... Musical .... 1985 .... Love Is Sharing
E-9254 ..... Figurine .... 1994 .... Praise The Lord Anyhow
E-9268 ..... Figurine .... 1990 .... Nobody's Perfect!
E-9273 ..... Figurine .... 1987 .... Let Love Reign
E-9274 ..... Figurine .... 1986 .... Taste And See That The Lord Is Good
12459 .... Figurine .... 1989 .... Waddle I Do Without You
12467 .... Figurine .... 1988 .... The Lord Will Carry You Through
15504 .... Musical .... 1989 .... God Sent You Just In Time

RETIRED continued

100102..... Figurine........... 1990 .... Make Me A Blessing
100129..... Figurine........... 1988 .... Lord Keep Me On My Toes
100188..... Figurine........... 1993 .... I'm A Possibility
100196..... Figurine........... 1991 .... The Spirit Is Willing But The Flesh Is Weak
100269..... Figurine........... 1989 .... Help Lord, I'm In A Spot
100528..... Figurine........... 1991 .... Scent From Above
101702..... Musical............ 1992 .... Our First Christmas Together
101842..... Figurine........... 1991 .... Smile Along The Way
101850..... Figurine........... 1992 .... Lord, Help Us Keep Our Act Together
102423..... Ornament .... 1990 .... Lord, Keep Me On My Toes
105945..... Figurine........... 1993 .... Showers Of Blessings
109584..... Figurine........... 1992 .... Happiness Divine
112402..... Musical............ 1993 .... I'm Sending You A White Christmas
113980..... Ornament .... 1991 .... Rejoice O Earth
520640..... Figurine........... 1991 .... I'm So Glad You Fluttered Into My Life
520683..... Figurine........... 1992 .... Sending You Showers Of Blessings
520772..... Figurine........... 1990 .... Many Moons In Same Canoe, Blessum You
520799..... Figurine........... 1992 .... Someday My Love
521396..... Figurine........... 1993 .... Faith Is A Victory
521566..... Ornament .... 1992 .... Glide Through The Holidays
521590..... Ornament .... 1994 .... Don't Let The Holidays Get You Down
522112..... Figurine........... 1993 .... Don't Let The Holidays Get You Down
522260..... Figurine........... 1994 .... To Be With You Is Uplifting
523747..... Figurine........... 1994 .... Blessings From Above
524271..... Figurine........... 1994 .... Friendship Grows When You Plant A Seed

###############

SUSPENDED –

"A figurine or collectible that has been removed from production for an unspecified period of time. A piece designated as Suspended cannot be moved to Retired status without first being "re-introduced" to the Collection. There is no time limit on how long a collectible may be Suspended from the Collection." - ENESCO

E-0501 ..... Figurine .... 1986 .... Sharing Our Season Together
E-0502 ..... Figurine .... 1986 .... Jesus Is The Light That Shines
E-0503 ..... Figurine .... 1986 .... Blessings From My House To Yours
E-0507 ..... Figurine .... 1987 .... God Sent His Son
E-0508 ..... Figurine .... 1986 .... Prepare Ye The Way Of The Lord
E-0509 ..... Figurine .... 1987 .... Bringing God's Blessing To You
E-0511 ..... Figurine .... 1993 .... Tubby's First Christmas
E-0512 ..... Figurine .... 1990 .... It's A Perfect Boy
E-0515 ..... Ornament .... 1988 .... To A Special Dad
E-0517 ..... Ornament .... 1990 .... The Perfect Grandpa
E-0520 ..... Musical .... 1986 .... Wee Three Kings
E-0521 ..... Frame .... 1987 .... Blessed Are The Pure In Heart
E-0526 ..... Figurine .... 1985 .... He Upholdeth Those Who Call
E-0531 ..... Ornament .... 1986 .... O Come All Ye Faithful
E-0533 ..... Ornament .... 1988 .... Tell Me The Story Of Jesus
E-0535 ..... Ornament .... 1986 .... Love Is Patient
E-0536 ..... Ornament .... 1986 .... Love Is Patient
E-0537 ..... Ornament .... 1985 .... Jesus Is The Light
E-0539 ..... Doll .... 1988 .... Katie Lynne
E-1375B .. Figurine .... 1984 .... Prayer Changes Things
E-1377A .. Figurine .... 1984 .... He Leadeth Me
E-1377B .. Figurine .... 1984 .... He Careth For You
E-1379A .. Figurine .... 1984 .... Love Is Kind
E-1379B .. Figurine .... 1984 .... God Understands
E-1381 ..... Figurine .... 1984 .... Jesus Is The Answer
E-2010 ..... Figurine .... 1984 .... We Have Seen His Star
E-2012 ..... Figurine .... 1984 .... Jesus Is Born
E-2013 ..... Figurine .... 1984 .... Unto Us A Child Is Born
E-2343 ..... Ornament .... 1988 .... Joy To The World
E-2344 ..... Cndl Clmb ...... 1985 .... Joy To The World
E-2345 ..... Figurine .... 1984 .... May Your Christmas Be Cozy
E-2346 ..... Musical .... 1989 .... Let Heaven And Nature Sing
E-2348 ..... Figurine .... 1988 .... May Your Christmas Be Warm
E-2349 ..... Figurine .... 1985 .... Tell Me The Story Of Jesus
E-2350 ..... Figurine .... 1984 .... Dropping In For Christmas
E-2352 ..... Musical .... 1984 .... O Come All Ye Faithful
E-2355 ..... Musical .... 1984 .... I'll Play My Drum For Him
E-2356 ..... Figurine .... 1985 .... I'll Play My Drum For Him
E-2361 ..... Figurine .... 1986 .... Christmas Joy From Head To Toe
E-2362 ..... Ornament .... 1988 .... Baby's First Christmas
E-2364 ..... Figurine .... 1989 .... Goat
E-2365 ..... Figurine .... 1984 .... The First Noel
E-2366 ..... Figurine .... 1984 .... The First Noel
E-2367 ..... Ornament .... 1984 .... The First Noel
E-2372 ..... Ornament .... 1985 .... Baby's First Christmas
E-2377 ..... Figurine .... 1985 .... Our First Christmas Together
E-2378 ..... Plate .... 1985 .... Our First Christmas Together
E-2381 ..... Ornament .... 1984 .... Mouse With Cheese
E-2385 ..... Ornament .... 1991 .... Our First Christmas Together

SUSPENDED continued

E-2386 ..... Ornaments ...... 1984 .... Camel, Donkey, Cow
E-2801 ..... Figurine .... 1984 .... Jesus Is Born
E-2802 ..... Figurine .... 1984 .... Christmas Is The Time To Share
E-2803 ..... Figurine .... 1984 .... Crown Him Lord Of All
E-2804 ..... Figurine .... 1984 .... Peace On Earth
E-2807 ..... Musical .... 1984 .... Crown Him Lord Of All
E-2808 ..... Musical .... 1984 .... Unto Us A Child Is Born
E-2809 ..... Musical .... 1985 .... Jesus Is Born
E-2810 ..... Musical .... 1993 .... Come Let Us Adore Him
E-2823 ..... Figurine .... 1987 .... To God Be The Glory
E-2826 ..... Figurine .... 1986 .... May Your Birthday Be A Blessing
E-2827 ..... Figurine .... 1986 .... I Get A Kick Out Of You
E-2834 ..... Figurine .... 1991 .... Sharing Our Joy Together
E-2840 ..... Figurine .... 1988 .... Baby's First Step
E-2851 ..... Doll .... 1989 .... Kristy
E-3104 ..... Figurine .... 1991 .... Blessed Are The Pure In Heart
E-3105 ..... Figurine .... 1984 .... He Watches Over Us All
E-3108 ..... Figurine .... 1984 .... The Hand That Rocks The Future
E-3119 ..... Figurine .... 1984 .... It's What's Inside That Counts
E-3120 ..... Figurine .... 1986 .... To Thee With Love
E-4720 ..... Figurine .... 1987 .... The Lord Bless You And Keep You
E-4722 ..... Figurine .... 1985 .... Love Cannot Break A True Friendship
E-4723 ..... Figurine .... 1984 .... Peace Amid The Storm
E-4725 ..... Figurine .... 1984 .... Peace On Earth
E-4726 ..... Musical .... 1984 .... Peace On Earth
E-5200 ..... Figurine .... 1984 .... Bear Ye One Another's Burdens
E-5201 ..... Figurine .... 1984 .... Love Lifted Me
E-5202 ..... Figurine .... 1984 .... Thank You For Coming To My Ade
E-5203 ..... Figurine .... 1984 .... Let Not The Sun Go Down Upon Your Wrath
E-5205 ..... Musical .... 1985 .... My Guardian Angel
E-5206 ..... Musical .... 1988 .... My Guardian Angel
E-5207 ..... Night Light ..... 1984 .... My Guardian Angel
E-5208 ..... Bell .... 1985 .... Jesus Loves Me
E-5209 ..... Bell .... 1985 .... Jesus Loves Me
E-5210 ..... Bell .... 1984 .... Prayer Changes Things
E-5213 ..... Figurine .... 1989 .... God Is Love
E-5214 ..... Figurine .... 1984 .... Prayer Changes Things
E-5216 ..... Plate .... 1987 .... The Lord Bless You And Keep You
E-5376 ..... Figurine .... 1986 .... May Your Christmas Be Blessed
E-5378 ..... Figurine .... 1989 .... Joy To The World
E-5380 ..... Figurine .... 1986 .... A Monarch Is Born
E-5381 ..... Figurine .... 1987 .... His Name Is Jesus
E-5382 ..... Figurines .... 1986 .... For God So Loved The World
E-5385 ..... Figurine .... 1986 .... Oh Worship The Lord
E-5386 ..... Figurine .... 1986 .... Oh Worship The Lord
E-5389 ..... Ornament .... 1986 .... Peace On Earth
E-5390 ..... Ornament .... 1989 .... May God Bless You With A Perfect Holiday Season
E-5391 ..... Ornament .... 1989 .... Love Is Kind
E-5394 ..... Musical .... 1986 .... Wishing You A Merry Christmas
E-5397 ..... Doll .... 1991 .... Timmy
E-5619 ..... Figurine .... 1985 .... Come Let Us Adore Him
E-5620 ..... Bell .... 1985 .... We Have Seen His Star
E-5623 ..... Bell .... 1984 .... Jesus Is Born
E-5627 ..... Ornament .... 1985 .... But Love Goes On Forever

SUSPENDED continued

E-5628 ..... Ornament .... 1985 .... But Love Goes On Forever
E-5630 ..... Ornament .... 1985 .... Unto Us A Child Is Born
E-5631 ..... Ornament .... 1985 .... Baby's First Christmas
E-5632 ..... Ornament .... 1985 .... Baby's First Christmas
E-5633 ..... Ornaments ...... 1984 .... Come Let Us Adore Him
E-5634 ..... Ornaments ...... 1984 .... Wee Three Kings
E-5639 ..... Figurine .... 1985 .... Isn't He Wonderful
E-5640 ..... Figurine .... 1985 .... Isn't He Wonderful
E-5641 ..... Figurine .... 1985 .... They Followed The Star
E-5642 ..... Musical .... 1985 .... Silent Knight
E-6118 ..... Cndl Clmb ...... 1988 .... But Love Goes On Forever
E-6214B .. Doll .... 1985 .... Mikey
E-6214G .. Doll .... 1985 .... Debbie
E-6613 ..... Figurine .... 1987 .... God Sends The Gift Of His Love
E-6901 ..... Plaque .... 1986 .... Collection Plaque
E-7153 ..... Figurine .... 1986 .... God Is Love, Dear Valentine
E-7154 ..... Figurine .... 1986 .... God Is Love, Dear Valentine
E-7155 ..... Figurine .... 1984 .... Thanking Him For You
E-7159 ..... Figurine .... 1985 .... Lord Give Me Patience
E-7160 ..... Figurine .... 1986 .... The Perfect Grandpa
E-7161 ..... Figurine .... 1984 .... His Sheep Am I
E-7162 ..... Figurine .... 1984 .... Love Is Sharing
E-7163 ..... Figurine .... 1984 .... God Is Watching Over You
E-7164 ..... Figurine .... 1984 .... Bless This House
E-7165 ..... Figurine .... 1987 .... Let The Whole World Know
E-7166 ..... Frame .... 1993 .... The Lord Bless You And Keep You
E-7167 ..... Box .... 1985 .... The Lord Bless You And Keep You
E-7168 ..... Frame .... 1984 .... My Guardian Angel
E-7169 ..... Frame .... 1984 .... My Guardian Angel
E-7170 ..... Frame .... 1985 .... Jesus Loves Me
E-7171 ..... Frame .... 1985 .... Jesus Loves Me
E-7172 ..... Plate .... 1985 .... Rejoicing With You
E-7175 ..... Bell .... 1985 .... The Lord Bless You And Keep You
E-7176 ..... Bell .... 1985 .... The Lord Bless You And Keep You
E-7177 ..... Frame .... 1987 .... The Lord Bless You And Keep You
E-7178 ..... Frame .... 1987 .... The Lord Bless You And Keep You
E-7179 ..... Bell .... 1993 .... The Lord Bless You And Keep You
E-7181 ..... Bell .... 1988 .... Mother Sew Dear
E-7183 ..... Bell .... 1988 .... The Purr-fect Grandma
E-7184 ..... Musical .... 1993 .... The Purr-fect Grandma
E-7186 ..... Musical .... 1986 .... Let The Whole World Know
E-7241 ..... Frame .... 1986 .... Mother Sew Dear
E-7242 ..... Frame .... 1988 .... The Purr-fect Grandma
E-9251 ..... Figurine .... 1985 .... Love Is Patient
E-9252 ..... Figurine .... 1989 .... Forgiving Is Forgetting
E-9253 ..... Figurine .... 1985 .... The End Is In Sight
E-9259 ..... Figurine .... 1990 .... We're In It Together
E-9260 ..... Figurine .... 1987 .... God's Promises Are Sure
E-9261 ..... Figurine .... 1986 .... Seek Ye The Lord
E-9262 ..... Figurine .... 1986 .... Seek Ye The Lord
E-9263 ..... Figurine .... 1985 .... How Can Two Walk Together Except They Agree
E-9266 ..... Box .... 1988 .... I'm Falling For Somebunny
E-9266 ..... Box .... 1988 .... Our Love Is Heaven Scent
E-9267 ..... Figurines .... 1991 .... Animal Collection
E-9267A .. Figurine .... 1991 .... Teddy Bear

SUSPENDED continued

E-9267B .. Figurine .... 1991 .... Dog
E-9267C .. Figurine .... 1991 .... Bunny
E-9267D .. Figurine .... 1991 .... Cat
E-9267E .. Figurine .... 1991 .... Lamb
E-9267F ... Figurine .... 1991 .... Pig
E-9275 ..... Plate .... 1984 .... Jesus Loves Me
E-9276 ..... Plate .... 1984 .... Jesus Loves Me
E-9280 ..... Box .... 1985 .... Jesus Loves Me
E-9281 ..... Box .... 1985 .... Jesus Loves Me
E-9282 ..... Figurines .... 1990 .... To Somebunny Special
You're Worth Your Weight In Gold
Especially For Ewe
E-9282A .. Figurine .... 1990 .... To Somebunny Special
E-9282B .. Figurine .... 1990 .... You're Worth Your Weight In Gold
E-9282C .. Figurine .... 1990 .... Especially For Ewe
E-9283A .. Box .... 1984 .... Forever Friends - Dog
E-9283B .. Box .... 1984 .... Forever Friends - Cat
E-9285 ..... Figurine .... 1985 .... If God Be For Us, Who Can Be Against Us
E-9287 ..... Figurine .... 1986 .... Peace On Earth
E-9288 ..... Figurine .... 1986 .... Sending You A Rainbow
E-9289 ..... Figurine .... 1987 .... Trust In The Lord
12009 .... Figurine .... 1991 .... Love Covers All
12017 .... Frame .... 1987 .... Loving You
12025 .... Frame .... 1987 .... Loving You
12033 .... Frame .... 1987 .... God's Precious Gift
12041 .... Frame .... 1992 .... God's Precious Gift
12149 .... Figurine .... 1989 .... Part Of Me Wants To Be Good
12157 .... Figurine .... 1990 .... This Is The Day Which The Lord Has Made
12165 .... Musical .... 1989 .... Lord, Keep My Life In Tune
12173 .... Figurine .... 1990 .... There's A Song In My Heart
12203 .... Figurine .... 1986 .... Get Into The Habit Of Prayer
12211 .... Figurine .... 1987 .... Baby's First Haircut
12254 .... Thimble .... 1990 .... Love Covers All
12297 .... Figurine .... 1987 .... It Is Better To Give Than To Receive
12335 .... Figurine .... 1988 .... You Can Fly
12343 .... Figurine .... 1986 .... Jesus Is Coming Soon
12351 .... Figurine .... 1988 .... Halo, And Merry Christmas
12378 .... Figurine .... 1990 .... Happiness Is The Lord
12386 .... Figurine .... 1990 .... Lord Give Me A Song
12394 .... Figurine .... 1990 .... He Is My Song
12408 .... Musical .... 1987 .... We Saw A Star
12424 .... Doll .... 1986 .... Aaron
12432 .... Doll .... 1986 .... Bethany
12475 .... Doll .... 1986 .... P.D.
12483 .... Doll .... 1986 .... Trish
12580 .... Musical .... 1990 .... Lord Keep My Life In Tune
15482 .... Figurine .... 1994 .... May Your Christmas Be Delightful
15776 .... Figurine .... 1992 .... May You Have The Sweetest Christmas
15784 .... Figurine .... 1992 .... The Story Of God's Love
15792 .... Figurine .... 1992 .... Tell Me A Story
15806 .... Figurine .... 1992 .... God Gave His Best
15814 .... Musical .... 1992 .... Silent Night
15822 .... Ornament .... 1989 .... May Your Christmas Be Happy
15830 .... Ornament .... 1989 .... Happiness Is The Lord
15849 .... Ornament .... 1993 .... May Your Christmas Be Delightful

SUSPENDED continued

15857 .... Ornament .... 1993 .... Honk If You Love Jesus
16012 .... Figurine .... 1989 .... Baby's First Trip
16020 .... Night Light ..... 1989 .... God Bless You With Rainbows
100021 ..... Figurine .... 1988 .... To My Favorite Paw
100056 ..... Figurine .... 1991 .... Sending My Love
100145 ..... Figurine .... 1990 .... God Bless The Day We Found You (Daughter)
100153 ..... Figurine .... 1990 .... God Bless The Day We Found You (Son)
100161 ..... Figurine .... 1990 .... Serving The Lord (Girl)
100285 ..... Musical .... 1993 .... Heaven Bless You
100293 ..... Figurine .... 1990 .... Serving The Lord (Boy)
100544 ..... Figurine .... 1989 .... Brotherly Love
100625 ..... Thimble .... 1989 .... God Is Love, Dear Valentine
100633 ..... Thimble .... 1991 .... The Lord Bless You And Keep You
100668 ..... Thimbles .... 1988 .... Clown Thimbles
102288 ..... Ornament .... 1993 .... Shepherd Of Love
102296 ..... Figurines .... 1992 .... Mini Animal Figurines
102369 ..... Figurine .... 1992 .... Wedding Arch
102415 ..... Ornament .... 1989 .... It's A Perfect Boy
102431 ..... Ornament .... 1988 .... Serve With A Smile
102458 ..... Ornament .... 1988 .... Serve With A Smile
102474 ..... Ornament .... 1991 .... Rocking Horse
102490 ..... Figurine .... 1988 .... Sharing Our Christmas Together
102962 ..... Figurine .... 1989 .... It's The Birthday Of A King
104027 ..... Figurine .... 1990 .... Love Is The Glue That Mends
104396 ..... Figurine .... 1990 .... Happy Days Are Here Again
104418 ..... Figurine .... 1993 .... Friends To The End
104825 ..... Figurine .... 1990 .... Sitting Pretty
105635 ..... Figurine .... 1991 .... Have I Got News For You
105643 ..... Figurine .... 1991 .... Something's Missing When You're Not Around
105813 ..... Figurine .... 1990 .... To Tell The Tooth You're Special
105953 ..... Figurine .... 1993 .... Brighten Someone's Day
106151 ..... Figurine .... 1991 .... We're Pulling For You
106216 ..... Figurine .... 1990 .... Lord Help Me Make The Grade
106836 ..... Figurine .... 1993 .... Happy Birthday Poppy
109487 ..... Figurine .... 1991 .... Believe The Impossible
109746 ..... Musical .... 1993 .... Peace On Earth
109754 ..... Figurine .... 1994 .... Wishing You A Yummy Christmas
111120 ..... Ornament .... 1990 .... I'm A Possibility
111333 ..... Figurine .... 1991 .... O Come Let Us Adore Him
112372 ..... Ornament .... 1992 .... I'm Sending You A White Christmas
113964 ..... Ornament .... 1993 .... Smile Along The Way
113972 ..... Ornament .... 1991 .... God Sent You Just In Time
113999 ..... Ornament .... 1991 .... Cheers To The Leader
114006 ..... Ornament .... 1991 .... My Love Will Never Let You Go
115290 ..... Figurine .... 1991 .... Our First Christmas Together
429570 ..... Musical Doll ... 1994 .... The Eyes Of The Lord Are Upon You
429589 ..... Musical Doll ... 1994 .... The Eyes Of The Lord Are Upon You
520357 ..... Figurine .... 1993 .... Jesus The Savior Is Born
520691 ..... Musical .... 1993 .... Lord, Keep My Life In Balance
520705 ..... Figurine .... 1994 .... Baby's First Pet
520756 ..... Figurine .... 1993 .... Jesus Is The Only Way
520802 ..... Figurine .... 1991 .... My Days Are Blue Without You
520810 ..... Figurine .... 1991 .... We Need A Good Friend Through The Ruff Times
520853 ..... Figurine .... 1991 .... I Belong To The Lord
521043 ..... Figurine .... 1993 .... To My Favorite Fan

SUSPENDED continued

521205.....Figurine...........1993 ....Hope You're Up And On The Trail Again
521272.....Figurine...........1994 ....Take Heed When You Stand
521280.....Figurine...........1994 ....Happy Trip
521302.....Ornament ....1994 ....May All Your Christmases Be White
521310.....Figurine...........1993 ....Yield Not To Temptation
521434.....Figurine...........1993 ....To A Very Special Mom And Dad
521574.....Ornament ....1994 ....Dashing Through The Snow
521868.....Figurine...........1991 ....The Greatest Of These Is Love
521949.....Figurine...........1993 ....Wishing You A Cozy Season
521957.....Figurine...........1993 ....High Hopes
522031.....Figurine...........1993 ....Thank The Lord For Everything
522104.....Figurine...........1994 ....It's No Yolk When I Say I Love You
522244.....Musical............1994 ....Do Not Open Till Christmas
522252.....Figurine...........1993 ....He Is The Star Of The Morning
522856.....Figurine...........1992 ....Have A Beary Merry Christmas
522953.....Ornament ....1994 ....I Believe In The Old Rugged Cross
522988.....Figurine...........1993 ....Isn't He Precious
522996.....Figurine...........1993 ....Some Bunny's Sleeping
523097.....Figurine...........1993 ....Jesus Is The Sweetest Name I Know
523224.....Ornament ....1994 ....Happy Trails Is Trusting Jesus
523763.....Figurine...........1994 ....I Can't Spell Success Without You
524484.....Figurines ....1994 ....Not A Creature Was Stirring
524875.....Figurine...........1993 ....Happy Birthday Dear Jesus
524883.....Figurine...........1992 ....Christmas Fireplace
526568.....Figurine...........1992 ....Bless Those Who Serve Their Country (Navy)
526576.....Figurine...........1992 ....Bless Those Who Serve Their Country (Army)
526584.....Figurine...........1992 ....Bless Those Who Serve Their Country (Air Force)
526959.....Figurine...........1994 ....We Have Come From Afar
527165.....Ornament ....1993 ....The Good Lord Always Delivers
527289.....Figurine...........1992 ....Bless Those Who Serve Their Country (Girl Soldier)
527297.....Figurine...........1992 ....Bless Those Who Serve Their Country (Soldier)
527521.....Figurine...........1992 ....Bless Those Who Serve Their Country (Marine)

################

RE-INTRODUCED –

1987 ....I Believe In Miracles ....Figurine...........E-7156 as E-7156R
1992 ....Jesus Is The Answer ....Figurine...........E-1381 as E-1381R

MOVED FROM SUSPENDED LIST TO RETIRED LIST

E-7156.....I Believe In Miracles

- E-7156 Suspended in 1985.
- E-7156 Re-introduced in 1987 as E-7156R.
- Both E-7156 & E-7156R Retired in 1992.

DATED ANNUALS

E-0505 ..... Plate .... 1983 .... Christmastime Is For Sharing
E-0513 ..... Ornament .... 1983 .... Surround Us With Joy
E-0518 ..... Ornament .... 1983 .... Blessed Are The Pure In Heart
E-0522 ..... Bell .... 1983 .... Surrounded With Joy
E-2357 ..... Plate .... 1982 .... I'll Play My Drum For Him
E-2358 ..... Bell .... 1982 .... I'll Play My Drum For Him (only prototypes were dated)
E-2359 ..... Ornament .... 1982 .... I'll Play My Drum For Him
E-5383 ..... Figurine .... 1984 .... Wishing You A Merry Christmas
E-5387 ..... Ornament .... 1984 .... Wishing You A Merry Christmas
E-5392 ..... Ornament .... 1984 .... Blessed Are The Pure In Heart
E-5393 ..... Bell .... 1984 .... Wishing You A Merry Christmas
E-5396 ..... Plate .... 1984 .... The Wonder Of Christmas
E-5622 ..... Bell .... 1981 .... Let The Heavens Rejoice
E-5629 ..... Ornament .... 1981 .... Let The Heavens Rejoice
15237 .... Plate .... 1985 .... Tell Me The Story Of Jesus
15539 .... Figurine .... 1985 .... Baby's First Christmas
15547 .... Figurine .... 1985 .... Baby's First Christmas
15768 .... Ornament .... 1985 .... God Sent His Love
15865 .... Thimble .... 1985 .... God Sent His Love
15873 .... Bell .... 1985 .... God Sent His Love
15881 .... Figurine .... 1985 .... God Sent His Love
15903 .... Ornament .... 1985 .... Baby's First Christmas
15911 .... Ornament .... 1985 .... Baby's First Christmas
101834 ..... Plate .... 1986 .... I'm Sending You A White Christmas
102318 ..... Bell .... 1986 .... Wishing You A Cozy Christmas
102326 ..... Ornament .... 1986 .... Wishing You A Cozy Christmas
102334 ..... Thimble .... 1986 .... Wishing You A Cozy Christmas
102342 ..... Figurine .... 1986 .... Wishing You A Cozy Christmas
102350 ..... Ornament .... 1986 .... Our First Christmas Together
102466 ..... Ornament .... 1986 .... Reindeer Ornament
102504 ..... Ornament .... 1986 .... Baby's First Christmas
102512 ..... Ornament .... 1986 .... Baby's First Christmas
102954 ..... Plate .... 1987 .... My Peace I Give Unto Thee
104515 ..... Ornament .... 1987 .... Bear The Good News Of Christmas
109401 ..... Ornament .... 1987 .... Baby's First Christmas
109428 ..... Ornament .... 1987 .... Baby's First Christmas
109770 ..... Ornament .... 1987 .... Love Is The Best Gift Of All
109835 ..... Bell .... 1987 .... Love Is The Best Gift Of All
109843 ..... Thimble .... 1987 .... Love Is The Best Gift Of All
110930 ..... Figurine .... 1987 .... Love Is The Best Gift Of All
112399 ..... Ornament .... 1987 .... Our First Christmas Together
115282 ..... Ornament .... 1988 .... Baby's First Christmas
115304 ..... Bell .... 1988 .... Time To Wish You A Merry Christmas
115312 ..... Thimble .... 1988 .... Time To Wish You A Merry Christmas
115320 ..... Ornament .... 1988 .... Time To Wish You A Merry Christmas
115339 ..... Figurine .... 1988 .... Time To Wish You A Merry Christmas
520233 ..... Ornament .... 1988 .... Our First Christmas Together
520241 ..... Ornament .... 1988 .... Baby's First Christmas
520276 ..... Ornament .... 1988 .... You Are My Gift Come True
520284 ..... Plate .... 1988 .... Merry Christmas, Deer
520292 ..... Ornament .... 1988 .... Hang On For The Holly Days
520411 ..... Ornament .... 1992 .... I'm Nuts About You
520438 ..... Ornament .... 1991 .... Sno-Bunny Falls For You Like I Do
520462 ..... Ornament .... 1989 .... Christmas Is Ruff Without You

DATED ANNUALS continued

520489..... Ornament .... 1993 .... Slow Down And Enjoy The Holidays
520497..... Ornament .... 1990 .... Wishing You A Purr-fect Holiday
521558..... Ornament .... 1989 .... Our First Christmas Together
522546..... Figurine .... 1989 .... Oh Holy Night
522554..... Thimble .... 1989 .... Oh Holy Night
522821..... Bell .... 1989 .... Oh Holy Night
522848..... Ornament .... 1989 .... Oh Holy Night
522945..... Ornament .... 1991 .... Our First Christmas Together
523003..... Plate .... 1989 .... May Your Christmas Be A Happy Home
523062..... Ornament .... 1989 .... Peace On Earth
523194..... Ornament .... 1989 .... Baby's First Christmas
523208..... Ornament .... 1989 .... Baby's First Christmas
523534..... Egg .... 1991 .... I Will Cherish The Old Rugged Cross
523704..... Ornament .... 1990 .... May Your Christmas Be A Happy Home
523771..... Ornament .... 1990 .... Baby's First Christmas
523798..... Ornament .... 1990 .... Baby's First Christmas
523801..... Plate .... 1990 .... Wishing You A Yummy Christmas
523828..... Bell .... 1990 .... Once Upon A Holy Night
523836..... Figurine .... 1990 .... Once Upon A Holy Night
523844..... Thimble .... 1990 .... Once Upon A Holy Night
523852..... Ornament .... 1990 .... Once Upon A Holy Night
523860..... Plate .... 1991 .... Blessings From Me To Thee
524166..... Figurine .... 1991 .... May Your Christmas Be Merry
524174..... Ornament .... 1991 .... May Your Christmas Be Merry
524182..... Bell .... 1991 .... May Your Christmas Be Merry
524190..... Thimble .... 1991 .... May Your Christmas Be Merry
525324..... Ornament .... 1990 .... Our First Christmas Together
525960..... Egg .... 1992 .... We Are God's Workmanship
526940..... Ornament .... 1991 .... May Your Christmas Be Merry
527084..... Ornament .... 1991 .... Baby's First Christmas
527092..... Ornament .... 1991 .... Baby's First Christmas
527475..... Ornament .... 1992 .... Baby's First Christmas
527483..... Ornament .... 1992 .... Baby's First Christmas
527688..... Figurine .... 1992 .... But The Greatest Of These Is Love
527696..... Ornament .... 1992 .... But The Greatest Of These Is Love
527718..... Thimble .... 1992 .... But The Greatest Of These Is Love
527726..... Bell .... 1992 .... But The Greatest Of These Is Love
527734..... Ornament .... 1992 .... But The Greatest Of These Is Love
527742..... Plate .... 1992 .... But The Greatest Of These Is Love
528617..... Egg .... 1993 .... Make A Joyful Noise
528870..... Ornament .... 1992 .... Our First Christmas Together
529095..... Egg .... 1994 .... A Reflection Of His Love
529206..... Ornament .... 1994 .... Our First Christmas Together
530166..... Figurine .... 1993 .... Wishing You The Sweetest Christmas
530174..... Bell .... 1993 .... Wishing You The Sweetest Christmas
530182..... Thimble .... 1993 .... Wishing You The Sweetest Christmas
530190..... Ornament .... 1993 .... Wishing You The Sweetest Christmas
530204..... Plate .... 1993 .... Wishing You The Sweetest Christmas
530212..... Ornament .... 1993 .... Wishing You The Sweetest Christmas
530255..... Ornament .... 1994 .... Baby's First Christmas
530263..... Ornament .... 1994 .... Baby's First Christmas
530387..... Ornament .... 1994 .... You're As Pretty As A Christmas Tree
530395..... Ornament .... 1994 .... You're As Pretty As A Christmas Tree
530409..... Plate .... 1994 .... You're As Pretty As A Christmas Tree

DATED ANNUALS continued

530425..... Figurine........... 1994 .... You're As Pretty As A Christmas Tree
530506..... Ornament .... 1993 .... Our First Christmas Together
530859..... Ornament .... 1993 .... Baby's First Christmas
530867..... Ornament .... 1993 .... Baby's First Christmas
530972..... Ornament .... 1994 .... You Are Always In My Heart
531359..... Plate .... 1994 .... Bring The Little Ones To Jesus
531766..... Plate .... 1994 .... Thinking Of You Is What I Really Like To Do
604216..... Bell .... 1994 .... You're As Pretty As A Christmas Tree

###############

TWO-YEAR COLLECTIBLES

408735..... Musical Jack-in-the-Box .... 1990, 1991 ...... The Voice Of Spring
408743..... Musical Jack-in-the-Box .... 1990, 1991 ...... Summer's Joy
408751..... Musical Jack-in-the-Box .... 1990, 1991 ...... Autumn's Praise
408778..... Musical Jack-in-the-Box .... 1990, 1991 ...... Winter's Song
408786..... Doll .... 1990, 1991 ...... The Voice Of Spring
408794..... Doll .... 1990, 1991 ...... Summer's Joy
408808..... Doll .... 1990, 1991 ...... Autumn's Praise
408816..... Doll .... 1990, 1991 ...... Winter's Song
417777..... Musical Jack-in-the-Box .... 1991, 1992 ...... May You Have An Old Fashioned Christmas
417785..... Doll .... 1991, 1992 ...... May You Have An Old Fashioned Christmas
422282..... Musical Jack-in-the-Box .... 1991, 1992 ...... You Have Touched So Many Hearts
427527..... Doll .... 1991, 1992 ...... You Have Touched So Many Hearts

###############

ANNUALS that are not dated

E-2838 ..... Figurine .... 1987 .... This Is The Day Which The Lord Hath Made
12068 .... Figurine .... 1985 .... The Voice Of Spring
12076 .... Figurine .... 1985 .... Summer's Joy
12084 .... Figurine .... 1986 .... Autumn's Praise
12092 .... Figurine .... 1986 .... Winter's Song
12106 .... Plate .... 1985 .... The Voice Of Spring
12114 .... Plate .... 1985 .... Summer's Joy
12122 .... Plate .... 1986 .... Autumn's Praise
12130 .... Plate .... 1986 .... Winter's Song
100536 ..... Figurine .... 1987 .... I Picked A Very Special Mom
100641 ..... Thimbles .... 1986 .... Four Seasons
102903 ..... Figurine .... 1987 .... We Are All Precious In His Sight
102938 ..... Figurine .... 1986 .... God Bless America
107999 ..... Figurine .... 1987 .... He Walks With Me
114022 ..... Figurine .... 1988 .... The Good Lord Has Blessed Us Tenfold
115231 ..... Figurine .... 1988 .... You Are My Main Event
115479 ..... Figurine .... 1988 .... Blessed Are They That Overcome
520470 ..... Ornament .... 1994 .... Take A Bow 'Cuz You're My Christmas Star
520861 ..... Figurine .... 1989 .... Sharing Begins In The Heart
522376 ..... Figurine .... 1989 .... His Love Will Shine On You
523291 ..... Wall Hanging . 1994 .... Blessed Are The Merciful
523313 ..... Wall Hanging . 1993 .... Blessed Are The Meek
523321 ..... Wall Hanging . 1993 .... Blessed Are The Ones Who Hunger
523348 ..... Wall Hanging . 1994 .... Blessed Are The Peacemakers
523380 ..... Wall Hanging . 1992 .... Blessed Are The Ones Who Mourn
523399 ..... Wall Hanging . 1995 .... Blessed Are The Pure In Heart
523437 ..... Wall Hanging . 1992 .... Blessed Are The Humble
523526 ..... Figurine .... 1990 .... I'm A PRECIOUS MOMENTS Fan
523593 ..... Figurine .... 1993 .... The Lord Will Provide
524158 ..... Figurine .... 1994 .... Lord, Teach Us To Pray
524263 ..... Figurine .... 1991 .... HE Loves Me
524379 ..... Figurine .... 1994 .... So Glad I Picked You As A Friend
524522 ..... Figurine .... 1990 .... Always In His Care
525049 ..... Figurine .... 1990 .... Good Friends Are Forever
525057 ..... Ornament .... 1990 .... Bundles Of Joy
526185 ..... Figurine .... 1992 .... You Are My Happiness
527114 ..... Figurine .... 1991 .... Sharing A Gift Of Love
527122 ..... Figurine .... 1991 .... You Can Always Bring A Friend
527173 ..... Figurine .... 1992 .... A Universal Love
527319 ..... Figurine .... 1992 .... An Event Worth Wading For
527564 ..... Figurine .... 1992 .... God Bless The USA
527777 ..... Figurine .... 1992 .... This Land Is Our Land
528862 ..... Figurine .... 1993 .... America, You're Beautiful
529648 ..... Ornament .... 1992 .... The Magic Starts With You
529931 ..... Figurine .... 1993 .... Happiness Is At Our Fingertips
529974 ..... Ornament .... 1993 .... An Event For All Seasons
529982 ..... Figurine .... 1994 .... Memories Are Made Of This
530026 ..... Figurine .... 1993 .... You're My Number One Friend
530158 ..... Figurine .... 1993 .... An Event For All Seasons
530786 ..... Figurine .... 1993 .... 15 Happy Years Together, What A Tweet!
530840 ..... Ornament .... 1993 .... 15 Years, Tweet Music Together
531111 ..... Figurine .... 1994 .... It Is No Secret What God Can Do
617334 ..... Tree Topper ..... 1990 .... Rejoice O Earth

################

QUIKREFERENCE • outline of the Annuals

(• indicates a completed series)

• JOY OF CHRISTMAS PLATE SERIES (Series of 4, Dated)

E-2357	1982	I'll Play My Drum For Him
E-0505	1983	Christmastime Is For Sharing
E-5396	1984	The Wonder Of Christmas
15237	1985	Tell Me The Story Of Jesus

• THE FOUR SEASONS PLATES (Set of 4, Unnumbered Certificate)

12106	1985	The Voice Of Spring
12114	1985	Summer's Joy
12122	1986	Autumn's Praise
12130	1986	Winter's Song

• THE FOUR SEASONS FIGURINES (Set of 4, Unnumbered Certificate)

12068	1985	The Voice Of Spring
12076	1985	Summer's Joy
12084	1986	Autumn's Praise
12092	1986	Winter's Song

• THE FOUR SEASONS THIMBLES (Set of 4)

100641	1986	Four Seasons Thimbles

• CHRISTMAS LOVE PLATE SERIES (Series of 4, Dated)

101834	1986	I'm Sending You A White Christmas
102954	1987	My Peace I Give To Thee
520284	1988	Merry Christmas, Deer
523003	1989	May Your Christmas Be A Happy Home

• CHRISTMAS BLESSINGS PLATE SERIES (Series of 4, Dated)

523801	1990	Wishing You A Yummy Christmas
523860	1991	Blessings From Me To Thee
527742	1992	But The Greatest Of These Is Love
530204	1993	Wishing You The Sweetest Christmas

CHAPEL WINDOW COLLECTION - BEATITUDE SERIES (Announced Series of 7)

523437	1992	Blessed Are The Humble
523380	1992	Blessed Are The Ones Who Mourn
523313	1993	Blessed Are The Meek
523321	1993	Blessed Are The Ones Who Hunger
523291	1994	Blessed Are The Merciful
523348	1994	Blessed Are The Peacemakers
523399	1995	Blessed Are The Pure In Heart

NATIONAL DAY OF PRAYER FIGURINES

527564	1992	God Bless The USA
528862	1993	America, You're Beautiful
524158	1994	Lord, Teach Us To Pray

DISTINGUISHED SERVICE RETAILER (DSR) OPEN HOUSE ORNAMENTS

529648	1992	The Magic Starts With You
529974	1993	An Event For All Seasons
520470	1994	Take A Bow 'Cuz You're My Christmas Star

SPRING CATALOG FIGURINES

529931	1993	Happiness Is At Our Fingertips
524379	1994	So Glad I Picked You As A Friend

SPECIAL EASTER SEAL FIGURINES

107999	1987	He Walks With Me
115479	1988	Blessed Are They That Overcome
522376	1989	His Love Will Shine On You
524522	1990	Always In His Care
527114	1991	Sharing A Gift Of Love
527173	1992	A Universal Love
530026	1993	You're My Number One Friend
531111	1994	It Is No Secret What God Can Do

SPECIAL EVENTS FIGURINES

115231	1988	You Are My Main Event
520861	1989	Sharing Begins In The Heart
523526	1990	I'm A PRECIOUS MOMENTS Fan
525049	1990	Good Friends Are Forever (Rosebud Understamp)
527122	1991	You Can Always Bring A Friend
527319	1992	An Event Worth Wading For
530158	1993	An Event For All Seasons
529982	1994	Memories Are Made Of This

• TRADITIONAL ANNUAL BELLS 1981 - 1993 (Dated)

E-5622	1981	Let The Heavens Rejoice
E-2358	1982	I'll Play My Drum For Him
E-0522	1983	Surrounded With Joy
E-5393	1984	Wishing You A Merry Christmas
15873	1985	God Sent His Love
102318	1986	Wishing You A Cozy Christmas
109835	1987	Love Is The Best Gift Of All
115304	1988	Time To Wish You A Merry Christmas
522821	1989	Oh Holy Night
523828	1990	Once Upon A Holy Night
524182	1991	May Your Christmas Be Merry
527726	1992	But The Greatest Of These Is Love
530174	1993	Wishing You The Sweetest Christmas

RESTYLED ANNUAL BELLS (Dated)

604216	1994	You're As Pretty As A Christmas Tree

• ANNUAL BABY'S FIRST CHRISTMAS ORNAMENTS – UNISEX (Dated)

E-0518	1983	Blessed Are The Pure In Heart
E-5392	1984	Blessed Are The Pure In Heart

• ANNUAL THIMBLES 1985 - 1993 (Dated)

15865	1985	God Sent His Love
102334	1986	Wishing You A Cozy Christmas
109843	1987	Love Is The Best Gift Of All
115312	1988	Time To Wish You A Merry Christmas
522554	1989	Oh Holy Night
523844	1990	Once Upon A Holy Night
524190	1991	May Your Christmas Be Merry
527718	1992	But The Greatest Of These Is Love
530182	1993	Wishing You The Sweetest Christmas

(1993 marked the end of the Annual Thimbles.)

QUIKREFERENCE • outline of the Annuals

ANNUAL ORNAMENTS (Dated)

E-5629	1981	Let The Heavens Rejoice
E-2359	1982	I'll Play My Drum For Him
E-0513	1983	Surround Us With Joy
E-5387	1984	Wishing You A Merry Christmas
15768	1985	God Sent His Love
102326	1986	Wishing You A Cozy Christmas
109770	1987	Love Is The Best Gift Of All
115320	1988	Time To Wish You A Merry Christmas
520276	1988	You Are My Gift Come True
522848	1989	Oh Holy Night
523852	1990	Once Upon A Holy Night
524174	1991	May Your Christmas Be Merry
527696	1992	But The Greatest Of These Is Love
530212	1993	Wishing You The Sweetest Christmas
530395	1994	You're As Pretty As A Christmas Tree

ANNUAL FIGURINES (Dated)

E-5383	1984	Wishing You A Merry Christmas
15539	1985	Baby's First Christmas (Boy)
15547	1985	Baby's First Christmas (Girl)
15881	1985	God Sent His Love
102342	1986	Wishing You A Cozy Christmas
110930	1987	Love Is The Best Gift Of All
115339	1988	Time To Wish You A Merry Christmas
522546	1989	Oh Holy Night
523836	1990	Once Upon A Holy Night
524166	1991	May Your Christmas Be Merry
527688	1992	But The Greatest Of These Is Love
530166	1993	Wishing You The Sweetest Christmas
530425	1994	You're As Pretty As A Christmas Tree

ANNUAL BABY'S FIRST CHRISTMAS ORNAMENTS – GIRL (Dated)

15911	1985	Baby's First Christmas
102504	1986	Baby's First Christmas
109401	1987	Baby's First Christmas
520241	1988	Baby's First Christmas
523208	1989	Baby's First Christmas
523771	1990	Baby's First Christmas
527092	1991	Baby's First Christmas
527475	1992	Baby's First Christmas
530867	1993	Baby's First Christmas
530255	1994	Baby's First Christmas

ANNUAL BABY'S FIRST CHRISTMAS ORNAMENTS – BOY (Dated)

15903	1985	Baby's First Christmas
102512	1986	Baby's First Christmas
109428	1987	Baby's First Christmas
115282	1988	Baby's First Christmas
523194	1989	Baby's First Christmas
523798	1990	Baby's First Christmas
527084	1991	Baby's First Christmas
527483	1992	Baby's First Christmas
530859	1993	Baby's First Christmas
530263	1994	Baby's First Christmas

ANNUAL OUR FIRST CHRISTMAS TOGETHER ORNAMENTS (Dated)

102350	1986	Our First Christmas Together
112399	1987	Our First Christmas Together
520233	1988	Our First Christmas Together
521558	1989	Our First Christmas Together
525324	1990	Our First Christmas Together
522945	1991	Our First Christmas Together
528870	1992	Our First Christmas Together
530506	1993	Our First Christmas Together
529206	1994	Our First Christmas Together

ANNUAL BIRTHDAY COLLECTION ORNAMENTS (Dated)

102466	1986	Reindeer
104515	1987	Bear The Good News Of Christmas
520292	1988	Hang On For The Holly Days
520462	1989	Christmas Is Ruff Without You
520497	1990	Wishing You A Purr-fect Holiday
520438	1991	Sno-Bunny Falls For You Like I Do
520411	1992	I'm Nuts About You
520489	1993	Slow Down And Enjoy The Holidays
530972	1994	You Are Always In My Heart

ANNUAL MASTERPIECE ORNAMENT SERIES (Dated)

523062	1989	Peace On Earth
523704	1990	May Your Christmas Be A Happy Home
526940	1991	May Your Christmas Be Merry
527734	1992	But The Greatest Of These Is Love
530190	1993	Wishing You The Sweetest Christmas
530387	1994	You're As Pretty As A Christmas Tree

• ANNUAL EGGS (Dated)

523534	1991	I Will Cherish The Old Rugged Cross
525960	1992	We Are God's Workmanship
528617	1993	Make A Joyful Noise
529095	1994	A Reflection Of His Love

(1994 marks the end of the Annual Eggs.)

QUIKREFERENCE • outline of the Series

(• indicates a completed series)

• MOTHER'S LOVE PLATE SERIES (Series of 4, Individually Numbered)

E-5217 Mother Sew Dear
E-7173 The Purr-fect Grandma
E-9256 The Hand That Rocks The Future
E-2848 Loving Thy Neighbor

• INSPIRED THOUGHTS PLATE SERIES (Series of 4, Individually Numbered)

E-5215 Love One Another
E-7174 Make A Joyful Noise
E-9257 I Believe In Miracles
E-2847 Love Is Kind

• CHRISTMAS COLLECTION PLATE SERIES (Series of 4, Individually Numbered)

E-5646 Come Let Us Adore Him
E-2347 Let Heaven And Nature Sing
E-0538 Wee Three Kings
E-5395 Unto Us A Child Is Born

• BRIDAL SERIES (Series of 8)

E-2831 Bridesmaid
E-2836 Groomsman
E-2835 Flower Girl
E-2833 Ringbearer
E-2845 Junior Bridesmaid
E-2837 Groom
E-2846 Bride
E-2838 This Is The Day Which The Lord Hath Made

• HEAVENLY HALOS SERIES (Series of 4)

E-9260 God's Promises Are Sure
E-9274 Taste And See That The Lord Is Good
E-9288 Sending You A Rainbow
E-9289 Trust In The Lord

• CLOWN SERIES (Series of 4)

12262 I Get A Bang Out Of You
12459 Waddle I Do Without You
12467 The Lord Will Carry You Through
12270 Lord Keep Me On The Ball

• REJOICE IN THE LORD BAND SERIES (Series of 6)

12165 Lord, Keep My Life In Tune
12173 There's A Song In My Heart
12378 Happiness Is The Lord
12386 Lord Give Me A Song
12394 He Is My Song
12580 Lord, Keep My Life In Tune

• BLESS THOSE WHO SERVE THEIR COUNTRY (Series of 6)

526568 Navy
526576 Army
526584 Air Force
527521 Marine
527289 Girl Soldier
527297 African-American Soldier

• CALENDAR GIRL SERIES (Series of 12)

109983 January Girl
109991 February Girl
110019 March Girl
110027 April Girl
110035 May Girl
110043 June Girl
110051 July Girl
110078 August Girl
110086 September Girl
110094 October Girl
110108 November Girl
110116 December Girl

• "BABY'S FIRST" SERIES (Series of 8)

E-2840 Baby's First Step
E-2841 Baby's First Picture
12211 Baby's First Haircut
16012 Baby's First Trip
520705 Baby's First Pet
524077 Baby's First Meal
527238 Baby's First Word
524069 Baby's First Birthday

• THE FAMILY CHRISTMAS SCENE SERIES (Series of 7)

15776 May You Have The Sweetest Christmas
15784 The Story Of God's Love
15792 Tell Me A Story
15806 God Gave His Best
15814 Silent Night
522856 Have A Beary Merry Christmas
524883 Christmas Fireplace

THE BIRTHDAY CIRCUS TRAIN SERIES

15938 May Your Birthday Be Warm (Baby)
15946 Happy Birthday Little Lamb (Age 1)
15962 God Bless You On Your Birthday (Age 2)
15954 Heaven Bless Your Special Day (Age 3)
15970 May Your Birthday Be Gigantic (Age 4)
15989 This Day Is Something To Roar About (Age 5)
15997 Keep Looking Up (Age 6)
109479 Wishing You Grrr-eatness (Age 7)
109460 Isn't Eight Just Great (Age 8)
521833 Being Nine Is Just Divine (Age 9)
521825 May Your Birthday Be Mammoth (Age 10)
16004 Bless The Days Of Our Youth

MOTHER'S DAY SERIES

531766 Thinking Of You Is What I Really Like To Do

THE GOOD SAMARITAN SERIES

603864 Nothing Can Dampen The Spirit Of Caring

THE CLUBS

"Symbols of Membership" are received with enrollment in the Clubs. Charter members who renew receive "Symbols of Charter Membership." All members have the option to purchase "Membership Pieces" that are crafted exclusively for Club Members.

The Enesco PRECIOUS MOMENTS Collectors' Club is on a calendar year basis. Collectors renewing or joining by December 31 receive that year's Symbol of Membership. Order forms for the Membership Pieces must be taken to an authorized Enesco PRECIOUS MOMENTS Retailer by March 31 of the following year.

The Enesco PRECIOUS MOMENTS Birthday Club's year runs from July 1 to June 30. Order forms for the Membership Pieces must be redeemed by September 30.

Currently The Enesco PRECIOUS MOMENTS Collectors' Club membership fees - including 3rd Class delivery of the GOODNEWSLETTER - are: new 1 year $26.00 and new 2 year $50.00. For 1st Class delivery of the GOODNEWSLETTER the rates are $28.00 and $54.00, respectively. The Enesco PRECIOUS MOMENTS Birthday Club membership fees are: new 1 year $17.50 and new 2 year $32.00.

The address for The Enesco PRECIOUS MOMENTS Collector's Club is: One Enesco Plaza, P.O. Box 1466, Elk Grove Village, IL 60009-1466. The address for The Enesco PRECIOUS MOMENTS Birthday Club is: One Enesco Plaza, P.O. Box 1529, Elk Grove Village, IL 60009-1529.

THE ENESCO PRECIOUS MOMENTS BIRTHDAY CLUB

SYMBOLS OF CHARTER MEMBERSHIP

B-0001 1986 Our Club Can't Be Beat
B-0102 1987 A Smile's The Cymbal Of Joy
B-0103 1988 The Sweetest Club Around
B-0104 1989 Have A Beary Special Birthday
B-0105 1990 Our Club Is A Tough Act To Follow
B-0106 1991 Jest To Let You Know You're Tops
B-0107 1992 All Aboard For Birthday Club Fun
B-0108 1993 Happiness Is Belonging

SYMBOLS OF MEMBERSHIP

B-0002 1987 A Smile's The Cymbal Of Joy
B-0003 1988 The Sweetest Club Around
B-0004 1989 Have A Beary Special Birthday
B-0005 1990 Our Club Is A Tough Act To Follow
B-0006 1991 Jest To Let You Know You're Tops
B-0007 1992 All Aboard For Birthday Club Fun
B-0008 1993 Happiness Is Belonging

MEMBERSHIP PIECES

BC-861 Fishing For Friends
BC-871 Hi Sugar!
BC-881 Somebunny Cares
BC-891 Can't Bee Hive Myself Without You
BC-901 Collecting Makes Good Scents
BC-902 I'm Nuts Over My Collection
BC-911 Love Pacifies
BC-912 True Blue Friends
BC-921 Every Man's House Is His Castle
BC-922 I Got You Under My Skin
BC-931 Put A Little Punch In Your Birthday
BC-932 Owl Always Be Your Friend
BC-941 God Bless Our Home

THE ENESCO PRECIOUS MOMENTS COLLECTORS' CLUB

SYMBOLS OF CHARTER MEMBERSHIP

E-0001 1981 But Love Goes On Forever
E-0102 1982 But Love Goes On Forever
E-0103 1983 Let Us Call The Club To Order
E-0104 1984 Join In On The Blessings
E-0105 1985 Seek And Ye Shall Find
E-0106 1986 Birds Of A Feather Collect Together
E-0107 1987 Sharing Is Universal
E-0108 1988 A Growing Love
C-0109 1989 Always Room For One More
C-0110 1990 My Happiness
C-0111 1991 Sharing The Good News Together
C-0112 1992 The Club That's Out Of This World
C-0113 1993 Loving, Caring & Sharing Along The Way
C-0114 1994 You Are The End Of My Rainbow

SYMBOLS OF MEMBERSHIP

E-0202 1982 But Love Goes On Forever
E-0303 1983 Let Us Call The Club To Order
E-0404 1984 Join In On The Blessings
E-0005 1985 Seek And Ye Shall Find
E-0006 1986 Birds Of A Feather Collect Together
E-0007 1987 Sharing Is Universal
E-0008 1988 A Growing Love
C-0009 1989 Always Room For One More
C-0010 1990 My Happiness
C-0011 1991 Sharing The Good News Together
C-0012 1992 The Club That's Out Of This World
C-0013 1993 Loving, Caring & Sharing Along The Way
C-0014 1994 You Are The End Of My Rainbow

THE ENESCO PRECIOUS MOMENTS COLLECTORS' CLUB SM

SHARING SEASON ORNAMENTS

PM-864 1986 Birds Of A Feather Collect Together
PM-008 1987 Sharing Season Ornament
520349 1988 A Growing Love
522961 1989 Always Room For One More
PM-904 1990 My Happiness
PM-037 1991 Sharing The Good News Together
PM-038 1992 The Club That's Out Of This World

MEMBERS' ONLY ORNAMENT

PM-040 1993 Loving, Caring & Sharing

MEMBERSHIP PIECES

PM-811 Hello Lord, It's Me Again
PM-821 Smile, God Loves You
PM-822 Put On A Happy Face
PM-831 Dawn's Early Light
PM-841 God's Ray Of Mercy
PM-842 Trust In The Lord To The Finish
PM-851 The Lord Is My Shepherd
PM-852 I Love To Tell The Story
PM-861 Grandma's Prayer
PM-862 I'm Following Jesus
PM-871 Feed My Sheep
PM-872 In His Time
PM-873 Loving You Dear Valentine
PM-874 Loving You Dear Valentine
PM-881 God Bless You For Touching My Life
PM-882 You Just Cannot Chuck A Good Friendship
PM-890 Beatitude Ornament Series (Set of 7)
PM-891 You Will Always Be My Choice
PM-892 Mow Power To Ya
PM-901 Ten Years And Still Going Strong
PM-902 You Are A Blessing To Me
PM-911 One Step At A Time
PM-912 Lord Keep Me In Teepee Top Shape
PM-921 Only Love Can Make A Home
PM-922 Sowing The Seeds Of Love
PM-931 His Little Treasure
PM-932 Loving
PM-941 Caring

COMMEMORATIVE PIECES:

12440 God Bless Our Years Together
527386 This Land Is Our Land

Individually, the seven Beatitude Ornaments are:
PM-190 Blessed are the Poor in Spirit, for Theirs is The Kingdom of Heaven
PM-290 Blessed are They that Mourn, for They Shall be Comforted
PM-390 Blessed are the Meek, for They Shall Inherit the Earth
PM-490 Blessed are They that Hunger and Thirst for Righteousness, for They Shall be Filled
PM-590 Blessed are the Merciful, for They Shall Obtain Mercy
PM-690 Blessed are the Pure in Heart, for They Shall See God
PM-790 Blessed are the Peacemakers, for they will be Called Sons of God

QUIKREFERENCE • CALENDAR

	1981		1982	
RETIRED	E-1378	God Loveth A Cheerful Giver	E-1374B	Praise The Lord Anyhow
	E-2011	Come Let Us Adore Him		
SUSPENDED				
ANNUALS	E-5622	Let The Heavens Rejoice	E-2357	I'll Play My Drum For Him
	E-5629	Let The Heavens Rejoice	E-2358	I'll Play My Drum For Him
			E-2359	I'll Play My Drum For Him

	1983	1984
RETIRED	E-3112 God's Speed E-3118 Eggs Over Easy	E-1373B Smile, God Loves You E-1380G His Burden Is Light E-1380B O, How I Love Jesus E-2368 The First Noel E-2806 Christmas Is A Time To Share E-5211 God Understands E-6120 We Have Seen His Star
SUSPENDED		E-1375B Prayer Changes Things E-1377A He Leadeth Me E-1377B He Careth For You E-1379A Love Is Kind E-1379B God Understands E-1381 Jesus Is The Answer E-2010 We Have Seen His Star E-2012 Jesus Is Born E-2013 Unto Us A Child Is Born E-2345 May Your Christmas Be Cozy E-2350 Dropping In For Christmas E-2352 O Come All Ye Faithful E-2355 I'll Play My Drum For Him E-2365 The First Noel E-2366 The First Noel E-2367 The First Noel E-2381 Mouse with Cheese E-2386 Camel, Donkey, Cow Ornaments E-2801 Jesus Is Born E-2802 Christmas Is The Time To Share E-2803 Crown Him Lord Of All E-2804 Peace On Earth E-2807 Crown Him Lord Of All E-2808 Unto Us A Child Is Born E-3105 He Watches Over Us All E-3108 The Hand That Rocks The Future E-3119 It's What's Inside That Counts E-4723 Peace Amid The Storm E-4725 Peace On Earth E-4726 Peace On Earth E-5200 Bear Ye One Another's Burdens E-5201 Love Lifted Me E-5202 Thank You For Coming To My Ade E-5203 Let Not The Sun Go Down Upon Your Wrath E-5207 My Guardian Angel E-5210 Prayer Changes Things E-5214 Prayer Changes Things E-5623 Jesus Is Born E-5633 Come Let Us Adore Him E-5634 Wee Three Kings E-7155 Thanking Him For You E-7161 His Sheep Am I E-7162 Love Is Sharing E-7163 God Is Watching Over You E-7164 Bless This House E-7168 My Guardian Angel E-7169 My Guardian Angel E-9275 Jesus Loves Me E-9276 Jesus Loves Me E-9283A Forever Friends - Dog E-9283B Forever Friends - Cat
ANNUALS	E-0505 Christmastime Is For Sharing E-0513 Surround Us With Joy E-0518 Blessed Are The Pure In Heart E-0522 Surrounded With Joy	E-5383 Wishing You A Merry Christmas E-5387 Wishing You A Merry Christmas E-5392 Baby's First Christmas E-5393 Wishing You A Merry Christmas E-5396 The Wonder Of Christmas

QUIKREFERENCE • CALENDAR

1985

RETIRED

- E-2376 Dropping Over For Christmas
- E-2805 Wishing You A Season Filled With Joy
- E-2850 Mother Sew Dear
- E-3107 Blessed Are The Peacemakers
- E-3111 Be Not Weary In Well Doing
- E-7185 Love Is Sharing

SUSPENDED

- E-0526 He Upholdeth Those Who Call
- E-0537 Jesus Is The Light
- E-2344 Joy To The World
- E-2349 Tell Me The Story Of Jesus
- E-2356 I'll Play My Drum For Him
- E-2372 Baby's First Christmas
- E-2377 Our First Christmas Together
- E-2378 Our First Christmas Together
- E-2809 Jesus Is Born
- E-4722 Love Cannot Break A True Friendship
- E-5205 My Guardian Angel
- E-5208 Jesus Loves Me
- E-5209 Jesus Loves Me
- E-5619 Come Let Us Adore Him
- E-5620 We Have Seen His Star
- E-5627 But Love Goes On Forever
- E-5628 But Love Goes On Forever
- E-5630 Unto Us A Child Is Born
- E-5631 Baby's First Christmas
- E-5632 Baby's First Christmas
- E-5639 Isn't He Wonderful
- E-5640 Isn't He Wonderful
- E-5641 They Followed The Star
- E-5642 Silent Knight
- E-6214B Mikey
- E-6214G Debbie
- E-7156 I Believe In Miracles
- E-7159 Lord Give Me Patience
- E-7167 The Lord Bless You And Keep You
- E-7170 Jesus Loves Me
- E-7171 Jesus Loves Me
- E-7172 Rejoicing With You
- E-7175 The Lord Bless You And Keep You
- E-7176 The Lord Bless You And Keep You
- E-9251 Love Is Patient
- E-9253 The End Is In Sight
- E-9263 How Can Two Walk Together Except They Agree
- E-9280 Jesus Loves Me
- E-9281 Jesus Loves Me
- E-9285 If God Be For Us, Who Can Be Against Us

ANNUALS

- 12068 The Voice Of Spring*
- 12076 Summer's Joy*
- 12106 The Voice Of Spring*
- 12114 Summer's Joy*

- 15237 Tell Me The Story Of Jesus
- 15539 Baby's First Christmas
- 15547 Baby's First Christmas
- 15768 God Sent His Love
- 15865 God Sent His Love
- 15873 God Sent His Love
- 15881 God Sent His Love
- 15903 Baby's First Christmas
- 15911 Baby's First Christmas

*Not Dated

1986

RETIRED

- E-0519 Sharing Our Season Together
- E-0532 Let Heaven And Nature Sing
- E-2353 O Come All Ye Faithful
- E-2369 Dropping In For Christmas
- E-2841 Baby's First Picture
- E-7157 There Is Joy In Serving Jesus
- E-9274 Taste And See That The Lord Is Good

SUSPENDED

- E-0501 Sharing Our Season Together
- E-0502 Jesus Is The Light That Shines
- E-0503 Blessings From My House To Yours
- E-0508 Prepare Ye The Way Of The Lord
- E-0520 Wee Three Kings
- E-0531 O Come All Ye Faithful
- E-0535 Love Is Patient
- E-0536 Love Is Patient
- E-2361 Christmas Joy From Head To Toe
- E-2826 May Your Birthday Be A Blessing
- E-2827 I Get A Kick Out Of You
- E-3120 To Thee With Love
- E-5376 May Your Christmas Be Blessed
- E-5380 A Monarch Is Born
- E-5382 For God So Loved The World
- E-5385 Oh Worship The Lord
- E-5386 Oh Worship The Lord
- E-5389 Peace On Earth
- E-5394 Wishing You A Merry Christmas
- E-6901 Collection Plaque
- E-7153 God Is Love, Dear Valentine
- E-7154 God Is Love, Dear Valentine
- E-7160 The Perfect Grandpa
- E-7186 Let The Whole World Know
- E-7241 Mother Sew Dear
- E-9261 Seek Ye The Lord
- E-9262 Seek Ye The Lord
- E-9287 Peace On Earth
- E-9288 Sending You A Rainbow
- 12203 Get Into The Habit Of Prayer
- 12343 Jesus Is Coming Soon
- 12424 Aaron
- 12432 Bethany
- 12475 P.D.
- 12483 Trish

ANNUALS

- 12084 Autumn's Praise*
- 12092 Winter's Song*
- 12122 Autumn's Praise*
- 12130 Winter's Song*
- 100641 Four Seasons Thimbles*
- 102938 God Bless America*

- 101834 I'm Sending You A White Christmas
- 102318 Wishing You A Cozy Christmas
- 102326 Wishing You A Cozy Christmas
- 102334 Wishing You A Cozy Christmas
- 102342 Wishing You A Cozy Christmas
- 102350 Our First Christmas Together
- 102466 Reindeer Ornament
- 102504 Baby's First Christmas
- 102512 Baby's First Christmas

*Not Dated

1987

RETIRED

E-0530	His Eye Is On The Sparrow
E-2351	Holy Smokes
E-5377	Love Is Kind
E-5388	Joy To The World
E-9273	Let Love Reign

SUSPENDED

E-0507	God Sent His Son
E-0509	Bringing God's Blessing To You
E-0521	Blessed Are The Pure In Heart
E-2823	To God Be The Glory
E-4720	The Lord Bless You And Keep You
E-5216	The Lord Bless You And Keep You
E-5381	His Name Is Jesus
E-6613	God Sends The Gift Of His Love
E-7165	Let The Whole World Know
E-7177	The Lord Bless You And Keep You
E-7178	The Lord Bless You And Keep You
E-9260	God's Promises Are Sure
E-9289	Trust In The Lord
12017	Loving You
12025	Loving You
12033	God's Precious Gift
12211	Baby's First Haircut
12297	It Is Better To Give Than To Receive
12408	We Saw A Star

ANNUALS

E-2838	This Is The Day Which The Lord Hath Made*
100536	I Picked A Very Special Mom*
102903	We Are All Precious In His Sight*
107999	He Walks With Me*
102954	My Peace I Give Unto Thee
104515	Bear The Good News Of Christmas
109401	Baby's First Christmas
109428	Baby's First Christmas
109770	Love Is The Best Gift Of All
109835	Love Is The Best Gift Of All
109843	Love Is The Best Gift Of All
110930	Love Is The Best Gift Of All
112399	Our First Christmas Together

*Not Dated

1988

RETIRED

E-1373G	Jesus Is The Light
E-2371	Unicorn
E-2822	This Is Your Day To Shine
E-5645	Rejoice O Earth
12467	The Lord Will Carry You Through
100129	Lord Keep Me On My Toes

SUSPENDED

E-0515	To A Special Dad
E-0533	Tell Me The Story Of Jesus
E-0539	Katie Lynne
E-2343	Joy To The World
E-2348	May Your Christmas Be Warm
E-2362	Baby's First Christmas
E-2840	Baby's First Step
E-5206	My Guardian Angel
E-6118	But Love Goes On Forever
E-7181	Mother Sew Dear
E-7183	The Purr-fect Grandma
E-7242	The Purr-fect Grandma
E-9266	I'm Falling For Somebunny
E-9266	Our Love Is Heaven Scent
12335	You Can Fly
12351	Halo, And Merry Christmas
100021	To My Favorite Paw
100668	Clown Thimbles
102431	Serve With A Smile
102458	Serve With A Smile
102490	Sharing Our Christmas Together

ANNUALS

114022	The Good Lord Blessed Us Tenfold*
115231	You Are My Main Event*
115479	Blessed Are They That Overcome*
115282	Baby's First Christmas
115304	Time To Wish You A Merry Christmas
115312	Time To Wish You A Merry Christmas
115320	Time To Wish You A Merry Christmas
115339	Time To Wish You A Merry Christmas
520233	Our First Christmas Together
520241	Baby's First Christmas
520276	You Are My Gift Come True
520284	Merry Christmas, Deer
520292	Hang On For The Holly Days

*Not Dated

QUIKREFERENCE • CALENDAR

RETIRED

1989		1990	
E-0506	Surrounded With Joy	E-0504	Christmastime Is For Sharing
E-0525	You Can't Run Away From God	E-9268	Nobody's Perfect!
E-0534	To Thee With Love	100102	Make Me A Blessing
12459	Waddle I Do Without You	102423	Lord, Keep Me On My Toes
15504	God Sent You Just In Time	520772	Many Moons In Same Canoe, Blessum You
100269	Help Lord, I'm In A Spot		

SUSPENDED

1989		1990	
E-2346	Let Heaven And Nature Sing	E-0512	It's A Perfect Boy
E-2364	Goat	E-0517	The Perfect Grandpa
E-2851	Kristy	E-9259	We're In It Together
E-5213	God Is Love	E-9282A	To Somebunny Special
E-5378	Joy To The World	E-9282B	You're Worth Your Weight In Gold
E-5390	May God Bless You With A Perfect Holiday Season	E-9282C	Especially For Ewe
E-5391	Love Is Kind	12157	This Is The Day The Lord Has Made
E-9252	Forgiving Is Forgetting	12173	There's A Song In My Heart
12149	Part Of Me Wants To Be Good	12254	Love Covers All
12165	Lord, Keep My Life In Tune	12378	Happiness Is The Lord
15822	May Your Christmas Be Happy	12386	Lord Give Me A Song
15830	Happiness Is The Lord	12394	He Is My Song
16012	Baby's First Trip	12580	Lord Keep My Life In Tune
16020	God Bless You With Rainbows	100145	God Bless The Day We Found You
100544	Brotherly Love	100153	God Bless The Day We Found You
100625	God Is Love, Dear Valentine	100161	Serving The Lord
102415	It's A Perfect Boy	100293	Serving The Lord
102962	It's The Birthday Of A King	104027	Love Is The Glue That Mends
		104396	Happy Days Are Here Again
		104825	Sitting Pretty
		105813	To Tell The Tooth You're Special
		106216	Lord Help Me Make The Grade
		111120	I'm A Possibility

ANNUALS

1989		1990	
		523526	I'm A PRECIOUS MOMENTS Fan*
		524522	Always In His Care*
		525049	Good Friends Are Forever*
520861	Sharing Begins In The Heart*	525057	Bundles Of Joy*
522376	His Love Will Shine On You*	617334	Rejoice O Earth*
520462	Christmas Is Ruff Without You	520497	Wishing You A Purr-fect Holiday
521558	Our First Christmas Together	523704	May Your Christmas Be A Happy Home
522546	Oh Holy Night	523771	Baby's First Christmas
522554	Oh Holy Night	523798	Baby's First Christmas
522821	Oh Holy Night	523801	Wishing You A Yummy Christmas
522848	Oh Holy Night	523828	Once Upon A Holy Night
523003	May Your Christmas Be A Happy Home	523836	Once Upon A Holy Night
523062	Peace On Earth	523844	Once Upon A Holy Night
523194	Baby's First Christmas	523852	Once Upon A Holy Night
523208	Baby's First Christmas	525324	Our First Christmas Together

*Not Dated

RETIRED

1991

E-2375	Dropping Over For Christmas
100196	The Spirit Is Willing But The Flesh Is Weak
100528	Scent From Above
101842	Smile Along The Way
113980	Rejoice O Earth
520640	I'm So Glad You Fluttered Into My Life

1992

JANUARY:

E-7156	I Believe In Miracles
E-7156R	I Believe In Miracles
101850	Lord, Help Us Keep Our Act Together

AUGUST:

101702	Our First Christmas Together
109584	Happiness Divine
520683	Sending You Showers Of Blessings
520799	Someday My Love
521566	Glide Through The Holidays

SUSPENDED

1991

E-2385	Our First Christmas Together
E-2834	Sharing Our Joy Together
E-3104	Blessed Are The Pure In Heart
E-5397	Timmy
E-9267	Animal Collection
E-9267A	Teddy Bear
E-9267B	Dog
E-9267C	Bunny
E-9267D	Cat
E-9267E	Lamb
E-9267F	Pig
12009	Love Covers All
100056	Sending My Love
100633	The Lord Bless You And Keep You
102474	Rocking Horse
105635	Have I Got News For You
105643	Something's Missing When You're Not Around
106151	We're Pulling For You
109487	Believe The Impossible
111333	O Come Let Us Adore Him
113972	God Sent You Just In Time
113999	Cheers To The Leader
114006	My Love Will Never Let You Go
115290	Our First Christmas Together
520802	My Days Are Blue Without You
520810	We Need A Good Friend Through The Ruff Times
520853	I Belong To The Lord
521868	The Greatest Of These Is Love

1992

12041	God's Precious Gift
15776	May You Have The Sweetest Chirstmas
15784	The Story Of God's Love
15792	Tell Me A Story
15806	God Gave His Best
15814	Silent Night
102296	Mini Animal Figurines
102369	Wedding Arch
112372	I'm Sending You A White Christmas
522856	Have A Beary Merry Christmas
524883	Christmas Fireplace
526568	Bless Those Who Serve Their Country - Navy
526576	Bless Those Who Serve Their Country - Army
526584	Bless Those Who Serve Their Country - Air Force
527289	Bless Those Who Serve Their Country - Girl Soldier
527297	Bless Those Who Serve Their Country - African-American Soldier
527521	Bless Those Who Serve Their Country - Marine

ANNUALS

1991

524263	HE Loves Me*
527114	Sharing A Gift Of Love*
527122	You Can Always Bring A Friend*
520438	Sno-Bunny Falls For You Like I Do
522945	Our First Christmas Together
523534	I Will Cherish The Old Rugged Cross
523860	Blessings From Me To Thee
524166	May Your Christmas Be Merry
524174	May Your Christmas Be Merry
524182	May Your Christmas Be Merry
524190	May Your Christmas Be Merry
526940	May Your Christmas Be Merry
527084	Baby's First Christmas
527092	Baby's First Christmas

*Not Dated

1992

523380	Blessed Are The Ones Who Mourn*
523437	Blessed Are The Humble*
526185	You Are My Happiness*
527173	A Universal Love*
527319	An Event Worth Wading For*
527564	God Bless The USA*
527777	This Land Is Our Land*
529648	The Magic Starts With You*
520411	I'm Nuts About You
525960	We Are God's Workmanship
527475	Baby's First Christmas
527483	Baby's First Christmas
527688	But The Greatest Of These Is Love
527696	But The Greatest Of These Is Love
527718	But The Greatest Of These Is Love
527726	But The Greatest Of These Is Love
527734	But The Greatest Of These Is Love
527742	But The Greatest Of These Is Love
528870	Our First Christmas Together

*Not Dated

QUIKREFERENCE • CALENDAR

1993

RETIRED

MAY:

E-1375A	Love Lifted Me
E-3110B	Loving Is Sharing
105945	Showers Of Blessings
521396	Faith Is A Victory

OCTOBER:

E-2374	Bundles Of Joy
100188	I'm A Possibility
112402	I'm Sending You A White Christmas
522112	Don't Let The Holidays Get You Down

SUSPENDED

E-0511	Tubby's First Christmas
E-2810	Come Let Us Adore Him
E-7166	The Lord Bless You And Keep You
E-7179	The Lord Bless You And Keep You
E-7184	The Purr-fect Grandma
15849	May Your Christmas Be Delightful
15857	Honk If You Love Jesus
100285	Heaven Bless You
102288	Shepherd Of Love
104418	Friends To The End
105953	Brighten Someone's Day
106836	Happy Birthday Poppy
109746	Peace On Earth
113964	Smile Along The Way
520357	Jesus The Savior Is Born
520691	Lord, Keep My Life In Balance
520756	Jesus Is The Only Way
521043	To My Favorite Fan
521205	Hope You're Up And On The Trail Again
521310	Yield Not To Temptation
521434	To A Very Special Mom And Dad
521949	Wishing You A Cozy Season
521957	High Hopes
522031	Thank The Lord For Everything
522252	He Is The Star Of The Morning
522988	Isn't He Precious
522996	Some Bunny's Sleeping
523097	Jesus Is The Sweetest Name I Know
524875	Happy Birthday Dear Jesus
527165	The Good Lord Always Delivers

ANNUALS

523313	Blessed Are The Meek*
523321	Blessed Are The Ones Who Hunger*
523593	The Lord Will Provide*
528862	America, You're Beautiful*
529931	Happiness Is At Our Fingertips*
529974	An Event For All Seasons*
530026	You're My Number One Friend*
530158	An Event For All Seasons*
530786	15 Happy Years Together, What A Tweet!*
530840	15 Years, Tweet Music Together*

520489	Slow Down And Enjoy The Holidays
528617	Make A Joyful Noise
530166	Wishing You The Sweetest Christmas
530174	Wishing You The Sweetest Christmas
530182	Wishing You The Sweetest Christmas
530190	Wishing You The Sweetest Christmas
530204	Wishing You The Sweetest Christmas
530212	Wishing You The Sweetest Christmas
530506	Our First Christmas Together
530859	Baby's First Christmas
530867	Baby's First Christmas

*Not Dated

1994

RETIRED

E-3116	Thee I Love
E-9254	Praise The Lord Anyhow
521590	Don't Let The Holidays Get You Down
522260	To Be With You Is Uplifting
523747	Blessings From Above
524271	Friendship Grows When You Plant A Seed

SUSPENDED

15482	May Your Christmas Be Delightful
109754	Wishing You A Yummy Christmas
429570	The Eyes Of The Lord Are Upon You
429589	The Eyes Of The Lord Are Upon You
520705	Baby's First Pet
521272	Take Heed When You Stand
521280	Happy Trip
521302	May All Your Christmases Be White
521574	Dashing Through The Snow
522104	It's No Yolk When I Say I Love You
522244	Do Not Open Till Christmas
522953	I Believe In The Old Rugged Cross
523224	Happy Trails Is Trusting Jesus
523763	I Can't Spell Success Without You
524484	Not A Creature Was Stirring
526959	We Have Come From Afar

ANNUALS

520470	Take A Bow 'Cuz You're My Christmas Star*
523291	Blessed Are The Merciful*
523348	Blessed Are The Peacemakers*
524158	Lord, Teach Us To Pray*
524379	So Glad I Picked You As A Friend*
529982	Memories Are Made Of This*
531111	It Is No Secret What God Can Do*

529095	A Reflection Of His Love
529206	Our First Christmas Together
530255	Baby's First Christmas
530263	Baby's First Christmas
530387	You're As Pretty As A Christmas Tree
530395	You're As Pretty As A Christmas Tree
530409	You're As Pretty As A Christmas Tree
530425	You're As Pretty As A Christmas Tree
530972	You Are Always In My Heart
531359	Bring The Little Ones To Jesus
531766	Thinking Of You Is What I Really Like To Do
604216	You're As Pretty As A Christmas Tree

*Not Dated

HOW TO READ A GREENBOOK LISTING

GREENBOOK Listings are in Enesco Item Number order.

Enesco Item Numbers can be found on the understamp of most pieces produced from 1982 to the present.

If you don't know the Enesco Item Number, but you do know the Inspirational Title, use the ALPHA-LOG™ to obtain the Enesco Item Number. If you don't know the Enesco Item Number or the Inspirational Title, use the ARTCHART™ to obtain the Enesco Item Number.

Collectors' Club and Birthday Club pieces are included at the end of the Listings in their own separate sections. Sugar Town, Two By Two and Sammy Circus pieces are not included in these Listings. These pieces are presented in a different format. Check the Table Of Contents for where they appear.

The following is a step-by-step explanation of how to read a GREENBOOK Listing using the figurine E-1374B, *Praise The Lord Anyhow*, as an example:

PRAISE THE LORD ANYHOW Figurine One of the "Original 21"

E-1374B	79 Boy w/Dog & Ice Cream Cone	UPP	$ 8.00	5.00"	NM	Retired/Sec	$120.00
19	81	UPP	11.00		TRI	Retired/Sec	95.00
	82	UPP	17.00		HRG	Retired/Sec	75.00

Variations exist in the color of the dog's nose (brown/black) and the flavor of ice cream.

This portion of a listing is the **INSPIRATIONAL TITLE.**

PRAISE THE LORD ANYHOW **Figurine** One of the "Original 21"

E-1374B	79 Boy w/Dog & Ice Cream Cone	UPP	$ 8.00	5.00"	NM	Retired/Sec	$120.00
19	81	UPP	11.00		TRI	Retired/Sec	95.00
	82	UPP	17.00		HRG	Retired/Sec	75.00

Variations exist in the color of the dog's nose (brown/black) and the flavor of ice cream.

This portion of a listing is the **TYPE OF PRODUCT**.

PRAISE THE LORD ANYHOW Figurine **One of the "Original 21"**

E-1374B	79 Boy w/Dog & Ice Cream Cone	UPP	$ 8.00	5.00"	NM	Retired/Sec	$120.00
19	81	UPP	11.00		TRI	Retired/Sec	95.00
	82	UPP	17.00		HRG	Retired/Sec	75.00

Variations exist in the color of the dog's nose (brown/black) and the flavor of ice cream.

This portion of a listing is reserved for **ADDITIONAL INFORMATION**. For example, if the piece is one of the "Original 21" that will be noted here. Other information appearing here includes series or set information, if a piece is dated, the tune if it's a musical, if it has a certificate, if it's individually numbered, or if the piece is a Nativity Addition.

... continued on next page

HOW TO READ A GREENBOOK LISTING continued

PRAISE THE LORD ANYHOW Figurine One of the "Original 21"

E-1374B	79 Boy w/Dog & Ice Cream Cone	UPP	$ 8.00	5.00"	NM	Retired/Sec	$120.00
19	81	UPP	11.00		TRI	Retired/Sec	95.00
	82	UPP	17.00		HRG	Retired/Sec	75.00

Variations exist in the color of the dog's nose (brown/black) and the flavor of ice cream.

This portion of a listing is the **ENESCO ITEM NUMBER**. It appears in brochures, catalogs, ads, and on the understamp of most pieces produced from 1982 to the present. It is a quick and *absolute* means of identification.

PRAISE THE LORD ANYHOW Figurine One of the "Original 21"

E-1374B	79 Boy w/Dog & Ice Cream Cone	UPP	$ 8.00	5.00"	NM	Retired/Sec	$120.00
19	81	UPP	11.00		TRI	Retired/Sec	95.00
	82	UPP	17.00		HRG	Retired/Sec	75.00

Variations exist in the color of the dog's nose (brown/black) and the flavor of ice cream.

This portion of a listing is the **GREENBOOK ARTCHART™ NUMBER**.

PRAISE THE LORD ANYHOW Figurine One of the "Original 21"

E-1374B	79 Boy w/Dog & Ice Cream Cone	UPP	$ 8.00	5.00"	NM	Retired/Sec	$120.00
19	81	UPP	11.00		TRI	Retired/Sec	95.00
	82	UPP	17.00		HRG	Retired/Sec	75.00

Variations exist in the color of the dog's nose (brown/black) and the flavor of ice cream.

This portion of a listing is the **YEAR OF ISSUE**. The GREENBOOK lists the year of issue for each change in Annual Production Symbol. A very common error made by collectors is to mistake the copyright date for the year of issue because the copyright date appears on the understamp written out as © 19XX. ***In other words, in order to determine what year your piece was produced, you must refer to the Annual Production Symbol, not the © date.***

PRAISE THE LORD ANYHOW Figurine One of the "Original 21"

E-1374B	79 Boy w/Dog & Ice Cream Cone	UPP	$ 8.00	5.00"	NM	Retired/Sec	$120.00
19	81	UPP	11.00		TRI	Retired/Sec	95.00
	82	UPP	17.00		HRG	Retired/Sec	75.00

Variations exist in the color of the dog's nose (brown/black) and the flavor of ice cream.

This portion of a listing is the **DESCRIPTIVE TITLE**.

PRAISE THE LORD ANYHOW Figurine One of the "Original 21"

E-1374B	79 Boy w/Dog & Ice Cream Cone	UPP	$ 8.00	5.00"	NM	Retired/Sec	$120.00
19	81	UPP	11.00		TRI	Retired/Sec	95.00
	82	UPP	17.00		HRG	Retired/Sec	75.00

Variations exist in the color of the dog's nose (brown/black) and the flavor of ice cream.

This portion of a listing is the **EDITION SIZE**. Editions are either limited or open (unlimited). The GREENBOOK identifies editions that are limited in one of five ways. They are: 1) A Specific Number - i.e. 15,000, 2) By Year (Annual), 3) Two-Year Collectible (2yr), 4) Available to Club Members Only (MemOnly), or 5) An Unspecified Production Period (UPP).

PRAISE THE LORD ANYHOW	Figurine	One of the "Original 21"					
E-1374B	79 Boy w/Dog & Ice Cream Cone	UPP	**$ 8.00**	5.00"	NM	Retired/Sec	$120.00
19	81	UPP	**11.00**		TRI	Retired/Sec	95.00
	82	UPP	**17.00**		HRG	Retired/Sec	75.00

Variations exist in the color of the dog's nose (brown/black) and the flavor of ice cream.

This portion of a listing is the **ISSUE PRICE** (Suggested Retail Price). GREENBOOK Listings include issue prices for each piece when it was first introduced and for each year the Annual Production Symbol is/was changed.

PRAISE THE LORD ANYHOW	Figurine	One of the "Original 21"					
E-1374B	79 Boy w/Dog & Ice Cream Cone	UPP	$ 8.00	**5.00"**	NM	Retired/Sec	$120.00
19	81	UPP	11.00		TRI	Retired/Sec	95.00
	82	UPP	17.00		HRG	Retired/Sec	75.00

Variations exist in the color of the dog's nose (brown/black) and the flavor of ice cream.

This portion of a listing is the **SIZE** in inches; diameter for plates and plaques, height for figurines, bells...

PRAISE THE LORD ANYHOW	Figurine	One of the "Original 21"					
E-1374B	79 Boy w/Dog & Ice Cream Cone	UPP	$ 8.00	5.00"	**NM**	Retired/Sec	$120.00
19	81	UPP	11.00		**TRI**	Retired/Sec	95.00
	82	UPP	17.00		**HRG**	Retired/Sec	75.00

Variations exist in the color of the dog's nose (brown/black) and the flavor of ice cream.

This portion of a listing is the **ANNUAL PRODUCTION SYMBOL**. Since mid-1981, Enesco has indicated when PRECIOUS MOMENTS collectibles were produced by including an Annual Production Symbol as part of the understamp. Pieces produced prior to mid-1981 have no Annual Production Symbol and are termed "No Marks."

The GREENBOOK defines "No Mark" as prior to mid-1981.

There are also "Unmarked" PRECIOUS MOMENTS collectibles. It was not until 1984 that some product types such as plates and ornaments were marked with an Annual Production Symbol. The GREENBOOK terms 1981, 1982, and 1983 pieces that fall into this category as "Unmarked." "Unmarked" pieces are designated as "UM" in the listings. HINT: Most "Unmarked" pieces (vs. "No Mark") will have the Enesco Item Number on the understamp but not an Annual Production Symbol.

An "Unmarked" piece can also be a production error. Some pieces simply miss getting marked!

The following page outlines and illustrates the different Annual Production Symbols and their meanings as well as the Special Production Symbols.

... continued on next page

HOW TO READ A GREENBOOK LISTING continued

ANNUAL PRODUCTION SYMBOLS:

Year	Name	Symbol	Code	Meaning
Prior to 1981	**"No Mark"**	----	NM	
1981	**Triangle**		TRI	Symbol of the Triune - God, the Father, Son, & Holy Spirit.
1982	**Hourglass**		HRG	Represents the time we have on earth to serve the Lord.
1983	**Fish**		FSH	Earliest symbol used by believers of the early apostolic church.
1984	**Cross**		CRS	Symbol of Christianity recognized worldwide.
1985	**Dove**		DVE	Symbol of love and peace.
1986	**Olive Branch**		OLB	Symbol of peace & understanding.
1987	**Cedar Tree**		CED	Symbol of strength, beauty, and preservation.
1988	**Flower**		FLW	Represents God's love toward His children.
1989	**Bow & Arrow**		B&A	Represents the power of the Bible.
1990	**Flame**		FLM	For those who have gone through the fire of life & found comfort in believing.
1991	**Vessel**		VSL	A reminder of God's love which flows through the vessel of life.
1992	**G-Clef**		G/CL	Symbolizes the harmony of God's love.
1993	**Butterfly**		BFY	Represents the rebirth of man who comes from darkness into the light.
1994	**Trumpet**		TRP	Represents Precious Moments as a voice to our nation with a message of loving, caring and sharing. The trumpet is the battle cry to war and the heralder of victory.

SPECIAL PRODUCTION SYMBOLS:

---	**Diamond**		DIA	Appeared on one piece only - #103004, *"We Belong To The Lord,"* the Damien-Dutton figurine.
---	**Easter Seal Lily**		---	Appears on figurines benefiting the National Easter Seal Society.
---	**Rosebud**		---	Appeared on one figurine only - #525049, *"Good Friends Are Forever,"* a Special Events figurine.
1991	**'91 Flag**		FLG	Appeared on all *"Bless Those Who Serve Their Country"* figurines crafted in 1991.
1992	**'92 Flag**		FLG/*	Appeared on all *"Bless Those Who Serve Their Country"* figurines crafted in 1992.

... continued on next page

HOW TO READ A GREENBOOK LISTING continued

PRAISE THE LORD ANYHOW Figurine One of the "Original 21"

E-1374B							
19	79 Boy w/Dog & Ice Cream Cone	UPP	$ 8.00	5.00"	NM	**Retired/Sec**	$120.00
	81	UPP	11.00		TRI	**Retired/Sec**	95.00
	82	UPP	17.00		HRG	**Retired/Sec**	75.00

Variations exist in the color of the dog's nose (brown/black) and the flavor of ice cream.

This portion of a listing is the **MARKET STATUS**. Enesco periodically retires and suspends individual pieces. As a result, GREENBOOK uses nine different classifications of availability or market status. They are:

PRIMARY Piece available from retailers at issue price.

SECONDARY Piece *not* generally available from retailers at issue price.

RETIRED/PRIMARY Piece with specific Enesco Item Number will never be produced again. Piece still available from retailers at issue price.

RETIRED/SECONDARY Piece with specific Enesco Item Number will never be produced again. Piece *not* generally available from retailers at issue price.

SUSPENDED/PRIMARY Piece with specific Enesco Item Number not currently being produced but may be re-sculptured and re-introduced in the future. Piece still available from retailers at issue price.

SUSPENDED/SECONDARY Piece with specific Enesco Item Number not currently being produced but may be re-sculptured and re-introduced in the future. Piece *not* generally available from retailers at issue price.

SUSPENDED/RETIRED/SECONDARY Piece with specific Enesco Item Number was suspended, re-sculptured and re-introduced, and subsequently retired. Piece *not* generally available from retailers at issue price.

DISCONTINUED/PRIMARY Production ceased on piece with specific Enesco Item Number. Piece still available from retailers at issue price.

DISCONTINUED/SECONDARY Production ceased on piece with specific Enesco Item Number. Piece *not* generally available from retailers at issue price.

PRAISE THE LORD ANYHOW Figurine One of the "Original 21"

E-1374B							
19	79 Boy w/Dog & Ice Cream Cone	UPP	$ 8.00	5.00"	NM	Retired/Sec	**$120.00**
	81	UPP	11.00		TRI	Retired/Sec	**95.00**
	82	UPP	17.00		HRG	Retired/Sec	**75.00**

Variations exist in the color of the dog's nose (brown/black) and the flavor of ice cream.

This portion of a listing is the **GREENBOOK TRUMARKET™ PRICE**. It reflects the current primary and secondary market prices for each piece. The prices reported ***are not absolute*** but are a reliable guide based on a system that relies on constant monitoring of actual trades made in the market-place by collectors over the past year.

CHEAT SHEET

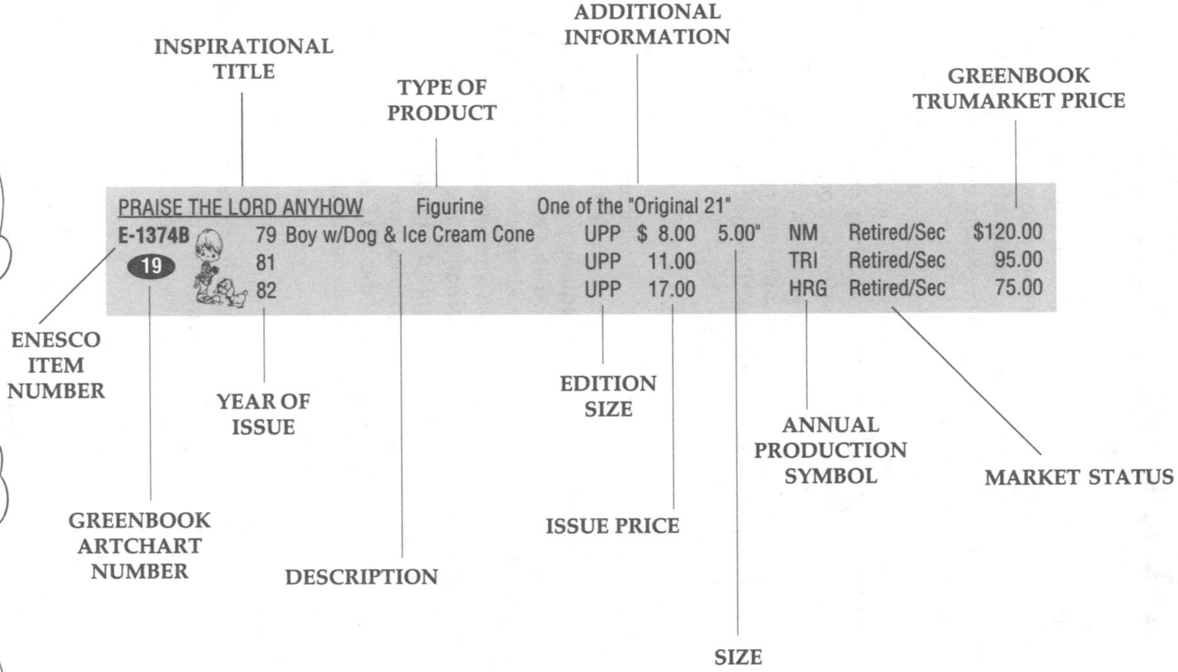

INSPIRATIONAL TITLE
TYPE OF PRODUCT
ADDITIONAL INFORMATION
GREENBOOK TRUMARKET PRICE

PRAISE THE LORD ANYHOW			Figurine	One of the "Original 21"					
E-1374B	79	Boy w/Dog & Ice Cream Cone		UPP	$ 8.00	5.00"	NM	Retired/Sec	$120.00
19	81			UPP	11.00		TRI	Retired/Sec	95.00
	82			UPP	17.00		HRG	Retired/Sec	75.00

ENESCO ITEM NUMBER
GREENBOOK ARTCHART NUMBER
YEAR OF ISSUE
DESCRIPTION
EDITION SIZE
ISSUE PRICE
SIZE
ANNUAL PRODUCTION SYMBOL
MARKET STATUS

GLOSSARY continued

Original 21 -

The term "Original 21" has become one of the buzz-words of Precious Moments collecting, and many collectors, although they may not attempt to own every one of the thousand or so porcelains in the Enesco Precious Moments Collection, do attempt to own each of the "Original 21" figurines -- the first twenty-one inspirational figurines which became the foundation of the Enesco Precious Moments Collection.

These figurines are numbered E-1372B through E-1381 and E-2010 through E-2013 with the last four being the first Christmas figurines in the Collection. As you look over the current secondary market values and activity on these pieces, you will note that these pieces are consistently excellent performers on the secondary market. Since the bulk of them are retired and suspended, and they are in high demand because of being "originals," the secondary market has continued to rise steadily, year after year. At this time, only four pieces of the "Original 21" remain in the Collection on the primary market.

Certificates Of Authenticity -

In the tradition of collectible plate and doll manufacturers, when Enesco introduced plates and dolls to the Precious Moments Collection, a Certificate of Authenticity was included with each of these limited edition pieces. To date, there has been no variation in secondary market values noted when a piece which should have a Certificate of Authenticity is missing it, but collectors would be well advised to save these certificates. Where the Enesco Precious Moments Collection is concerned, Certificates of Authenticity, which simply recognize the particular piece as part of the Collection, can be found on the following: limited edition plates (not including dated plates), porcelain bisque dolls, and some figurines, including the Four Seasons and the first version of "Uncle Sam." It appears as though Certificates of Authenticity were an idea which was experimented with, but not continued, as they have not been included with new introductions recently.

Precious Moments Collectors' Centers -

The Precious Moments Collectors' Center was the predecessor of the DSR store. Like the DSR stores, Centers were the "redemption center" for Members Only coupons, and were the "highest" level available in retail sales of Precious Moments.

Individually Numbered Limited Editions -

On some Precious Moments collectibles, such as plates and 9" Easter Seals figurines, the decision was made to market them as numbered, limited edition collectibles. These pieces are limited to a specific number produced. For example, the three original plate series were numbered -- limited in production to 15,000 pieces. There are also some numbered, limited edition dolls in the collection, including "Tammy" & "Cubby," the bride and groom dolls, which were limited in production to 5,000 of each doll. On numbered, limited edition plates, the plates are hand-numbered on the decal on the back of the plate. On numbered, limited edition figurines, the number is hand-written on the bottom of the figurine. On dolls, the number can be found underneath the shoe - written on the fabric of the doll's foot.

... continued on page 266

GREENBOOK LISTINGS™

The GREENBOOK LISTINGS are where specific factual information as well as GREENBOOK TRUMARKET PRICES for each collectible can be found.

GREENBOOK Listings are in Enesco Item Number order. Enesco Item Numbers can be found on the understamp of most pieces produced from 1982 to the present. If you don't know the Enesco Item Number, but you do know the Inspirational Title, use the ALPHA-LOG to obtain the Enesco Item Number. If you don't know the Enesco Item Number or the Inspirational Title, use the ARTCHART to obtain the Enesco Item Number.

Collectors' Club and Birthday Club pieces are included at the end of the Listings in their own separate section.

Sugar Town, Two By Two and Sammy's Circus pieces are not included in the Listings. These pieces are presented in a different format. Check the Table Of Contents for where they appear.

SHARING OUR SEASON TOGETHER Figurine

E-0501 (118)	Yr	Description	Mark	Price	Size	Sym	Status	Value
	83	Boy Pushing Girl on Sled	UPP	$50.00	4.90"	FSH	Susp/Sec	$155.00
	84		UPP	50.00		CRS	Susp/Sec	140.00
	85		UPP	50.00		DVE	Susp/Sec	138.00
	86		UPP	50.00		OLB	Susp/Sec	135.00

JESUS IS THE LIGHT THAT SHINES Figurine

E-0502 (119)	Yr	Description	Mark	Price	Size	Sym	Status	Value
	83	Boy with Candle & Mouse	UPP	$22.50	5.25"	FSH	Susp/Sec	$68.00
	84		UPP	23.00		CRS	Susp/Sec	58.00
	85		UPP	23.00		DVE	Susp/Sec	52.00
	86		UPP	23.00		OLB	Susp/Sec	50.00

BLESSINGS FROM MY HOUSE TO YOURS Figurine

E-0503 (120)	Yr	Description	Mark	Price	Size	Sym	Status	Value
	83	Girl in Snow Looking at	UPP	$27.00	5.80"	FSH	Susp/Sec	$82.00
	84	Birdhouse	UPP	27.00		CRS	Susp/Sec	75.00
	85		UPP	27.00		DVE	Susp/Sec	72.00
	86		UPP	27.00		OLB	Susp/Sec	70.00

CHRISTMASTIME IS FOR SHARING Figurine

E-0504 (121)	Yr	Description	Mark	Price	Size	Sym	Status	Value
	83	Boy Giving Teddy to	UPP	$37.00	5.25"	FSH	Ret'd/Sec	$105.00
	84	a Poor Boy	UPP	37.00		CRS	Ret'd/Sec	95.00
	85		UPP	37.00		DVE	Ret'd/Sec	90.00
	86		UPP	37.00		OLB	Ret'd/Sec	85.00
	87		UPP	40.00		CED	Ret'd/Sec	85.00
	88		UPP	40.00		FLW	Ret'd/Sec	82.00
	89		UPP	47.50		B&A	Ret'd/Sec	82.00
	90		UPP	50.00		FLM	Ret'd/Sec	80.00

CHRISTMASTIME IS FOR SHARING Plate, Dated — Second Issue "Joy Of Christmas" Series

E-0505 (121)	Yr	Description	Mark	Price	Size	Sym	Status	Value
	83	Boy Giving Teddy to a Poor Boy	Annual	$40.00	8.50"	UM	Secondary	$78.00

SURROUNDED WITH JOY Figurine

E-0506 (122)	Yr	Description	Mark	Price	Size	Sym	Status	Value
	83	Boy with Wreath	UPP	$21.00	4.15"	FSH	Ret'd/Sec	$85.00
	84		UPP	21.00		CRS	Ret'd/Sec	80.00
	85		UPP	21.00		DVE	Ret'd/Sec	78.00
	86		UPP	21.00		OLB	Ret'd/Sec	75.00
	87		UPP	23.00		CED	Ret'd/Sec	72.00
	88		UPP	23.00		FLW	Ret'd/Sec	72.00
	89		UPP	27.50		B&A	Ret'd/Sec	70.00

GOD SENT HIS SON Figurine

E-0507 (123)	Yr	Description	Mark	Price	Size	Sym	Status	Value
	83	Girl Looking into Manger	UPP	$32.50	5.50"	FSH	Susp/Sec	$85.00
	84		UPP	32.50		CRS	Susp/Sec	78.00
	85		UPP	32.50		DVE	Susp/Sec	75.00
	86		UPP	32.50		OLB	Susp/Sec	75.00
	87		UPP	37.00		CED	Susp/Sec	72.00

PREPARE YE THE WAY OF THE LORD Figurine — 6 Piece Set

E-0508 (124)	Yr	Description	Mark	Price	Size	Sym	Status	Value
	83	Angels Preparing Manger	UPP	$75.00	5.75"	FSH	Susp/Sec	$145.00
	84		UPP	75.00		CRS	Susp/Sec	135.00
	85		UPP	75.00		DVE	Susp/Sec	130.00
	86		UPP	75.00		OLB	Susp/Sec	125.00

BRINGING GOD'S BLESSING TO YOU Figurine

E-0509 (125)	Yr	Description	Mark	Price	Size	Sym	Status	Value
	83	Girl Angel Pushing Jesus	UPP	$35.00	5.50"	FSH	Susp/Sec	$88.00
	84	in Buggy	UPP	35.00		CRS	Susp/Sec	80.00
	85		UPP	35.00		DVE	Susp/Sec	75.00
	86		UPP	35.00		OLB	Susp/Sec	70.00
	87		UPP	38.50		CED	Susp/Sec	68.00

TUBBY'S FIRST CHRISTMAS Figurine Nativity Addition

E-0511

126

83	Rooster & Bird on Pig	UPP	$12.00	3.25"	FSH	Susp/Sec	$45.00
84		UPP	12.00		CRS	Susp/Sec	40.00
85		UPP	12.00		DVE	Susp/Sec	40.00
86		UPP	12.00		OLB	Susp/Sec	38.00
87		UPP	13.50		CED	Susp/Sec	38.00
88		UPP	13.50		FLW	Susp/Sec	35.00
89		UPP	15.00		B&A	Susp/Sec	35.00
90		UPP	16.50		FLM	Susp/Sec	32.00
91		UPP	16.50		VSL	Susp/Sec	32.00
92		UPP	16.50		G/CL	Susp/Sec	30.00
93		UPP	16.50		BFY	Susp/Sec	28.00

IT'S A PERFECT BOY Figurine Nativity Addition

E-0512

127

83	Boy Angel with Red Cross	UPP	$18.50	4.75"	FSH	Susp/Sec	$62.00
84	Bag	UPP	18.50		CRS	Susp/Sec	58.00
85		UPP	18.50		DVE	Susp/Sec	58.00
86		UPP	18.50		OLB	Susp/Sec	55.00
87		UPP	21.00		CED	Susp/Sec	55.00
88		UPP	21.00		FLW	Susp/Sec	52.00
89		UPP	25.00		B&A	Susp/Sec	50.00
90		UPP	27.50		FLM	Susp/Sec	48.00

SURROUND US WITH JOY Ornament, Dated

E-0513

122

83	Boy with Wreath	Annual	$ 9.00	3.00"	FSH	Secondary	$65.00

MOTHER SEW DEAR Ornament

E-0514

30

83	Mother Needlepointing	UPP	$ 9.00	3.00"	FSH	Secondary	$35.00
84		UPP	10.00		CRS*	Secondary	28.00
85		UPP	10.00		DVE	Secondary	25.00
86		UPP	10.00		OLB	Secondary	22.00
87		UPP	11.00		CED	Secondary	22.00
88		UPP	11.00		FLW	Secondary	20.00
89		UPP	13.50		B&A	Secondary	20.00
90		UPP	15.00		FLM	Secondary	18.00
91		UPP	15.00		VSL	Secondary	18.00
92		UPP	15.00		G/CL	Primary	16.00
93		UPP	15.00		BFY	Primary	16.00
94		OPEN	16.00		TRP	Primary	16.00

* Stamped Ink CRS @ $38.00.

TO A SPECIAL DAD Ornament

E-0515

59

83	Boy in Dad's Duds	UPP	$ 9.00	3.00"	FSH	Susp/Sec	$55.00
84		UPP	10.00		CRS*	Susp/Sec	45.00
85		UPP	10.00		DVE	Susp/Sec	42.00
86		UPP	10.00		OLB	Susp/Sec	40.00
87		UPP	11.00		CED	Susp/Sec	40.00
88		UPP	11.00		FLW	Susp/Sec	38.00

* Stamped Ink CRS @ $55.00.

THE PURR-FECT GRANDMA Ornament

E-0516

33

83	Grandma in Rocker	UPP	$ 9.00	3.00"	FSH	Secondary	$35.00
84		UPP	10.00		CRS*	Secondary	28.00
85		UPP	10.00		DVE	Secondary	25.00
86		UPP	10.00		OLB	Secondary	22.00
87		UPP	11.00		CED	Secondary	20.00
88		UPP	11.00		FLW	Secondary	20.00
89		UPP	13.50		B&A	Secondary	18.00
90		UPP	15.00		FLM	Secondary	18.00
91		UPP	15.00		VSL	Secondary	18.00
92		UPP	15.00		G/CL	Secondary	16.00
93		UPP	15.00		BFY	Primary	16.00
94		OPEN	16.00		TRP	Primary	16.00

*Stamped Ink CRS @ $35.00

THE PERFECT GRANDPA Ornament
E-0517
109

83	Grandpa in Rocking Chair	UPP	$ 9.00	3.00"	FSH	Susp/Sec	$45.00
84		UPP	10.00		CRS*	Susp/Sec	38.00
85		UPP	10.00		DVE	Susp/Sec	38.00
86		UPP	10.00		OLB	Susp/Sec	35.00
87		UPP	11.00		CED	Susp/Sec	35.00
88		UPP	11.00		FLW	Susp/Sec	32.00
89		UPP	13.50		B&A	Susp/Sec	32.00
90		UPP	15.00		FLM	Susp/Sec	30.00

* Stamped Ink CRS @ $48.00.

BLESSED ARE THE PURE IN HEART Ornament, Dated
E-0518
28

83	Baby in Cradle	Annual	$ 9.00	2.00"	FSH	Secondary	$42.00

SHARING OUR SEASON TOGETHER Musical TUNE: Winter Wonderland
E-0519
118

83	Boy Pushing Girl on Sled	UPP	$70.00	6.00"	FSH	Ret'd/Sec	$165.00
84		UPP	70.00		CRS	Ret'd/Sec	155.00
85		UPP	70.00		DVE	Ret'd/Sec	145.00
86		UPP	70.00		OLB	Ret'd/Sec	135.00

WEE THREE KINGS Musical TUNE: We Three Kings
E-0520
66

83	Three Kings	UPP	$60.00	7.00"	FSH	Susp/Sec	$135.00
84		UPP	60.00		CRS	Susp/Sec	125.00
85		UPP	60.00		DVE	Susp/Sec	120.00
86		UPP	60.00		OLB	Susp/Sec	115.00

BLESSED ARE THE PURE IN HEART Frame
E-0521
28

83	Baby in Cradle	UPP	$18.00	4.50"	FSH	Susp/Sec	$55.00
84		UPP	19.00		CRS	Susp/Sec	50.00
85		UPP	19.00		DVE	Susp/Sec	48.00
86		UPP	19.00		OLB	Susp/Sec	48.00
87		UPP	21.00		CED	Susp/Sec	45.00

SURROUNDED WITH JOY Bell, Dated
E-0522
122

83	Boy with Wreath	Annual	$18.00	5.15"	UM	Secondary	$70.00
					FSH	Secondary	65.00

ONWARD CHRISTIAN SOLDIERS Figurine
E-0523
128

*	Knight in Armor	UPP	$24.00	6.25"	UM	Secondary	$115.00
83		UPP	24.00		FSH	Secondary	62.00
84		UPP	24.00		CRS	Secondary	50.00
85		UPP	24.00		DVE	Secondary	45.00
86		UPP	24.00		OLB	Secondary	42.00
87		UPP	27.00		CED	Secondary	42.00
88		UPP	30.00		FLW	Secondary	40.00
89		UPP	33.00		B&A	Secondary	40.00
90		UPP	35.00		FLM	Secondary	40.00
91		UPP	35.00		VSL	Secondary	40.00
92		UPP	35.00		G/CL	Secondary	38.00
93		UPP	35.00		BFY	Primary	35.00
94		OPEN	35.00		TRP	Primary	35.00

* UNMARKED pieces could have been produced in any of the years of production.
Also exists with a DECAL FISH @ $115.00 .

YOU CAN'T RUN AWAY FROM GOD Figurine
E-0525
129

83	Boy and Dog Running Away	UPP	$28.50	5.15"	HRG	Ret'd/Sec	$155.00
83		UPP	28.50		FSH*	Ret'd/Sec	100.00
84		UPP	28.50		CRS	Ret'd/Sec	95.00
85		UPP	28.50		DVE	Ret'd/Sec	88.00
86		UPP	28.50		OLB	Ret'd/Sec	85.00
87		UPP	32.50		CED	Ret'd/Sec	80.00
88		UPP	35.00		FLW	Ret'd/Sec	78.00
89		UPP	38.50		B&A	Ret'd/Sec	75.00

* Also exists with a DECAL FISH @ $115.00.

HE UPHOLDETH THOSE WHO CALL Figurine

E-0526 (130)

*	Angel Catching Skater	UPP	$28.50	5.15"	UM	Susp/Sec	$130.00
83		UPP	28.50		FSH	Susp/Sec	80.00
84		UPP	35.00		CRS	Susp/Sec	75.00
85		UPP	35.00		DVE	Susp/Sec	72.00

*UNMARKED pieces could have been produced in any of the years of production.
Also exists with a removable INKED FISH @ $135.00.

Fall 1986 GOODNEWSLETTER announced Sam had wanted this piece to be titled "He UpholdethThose Who Fall" and went on to say if/when the piece was brought back from Suspension the title would be changed to "...Fall." From that point on, in much of their written literature, Enesco began referring to the suspended figurine as "...Fall." This has confused many collectors. Thinking the understamp should say "...Fall," they presume their "...Call" piece is an error or variation. See 6th Edition, page 220.

HIS EYE IS ON THE SPARROW Figurine

E-0530 (131)

83	Girl with Bird in Hand	UPP	$28.50	5.25"	FSH	Ret'd/Sec	$120.00
84		UPP	28.50		CRS	Ret'd/Sec	110.00
85		UPP	28.50		DVE	Ret'd/Sec	105.00
86		UPP	28.50		OLB	Ret'd/Sec	105.00
87		UPP	32.50		CED	Ret'd/Sec	100.00

O COME ALL YE FAITHFUL Ornament

E-0531 (86)

83	Boy Caroller	UPP	$ 9.00	3.25"	FSH	Susp/Sec	$60.00
84		UPP	10.00		CRS	Susp/Sec	55.00
85		UPP	10.00		DVE	Susp/Sec	50.00
86		UPP	10.00		OLB	Susp/Sec	48.00

LET HEAVEN AND NATURE SING Ornament

E-0532 (81)

83	Angel with Book and Songbird	UPP	$ 9.00	3.10"	FSH	Ret'd/Sec	$55.00
84		UPP	10.00		CRS	Ret'd/Sec	45.00
85		UPP	10.00		DVE	Ret'd/Sec	40.00
86		UPP	10.00		OLB	Ret'd/Sec	35.00

TELL ME THE STORY OF JESUS Ornament

E-0533 (83)

83	Girl with Doll Reading Book	UPP	$ 9.00	3.00"	FSH	Susp/Sec	$62.00
84		UPP	10.00		CRS	Susp/Sec	52.00
85		UPP	10.00		DVE	Susp/Sec	50.00
86		UPP	10.00		OLB	Susp/Sec	45.00
87		UPP	11.00		CED	Susp/Sec	42.00
88		UPP	12.50		FLW	Susp/Sec	40.00

TO THEE WITH LOVE Ornament

E-0534 (43)

83	Girl with Box of Kittens	UPP	$ 9.00	3.25"	FSH	Ret'd/Sec	$55.00
84		UPP	10.00		CRS	Ret'd/Sec	50.00
85		UPP	10.00		DVE	Ret'd/Sec	48.00
86		UPP	10.00		OLB	Ret'd/Sec	45.00
87		UPP	11.00		CED*	Ret'd/Sec	42.00
88		UPP	12.50		FLW	Ret'd/Sec	40.00
89		UPP	13.50		B&A	Ret'd/Sec	32.00

* There are CEDAR TREE pieces w/two hooks from the Retailers Wreath, #111465. For further information, see 6th Ed., pg. 209.

LOVE IS PATIENT Ornament

E-0535 (132)

83	Boy with Slate	UPP	$ 9.00	2.75"	FSH	Susp/Sec	$60.00
84		UPP	10.00		CRS	Susp/Sec	55.00
85		UPP	10.00		DVE	Susp/Sec	52.00
86		UPP	10.00		OLB	Susp/Sec	50.00

LOVE IS PATIENT Ornament

E-0536 (133)

83	Girl with Slate	UPP	$ 9.00	3.10"	FSH	Susp/Sec	$70.00
84		UPP	10.00		CRS	Susp/Sec	65.00
85		UPP	10.00		DVE	Susp/Sec	62.00
86		UPP	10.00		OLB	Susp/Sec	60.00

JESUS IS THE LIGHT THAT SHINES — Ornament
E-0537 (119)

Yr	Description	Edition	Issue Price	Size	Mark	Status	Price
83	Boy in Night Cap with Candle	UPP	$ 9.00	3.00"	FSH	Susp/Sec	$75.00
84		UPP	10.00		CRS	Susp/Sec	70.00
85		UPP	10.00		DVE	Susp/Sec	65.00

WEE THREE KINGS — Plate — Third Issue "Christmas Collection" Series — Individually Numbered
E-0538 (66)

Yr	Description	Edition	Issue Price	Size	Mark	Status	Price
83	Three Kings	15,000	$40.00	8.50"	UM	Secondary	$48.00
					FSH	Secondary	45.00
					OLB	Secondary	42.00

KATIE LYNNE — Doll
E-0539 (134)

Yr	Description	Edition	Issue Price	Size	Mark	Status	Price
83	Baby Collector's Doll	UPP	$150.00	16.00"	UM	Susp/Sec	$185.00
83		UPP	150.00		FSH	Susp/Sec	180.00
84		UPP	165.00		CRS	Susp/Sec	175.00
85		UPP	165.00		DVE	Susp/Sec	175.00
86		UPP	165.00		OLB	Susp/Sec	175.00
87		UPP	175.00		CED	Susp/Sec	175.00
88		UPP	175.00		FLW	Susp/Sec	175.00

JESUS LOVES ME — Figurine — One of the "Original 21"
E-1372B (1)

Yr	Description	Edition	Issue Price	Size	Mark	Status	Price
79	Boy with Teddy	UPP	$ 7.00	4.50"	NM	Secondary	$105.00
81		UPP	10.00		TRI	Secondary	65.00
82		UPP	15.00		HRG	Secondary	48.00
83		UPP	15.00		FSH	Secondary	35.00
84		UPP	17.00		CRS	Secondary	32.00
85		UPP	17.00		DVE	Secondary	32.00
86		UPP	17.00		OLB	Secondary	30.00
87		UPP	19.00		CED	Secondary	30.00
88		UPP	21.00		FLW	Secondary	28.00
89		UPP	23.00		B&A	Secondary	28.00
90		UPP	25.00		FLM	Secondary	25.00
91		UPP	25.00		VSL	Secondary	25.00
92		UPP	25.00		G/CL	Secondary	25.00
93		UPP	25.00		BFY	Primary	25.00
94		OPEN	25.00		TRP	Primary	25.00

JESUS LOVES ME — Figurine — One of the "Original 21"
E-1372G (2)

Yr	Description	Edition	Issue Price	Size	Mark	Status	Price
79	Girl with Bunny	UPP	$ 7.00	4.50"	NM	Secondary	$125.00
81		UPP	10.00		TRI	Secondary	75.00
82		UPP	15.00		HRG	Secondary	50.00
83		UPP	15.00		FSH	Secondary	40.00
84		UPP	17.00		CRS	Secondary	38.00
85		UPP	17.00		DVE	Secondary	35.00
86		UPP	17.00		OLB	Secondary	32.00
87		UPP	19.00		CED	Secondary	30.00
88		UPP	21.00		FLW	Secondary	30.00
89		UPP	23.00		B&A	Secondary	28.00
90		UPP	25.00		FLM	Secondary	25.00
91		UPP	25.00		VSL	Secondary	25.00
92		UPP	25.00		G/CL	Primary	25.00
93		UPP	25.00		BFY	Primary	25.00
94		OPEN	25.00		TRP	Primary	25.00

SMILE, GOD LOVES YOU — Figurine — One of the "Original 21"
E-1373B (3)

Yr	Description	Edition	Issue Price	Size	Mark	Status	Price
79	Boy with Black* Eye	UPP	$ 7.00	4.50"	NM	Ret'd/Sec	$115.00
81		UPP	12.00		TRI	Ret'd/Sec	85.00
82		UPP	15.00		HRG	Ret'd/Sec	68.00
83		UPP	15.00		FSH	Ret'd/Sec	65.00
84		UPP	17.00		CRS	Ret'd/Sec	60.00

*"Brown Eye" Variation, add $20.00 to GREENBOOK TRUMARKET PRICE.

JESUS IS THE LIGHT — Figurine — One of the "Original 21"

E-1373G (4)

Yr	Description	Status	Issue Price	Size	Mark	Market	Value
79	Girl with Doll and Candle	UPP	$7.00	4.50"	NM	Ret'd/Sec	$130.00
81		UPP	10.00		TRI	Ret'd/Sec	85.00
82		UPP	15.00		HRG	Ret'd/Sec	68.00
83		UPP	15.00		FSH	Ret'd/Sec	60.00
84		UPP	17.00		CRS	Ret'd/Sec	58.00
85		UPP	17.00		DVE	Ret'd/Sec	55.00
86		UPP	17.00		OLB	Ret'd/Sec	48.00
87		UPP	19.00		CED	Ret'd/Sec	42.00
88		UPP	21.00		FLW	Ret'd/Sec	40.00

PRAISE THE LORD ANYHOW — Figurine — One of the "Original 21"

E-1374B (19)

Yr	Description	Status	Issue Price	Size	Mark	Market	Value
79	Boy with Dog	UPP	$8.00	5.00"	NM	Ret'd/Sec	$120.00
81	and Ice Cream Cone	UPP	11.00		TRI	Ret'd/Sec	95.00
82		UPP	17.00		HRG	Ret'd/Sec	75.00

Variations in the color of the dog's nose (brown/black) & the flavor of ice cream.

MAKE A JOYFUL NOISE — Figurine — One of the "Original 21"

E-1374G (5)

Yr	Description	Status	Issue Price	Size	Mark	Market	Value
79	Girl with Goose	UPP	$8.00	4.75"	NM	Secondary	$135.00
81		UPP	13.00		TRI	Secondary	80.00
82		UPP	17.00		HRG	Secondary	50.00
83		UPP	17.00		FSH	Secondary	40.00
84		UPP	19.00		CRS	Secondary	36.00
85		UPP	19.00		DVE	Secondary	35.00
86		UPP	19.00		OLB	Secondary	35.00
87		UPP	21.00		CED	Secondary	32.00
88		UPP	23.00		FLW	Secondary	32.00
89		UPP	25.00		B&A	Secondary	32.00
90		UPP	27.50		FLM	Secondary	30.00
91		UPP	27.50		VSL	Secondary	30.00
92		UPP	27.50		G/CL	Primary	30.00
93		UPP	30.00		BFY	Primary	30.00
94		OPEN	30.00		TRP	Primary	30.00

LOVE LIFTED ME — Figurine — One of the "Original 21"

E-1375A (6)

Yr	Description	Status	Issue Price	Size	Mark	Market	Value
79	Boy & Girl on Seesaw	UPP	$11.00	5.00"	NM	Ret'd/Sec	$160.00
81		UPP	17.00		TRI	Ret'd/Sec	115.00
82		UPP	21.00		HRG	Ret'd/Sec	95.00
83		UPP	21.00		FSH	Ret'd/Sec	85.00
84		UPP	22.50		CRS	Ret'd/Sec	80.00
85		UPP	22.50		DVE	Ret'd/Sec	78.00
86		UPP	22.50		OLB	Ret'd/Sec	75.00
87		UPP	25.00		CED	Ret'd/Sec	70.00
88		UPP	30.00		FLW	Ret'd/Sec	68.00
89		UPP	33.00		B&A	Ret'd/Sec	65.00
90		UPP	35.00		FLM	Ret'd/Sec	62.00
91		UPP	35.00		VSL	Ret'd/Sec	62.00
92		UPP	35.00		G/CL	Ret'd/Sec	60.00
93		UPP	37.50		BFY	Ret'd/Sec	58.00

PRAYER CHANGES THINGS — Figurine — One of the "Original 21"

E-1375B (7)

Yr	Description	Status	Issue Price	Size	Mark	Market	Value
79	Boy & Girl with Bluebirds	UPP	$11.00	5.00"	NM	Susp/Sec	$225.00
81	on Shovel	UPP	17.00		TRI	Susp/Sec	170.00
82		UPP	21.00		HRG	Susp/Sec	160.00
83		UPP	21.00		FSH	Susp/Sec	150.00
84		UPP	22.50		CRS	Susp/Sec	145.00

LOVE ONE ANOTHER — Figurine — One of the "Original 21"

E-1376 (8)

Yr	Description	Status	Issue	Size	Mark	Market	Value
79	Boy & Girl Sitting on Stump	UPP	$10.00	4.75"	NM	Secondary	$125.00
81		UPP	16.00		TRI	Secondary	80.00
82		UPP	21.00		HRG	Secondary	60.00
83		UPP	21.00		FSH	Secondary	50.00
84		UPP	22.50		CRS	Secondary	48.00
85		UPP	22.50		DVE	Secondary	45.00
86		UPP	22.50		OLB	Secondary	42.00
87		UPP	25.00		CED	Secondary	40.00
88		UPP	30.00		FLW	Secondary	40.00
89		UPP	33.00		B&A	Secondary	38.00
90		UPP	35.00		FLM	Secondary	38.00
91		UPP	35.00		VSL	Secondary	38.00
92		UPP	35.00		G/CL	Primary	37.50
93		UPP	37.50		BFY	Primary	37.50
94		OPEN	37.50		TRP	Primary	37.50

HE LEADETH ME — Figurine — One of the "Original 21"

E-1377A (9)

Yr	Description	Status	Issue	Size	Mark	Market	Value
79	Boy Leading Lamb	UPP	$ 9.00	4.75"	NM*	Susp/Sec	$130.00
81		UPP	15.00		TRI	Susp/Sec	110.00
82		UPP	19.00		HRG	Susp/Sec	95.00
83		UPP	19.00		FSH	Susp/Sec	90.00
84		UPP	20.00		CRS	Susp/Sec	85.00

**Classic Variation:* The incorrect Inspirational Title, "He Careth For You," is on the understamp decal of some NO MARK pieces. This is one of the most difficult to find of all the classic variations. The few known sales are in the $250.00 range.

HE CARETH FOR YOU — Figurine — One of the "Original 21"

E-1377B (10)

Yr	Description	Status	Issue	Size	Mark	Market	Value
79	Boy Helping Lamb	UPP	$ 9.00	4.00"	NM	Susp/Sec	$140.00
81		UPP	15.00		TRI	Susp/Sec	120.00
82		UPP	19.00		HRG	Susp/Sec	105.00
83		UPP	19.00		FSH	Susp/Sec	100.00
84		UPP	20.00		CRS	Susp/Sec	95.00

GOD LOVETH A CHEERFUL GIVER — Figurine — One of the "Original 21" — First Retirement - May 1981

E-1378 (20)

Yr	Description	Status	Issue	Size	Mark	Market	Value
79	Girl with Puppies	UPP	$15.00	5.15"	NM	Ret'd/Sec	$900.00

LOVE IS KIND — Figurine — One of the "Original 21"

E-1379A (11)

Yr	Description	Status	Issue	Size	Mark	Market	Value
79	Boy with Turtle	UPP	$ 8.00	4.50"	NM	Susp/Sec	$135.00
81		UPP	13.00		TRI	Susp/Sec	110.00
82		UPP	17.00		HRG	Susp/Sec	100.00
83		UPP	17.00		FSH	Susp/Sec	95.00
84		UPP	19.00		CRS	Susp/Sec	90.00

GOD UNDERSTANDS — Figurine — One of the "Original 21"

E-1379B (12)

Yr	Description	Status	Issue	Size	Mark	Market	Value
79	Boy with Report Card	UPP	$ 8.00	5.00"	NM	Susp/Sec	$135.00
81		UPP	13.00		TRI	Susp/Sec	115.00
82		UPP	17.00		HRG	Susp/Sec	105.00
83		UPP	17.00		FSH	Susp/Sec	95.00
84		UPP	19.00		CRS	Susp/Sec	90.00

O, HOW I LOVE JESUS — Figurine — One of the "Original 21"

E-1380B (13)

Yr	Description	Status	Issue	Size	Mark	Market	Value
79	Indian Boy	UPP	$ 8.00	4.75"	NM	Ret'd/Sec	$140.00
81		UPP	13.00		TRI	Ret'd/Sec	120.00
82		UPP	17.00		HRG	Ret'd/Sec	105.00
83		UPP	17.00		FSH	Ret'd/Sec	90.00
84		UPP	19.00		CRS	Ret'd/Sec	85.00

HIS BURDEN IS LIGHT — Figurine — One of the "Original 21"

E-1380G (14)

Yr	Description	Status	Issue	Size	Mark	Market	Value
79	Indian Girl	UPP	$ 8.00	4.75"	NM	Ret'd/Sec	$150.00
81		UPP	13.00		TRI	Ret'd/Sec	130.00
82		UPP	17.00		HRG	Ret'd/Sec	110.00
83		UPP	17.00		FSH	Ret'd/Sec	95.00
84		UPP	19.00		CRS	Ret'd/Sec	90.00

JESUS IS THE ANSWER Figurine One of the "Original 21"

E-1381 (15)	79	Boy Patching World	UPP	$11.50	4.50"	NM	Susp/Sec	$180.00
	81		UPP	19.00		TRI	Susp/Sec	165.00
	82		UPP	21.00		HRG	Susp/Sec	150.00
	83		UPP	21.00		FSH	Susp/Sec	145.00
	84		UPP	22.50		CRS	Susp/Sec	140.00

E-1381 was re-sculptured and re-introduced in April 1992 as E-1381R below (See 7th Ed., pg. 229):

JESUS IS THE ANSWER Figurine

E-1381R (611)	92	Boy Holding a Stethoscope	UPP	$55.00	4.50"	G/CL	Secondary	$62.00
	93	to a Bandaged World	UPP	55.00		BFY	Primary	55.00
	94		OPEN	55.00		TRP	Primary	55.00

In this re-sculptured figurine the globe reflects boundary changes & new nations that have emerged as a result of political changes around/world. The figurine will benefit research at St. Jude's Children's Hospital.

WE HAVE SEEN HIS STAR Figurine One of the "Original 21"

E-2010 (16)	79	Boy Holding Lamb	UPP	$ 8.00	5.50"	NM	Susp/Sec	$118.00
	82		UPP	17.00		HRG	Susp/Sec	85.00
	83		UPP	17.00		FSH	Susp/Sec	80.00
	84		UPP	19.00		CRS	Susp/Sec	78.00

COME LET US ADORE HIM Figurine One of the "Original 21" First Retirement - May 1981

E-2011 (21)	79	Boy with Manger Baby	UPP	$10.00	5.00"	NM	Ret'd/Sec	$310.00

JESUS IS BORN Figurine One of the "Original 21"

E-2012 (17)	79	Boy & Girl Playing Angels	UPP	$12.00	6.25"	NM	Susp/Sec	$140.00
	82		UPP	22.50		HRG	Susp/Sec	115.00
	83		UPP	22.50		FSH	Susp/Sec	105.00
	84		UPP	25.00		CRS	Susp/Sec	100.00

UNTO US A CHILD IS BORN Figurine One of the "Original 21"

E-2013 (18)	79	Boy & Girl Reading Book	UPP	$12.00	4.75"	NM	Susp/Sec	$125.00
	82		UPP	22.50		HRG	Susp/Sec	105.00
	84		UPP	22.50		CRS	Susp/Sec	90.00

JOY TO THE WORLD Ornament

E-2343 (79)	82	Boy Angel Playing Trumpet	UPP	$ 9.00	2.00"	UM	Susp/Sec	$60.00
	84		UPP	10.00		CRS	Susp/Sec	55.00
	85		UPP	10.00		DVE	Susp/Sec	50.00
	86		UPP	10.00		OLB	Susp/Sec	45.00
	87		UPP	11.00		CED	Susp/Sec	42.00
	88		UPP	12.50		FLW	Susp/Sec	40.00

JOY TO THE WORLD Candle Climbers Set of 2

E-2344 (79)	82	Boy Angel Playing Trumpet	UPP	$20.00	2.50"	UM	Susp/Sec	$110.00
	84		UPP	20.00		CRS	Susp/Sec	100.00
	85		UPP	22.50		DVE	Susp/Sec	90.00

MAY YOUR CHRISTMAS BE COZY Figurine

E-2345 (80)	82	Boy in Pajamas with Teddy	UPP	$23.00	4.25"	HRG	Susp/Sec	$85.00
	83		UPP	23.00		FSH	Susp/Sec	78.00
	84		UPP	25.00		CRS	Susp/Sec	75.00

LET HEAVEN AND NATURE SING Musical TUNE: Joy To The World

E-2346 (81)	*	Angel with Friends Carolling	UPP	$50.00	6.00"	UM	Susp/Sec	$165.00
	82		UPP	50.00		HRG	Susp/Sec	140.00
	83		UPP	55.00		FSH	Susp/Sec	138.00
	84		UPP	60.00		CRS	Susp/Sec	135.00
	85		UPP	60.00		DVE	Susp/Sec	132.00
	86		UPP	60.00		OLB	Susp/Sec	130.00
	87		UPP	65.00		CED	Susp/Sec	125.00
	88		UPP	70.00		FLW	Susp/Sec	120.00
	89		UPP	75.00		B&A	Susp/Sec	115.00

* UNMARKED pieces could have been produced in any of the years of production.

LET HEAVEN AND NATURE SING Plate Second Issue "Christmas Collection" Series Individually #'d

E-2347 (81)	82	Angel with Friends Carolling	15,000	$40.00	8.50"	UM	Secondary	$45.00
						CRS	Secondary	45.00
						DVE	Secondary	42.00
						OLB	Secondary	40.00

MAY YOUR CHRISTMAS BE WARM Figurine

E-2348 (82)	82	Boy Next to a Potbelly Stove	UPP	$30.00	4.75"	HRG	Susp/Sec	$130.00
	83		UPP	30.00		FSH	Susp/Sec	115.00
	84		UPP	33.00		CRS	Susp/Sec	110.00
	85		UPP	33.00		DVE	Susp/Sec	105.00
	86		UPP	33.00		OLB	Susp/Sec	100.00
	87		UPP	37.00		CED	Susp/Sec	98.00
	88		UPP	37.00		FLW	Susp/Sec	95.00

TELL ME THE STORY OF JESUS Figurine

E-2349 (83)	82	Girl Reading Book to Doll	UPP	$30.00	5.00"	HRG	Susp/Sec	$120.00
	83		UPP	30.00		FSH	Susp/Sec	105.00
	84		UPP	33.00		CRS	Susp/Sec	100.00
	85		UPP	33.00		DVE	Susp/Sec	95.00

DROPPING IN FOR CHRISTMAS Figurine

E-2350 (84)	82	Boy Ice Skater in Santa Cap	UPP	$18.00	5.15"	HRG	Susp/Sec	$80.00
	83		UPP	18.00		FSH	Susp/Sec	75.00
	84		UPP	18.00		CRS	Susp/Sec	72.00

HOLY SMOKES Figurine

E-2351 (85)	82	Two Angels with Candles	UPP	$27.00	5.75"	HRG	Ret'd/Sec	$135.00
	83		UPP	27.00		FSH	Ret'd/Sec	120.00
	84		UPP	30.00		CRS	Ret'd/Sec	115.00
	85		UPP	30.00		DVE	Ret'd/Sec	110.00
	86		UPP	30.00		OLB	Ret'd/Sec	100.00
	87		UPP	33.50		CED	Ret'd/Sec	98.00

O COME ALL YE FAITHFUL Musical TUNE: O Come All Ye Faithful

E-2352 (86)	82	Boy Carolling by Lamp Post	UPP	$45.00	7.25"	UM	Susp/Sec	$175.00
	82		UPP	45.00		HRG	Susp/Sec	140.00
	83		UPP	45.00		FSH	Susp/Sec	135.00
	84		UPP	50.00		CRS	Susp/Sec	130.00

O COME ALL YE FAITHFUL Figurine

E-2353 (86)	82	Boy Carolling by Lamp Post	UPP	$27.50	6.25"	HRG	Ret'd/Sec	$100.00
	83		UPP	27.50		FSH	Ret'd/Sec	80.00
	84		UPP	30.00		CRS	Ret'd/Sec	75.00
	85		UPP	30.00		DVE	Ret'd/Sec	72.00
	86		UPP	30.00		OLB	Ret'd/Sec	70.00

I'LL PLAY MY DRUM FOR HIM Musical TUNE: Little Drummer Boy

E-2355 (87)	82	Drummer Boy at Manger	UPP	$45.00	6.75"	HRG	Susp/Sec	$180.00
	83		UPP	45.00		FSH	Susp/Sec	162.00
	84		UPP	50.00		CRS	Susp/Sec	155.00

I'LL PLAY MY DRUM FOR HIM Figurine

E-2356 (87)	82	Drummer Boy at Manger	UPP	$30.00	5.50"	HRG	Susp/Sec	$125.00
	83		UPP	30.00		FSH	Susp/Sec	85.00
	84		UPP	33.00		CRS	Susp/Sec	80.00
	85		UPP	33.00		DVE	Susp/Sec	78.00

I'LL PLAY MY DRUM FOR HIM Plate, Dated First Issue "Joy of Christmas" Series

E-2357 (87)	82	Drummer Boy at Manger	Annual	$40.00	8.50"	UM	Secondary	$90.00

I'LL PLAY MY DRUM FOR HIM Bell, Dated?*

E-2358 (87)	82	Drummer Boy	Annual	$17.00	5.75"	UM	Secondary	$72.00

* Prototypes were dated, it appears actual production wasn't.

I'LL PLAY MY DRUM FOR HIM — Ornament, Dated

E-2359 (87)

82	Drummer Boy	Annual	$ 9.00	3.25"	HRG	Secondary	$105.00

I'LL PLAY MY DRUM FOR HIM — Figurine — Nativity Addition

E-2360 (87)

82	Drummer Boy	UPP	$16.00	5.00"	HRG	Secondary	$48.00
83		UPP	16.00		FSH	Secondary	38.00
84		UPP	17.00		CRS	Secondary	35.00
85		UPP	17.00		DVE	Secondary	32.00
86		UPP	17.00		OLB	Secondary	30.00
87		UPP	19.00		CED	Secondary	30.00
88		UPP	19.00		FLW	Secondary	30.00
89		UPP	23.00		B&A	Secondary	28.00
90		UPP	25.00		FLM	Secondary	27.00
91		UPP	25.00		VSL	Secondary	25.00
92		UPP	25.00		G/CL	Secondary	25.00
93		UPP	25.00		BFY	Primary	25.00
94		OPEN	25.00		TRP	Primary	25.00

CHRISTMAS JOY FROM HEAD TO TOE — Figurine

E-2361 (88)

82	Girl with Stocking	UPP	$25.00	5.50"	HRG	Susp/Sec	$82.00
83		UPP	25.00		FSH	Susp/Sec	75.00
84		UPP	27.50		CRS	Susp/Sec	70.00
85		UPP	27.50		DVE	Susp/Sec	68.00
86		UPP	27.50		OLB	Susp/Sec	65.00

BABY'S FIRST CHRISTMAS — Ornament

E-2362 (89)

82	Baby Girl in Christmas	UPP	$ 9.00	3.50"	UM*	Susp/Sec	$50.00
84	Stocking	UPP	10.00		CRS	Susp/Sec	40.00
85		UPP	10.00		DVE	Susp/Sec	35.00
86		UPP	10.00		OLB	Susp/Sec	32.00
87		UPP	10.00		CED	Susp/Sec	30.00
88		UPP	11.00		FLW	Susp/Sec	28.00

**Classic Variation: "Straight Hair."* UNMARKED pieces exist in four variations: 1) Straight hair and no caption, 2) Curly hair and no caption, 3) Straight hair with the caption, "Baby's First Christmas," and, 4) Curly hair with the caption, "Baby's First Christmas." Subsequent pieces (CROSS through FLOWER) were curly hair with the caption. The straight hair, with or without the caption, is considered the variation. The GREENBOOK TRUMARKET PRICE for an UNMARKED "Straight Hair" ornament is $65.00. Full color photo: 4th Ed., pg. 194 or 5th Ed., pg. 200. One color photo: 6th Ed., pg. 223.

CAMEL — Figurine — Nativity Addition

E-2363 (90)

82	Camel	UPP	$20.00	4.00"	HRG	Secondary	$50.00
83		UPP	20.00		FSH	Secondary	42.00
84		UPP	22.50		CRS	Secondary	40.00
85		UPP	22.50		DVE	Secondary	40.00
86		UPP	22.50		OLB	Secondary	38.00
87		UPP	25.00		CED	Secondary	38.00
88		UPP	25.00		FLW	Secondary	38.00
89		UPP	30.00		B&A	Secondary	35.00
90		UPP	32.50		FLM	Secondary	33.00
91		UPP	32.50		VSL	Secondary	33.00
92		UPP	32.50		G/CL	Primary	32.50
93		UPP	32.50		BFY	Primary	32.50
94		OPEN	32.50		TRP	Primary	32.50

GOAT — Figurine — Nativity Addition

E-2364 (91)

82	Goat	UPP	$10.00	3.00"	UM	Susp/Sec	$60.00
83		UPP	10.00		FSH	Susp/Sec	55.00
84		UPP	11.00		CRS	Susp/Sec	50.00
85		UPP	11.00		DVE	Susp/Sec	48.00
86		UPP	11.00		OLB	Susp/Sec	46.00
87		UPP	12.00		CED	Susp/Sec	45.00
88		UPP	12.00		FLW	Susp/Sec	42.00
89		UPP	15.00		B&A	Susp/Sec	40.00

THE FIRST NOEL Figurine Nativity Addition
E-2365
92

82	Boy Angel with Candle	UPP	$16.00	4.50"	UM	Susp/Sec	$80.00
82		UPP	16.00		HRG	Susp/Sec	72.00
83		UPP	16.00		FSH	Susp/Sec	62.00
84		UPP	17.00		CRS	Susp/Sec	60.00

THE FIRST NOEL Figurine Nativity Addition
E-2366
93

82	Girl Angel Praying	UPP	$16.00	4.50"	UM	Susp/Sec	$85.00
82		UPP	16.00		HRG	Susp/Sec	75.00
83		UPP	16.00		FSH	Susp/Sec	68.00
84		UPP	17.00		CRS	Susp/Sec	65.00

THE FIRST NOEL Ornament
E-2367
92

82	Boy Angel with Candle	UPP	$ 9.00	3.10"	HRG	Susp/Sec	$70.00
83		UPP	9.00		FSH	Susp/Sec	65.00
84		UPP	10.00		CRS	Susp/Sec	60.00

THE FIRST NOEL Ornament
E-2368
93

82	Girl Angel Praying	UPP	$ 9.00	3.00"	HRG	Ret'd/Sec	$75.00
83		UPP	9.00		FSH	Ret'd/Sec	50.00
84		UPP	10.00		CRS	Ret'd/Sec	42.00

DROPPING IN FOR CHRISTMAS Ornament
E-2369
84

82	Boy Ice Skater in Santa Cap	UPP	$ 9.00	3.50"	UM	Ret'd/Sec	$60.00
82		UPP	9.00		HRG	Ret'd/Sec	50.00
83		UPP	9.00		FSH	Ret'd/Sec	48.00
84		UPP	10.00		CRS	Ret'd/Sec	45.00
85		UPP	10.00		DVE	Ret'd/Sec	42.00
86		UPP	10.00		OLB	Ret'd/Sec	40.00

UNICORN Ornament
E-2371
94

82	Unicorn	UPP	$10.00	3.00"	UM	Ret'd/Sec	$65.00
84		UPP	10.00		CRS	Ret'd/Sec	50.00
85		UPP	11.00		DVE	Ret'd/Sec	45.00
86		UPP	11.00		OLB	Ret'd/Sec	45.00
87		UPP	12.00		CED	Ret'd/Sec	42.00
88		UPP	13.00		FLW	Ret'd/Sec	40.00

BABY'S FIRST CHRISTMAS Ornament
E-2372
95

82	Boy Holding Block	UPP	$ 9.00	2.75"	UM*	Susp/Sec	$45.00
84		UPP	10.00		CRS	Susp/Sec	40.00
85		UPP	10.00		DVE	Susp/Sec	35.00

* Exists with and without caption, "Baby's First Christmas," in UNMARKED version.

BUNDLES OF JOY Figurine
E-2374
96

82	Girl with Presents	UPP	$27.50	6.75"	HRG	Ret'd/Sec	$118.00
83		UPP	27.50		FSH	Ret'd/Sec	100.00
84		UPP	30.00		CRS	Ret'd/Sec	90.00
85		UPP	30.00		DVE	Ret'd/Sec	90.00
86		UPP	30.00		OLB	Ret'd/Sec	85.00
87		UPP	33.50		CED	Ret'd/Sec	85.00
88		UPP	33.50		FLW	Ret'd/Sec	80.00
89		UPP	40.00		B&A	Ret'd/Sec	80.00
90		UPP	45.00		FLM	Ret'd/Sec	80.00
91		UPP	45.00		VSL	Ret'd/Sec	78.00
92		UPP	45.00		G/CL	Ret'd/Sec	75.00
93		UPP	45.00		BFY	Ret'd/Sec	72.00

DROPPING OVER FOR CHRISTMAS Figurine

E-2375

97

82	Girl with Pie	UPP	$30.00	5.15"	HRG	Ret'd/Sec	$115.00
83		UPP	30.00		FSH	Ret'd/Sec	95.00
84		UPP	33.00		CRS	Ret'd/Sec	90.00
85		UPP	33.00		DVE	Ret'd/Sec	85.00
86		UPP	33.00		OLB	Ret'd/Sec	82.00
87		UPP	37.00		CED	Ret'd/Sec	82.00
88		UPP	37.00		FLW	Ret'd/Sec	80.00
89		UPP	42.50		B&A	Ret'd/Sec	80.00
90		UPP	45.00		FLM	Ret'd/Sec	78.00
91		UPP	45.00		VSL	Ret'd/Sec	75.00

DROPPING OVER FOR CHRISTMAS Ornament

E-2376

97

82	Girl with Pie	UPP	$ 9.00	3.00"	HRG	Ret'd/Sec	$60.00
83		UPP	9.00		FSH	Ret'd/Sec	50.00
84		UPP	10.00		CRS	Ret'd/Sec	46.00
85		UPP	10.00		DVE	Ret'd/Sec	42.00

OUR FIRST CHRISTMAS TOGETHER Figurine

E-2377

98

82	Girl Knitting Tie for Boy	UPP	$35.00	5.15"	HRG	Susp/Sec	$90.00
83		UPP	35.00		FSH	Susp/Sec	85.00
84		UPP	37.50		CRS	Susp/Sec	80.00
85		UPP	37.50		DVE	Susp/Sec	78.00

OUR FIRST CHRISTMAS TOGETHER Plate

E-2378

98

82	Girl Knitting Tie for Boy	UPP	$30.00	7.00"	UM	Susp/Sec	$50.00
84		UPP	30.00		CRS	Susp/Sec	42.00
85		UPP	30.00		DVE	Susp/Sec	40.00

MOUSE WITH CHEESE Ornament

E-2381

99

82	Mouse with Cheese	UPP	$ 9.00	2.50"	HRG	Susp/Sec	$140.00
83		UPP	9.00		FSH	Susp/Sec	130.00
84		UPP	10.00		CRS	Susp/Sec	125.00

OUR FIRST CHRISTMAS TOGETHER Ornament

E-2385

38

82	Bride and Groom	UPP	$10.00	4.00"	HRG	Susp/Sec	$50.00
83		UPP	10.00		FSH	Susp/Sec	42.00
84		UPP	10.00		CRS	Susp/Sec	40.00
85		UPP	11.00		DVE	Susp/Sec	38.00
86		UPP	11.00		OLB	Susp/Sec	35.00
87		UPP	12.00		CED	Susp/Sec	32.00
88		UPP	13.00		FLW	Susp/Sec	32.00
89		UPP	15.00		B&A	Susp/Sec	30.00
90		UPP	15.00		FLM	Susp/Sec	30.00
91		UPP	15.00		VSL	Susp/Sec	30.00

CAMEL, DONKEY, AND COW Ornaments Set of 3

E-2386

100

*	Camel, Donkey, Cow	UPP	$25.00	2.25"	UM	Susp/Sec	$100.00
82	Mixed sets UM/HRG are common. Use lower value.	UPP	25.00		HRG	Susp/Sec	90.00
83		UPP	25.00		FSH	Susp/Sec	85.00
84		UPP	27.50		CRS	Susp/Sec	75.00

* UNMARKED pieces could have been produced in any of the years of production.

HOUSE SET AND PALM TREE Figurines Set of 3 Mini Nativity Addition

E-2387

101

82	Mini Houses and Palm Tree	UPP	$45.00	3.00"	HRG	Secondary	$125.00
83		UPP	45.00		FSH	Secondary	90.00
84		UPP	50.00		CRS	Secondary	88.00
85		UPP	50.00		DVE	Secondary	85.00
86		UPP	50.00		OLB	Secondary	82.00
87		UPP	55.00		CED	Secondary	82.00
88		UPP	55.00		FLW	Secondary	80.00
89		UPP	65.00		B&A	Secondary	75.00
90		UPP	70.00		FLM	Secondary	75.00
91		UPP	70.00		VSL	Secondary	75.00
92		UPP	70.00		G/CL	Primary	75.00
93		UPP	70.00		BFY	Primary	75.00
94		OPEN	75.00		TRP	Primary	75.00

COME LET US ADORE HIM Figurines Set of 11

E-2395

22

82	Mini Nativity Set	UPP	$80.00	3.50"	HRG*	Secondary	$160.00
83		UPP	80.00		FSH	Secondary	140.00
84		UPP	90.00		CRS	Secondary	135.00
85		UPP	90.00		DVE	Secondary	130.00
86		UPP	90.00		OLB	Secondary	128.00
87		UPP	90.00		CED	Secondary	125.00
88		UPP	95.00		FLW	Secondary	125.00
89		UPP	110.00		B&A	Secondary	125.00
90		UPP	120.00		FLM	Secondary	125.00
91		UPP	120.00		VSL	Secondary	125.00
92		UPP	120.00		G/CL	Primary	125.00
93		UPP	120.00		BFY	Primary	125.00
94		OPEN	125.00		TRP	Primary	125.00

* *Classic Variation: "Turban Nativity."* Termed the "Turban Nativity," the shepherd holding a lamb was replaced in some HOURGLASS sets with a shepherd wearing a turban. "Turban Boy" shepherds were also shipped individually to retailers as replacement pieces, so collectors were sometimes able to add the "Turban Boy" as a twelfth piece to this eleven piece mini Nativity Set. The GREENBOOK TRUMARKET PRICE for the "Turban Nativity" is $215.00. The GREENBOOKTRUMARKET PRICE for the individual "Turban Boy" piece is $90.00.
Full color photo: 4th Ed., pg. 194 or 5th Ed., pg. 199. One color photo 6th Ed., pg. 221.

COME LET US ADORE HIM Figurines Set of 9

E-2800

22

80	Nativity Set	UPP	$60.00	4.75"	NM	Disc/Sec	$205.00
81		UPP	70.00		TRI	Disc/Sec	185.00
82		UPP	80.00		HRG	Disc/Sec	175.00
83		UPP	80.00		FSH	Disc/Sec	155.00
84		UPP	90.00		CRS	Disc/Sec	150.00
85		UPP	90.00		DVE	Disc/Sec	145.00

Mixed sets TRI/HRG and HRG/FSH are common. Take lower value.

Re-sculptured - See #104000, page 218.

JESUS IS BORN Figurine

E-2801

23

80	Angels in Chariot	UPP	$37.00	5.75"	NM	Susp/Sec	$350.00
81		UPP	45.00		TRI	Susp/Sec	325.00
82		UPP	50.00		HRG	Susp/Sec	315.00
83		UPP	50.00		FSH	Susp/Sec	295.00
84		UPP	55.00		CRS	Susp/Sec	285.00

CHRISTMAS IS A TIME TO SHARE Figurine

E-2802

24

80	Boy Giving Toy Lamb	UPP	$20.00	5.00"	NM	Susp/Sec	$100.00
81		UPP	22.50		TRI	Susp/Sec	90.00
82		UPP	25.00		HRG	Susp/Sec	80.00
83		UPP	25.00		FSH	Susp/Sec	78.00
84		UPP	27.50		CRS	Susp/Sec	75.00
*					DVE	Susp/Sec	70.00

*Piece was suspended in 1984 yet exists in a DOVE Annual Production Symbol.

CROWN HIM LORD OF ALL Figurine

E-2803 (25)

80	Boy Holding Crown at Manger	UPP	$20.00	4.50"	NM	Susp/Sec	$100.00
81		UPP	22.50		TRI	Susp/Sec	90.00
82		UPP	25.00		HRG	Susp/Sec	80.00
83		UPP	25.00		FSH	Susp/Sec	75.00
84		UPP	27.50		CRS	Susp/Sec	72.00
*					DVE	Susp/Sec	70.00

*Piece was suspended in 1984 yet exists in a DOVE Annual Production Symbol.

PEACE ON EARTH Figurine

E-2804 (26)

80	Boy Angel on Globe	UPP	$20.00	6.00"	NM	Susp/Sec	$165.00
81	with Teddy	UPP	22.50		TRI	Susp/Sec	150.00
82		UPP	25.00		HRG	Susp/Sec	140.00
83		UPP	25.00		FSH	Susp/Sec	135.00
84		UPP	27.50		CRS	Susp/Sec	130.00

WISHING YOU A SEASON FILLED WITH JOY Figurine

E-2805 (27)

80	Boy in Santa Cap with Dog	UPP	$20.00	4.25"	NM	Ret'd/Sec	$125.00
81		UPP	22.50		TRI	Ret'd/Sec	115.00
82		UPP	25.00		HRG	Ret'd/Sec	100.00
83		UPP	25.00		FSH	Ret'd/Sec	90.00
84		UPP	27.50		CRS	Ret'd/Sec	85.00
85		UPP	27.50		DVE	Ret'd/Sec	80.00

NM thru CRS have only one dog's eye painted. DVE exists w/both one & two eyes painted.

CHRISTMAS IS A TIME TO SHARE Musical TUNE: Away in a Manger

E-2806 (24)

80	Boy Giving Toy Lamb	UPP	$35.00	6.00"	NM	Ret'd/Sec	$180.00
81	to Baby Jesus	UPP	35.00		TRI	Ret'd/Sec	165.00
82		UPP	40.00		HRG	Ret'd/Sec	160.00
83		UPP	45.00		FSH	Ret'd/Sec	155.00
84		UPP	50.00		CRS	Ret'd/Sec	150.00

CROWN HIM LORD OF ALL Musical TUNE: O Come All Ye Faithful

E-2807 (25)

80	Boy Kneeling at Manger	UPP	$35.00	5.50"	NM	Susp/Sec	$130.00
81	with Crown	UPP	40.00		TRI	Susp/Sec	115.00
82		UPP	45.00		HRG	Susp/Sec	105.00
83		UPP	45.00		FSH	Susp/Sec	100.00
84		UPP	50.00		CRS	Susp/Sec	95.00

UNTO US A CHILD IS BORN Musical TUNE: Jesus Loves Me

E-2808 (18)

80	Boy and Girl Reading Book	UPP	$35.00	5.75"	NM	Susp/Sec	$135.00
81		UPP	40.00		TRI	Susp/Sec	120.00
82		UPP	45.00		HRG	Susp/Sec	110.00
83		UPP	45.00		FSH	Susp/Sec	105.00
84		UPP	50.00		CRS	Susp/Sec	100.00

JESUS IS BORN Musical TUNE: Hark! The Herald Angels Sing

E-2809 (17)

80	Boy and Girl Playing Angels	UPP	$35.00	7.00"	NM	Susp/Sec	$145.00
81		UPP	45.00		TRI	Susp/Sec	135.00
82		UPP	45.00		HRG	Susp/Sec	125.00
83		UPP	45.00		FSH	Susp/Sec	120.00
84		UPP	50.00		CRS	Susp/Sec	115.00
85		UPP	50.00		DVE	Susp/Sec	110.00

COME LET US ADORE HIM — Musical — TUNE: Joy To The World

E-2810

22

80	Nativity Scene	UPP	$45.00	6.50"	NM	Susp/Sec	$155.00
81		UPP	45.00		TRI	Susp/Sec	140.00
82		UPP	60.00		HRG	Susp/Sec	135.00
83		UPP	60.00		FSH	Susp/Sec	130.00
84		UPP	65.00		CRS	Susp/Sec	130.00
85		UPP	65.00		DVE	Susp/Sec	130.00
86		UPP	65.00		OLB	Susp/Sec	125.00
87		UPP	70.00		CED	Susp/Sec	125.00
88		UPP	70.00		FLW	Susp/Sec	125.00
89		UPP	80.00		B&A	Susp/Sec	120.00
90		UPP	85.00		FLM	Susp/Sec	120.00
91		UPP	85.00		VSL	Susp/Sec	120.00
92		UPP	85.00		G/CL	Susp/Sec	120.00
93		UPP	100.00		BFY	Susp/Sec	115.00

YOU HAVE TOUCHED SO MANY HEARTS — Figurine

E-2821

161

84	Girl with Hearts	UPP	$25.00	5.50"	FSH	Secondary	$60.00
84		UPP	25.00		CRS	Secondary	50.00
85		UPP	25.00		DVE	Secondary	48.00
86		UPP	25.00		OLB	Secondary	45.00
87		UPP	27.50		CED	Secondary	45.00
88		UPP	30.00		FLW	Secondary	42.00
89		UPP	33.00		B&A	Secondary	40.00
90		UPP	35.00		FLM	Secondary	38.00
91		UPP	35.00		VSL	Secondary	38.00
92		UPP	35.00		G/CL	Primary	37.50
93		UPP	35.00		BFY	Primary	37.50
94		OPEN	37.50		TRP	Primary	37.50

THIS IS YOUR DAY TO SHINE — Figurine

E-2822

162

84	Girl Polishing Table	UPP	$37.50	6.00"	FSH	Ret'd/Sec	$155.00
84		UPP	37.50		CRS	Ret'd/Sec	100.00
85		UPP	37.50		DVE	Ret'd/Sec	95.00
86		UPP	37.50		OLB	Ret'd/Sec	90.00
87		UPP	40.00		CED	Ret'd/Sec	88.00
88		UPP	40.00		FLW	Ret'd/Sec	85.00

TO GOD BE THE GLORY — Figurine

E-2823

163

84	Boy Holding Picture Frame	UPP	$40.00	5.50"	FSH	Susp/Sec	$100.00
84		UPP	40.00		CRS	Susp/Sec	85.00
85		UPP	40.00		DVE	Susp/Sec	82.00
86		UPP	40.00		OLB	Susp/Sec	80.00
87		UPP	45.00		CED	Susp/Sec	78.00

TO A VERY SPECIAL MOM — Figurine

E-2824

164

84	Girl with Floppy Hat	UPP	$27.50	5.75"	CRS	Secondary	$60.00
85		UPP	27.50		DVE	Secondary	50.00
86		UPP	27.50		OLB	Secondary	48.00
87		UPP	30.00		CED	Secondary	45.00
88		UPP	32.50		FLW	Secondary	42.00
89		UPP	35.00		B&A	Secondary	40.00
90		UPP	37.50		FLM	Secondary	38.00
91		UPP	37.50		VSL	Secondary	38.00
92		UPP	37.50		G/CL	Secondary	38.00
93		UPP	37.50		BFY	Primary	37.50
94		OPEN	37.50		TRP	Primary	37.50

TO A VERY SPECIAL SISTER Figurine

E-2825	84 Girl Putting Bows in	UPP	$37.50	5.50"	CRS	Secondary	$75.00
165	85 Sister's Hair	UPP	37.50		DVE	Secondary	62.00
	86	UPP	37.50		OLB	Secondary	60.00
	87	UPP	40.00		CED	Secondary	58.00
	88	UPP	40.00		FLW	Secondary	55.00
	89	UPP	45.00		B&A	Secondary	52.00
	90	UPP	50.00		FLM	Secondary	52.00
	91	UPP	50.00		VSL	Secondary	52.00
	92	UPP	50.00		G/CL	Secondary	50.00
	93	UPP	50.00		BFY	Primary	50.00
	94	OPEN	50.00		TRP	Primary	50.00

MAY YOUR BIRTHDAY BE A BLESSING Figurine

E-2826	84 Girl at Table with Dolls	UPP	$37.50	5.25"	FSH	Susp/Sec	$130.00
166	84	UPP	37.50		CRS	Susp/Sec	100.00
	85	UPP	37.50		DVE	Susp/Sec	95.00
	86	UPP	37.50		OLB	Susp/Sec	85.00

I GET A KICK OUT OF YOU Figurine

E-2827	84 Girl with Bucket on Head	UPP	$50.00	4.75"	FSH	Susp/Sec	$175.00
167	84	UPP	50.00		CRS	Susp/Sec	155.00
	85	UPP	50.00		DVE	Susp/Sec	140.00
	86	UPP	50.00		OLB	Susp/Sec	135.00

PRECIOUS MEMORIES Figurine

E-2828	84 Girl at Trunk with	UPP	$45.00	5.50"	CRS	Secondary	$85.00
168	85 Wedding Gown	UPP	45.00		DVE	Secondary	78.00
	86	UPP	45.00		OLB	Secondary	75.00
	87	UPP	50.00		CED	Secondary	72.00
	88	UPP	50.00		FLW	Secondary	70.00
	89	UPP	55.00		B&A	Secondary	68.00
	90	UPP	60.00		FLM	Secondary	68.00
	91	UPP	60.00		VSL	Secondary	65.00
	92	UPP	60.00		G/CL	Secondary	65.00
	93	UPP	65.00		BFY	Primary	65.00
	94	OPEN	65.00		TRP	Primary	65.00

I'M SENDING YOU A WHITE CHRISTMAS Figurine

E-2829	84 Girl Mailing Snowball	UPP	$37.50	5.00"	CRS	Secondary	$85.00
169	85	UPP	37.50		DVE	Secondary	67.00
	86	UPP	37.50		OLB	Secondary	65.00
	87	UPP	40.00		CED	Secondary	62.00
	88	UPP	45.00		FLW	Secondary	60.00
	89	UPP	47.50		B&A	Secondary	55.00
	90	UPP	50.00		FLM	Secondary	55.00
	91	UPP	50.00		VSL	Secondary	52.00
	92	UPP	50.00		G/CL	Secondary	50.00
	93	UPP	50.00		BFY	Secondary	50.00
	94	OPEN	50.00		TRP	Primary	50.00

BRIDESMAID Figurine First Issue "Bridal" Series

E-2831	84 Bridesmaid	UPP	$13.50	4.25"	CRS	Secondary	$35.00
170	85	UPP	13.50		DVE	Secondary	30.00
	86	UPP	13.50		OLB	Secondary	30.00
	87	UPP	15.00		CED	Secondary	28.00
	88	UPP	16.00		FLW	Secondary	27.00
	89	UPP	17.50		B&A	Secondary	25.00
	90	UPP	19.50		FLM	Secondary	25.00
	91	UPP	19.50		VSL	Secondary	23.00
	92	UPP	19.50		G/CL	Primary	22.50
	93	UPP	20.00		BFY	Primary	22.50
	94	OPEN	22.50		TRP	Primary	22.50

GOD BLESS THE BRIDE Figurine

E-2832

171

Year	Description	Status	Issue Price	Size	Mark	Market	Value
84	Bride with Flower Girl	UPP	$35.00	5.50"	CRS	Secondary	$62.00
85		UPP	35.00		DVE	Secondary	58.00
86		UPP	35.00		OLB	Secondary	55.00
87		UPP	38.50		CED	Secondary	55.00
88		UPP	40.00		FLW	Secondary	52.00
89		UPP	45.00		B&A	Secondary	52.00
90		UPP	50.00		FLM	Secondary	50.00
91		UPP	50.00		VSL	Secondary	50.00
92		UPP	50.00		G/CL	Primary	50.00
93		UPP	50.00		BFY	Primary	50.00
94		OPEN	50.00		TRP	Primary	50.00

RINGBEARER Figurine Fourth Issue "Bridal" Series

E-2833

208

Year	Description	Status	Issue Price	Size	Mark	Market	Value
85	Ringbearer	UPP	$11.00	3.00"	DVE	Secondary	$28.00
86		UPP	11.00		OLB	Secondary	24.00
87		UPP	12.00		CED	Secondary	22.00
88		UPP	13.00		FLW	Secondary	20.00
89		UPP	15.00		B&A	Secondary	18.00
90		UPP	16.50		FLM	Secondary	18.00
91		UPP	16.50		VSL	Secondary	17.00
92		UPP	16.50		G/CL	Primary	17.00
93		UPP	16.50		BFY	Primary	17.00
94		OPEN	17.00		TRP	Primary	17.00

SHARING OUR JOY TOGETHER Figurine

E-2834

268

Year	Description	Status	Issue Price	Size	Mark	Market	Value
86	Bridesmaid with Kitten	UPP	$31.00	5.50"	OLB	Susp/Sec	$65.00
87		UPP	35.00		CED	Susp/Sec	62.00
88		UPP	36.00		FLW	Susp/Sec	60.00
89		UPP	38.50		B&A	Susp/Sec	58.00
90		UPP	40.00		FLM	Susp/Sec	58.00
91		UPP	40.00		VSL	Susp/Sec	55.00

FLOWER GIRL Figurine Third Issue "Bridal" Series

E-2835

209

Year	Description	Status	Issue Price	Size	Mark	Market	Value
85	Flower Girl	UPP	$11.00	3.00"	DVE	Secondary	$30.00
86		UPP	11.00		OLB	Secondary	25.00
87		UPP	12.00		CED	Secondary	24.00
88		UPP	13.00		FLW	Secondary	22.00
89		UPP	15.00		B&A	Secondary	20.00
90		UPP	16.50		FLM	Secondary	20.00
91		UPP	16.50		VSL	Secondary	18.00
92		UPP	16.50		G/CL	Primary	17.00
93		UPP	16.50		BFY	Primary	17.00
94		OPEN	17.00		TRP	Primary	17.00

GROOMSMAN Figurine Second Issue "Bridal" Series

E-2836

172

Year	Description	Status	Issue Price	Size	Mark	Market	Value
84	Groomsman with Frog	UPP	$13.50	4.25"	CRS	Secondary	$35.00
85		UPP	13.50		DVE	Secondary	30.00
86		UPP	13.50		OLB	Secondary	28.00
87		UPP	13.50		CED	Secondary	27.00
88		UPP	16.00		FLW	Secondary	25.00
89		UPP	17.50		B&A	Secondary	23.00
90		UPP	19.50		FLM	Secondary	23.00
91		UPP	19.50		VSL	Secondary	23.00
92		UPP	19.50		G/CL	Primary	22.50
93		UPP	20.00		BFY	Primary	22.50
94		OPEN	22.50		TRP	Primary	22.50

GROOM Figurine Sixth Issue "Bridal" Series
E-2837
269

86	Groom	UPP	$15.00	4.50"	OLB*	Secondary	$30.00
87		UPP	17.00		CED	Secondary	30.00
88		UPP	18.00		FLW	Secondary	27.00
89		UPP	20.00		B&A	Secondary	25.00
90		UPP	22.50		FLM	Secondary	25.00
91		UPP	22.50		VSL	Primary	25.00
92		UPP	22.50		G/CL	Primary	25.00
93		UPP	25.00		BFY	Primary	25.00
94		OPEN	25.00		TRP	Primary	25.00

*Termed the "No Hands Groom," during the first year of production (OLIVE BRANCH) this piece was produced with no hands. The mold was changed for the subsequent years (CEDAR TREE to present) to show the boy's hands. Full color photograph: 5th Ed., pg. 198. One color photo: 6th Ed., pg. 222.

THIS IS THE DAY WHICH THE LORD HATH MADE Figurine Eighth & Final Issue "Bridal" Series
E-2838
312

87	Complete Wedding Party	Annual	$175.00	5.25"	CED	Secondary	$195.00

BABY'S FIRST STEP Figurine First Issue "Baby's First" Series
E-2840
173

84	Angel Carrying Baby	UPP	$35.00	5.25"	CRS	Susp/Sec	$90.00
85		UPP	35.00		DVE	Susp/Sec	85.00
86		UPP	35.00		OLB	Susp/Sec	80.00
87		UPP	38.50		CED	Susp/Sec	78.00
88		UPP	40.00		FLW	Susp/Sec	75.00

BABY'S FIRST PICTURE Figurine Second Issue "Baby's First" Series
E-2841
174

84	Angel Taking Baby's Picture	UPP	$45.00	5.00"	CRS	Ret'd/Sec	$165.00
85		UPP	45.00		DVE	Ret'd/Sec	155.00
86		UPP	45.00		OLB	Ret'd/Sec	145.00

JUNIOR BRIDESMAID Figurine Fifth Issue "Bridal" Series
E-2845
210

86	Junior Bridesmaid	UPP	$12.50	3.75"	OLB	Secondary	$30.00
87		UPP	14.00		CED	Secondary	25.00
88		UPP	15.00		FLW	Secondary	22.00
89		UPP	17.00		B&A	Secondary	22.00
90		UPP	18.50		FLM	Secondary	20.00
91		UPP	18.50		VSL	Secondary	20.00
92		UPP	18.50		G/CL	Primary	20.00
93		UPP	18.50		BFY	Primary	20.00
94		OPEN	20.00		TRP	Primary	20.00

BRIDE Figurine Seventh Issue "Bridal" Series
E-2846
313

87	Bride	UPP	$18.00	4.75"	CED	Secondary	$35.00
88		UPP	22.50		FLW	Secondary	30.00
89		UPP	25.00		B&A	Secondary	28.00
90		UPP	25.00		FLM	Secondary	27.00
91		UPP	25.00		VSL	Secondary	25.00
92		UPP	25.00		G/CL	Primary	25.00
93		UPP	25.00		BFY	Primary	25.00
94		OPEN	25.00		TRP	Primary	25.00

LOVE IS KIND Plate Fourth Issue "Inspired Thoughts" Series Individually Numbered
E-2847
175

84	Boy Pushing Girl on Swing	15,000	$40.00	8.50"	UM	Secondary	$50.00
					CRS	Secondary	45.00

LOVING THY NEIGHBOR Plate Fourth Issue "Mother's Love" Series Individually Numbered
E-2848
176

84	Mother Wrapping Bread	15,000	$40.00	8.50"	CRS	Secondary	$42.00

MOTHER SEW DEAR Doll
E-2850
30

84	Mother Needlepointing	UPP	$350.00	16.00"	UM	Ret'd/Sec	$350.00
84		UPP	350.00		CRS	Ret'd/Sec	350.00
85		UPP	350.00		DVE	Ret'd/Sec	350.00

KRISTY Doll
E-2851
177

84	Baby Collector Doll	UPP	$150.00	12.00"	CRS	Susp/Sec	$175.00
85		UPP	150.00		DVE	Susp/Sec	170.00
86		UPP	150.00		OLB	Susp/Sec	170.00
87		UPP	160.00		CED	Susp/Sec	170.00
88		UPP	160.00		FLW	Susp/Sec	170.00
89		UPP	170.00		B&A	Susp/Sec	170.00

BABY FIGURINES Figurines Set of 6 (Divide by 6 for an "each" value)
E-2852
178

84	Baby Figurines	UPP	$72.00	3.50"	CRS	Secondary	$168.00
85		UPP	72.00		DVE	Secondary	156.00
86		UPP	72.00		OLB	Secondary	150.00
87		UPP	81.00		CED	Secondary	138.00

In 1987, individual Enesco Item #s were assigned for each figurine in the above set of 6:

BABY FIGURINE Figurine
E-2852/A
401

87	Baby Boy Standing	UPP	$13.50	3.75"	CED	Secondary	$22.00
88		UPP	14.00		FLW	Secondary	21.00
89		UPP	15.00		B&A	Secondary	20.00
90		UPP	16.50		FLM	Secondary	18.00
91		UPP	16.50		VSL	Secondary	18.00
92		UPP	16.50		G/CL	Secondary	18.00
93		UPP	16.50		BFY	Primary	17.50
94		OPEN	17.50		TRP	Primary	17.50

BABY FIGURINE Figurine
E-2852/B
402

87	Baby Girl with Bow in Hair	UPP	$13.50	3.75"	CED	Secondary	$23.00
88		UPP	14.00		FLW	Secondary	21.00
89		UPP	15.00		B&A	Secondary	20.00
90		UPP	16.50		FLM	Secondary	20.00
91		UPP	16.50		VSL	Secondary	20.00
92		UPP	16.50		G/CL	Secondary	18.00
93		UPP	16.50		BFY	Primary	17.50
94		OPEN	17.50		TRP	Primary	17.50

BABY FIGURINE Figurine
E-2852/C
403

87	Baby Boy Sitting	UPP	$13.50	3.00"	CED	Secondary	$22.00
88		UPP	14.00		FLW	Secondary	21.00
89		UPP	15.00		B&A	Secondary	20.00
90		UPP	16.50		FLM	Secondary	20.00
91		UPP	16.50		VSL	Secondary	18.00
92		UPP	16.50		G/CL	Secondary	18.00
93		UPP	16.50		BFY	Primary	17.50
94		OPEN	17.50		TRP	Primary	17.50

BABY FIGURINE Figurine
E-2852/D
404

87	Baby Girl Clapping Hands	UPP	$13.50	3.25"	CED	Secondary	$23.00
88		UPP	14.00		FLW	Secondary	21.00
89		UPP	15.00		B&A	Secondary	20.00
90		UPP	16.50		FLM	Secondary	20.00
91		UPP	16.50		VSL	Secondary	20.00
92		UPP	16.50		G/CL	Secondary	18.00
93		UPP	16.50		BFY	Primary	17.50
94		OPEN	17.50		TRP	Primary	17.50

BABY FIGURINE Figurine
E-2852/E
405

87	Baby Boy Crawling	UPP	$13.50	2.75"	CED	Secondary	$22.00
88		UPP	14.00		FLW	Secondary	21.00
89		UPP	15.00		B&A	Secondary	20.00
90		UPP	16.50		FLM	Secondary	18.00
91		UPP	16.50		VSL	Secondary	18.00
92		UPP	16.50		G/CL	Secondary	18.00
93		UPP	16.50		BFY	Primary	17.50
94		OPEN	17.50		TRP	Primary	17.50

BABY FIGURINE Figurine
E-2852/F
406

Year	Description	Mark	Issue Price	Size	Mark	Market	Value
87	Baby Girl Lying Down	UPP	$13.50	2.50"	CED	Secondary	$23.00
88		UPP	14.00		FLW	Secondary	21.00
89		UPP	15.00		B&A	Secondary	20.00
90		UPP	16.50		FLM	Secondary	20.00
91		UPP	16.50		VSL	Secondary	20.00
92		UPP	16.50		G/CL	Secondary	18.00
93		UPP	16.50		BFY	Primary	17.50
94		OPEN	17.50		TRP	Primary	17.50

GOD BLESSED OUR YEARS TOGETHER WITH SO MUCH LOVE & HAPPINESS Figurine
E-2853
179

Year	Description	Mark	Issue Price	Size	Mark	Market	Value
84	Happy Anniversary	UPP	$35.00	5.50"	CRS	Secondary	$62.00
85		UPP	35.00		DVE	Secondary	55.00
86		UPP	35.00		OLB	Secondary	52.00
87		UPP	38.50		CED	Secondary	52.00
88		UPP	40.00		FLW	Secondary	50.00
89		UPP	45.00		B&A	Secondary	50.00
90		UPP	50.00		FLM	Secondary	50.00
91		UPP	50.00		VSL	Secondary	50.00
92		UPP	50.00		G/CL	Secondary	50.00
93		UPP	50.00		BFY	Secondary	50.00
94		OPEN	50.00		TRP	Primary	50.00

GOD BLESSED OUR YEAR TOGETHER WITH SO MUCH LOVE & HAPPINESS Figurine
E-2854
180

Year	Description	Mark	Issue Price	Size	Mark	Market	Value
84	First Anniversary	UPP	$35.00	5.50"	CRS	Secondary	$65.00
85		UPP	35.00		DVE	Secondary	55.00
86		UPP	35.00		OLB	Secondary	52.00
87		UPP	38.50		CED	Secondary	52.00
88		UPP	40.00		FLW	Secondary	50.00
89		UPP	45.00		B&A	Secondary	50.00
90		UPP	50.00		FLM	Secondary	50.00
91		UPP	50.00		VSL	Secondary	50.00
92		UPP	50.00		G/CL	Secondary	50.00
93		UPP	50.00		BFY	Secondary	50.00
94		OPEN	50.00		TRP	Primary	50.00

GOD BLESSED OUR YEARS TOGETHER WITH SO MUCH LOVE & HAPPINESS Figurine
E-2855
181

Year	Description	Mark	Issue Price	Size	Mark	Market	Value
84	5th Anniversary	UPP	$35.00	5.50"	CRS	Secondary	$62.00
85		UPP	35.00		DVE	Secondary	55.00
86		UPP	35.00		OLB	Secondary	52.00
87		UPP	38.50		CED	Secondary	50.00
88		UPP	40.00		FLW	Secondary	50.00
89		UPP	45.00		B&A	Secondary	50.00
90		UPP	50.00		FLM	Secondary	50.00
91		UPP	50.00		VSL	Secondary	50.00
92		UPP	50.00		G/CL	Secondary	50.00
93		UPP	50.00		BFY	Primary	50.00
94		OPEN	50.00		TRP	Primary	50.00

GOD BLESSED OUR YEARS TOGETHER WITH SO MUCH LOVE & HAPPINESS Figurine
E-2856
182

Year	Description	Mark	Issue Price	Size	Mark	Market	Value
84	10th Anniversary	UPP	$35.00	5.50"	CRS	Secondary	$62.00
85		UPP	35.00		DVE	Secondary	55.00
86		UPP	35.00		OLB	Secondary	52.00
87		UPP	38.50		CED	Secondary	50.00
88		UPP	40.00		FLW	Secondary	50.00
89		UPP	45.00		B&A	Secondary	50.00
90		UPP	50.00		FLM	Secondary	50.00
91		UPP	50.00		VSL	Secondary	50.00
92		UPP	50.00		G/CL	Secondary	50.00
93		UPP	50.00		BFY	Primary	50.00
94		OPEN	50.00		TRP	Primary	50.00

GOD BLESSED OUR YEARS TOGETHER WITH SO MUCH LOVE & HAPPINESS Figurine

E-2857 (183)

	Year	Description	Status	Price	Size	Mark	Market	Value
	84	25th Anniversary	UPP	$35.00	5.50"	CRS	Secondary	$65.00
	85		UPP	35.00		DVE	Secondary	58.00
	86		UPP	35.00		OLB	Secondary	55.00
	87		UPP	38.50		CED	Secondary	52.00
	88		UPP	40.00		FLW	Secondary	52.00
	89		UPP	45.00		B&A	Secondary	50.00
	90		UPP	50.00		FLM	Secondary	50.00
	91		UPP	50.00		VSL	Secondary	50.00
	92		UPP	50.00		G/CL	Secondary	50.00
	93		UPP	50.00		BFY	Secondary	50.00
	94		OPEN	50.00		TRP	Primary	50.00

GOD BLESSED OUR YEARS TOGETHER WITH SO MUCH LOVE & HAPPINESS Figurine

E-2859 (184)

	Year	Description	Status	Price	Size	Mark	Market	Value
	84	40th Anniversary	UPP	$35.00	5.50"	CRS	Secondary	$65.00
	85		UPP	35.00		DVE	Secondary	55.00
	86		UPP	35.00		OLB	Secondary	52.00
	87		UPP	38.50		CED	Secondary	50.00
	88		UPP	40.00		FLW	Secondary	50.00
	89		UPP	45.00		B&A	Secondary	50.00
	90		UPP	50.00		FLM	Secondary	50.00
	91		UPP	50.00		VSL	Secondary	50.00
	92		UPP	50.00		G/CL	Secondary	50.00
	93		UPP	50.00		BFY	Secondary	50.00
	94		OPEN	50.00		TRP	Primary	50.00

GOD BLESSED OUR YEARS TOGETHER WITH SO MUCH LOVE & HAPPINESS Figurine

E-2860 (185)

	Year	Description	Status	Price	Size	Mark	Market	Value
	84	50th Anniversary	UPP	$35.00	5.50"	CRS	Secondary	$65.00
	85		UPP	35.00		DVE	Secondary	55.00
	86		UPP	35.00		OLB	Secondary	55.00
	87		UPP	38.50		CED	Secondary	52.00
	88		UPP	40.00		FLW	Secondary	50.00
	89		UPP	45.00		B&A	Secondary	50.00
	90		UPP	50.00		FLM	Secondary	50.00
	91		UPP	50.00		VSL	Secondary	50.00
	92		UPP	50.00		G/CL	Primary	50.00
	93		UPP	50.00		BFY	Primary	50.00
	94		OPEN	50.00		TRP	Primary	50.00

BLESSED ARE THE PURE IN HEART Figurine

E-3104 (28)

	Year	Description	Status	Price	Size	Mark	Market	Value
	80	Rocking Cradle	UPP	$ 9.00	2.75"	NM	Susp/Sec	$55.00
	81		UPP	10.50		TRI	Susp/Sec	48.00
	82		UPP	12.00		HRG	Susp/Sec	45.00
	83		UPP	12.00		FSH	Susp/Sec	42.00
	84		UPP	13.50		CRS	Susp/Sec	40.00
	85		UPP	13.50		DVE	Susp/Sec	38.00
	86		UPP	13.50		OLB	Susp/Sec	35.00
	87		UPP	16.00		CED	Susp/Sec	32.00
	88		UPP	16.00		FLW	Susp/Sec	32.00
	89		UPP	17.50		B&A	Susp/Sec	30.00
	90		UPP	19.00		FLM	Susp/Sec	30.00
	91		UPP	19.00		VSL	Susp/Sec	30.00

HE WATCHES OVER US ALL Figurine

E-3105 (29)

	Year	Description	Status	Price	Size	Mark	Market	Value
	80	Boy on Crutches with Bible	UPP	$11.00	5.25"	NM	Susp/Sec	$90.00
	81		UPP	11.00		TRI	Susp/Sec	80.00
	82		UPP	15.00		HRG	Susp/Sec	70.00
	83		UPP	15.00		FSH	Susp/Sec	68.00
	84		UPP	17.00		CRS	Susp/Sec	65.00

MOTHER SEW DEAR — Figurine
E-3106 (30)

Yr	Description	Mark	Issue Price	Size	Mark Code	Market	Value
80	Mother Needlepointing	UPP	$13.00	5.00"	NM	Secondary	$80.00
81		UPP	13.00		TRI	Secondary	60.00
82		UPP	16.00		HRG	Secondary	50.00
83		UPP	16.00		FSH	Secondary	42.00
84		UPP	17.00		CRS	Secondary	38.00
85		UPP	17.00		DVE	Secondary	35.00
86		UPP	17.00		OLB	Secondary	32.00
87		UPP	21.00		CED	Secondary	32.00
88		UPP	22.50		FLW	Secondary	30.00
89		UPP	25.00		B&A	Secondary	30.00
90		UPP	27.50		FLM	Secondary	30.00
91		UPP	27.50		VSL	Secondary	30.00
92		UPP	27.50		G/CL	Secondary	30.00
93		UPP	30.00		BFY	Primary	30.00
94		OPEN	30.00		TRP	Primary	30.00

BLESSED ARE THE PEACEMAKERS — Figurine
E-3107 (31)

Yr	Description	Mark	Issue Price	Size	Mark Code	Market	Value
80	Boy Holding Cat & Dog	UPP	$13.00	5.25"	NM	Ret'd/Sec	$130.00
81		UPP	15.00		TRI	Ret'd/Sec	110.00
82		UPP	17.00		HRG	Ret'd/Sec	85.00
83		UPP	17.00		FSH	Ret'd/Sec	80.00
84		UPP	19.00		CRS	Ret'd/Sec	75.00
85		UPP	19.00		DVE	Ret'd/Sec	72.00

THE HAND THAT ROCKS THE FUTURE — Figurine
E-3108 (32)

Yr	Description	Mark	Issue Price	Size	Mark Code	Market	Value
80	Girl Rocking Cradle	UPP	$13.00	4.50"	NM	Susp/Sec	$100.00
81		UPP	15.00		TRI	Susp/Sec	85.00
82		UPP	17.00		HRG	Susp/Sec	78.00
83		UPP	17.00		FSH	Susp/Sec	75.00
84		UPP	19.00		CRS	Susp/Sec	70.00

THE PURR-FECT GRANDMA — Figurine
E-3109 (33)

Yr	Description	Mark	Issue Price	Size	Mark Code	Market	Value
80	Grandma in Rocker	UPP	$13.00	4.75"	NM	Secondary	$78.00
81		UPP	15.00		TRI	Secondary	65.00
82		UPP	17.00		HRG	Secondary	50.00
83		UPP	17.00		FSH	Secondary	42.00
84		UPP	19.00		CRS	Secondary	40.00
85		UPP	19.00		DVE	Secondary	38.00
86		UPP	19.00		OLB	Secondary	38.00
87		UPP	21.00		CED	Secondary	35.00
88		UPP	23.00		FLW	Secondary	32.00
89		UPP	25.00		B&A	Secondary	30.00
90		UPP	27.50		FLM	Secondary	30.00
91		UPP	27.50		VSL	Secondary	30.00
92		UPP	27.50		G/CL	Secondary	30.00
93		UPP	30.00		BFY	Primary	30.00
94		OPEN	30.00		TRP	Primary	30.00

LOVING IS SHARING — Figurine
E-3110B (34)

Yr	Description	Mark	Issue Price	Size	Mark Code	Market	Value
80	Boy Sharing with Puppy	UPP	$13.00	4.50"	NM	Ret'd/Sec	$145.00
81		UPP	15.00		TRI	Ret'd/Sec	115.00
82		UPP	17.00		HRG	Ret'd/Sec	100.00
83		UPP	17.00		FSH	Ret'd/Sec	85.00
84		UPP	19.00		CRS	Ret'd/Sec	80.00
85		UPP	19.00		DVE	Ret'd/Sec	75.00
86		UPP	19.00		OLB	Ret'd/Sec	75.00
87		UPP	21.00		CED	Ret'd/Sec	72.00
88		UPP	24.00		FLW	Ret'd/Sec	72.00
89		UPP	27.50		B&A	Ret'd/Sec	70.00
90		UPP	30.00		FLM	Ret'd/Sec	70.00
91		UPP	30.00		VSL	Ret'd/Sec	70.00
92		UPP	30.00		G/CL	Ret'd/Sec	70.00
93		UPP	30.00		BFY	Ret'd/Sec	70.00

LOVING IS SHARING Figurine
E-3110G
35

Year	Description	Status	Price	Size	Mark	Market	Value
80	Girl Sharing with Puppy	UPP	$13.00	4.50"	NM	Secondary	$95.00
81		UPP	15.00		TRI	Secondary	70.00
82		UPP	17.00		HRG	Secondary	52.00
83		UPP	17.00		FSH	Secondary	42.00
84		UPP	19.00		CRS	Secondary	40.00
85		UPP	19.00		DVE	Secondary	38.00
86		UPP	19.00		OLB	Secondary	35.00
87		UPP	21.00		CED	Secondary	32.00
88		UPP	24.00		FLW	Secondary	32.00
89		UPP	27.50		B&A	Secondary	30.00
90		UPP	30.00		FLM	Secondary	30.00
91		UPP	30.00		VSL	Secondary	30.00
92		UPP	30.00		G/CL	Secondary	30.00
93		UPP	30.00		BFY	Primary	30.00
94		OPEN	30.00		TRP	Primary	30.00

BE NOT WEARY IN WELL DOING Figurine
E-3111
36

Year	Description	Status	Price	Size	Mark	Market	Value
80	Girl Helper	UPP	$14.00	4.00"	NM*	Ret'd/Sec	$130.00
81		UPP	16.00		TRI	Ret'd/Sec	115.00
82		UPP	18.00		HRG	Ret'd/Sec	100.00
83		UPP	18.00		FSH	Ret'd/Sec	95.00
84		UPP	19.00		CRS	Ret'd/Sec	88.00
85		UPP	19.00		DVE	Ret'd/Sec	82.00

**Classic Variation.* Figurines exist in NO MARK versions with an error in the Inspirational Title on the understamp decal. Instead of "Be Not Weary In Well Doing," they read "Be Not Weary And Well Doing." The black and white boxes which the pieces were shipped in also have the incorrect title on the label. The GREENBOOK TRUMARKET PRICE for "...And Well Doing" is $190.00.
Full color photograph: 5th Ed., pg. 204.

GOD'S SPEED Figurine
E-3112
44

Year	Description	Status	Price	Size	Mark	Market	Value
80	Boy Jogging with Dog	UPP	$14.00	4.75"	NM	Ret'd/Sec	$105.00
81		UPP	16.00		TRI	Ret'd/Sec	85.00
82		UPP	18.00		HRG	Ret'd/Sec	80.00
83		UPP	18.00		FSH	Ret'd/Sec	70.00

Exists in a double mark TRIANGLE/HOURGLASS.

THOU ART MINE Figurine
E-3113
37

Year	Description	Status	Price	Size	Mark	Market	Value
80	Boy with Girl Writing	UPP	$16.00	5.00"	NM	Secondary	$90.00
81	in Sand	UPP	19.00		TRI	Secondary	72.00
82		UPP	22.50		HRG	Secondary	60.00
83		UPP	22.50		FSH	Secondary	55.00
84		UPP	25.00		CRS	Secondary	45.00
85		UPP	25.00		DVE	Secondary	42.00
86		UPP	25.00		OLB	Secondary	40.00
87		UPP	27.50		CED	Secondary	38.00
88		UPP	30.00		FLW	Secondary	38.00
89		UPP	33.00		B&A	Secondary	38.00
90		UPP	35.00		FLM	Secondary	38.00
91		UPP	35.00		VSL	Secondary	38.00
92		UPP	35.00		G/CL	Primary	37.50
93		UPP	37.50		BFY	Primary	37.50
94		OPEN	37.50		TRP	Primary	37.50

THE LORD BLESS YOU AND KEEP YOU Figurine

E-3114	80 Bride and Groom	UPP	$16.00	5.00"	NM	Secondary	$90.00
38	81	UPP	19.00		TRI	Secondary	70.00
	82	UPP	22.50		HRG	Secondary	58.00
	83	UPP	22.50		FSH	Secondary	55.00
	84	UPP	25.00		CRS	Secondary	50.00
	85	UPP	25.00		DVE	Secondary	48.00
	86	UPP	25.00		OLB	Secondary	45.00
	87	UPP	27.50		CED	Secondary	42.00
	88	UPP	32.50		FLW	Secondary	40.00
	89	UPP	37.50		B&A	Secondary	40.00
	90	UPP	37.50		FLM	Secondary	40.00
	91	UPP	37.50		VSL	Secondary	40.00
	92	UPP	37.50		G/CL	Secondary	40.00
	93	UPP	40.00		BFY	Primary	40.00
	94	OPEN	40.00		TRP	Primary	40.00

BUT LOVE GOES ON FOREVER Figurine

E-3115	80 Boy and Girl Angels on Cloud	UPP	$16.50	5.25"	NM	Secondary	$105.00
39	81	UPP	19.00		TRI	Secondary	75.00
	82	UPP	22.50		HRG	Secondary	60.00
	83	UPP	22.50		FSH	Secondary	50.00
	84	UPP	25.00		CRS	Secondary	45.00
	85	UPP	25.00		DVE	Secondary	45.00
	86	UPP	25.00		OLB	Secondary	42.00
	87	UPP	27.50		CED	Secondary	40.00
	88	UPP	30.00		FLW	Secondary	38.00
	89	UPP	33.00		B&A	Secondary	36.00
	90	UPP	35.00		FLM	Secondary	35.00
	91	UPP	35.00		VSL	Secondary	35.00
	92	UPP	35.00		G/CL	Primary	35.00
	93	UPP	35.00		BFY	Primary	35.00
	94	OPEN	35.00		TRP	Primary	35.00

THEE I LOVE Figurine

E-3116	80 Boy Carving Tree for Girl	UPP	$16.50	6.00"	NM	Ret'd/Sec	$135.00
40	81	UPP	19.00		TRI	Ret'd/Sec	100.00
	82	UPP	22.50		HRG	Ret'd/Sec	85.00
	83	UPP	22.50		FSH	Ret'd/Sec	80.00
	84	UPP	25.00		CRS	Ret'd/Sec	78.00
	85	UPP	25.00		DVE	Ret'd/Sec	75.00
	86	UPP	25.00		OLB	Ret'd/Sec	72.00
	87	UPP	27.50		CED	Ret'd/Sec	70.00
	88	UPP	32.50		FLW	Ret'd/Sec	68.00
	89	UPP	36.00		B&A	Ret'd/Sec	65.00
	90	UPP	37.50		FLM	Ret'd/Sec	62.00
	91	UPP	37.50		VSL	Ret'd/Sec	60.00
	92	UPP	37.50		G/CL	Ret'd/Sec	58.00
	93	UPP	40.00		BFY	Ret'd/Sec	55.00
	94	UPP	40.00		TRP	Ret'd/Sec	52.00

WALKING BY FAITH Figurine
E-3117
41

80	Boy Pulling Wagon with Girl	UPP	$35.00	7.25"	NM	Secondary	$125.00
81		UPP	40.00		TRI	Secondary	100.00
82		UPP	45.00		HRG	Secondary	95.00
83		UPP	45.00		FSH	Secondary	90.00
84		UPP	50.00		CRS	Secondary	85.00
85		UPP	50.00		DVE	Secondary	82.00
86		UPP	50.00		OLB	Secondary	80.00
87		UPP	55.00		CED	Secondary	78.00
88		UPP	60.00		FLW	Secondary	75.00
89		UPP	67.50		B&A	Secondary	75.00
90		UPP	70.00		FLM	Secondary	75.00
91		UPP	70.00		VSL	Secondary	75.00
92		UPP	70.00		G/CL	Primary	75.00
93		UPP	75.00		BFY	Primary	75.00
94		OPEN	75.00		TRP	Primary	75.00

EGGS OVER EASY Figurine
E-3118
45

80	Girl with Frypan	UPP	$12.00	5.00"	NM	Ret'd/Sec	$120.00
81		UPP	14.00		TRI	Ret'd/Sec	100.00
82		UPP	15.00		HRG	Ret'd/Sec	88.00
83		UPP	15.00		FSH	Ret'd/Sec	85.00

IT'S WHAT'S INSIDE THAT COUNTS Figurine
E-3119
42

80	Boy with Books	UPP	$13.00	5.25"	NM	Susp/Sec	$130.00
81		UPP	15.00		TRI	Susp/Sec	120.00
82		UPP	17.00		HRG	Susp/Sec	110.00
83		UPP	17.00		FSH	Susp/Sec	105.00
84		UPP	19.00		CRS	Susp/Sec	100.00

TO THEE WITH LOVE Figurine
E-3120
43

80	Girl with Box of Kittens	UPP	$13.00	5.75"	NM	Susp/Sec	$95.00
81		UPP	15.00		TRI	Susp/Sec	75.00
82		UPP	17.00		HRG	Susp/Sec	70.00
83		UPP	17.00		FSH	Susp/Sec	68.00
84		UPP	19.00		CRS	Susp/Sec	65.00
85		UPP	19.00		DVE	Susp/Sec	60.00
86		UPP	19.00		OLB	Susp/Sec	58.00
*					CED	Susp/Sec	55.00

* Piece was suspended in 1986 yet exists in a CEDAR TREE Annual Production Symbol.

Notes Along The Way ...

THE LORD BLESS YOU AND KEEP YOU Figurine

E-4720	81	Boy Graduate	UPP	$14.00	5.25"	NM	Susp/Sec	$45.00
46	81		UPP	14.00		TRI	Susp/Sec	38.00
	82		UPP	17.00		HRG	Susp/Sec	35.00
	83		UPP	17.00		FSH	Susp/Sec	35.00
	84		UPP	19.00		CRS	Susp/Sec	32.00
	85		UPP	19.00		DVE	Susp/Sec	32.00
	86		UPP	19.00		OLB	Susp/Sec	30.00
	87		UPP	22.50		CED	Susp/Sec	30.00

THE LORD BLESS YOU AND KEEP YOU Figurine

E-4721	81	Girl Graduate	UPP	$14.00	5.25"	NM	Secondary	$75.00
47	81		UPP	14.00		TRI	Secondary	60.00
	82		UPP	17.00		HRG	Secondary	54.00
	83		UPP	17.00		FSH	Secondary	45.00
	84		UPP	19.00		CRS	Secondary	42.00
	85		UPP	19.00		DVE	Secondary	40.00
	86		UPP	19.00		OLB	Secondary	35.00
	87		UPP	22.50		CED	Secondary	34.00
	88		UPP	24.00		FLW	Secondary	32.00
	89		UPP	27.00		B&A	Secondary	32.00
	90		UPP	30.00		FLM	Secondary	32.00
	91		UPP	30.00		VSL	Secondary	30.00
	92		UPP	30.00		G/CL	Secondary	30.00
	93		UPP	30.00		BFY	Secondary	30.00
	94		OPEN	30.00		TRP	Primary	30.00

LOVE CANNOT BREAK A TRUE FRIENDSHIP Figurine

E-4722	81	Girl with Piggy Bank	UPP	$22.50	5.00"	NM	Susp/Sec	$150.00
48	81		UPP	22.50		TRI	Susp/Sec	130.00
	82		UPP	25.00		HRG	Susp/Sec	120.00
	83		UPP	25.00		FSH	Susp/Sec	115.00
	84		UPP	27.50		CRS	Susp/Sec	110.00
	85		UPP	27.50		DVE	Susp/Sec	105.00

PEACE AMID THE STORM Figurine

E-4723	81	Boy Reading Holy Bible	UPP	$22.50	4.75"	NM	Susp/Sec	$105.00
49	81		UPP	22.50		TRI	Susp/Sec	85.00
	82		UPP	25.00		HRG	Susp/Sec	80.00
	83		UPP	25.00		FSH	Susp/Sec	75.00
	84		UPP	27.50		CRS	Susp/Sec	72.00

REJOICING WITH YOU Figurine

E-4724	81	Christening	UPP	$25.00	5.25"	NM	Secondary	$95.00
50	81		UPP	25.00		TRI	Secondary	75.00
	82		UPP	27.50		HRG	Secondary	65.00
	83		UPP	27.50		FSH	Secondary	58.00
	84		UPP	30.00		CRS	Secondary	55.00
	85		UPP	30.00		DVE	Secondary	52.00
	86		UPP	30.00		OLB	Secondary	50.00
	87		UPP	33.50		CED	Secondary	50.00
	88		UPP	37.50		FLW	Secondary	50.00
	89		UPP	40.00		B&A	Secondary	50.00
	90		UPP	45.00		FLM	Secondary	50.00
	91		UPP	45.00		VSL	Secondary	50.00
	92		UPP	45.00		G/CL	Primary	50.00
	93		UPP	50.00		BFY	Primary	50.00
	94		OPEN	50.00		TRP	Primary	50.00

Classic Variation: "No E" or "Bibl Error." During the first years of production the "e" was missing from the word Bible. It appears as though all NO MARK, TRIANGLE, and HOURGLASS pieces as well as some FISH pieces have this variation.

Full color photograph: 4th Ed., pg. 195 or 5th Ed., pg. 203.

PEACE ON EARTH — Figurine
E-4725
51

81	Choir Boys with Bandages	UPP	$25.00	5.25"	NM	Susp/Sec	$100.00
81		UPP	25.00		TRI	Susp/Sec	78.00
82		UPP	27.50		HRG	Susp/Sec	72.00
83		UPP	27.50		FSH	Susp/Sec	70.00
84		UPP	30.00		CRS	Susp/Sec	65.00

PEACE ON EARTH — Musical — TUNE: Jesus Loves Me
E-4726
51

81	Choir Boys with Bandages	UPP	$45.00	6.25"	NM	Susp/Sec	$145.00
81		UPP	45.00		TRI	Susp/Sec	120.00
82		UPP	45.00		HRG	Susp/Sec	125.00
83		UPP	45.00		FSH	Susp/Sec	110.00
84		UPP	50.00		CRS	Susp/Sec	105.00

BEAR YE ONE ANOTHER'S BURDENS — Figurine
E-5200
52

81	Sad Boy with Teddy	UPP	$20.00	4.74"	NM	Susp/Sec	$110.00
81		UPP	20.00		TRI	Susp/Sec	88.00
82		UPP	22.50		HRG	Susp/Sec	82.00
83		UPP	22.50		FSH	Susp/Sec	78.00
84		UPP	25.00		CRS	Susp/Sec	75.00

LOVE LIFTED ME — Figurine
E-5201
53

81	Boy Helping Friend	UPP	$25.00	5.50"	NM	Susp/Sec	$110.00
81		UPP	25.00		TRI	Susp/Sec	90.00
82		UPP	30.00		HRG	Susp/Sec	85.00
83		UPP	30.00		FSH	Susp/Sec	82.00
84		UPP	33.00		CRS	Susp/Sec	75.00

THANK YOU FOR COMING TO MY ADE — Figurine
E-5202
54

81	Lemonade Stand	UPP	$22.50	5.50"	NM	Susp/Sec	$150.00
81		UPP	22.50		TRI	Susp/Sec	125.00
82		UPP	27.50		HRG	Susp/Sec	115.00
83		UPP	27.50		FSH	Susp/Sec	110.00
84		UPP	30.00		CRS	Susp/Sec	105.00

LET NOT THE SUN GO DOWN UPON YOUR WRATH — Figurine
E-5203
55

81	Boy with Dog on Stairs	UPP	$22.50	6.75"	NM	Susp/Sec	$175.00
81		UPP	22.50		TRI	Susp/Sec	155.00
82		UPP	27.50		HRG	Susp/Sec	145.00
83		UPP	30.00		FSH	Susp/Sec	135.00
84		UPP	30.00		CRS	Susp/Sec	130.00

THE HAND THAT ROCKS THE FUTURE — Musical — TUNE: Mozart's Lullaby
E-5204
32

81	Girl Rocking Cradle	UPP	$30.00	5.50"	NM	Secondary	$100.00
81		UPP	30.00		TRI	Secondary	82.00
82		UPP	35.00		HRG	Secondary	75.00
83		UPP	35.00		FSH	Secondary	72.00
84		UPP	37.50		CRS	Secondary	70.00
85		UPP	37.50		DVE	Secondary	68.00
86		UPP	37.50		OLB	Secondary	65.00
87		UPP	40.00		CED	Secondary	62.00
88		UPP	45.00		FLW	Secondary	60.00
89		UPP	50.00		B&A	Secondary	60.00
90		UPP	55.00		FLM	Secondary	60.00
91		UPP	55.00		VSL	Secondary	60.00
92		UPP	55.00		G/CL	Secondary	60.00
93		UPP	60.00		BFY	Primary	60.00
94		OPEN	60.00		TRP	Primary	60.00

MY GUARDIAN ANGEL — Musical — TUNE: Brahm's Lullaby
E-5205
56

81	Boy Angel on Cloud	UPP	$22.50	5.50"	NM	Susp/Sec	$102.00
84		UPP	27.50		CRS	Susp/Sec	85.00
85		UPP	27.50		DVE	Susp/Sec	82.00

MY GUARDIAN ANGEL — Musical — TUNE: Brahm's Lullaby
E-5206 (57)

Year	Description	Mark	Price	Size	Mark	Status	Value
81	Girl Angel on Cloud	UPP	$22.50	5.50"	NM	Susp/Sec	$100.00
84		UPP	27.50		CRS	Susp/Sec	85.00
85		UPP	27.50		DVE	Susp/Sec	82.00
86		UPP	27.50		OLB	Susp/Sec	80.00
87		UPP	30.00		CED	Susp/Sec	78.00
88		UPP	33.00		FLW	Susp/Sec	75.00

MY GUARDIAN ANGELS — Night Light
E-5207 (39)

Year	Description	Mark	Price	Size	Mark	Status	Value
81	Boy & Girl Angels on Cloud	UPP	$30.00	3.50"	NM	Susp/Sec	$220.00
84		UPP	37.50		CRS	Susp/Sec	185.00

JESUS LOVES ME — Bell
E-5208 (1)

Year	Description	Mark	Price	Size	Mark	Status	Value
81	Boy with Teddy	UPP	$15.00	5.75"	NM	Susp/Sec	$55.00
84		UPP	19.00		CRS	Susp/Sec	50.00
85		UPP	19.00		DVE	Susp/Sec	48.00

JESUS LOVES ME — Bell
E-5209 (2)

Year	Description	Mark	Price	Size	Mark	Status	Value
81	Girl with Bunny	UPP	$15.00	5.75"	NM	Susp/Sec	$62.00
84		UPP	19.00		CRS	Susp/Sec	50.00
85		UPP	19.00		DVE	Susp/Sec	48.00

PRAYER CHANGES THINGS — Bell
E-5210 (58)

Year	Description	Mark	Price	Size	Mark	Status	Value
81	Girl Praying	UPP	$15.00	5.75"	NM	Susp/Sec	$55.00
84		UPP	19.00		CRS	Susp/Sec	48.00

GOD UNDERSTANDS — Bell
E-5211 (12)

Year	Description	Mark	Price	Size	Mark	Status	Value
81	Boy with Report Card	UPP	$15.00	5.75"	UM	Ret'd/Sec	$58.00
84		UPP	19.00		CRS	Ret'd/Sec	42.00

TO A SPECIAL DAD — Figurine
E-5212 (59)

Year	Description	Mark	Price	Size	Mark	Status	Value
81	Boy in Dad's Duds	UPP	$20.00	5.50"	NM	Secondary	$72.00
81	with Dog	UPP	20.00		TRI	Secondary	60.00
82		UPP	22.50		HRG	Secondary	48.00
83		UPP	22.50		FSH	Secondary	42.00
84		UPP	25.00		CRS	Secondary	42.00
85		UPP	25.00		DVE	Secondary	40.00
86		UPP	25.00		OLB	Secondary	38.00
87		UPP	27.50		CED	Secondary	38.00
88		UPP	30.00		FLW	Secondary	36.00
89		UPP	33.00		B&A	Secondary	35.00
90		UPP	35.00		FLM	Secondary	35.00
91		UPP	35.00		VSL	Secondary	35.00
92		UPP	35.00		G/CL	Primary	35.00
93		UPP	35.00		BFY	Primary	35.00
94		OPEN	35.00		TRP	Primary	35.00

GOD IS LOVE — Figurine
E-5213 (60)

Year	Description	Mark	Price	Size	Mark	Status	Value
81	Girl with Goose in Lap	UPP	$17.00	5.00"	NM	Susp/Sec	$110.00
81		UPP	17.00		TRI	Susp/Sec	75.00
82		UPP	20.00		HRG	Susp/Sec	65.00
83		UPP	20.00		FSH	Susp/Sec	62.00
84		UPP	22.50		CRS	Susp/Sec	60.00
85		UPP	22.50		DVE	Susp/Sec	58.00
86		UPP	22.50		OLB	Susp/Sec	55.00
87		UPP	25.00		CED	Susp/Sec	52.00
88		UPP	27.00		FLW	Susp/Sec	52.00
89		UPP	30.00		B&A	Susp/Sec	50.00

This piece was re-sculptured in 1985. On the original mold the girl had no chin.

PRAYER CHANGES THINGS Figurine

E-5214

61

81	Boy & Girl Praying at Table	UPP	$35.00	5.15"	NM	Susp/Sec	*
81	with Bible	UPP	35.00		TRI	Susp/Sec	*
82		UPP	35.00		HRG	Susp/Sec	*
83		UPP	35.00		FSH	Susp/Sec	$110.00
84		UPP	37.50		CRS	Susp/Sec	105.00
**					DVE	Susp/Sec	100.00

**Piece was suspended in 1984 yet exists in a DOVE. **Classic Variation: "Backwards Bible."* The first production of this figurine had the words "Holy Bible" inscribed on the back cover. Pieces with this error exist in NO MARK and TRIANGLE versions. Reportedly, NO MARK and TRIANGLE pieces also exist where the title is correctly placed, but these may be considered extremely rare. The majority of HOURGLASS pieces have the correctly placed title. TRUMARKET PRICES are as follows: Backwards NO MARK $175.00, Backwards TRIANGLE $160.00, Backwards HOURGLASS $145.00, and correct HOURGLASS $130.00. Full color photo: 4th Ed., pg. 195 or 5th Ed., pg. 202. One color photograph: 6th Ed., pg. 224.

LOVE ONE ANOTHER Plate First Issue "Inspired Thoughts" Series Individually Numbered

E-5215

8

81	Boy and Girl on Stump	15,000	$40.00	8.50"	UM	Secondary	$70.00

THE LORD BLESS YOU AND KEEP YOU Plate

E-5216

38

81	Bride and Groom	UPP	$30.00	7.00"	UM	Susp/Sec	$45.00
84		UPP	30.00		CRS	Susp/Sec	40.00
85		UPP	30.00		DVE	Susp/Sec	40.00
86		UPP	30.00		OLB	Susp/Sec	40.00
87		UPP	35.00		CED	Susp/Sec	40.00

MOTHER SEW DEAR Plate First Issue "Mother's Love" Series Individually Numbered

E-5217

30

81	Mother Needlepointing	15,000	$40.00	8.50"	UM	Secondary	$70.00

MAY YOUR CHRISTMAS BE BLESSED Figurine

E-5376

186

84	Girl with Long Hair & Bible	UPP	$37.50	5.75"	CRS	Susp/Sec	$75.00
85		UPP	37.50		DVE	Susp/Sec	70.00
86		UPP	37.50		OLB	Susp/Sec	68.00

LOVE IS KIND Figurine

E-5377

187

84	Girl with Mouse	UPP	$27.50	4.00"	CRS	Ret'd/Sec	$95.00
85		UPP	27.50		DVE	Ret'd/Sec	87.00
86		UPP	27.50		OLB	Ret'd/Sec	85.00
87		UPP	27.50		CED	Ret'd/Sec	80.00

JOY TO THE WORLD Figurine Nativity Addition

E-5378

188

84	Boy Playing Harp	UPP	$18.00	4.00"	CRS	Susp/Sec	$48.00
85		UPP	18.00		DVE	Susp/Sec	42.00
86		UPP	18.00		OLB	Susp/Sec	40.00
87		UPP	20.00		CED	Susp/Sec	38.00
88		UPP	20.00		FLW	Susp/Sec	38.00
89		UPP	25.00		B&A	Susp/Sec	36.00

ISN'T HE PRECIOUS Figurine Nativity Addition

E-5379

189

84	Girl with Broom	UPP	$20.00	5.00"	CRS	Secondary	$50.00
85		UPP	20.00		DVE	Secondary	40.00
86		UPP	20.00		OLB	Secondary	38.00
87		UPP	22.50		CED	Secondary	35.00
88		UPP	22.50		FLW	Secondary	35.00
89		UPP	27.50		B&A	Secondary	32.00
90		UPP	30.00		FLM	Secondary	32.00
91		UPP	30.00		VSL	Secondary	30.00
92		UPP	30.00		G/CL	Secondary	30.00
93		UPP	30.00		BFY	Primary	30.00
94		OPEN	30.00		TRP	Primary	30.00

With the opening of a new production facility in Indonesia, numerous pieces of whiteware (unpainted figurines) were inadvertently shipped to retailers. The few known sales of this piece range from $400.00 to $650.00. Full color photograph: 5th Ed., pg. 204.

A MONARCH IS BORN Figurine

E-5380 (190)

84	Boy with Butterfly at Manger	UPP	$33.00	5.00"	CRS	Susp/Sec	$80.00
85		UPP	33.00		DVE	Susp/Sec	72.00
86		UPP	33.00		OLB	Susp/Sec	68.00

HIS NAME IS JESUS Figurine

E-5381 (191)

84	Boys at Manger	UPP	$45.00	5.00"	CRS	Susp/Sec	$110.00
85		UPP	45.00		DVE	Susp/Sec	95.00
86		UPP	45.00		OLB	Susp/Sec	90.00
87		UPP	50.00		CED	Susp/Sec	88.00

FOR GOD SO LOVED THE WORLD Figurines Set of 4

E-5382 (192)

84	Deluxe 4 Piece Nativity	UPP	$70.00	5.00"	CRS	Susp/Sec	$140.00
85		UPP	70.00		DVE	Susp/Sec	125.00
86		UPP	70.00		OLB	Susp/Sec	120.00

WISHING YOU A MERRY CHRISTMAS Figurine, Dated

E-5383 (193)

84	Girl with Songbook	Annual	$17.00	4.75"	CRS	Secondary	$45.00

I'LL PLAY MY DRUM FOR HIM Figurine Mini Nativity Addition

E-5384 (87)

84	Drummer Boy	UPP	$10.00	3.50"	CRS	Secondary	$33.00
85		UPP	10.00		DVE	Secondary	25.00
86		UPP	10.00		OLB	Secondary	23.00
87		UPP	11.00		CED	Secondary	23.00
88		UPP	12.50		FLW	Secondary	20.00
89		UPP	13.50		B&A	Secondary	18.00
90		UPP	15.00		FLM	Secondary	16.00
91		UPP	15.00		VSL	Secondary	16.00
92		UPP	15.00		G/CL	Secondary	16.00
93		UPP	15.00		BFY	Primary	16.00
94		OPEN	16.00		TRP	Primary	16.00

OH WORSHIP THE LORD Figurine Mini Nativity Addition

E-5385 (194)

84	Boy Angel with Candle	UPP	$10.00	3.25"	CRS	Susp/Sec	$55.00
85		UPP	10.00		DVE	Susp/Sec	48.00
86		UPP	10.00		OLB	Susp/Sec	45.00

OH WORSHIP THE LORD Figurine Mini Nativity Addition

E-5386 (195)

84	Girl Angel Praying	UPP	$10.00	3.25"	CRS	Susp/Sec	$60.00
85		UPP	10.00		DVE	Susp/Sec	52.00
86		UPP	10.00		OLB	Susp/Sec	50.00

WISHING YOU A MERRY CHRISTMAS Ornament, Dated

E-5387 (193)

84	Girl with Songbook	Annual	$10.00	3.00"	CRS	Secondary	$40.00

JOY TO THE WORLD Ornament

E-5388 (188)

84	Boy Playing Harp	UPP	$10.00	2.50"	CRS	Ret'd/Sec	$48.00
85		UPP	10.00		DVE	Ret'd/Sec	45.00
86		UPP	10.00		OLB	Ret'd/Sec	42.00
87		UPP	11.00		CED	Ret'd/Sec	38.00

PEACE ON EARTH Ornament

E-5389 (196)

84	Boy in Choir	UPP	$10.00	3.00"	CRS	Susp/Sec	$45.00
85		UPP	10.00		DVE	Susp/Sec	38.00
86		UPP	10.00		OLB	Susp/Sec	35.00

MAY GOD BLESS YOU WITH A PERFECT SEASON Ornament

E-5390 (197)

84	Girl in Scarf and Hat	UPP	$10.00	3.00"	CRS	Susp/Sec	$40.00
85		UPP	10.00		DVE	Susp/Sec	38.00
86		UPP	10.00		OLB	Susp/Sec	35.00
87		UPP	10.00		CED	Susp/Sec	32.00
88		UPP	11.00		FLW	Susp/Sec	32.00
89		UPP	13.50		B&A	Susp/Sec	30.00

LOVE IS KIND Ornament
E-5391
198

Year	Description	Edition	Issue Price	Size	Mark	Status	Value
84	Girl with Gift	UPP	$10.00	2.50"	CRS	Susp/Sec	$42.00
85		UPP	10.00		DVE	Susp/Sec	40.00
86		UPP	10.00		OLB	Susp/Sec	35.00
87		UPP	10.00		CED	Susp/Sec	32.00
88		UPP	11.00		FLW	Susp/Sec	30.00
89		UPP	13.50		B&A	Susp/Sec	30.00

BLESSED ARE THE PURE IN HEART Ornament, Dated
E-5392
28

Year	Description	Edition	Issue Price	Size	Mark	Status	Value
84	Baby in Cradle	Annual	$10.00	2.00"	CRS	Secondary	$35.00

WISHING YOU A MERRY CHRISTMAS Bell, Dated
E-5393
193

Year	Description	Edition	Issue Price	Size	Mark	Status	Value
84	Girl with Songbook	Annual	$19.00	5.75"	CRS	Secondary	$50.00

WISHING YOU A MERRY CHRISTMAS Musical TUNE: We Wish You A Merry Christmas
E-5394
200

Year	Description	Edition	Issue Price	Size	Mark	Status	Value
84	Carollers with Puppy	UPP	$55.00	6.50"	CRS	Susp/Sec	$115.00
85		UPP	55.00		DVE	Susp/Sec	105.00
86		UPP	55.00		OLB	Susp/Sec	100.00

UNTO US A CHILD IS BORN Plate Fourth Issue "Christmas Collection" Series
Individually Numbered
E-5395
201

Year	Description	Edition	Issue Price	Size	Mark	Status	Value
84	Shepherds and Lambs on Hillside	15,000	$40.00	8.50"	UM	Secondary	$50.00
					CRS	Secondary	45.00

THE WONDER OF CHRISTMAS Plate, Dated Third Issue "Joy of Christmas" Series
E-5396
202

Year	Description	Edition	Issue Price	Size	Mark	Status	Value
84	Boy Pulling Girl and Tree on Sled	Annual	$40.00	8.50"	CRS	Secondary	$75.00

TIMMY Doll
E-5397
203

Year	Description	Edition	Issue Price	Size	Mark	Status	Value
84	Boy Jogger	UPP	$125.00	10.00"	CRS	Susp/Sec	$170.00
85		UPP	125.00		DVE	Susp/Sec	155.00
86		UPP	125.00		OLB	Susp/Sec	155.00
87		UPP	135.00		CED	Susp/Sec	150.00
88		UPP	135.00		FLW	Susp/Sec	150.00
89		UPP	145.00		B&A	Susp/Sec	150.00
90		UPP	150.00		FLM	Susp/Sec	150.00
91		UPP	150.00		VSL	Susp/Sec	150.00

COME LET US ADORE HIM Figurine
E-5619
62

Year	Description	Edition	Issue Price	Size	Mark	Status	Value
81	Manger Child	UPP	$10.00	2.00"	NM	Susp/Sec	$55.00
81		UPP	10.00		TRI	Susp/Sec	40.00
82		UPP	10.50		HRG	Susp/Sec	35.00
83		UPP	10.50		FSH	Susp/Sec	32.00
84		UPP	11.00		CRS	Susp/Sec	30.00
85		UPP	11.00		DVE	Susp/Sec	30.00

WE HAVE SEEN HIS STAR Bell
E-5620
16

Year	Description	Edition	Issue Price	Size	Mark	Status	Value
81	Boy Holding Lamb	UPP	$15.00	5.50"	UM	Susp/Sec	$55.00
84		UPP	15.00		CRS	Susp/Sec	48.00
85		UPP	19.00		DVE	Susp/Sec	45.00

DONKEY Figurine Nativity Addition

E-5621

63

Year	Description	Edition	Issue Price	Size	Mark	Market	Price
81	Donkey	UPP	$ 6.00	2.75"	UM	Secondary	$33.00
84		UPP	9.00		CRS	Secondary	22.00
85		UPP	9.00		DVE	Secondary	20.00
86		UPP	9.00		OLB	Secondary	18.00
87		UPP	11.00		CED	Secondary	17.00
88		UPP	11.00		FLW	Secondary	16.00
89		UPP	12.00		B&A	Secondary	15.00
90		UPP	13.50		FLM	Secondary	15.00
91		UPP	13.50		VSL	Secondary	15.00
92		UPP	13.50		G/CL	Secondary	15.00
93		UPP	13.50		BFY	Primary	15.00
94		OPEN	15.00		TRP	Primary	15.00

LET THE HEAVENS REJOICE Bell, Dated

E-5622

77

Year	Description	Edition	Issue Price	Size	Mark	Market	Price
81	Praying Angel Boy	Annual	$15.00	5.75"	UM	Secondary	$190.00

JESUS IS BORN Bell

E-5623

64

Year	Description	Edition	Issue Price	Size	Mark	Market	Price
81	Shepherd	UPP	$15.00	5.75"	UM	Susp/Sec	$55.00
84		UPP	19.00		CRS	Susp/Sec	48.00

THEY FOLLOWED THE STAR Figurines Set of 3

E-5624

65

Year	Description	Edition	Issue Price	Size	Mark	Market	Price
*	3 Kings on Camels	UPP	$130.00	8.75"	UM	Secondary	$275.00
81		UPP	130.00		TRI	Secondary	295.00
82		UPP	150.00		HRG	Secondary	250.00
83		UPP	150.00		FSH	Secondary	245.00
84		UPP	165.00		CRS	Secondary	240.00
85		UPP	165.00		DVE	Secondary	240.00
86		UPP	165.00		OLB	Secondary	235.00
87		UPP	175.00		CED	Secondary	235.00
88		UPP	175.00		FLW	Secondary	230.00
89		UPP	190.00		B&A	Secondary	230.00
90		UPP	200.00		FLM	Secondary	225.00
91		UPP	200.00		VSL	Secondary	225.00
92		UPP	200.00		G/CL	Primary	225.00
93		UPP	225.00		BFY	Primary	225.00
94		OPEN	225.00		TRP	Primary	225.00

* UNMARKED pieces could have been produced in any of the years of production.

BUT LOVE GOES ON FOREVER Ornament

E-5627

56

Year	Description	Edition	Issue Price	Size	Mark	Market	Price
*	Boy Angel on Cloud	UPP	$ 6.00	3.00"	UM	Susp/Sec	$130.00
81		UPP	6.00		TRI	Susp/Sec	135.00
82		UPP	6.00		HRG	Susp/Sec	125.00
83		UPP	9.00		FSH	Susp/Sec	110.00
84		UPP	10.00		CRS	Susp/Sec	100.00
85		UPP	10.00		DVE	Susp/Sec	95.00

* UNMARKED pieces could have been produced in any of the years of production.

BUT LOVE GOES ON FOREVER Ornament

E-5628

57

Year	Description	Edition	Issue Price	Size	Mark	Market	Price
*	Girl Angel on Cloud	UPP	$ 6.00	3.00"	UM	Susp/Sec	$140.00
81		UPP	6.00		TRI	Susp/Sec	150.00
82		UPP	6.00		HRG	Susp/Sec	130.00
83		UPP	9.00		FSH	Susp/Sec	110.00
84		UPP	10.00		CRS	Susp/Sec	105.00
85		UPP	10.00		DVE	Susp/Sec	105.00

* UNMARKED pieces could have been produced in any of the years of production.

LET THE HEAVENS REJOICE Ornament, Dated

E-5629

77

Year	Description	Edition	Issue Price	Size	Mark	Market	Price
81	Praying Angel Boy	Annual	$ 6.00	3.10"	TRI	Secondary	$240.00

Some ornaments are without the patch on the angel. The GREENBOOK TRUMARKET PRICE is $270.00.

UNTO US A CHILD IS BORN Ornament
E-5630
64

	Description		Issue Price	Size	Mark	Status	Value
81	Shepherd	UPP	$ 6.00	3.25"	NM	Susp/Sec	$70.00
81		UPP	6.00		TRI	Susp/Sec	65.00
82		UPP	6.00		HRG	Susp/Sec	55.00
83		UPP	9.00		FSH	Susp/Sec	52.00
84		UPP	10.00		CRS	Susp/Sec	50.00
85		UPP	10.00		DVE	Susp/Sec	48.00

BABY'S FIRST CHRISTMAS Ornament
E-5631
1

	Description		Issue Price	Size	Mark	Status	Value
*	Boy with Teddy	UPP	$ 6.00	3.00"	UM	Susp/Sec	$60.00
81		UPP	6.00		TRI	Susp/Sec	65.00
82		UPP	6.50		HRG	Susp/Sec	55.00
83		UPP	9.00		FSH	Susp/Sec	52.00
84		UPP	10.00		CRS	Susp/Sec	50.00
85		UPP	10.00		DVE	Susp/Sec	48.00

* UNMARKED pieces could have been produced in any of the years of production.

BABY'S FIRST CHRISTMAS Ornament
E-5632
2

	Description		Issue Price	Size	Mark	Status	Value
*	Girl with Bunny	UPP	$ 6.00	3.00"	UM	Susp/Sec	$65.00
81		UPP	6.00		TRI	Susp/Sec	70.00
82		UPP	6.50		HRG	Susp/Sec	62.00
83		UPP	9.00		FSH	Susp/Sec	58.00
84		UPP	10.00		CRS	Susp/Sec	55.00
85		UPP	10.00		DVE	Susp/Sec	52.00

* UNMARKED pieces could have been produced in any of the years of production.

COME LET US ADORE HIM Ornaments Set of 4
E-5633
22

	Description		Issue Price	Size	Mark	Status	Value
*	Jesus, Mary, Joseph & Lamb	UPP	$22.00	2.50"	UM	Susp/Sec	$145.00
81	Mixed sets TRI/HRG and HRG/FSH	UPP	22.00		TRI	Susp/Sec	150.00
82	are common. Take lower value.	UPP	25.00		HRG	Susp/Sec	140.00
83		UPP	31.50		FSH	Susp/Sec	130.00
84		UPP	31.50		CRS	Susp/Sec	125.00

* UNMARKED pieces could have been produced in any of the years of production.

WEE THREE KINGS Ornaments Set of 3
E-5634
66

	Description		Issue Price	Size	Mark	Status	Value
*	Three Kings	UPP	$19.00	3.50"	UM	Susp/Sec	$140.00
81	Mixed sets TRI/HRG and HRG/FSH	UPP	19.00		TRI	Susp/Sec	150.00
82	are common. Take lower value.	UPP	19.00		HRG	Susp/Sec	135.00
83		UPP	25.00		FSH	Susp/Sec	130.00
84		UPP	27.50		CRS	Susp/Sec	125.00

* UNMARKED pieces could have been produced in any of the years of production.

WEE THREE KINGS Figurines Set of 3 Nativity Addition
E-5635
66

	Description		Issue Price	Size	Mark	Status	Value
*	Three Kings	UPP	$40.00	5.50"	UM	Secondary	$115.00
81	Mixed sets TRI/HRG and HRG/FSH	UPP	40.00		TRI	Secondary	125.00
82	are common. Take lower value.	UPP	50.00		HRG	Secondary	110.00
83		UPP	50.00		FSH	Secondary	100.00
84		UPP	55.00		CRS	Secondary	95.00
85		UPP	55.00		DVE	Secondary	90.00
86		UPP	55.00		OLB	Secondary	85.00
87		UPP	60.00		CED	Secondary	85.00
88		UPP	60.00		FLW	Secondary	80.00
89		UPP	70.00		B&A	Secondary	78.00
90		UPP	75.00		FLM	Secondary	78.00
91		UPP	75.00		VSL	Secondary	75.00
92		UPP	75.00		G/CL	Primary	75.00
93		UPP	75.00		BFY	Primary	75.00
94		OPEN	75.00		TRP	Primary	75.00

* UNMARKED pieces could have been produced in any of the years of production.

REJOICE O EARTH Figurine Nativity Addition
E-5636
67

Year	Description	Status	Issue Price	Size	Mark	Market	Value
*	Angel with Trumpet	UPP	$15.00	5.00"	UM	Secondary	$60.00
81		UPP	15.00		TRI	Secondary	65.00
82		UPP	19.00		HRG	Secondary	50.00
83		UPP	19.00		FSH	Secondary	48.00
84		UPP	20.00		CRS	Secondary	45.00
85		UPP	20.00		DVE	Secondary	42.00
86		UPP	20.00		OLB	Secondary	40.00
87		UPP	22.50		CED	Secondary	38.00
88		UPP	22.50		FLW	Secondary	35.00
89		UPP	27.50		B&A	Secondary	33.00
90		UPP	30.00		FLM	Secondary	32.00
91		UPP	30.00		VSL	Secondary	30.00
92		UPP	30.00		G/CL	Primary	30.00
93		UPP	30.00		BFY	Primary	30.00
94		OPEN	30.00		TRP	Primary	30.00

* UNMARKED pieces could have been produced in any of the years of production.

THE HEAVENLY LIGHT Figurine Nativity Addition
E-5637
68

Year	Description	Status	Issue Price	Size	Mark	Market	Value
*	Angel with Flashlight	UPP	$15.00	4.85"	UM	Secondary	$60.00
81		UPP	15.00		TRI	Secondary	65.00
82		UPP	17.00		HRG	Secondary	50.00
83		UPP	17.00		FSH	Secondary	45.00
84		UPP	19.00		CRS	Secondary	42.00
85		UPP	19.00		DVE	Secondary	40.00
86		UPP	19.00		OLB	Secondary	38.00
87		UPP	21.00		CED	Secondary	35.00
88		UPP	21.00		FLW	Secondary	32.00
89		UPP	25.00		B&A	Secondary	30.00
90		UPP	27.50		FLM	Secondary	28.00
91		UPP	27.50		VSL	Secondary	27.50
92		UPP	27.50		G/CL	Primary	27.50
93		UPP	27.50		BFY	Primary	27.50
94		OPEN	27.50		TRP	Primary	27.50

* UNMARKED pieces could have been produced in any of the years of production.

COW Figurine Nativity Addition
E-5638
69

Year	Description	Status	Issue Price	Size	Mark	Market	Value
*	Cow with Bell	UPP	$16.00	3.50"	UM	Secondary	$54.00
84		UPP	21.00		CRS	Secondary	42.00
85		UPP	21.00		DVE	Secondary	40.00
86		UPP	22.50		OLB	Secondary	37.00
87		UPP	22.50		CED	Secondary	35.00
88		UPP	27.50		FLW	Secondary	35.00
89		UPP	30.00		B&A	Secondary	33.00
90		UPP	32.50		FLM	Secondary	33.00
91		UPP	32.50		VSL	Secondary	32.50
92		UPP	32.50		G/CL	Primary	32.50
93		UPP	32.50		BFY	Primary	32.50
94		OPEN	32.50		TRP	Primary	32.50

* UNMARKED pieces could have been produced in any of the years of production.

ISN'T HE WONDERFUL Figurine Nativity Addition
E-5639
70

Year	Description	Status	Issue Price	Size	Mark	Market	Value
*	Boy Angel Praying with Harp	UPP	$12.00	4.75"	UM	Susp/Sec	$65.00
81		UPP	12.00		TRI	Susp/Sec	70.00
82		UPP	15.00		HRG	Susp/Sec	62.00
83		UPP	15.00		FSH	Susp/Sec	60.00
84		UPP	17.00		CRS	Susp/Sec	58.00
85		UPP	17.00		DVE	Susp/Sec	55.00

* UNMARKED pieces could have been produced in any of the years of production.

<u>ISN'T HE WONDERFUL</u> Figurine Nativity Addition

E-5640

71

Year	Description	Production	Issue Price	Size	Mark	Status	Value
*	Girl Angel Praying with Harp	UPP	$12.00	4.75"	UM	Susp/Sec	$72.00
81		UPP	12.00		TRI	Susp/Sec	75.00
82		UPP	15.00		HRG	Susp/Sec	70.00
83		UPP	15.00		FSH	Susp/Sec	68.00
84		UPP	17.00		CRS	Susp/Sec	65.00
85		UPP	17.00		DVE	Susp/Sec	62.00

* UNMARKED pieces could have been produced in any of the years of production.

<u>THEY FOLLOWED THE STAR</u> Figurine

E-5641

72

Year	Description	Production	Issue Price	Size	Mark	Status	Value
*	"Follow Me" Angel with	UPP	$ 75.00	6.00"	UM	Susp/Sec	$210.00
81	Three Kings	UPP	75.00		TRI	Susp/Sec	215.00
82		UPP	90.00		HRG	Susp/Sec	195.00
83		UPP	90.00		FSH	Susp/Sec	190.00
84		UPP	100.00		CRS	Susp/Sec	185.00
85		UPP	100.00		DVE	Susp/Sec	180.00

* UNMARKED pieces could have been produced in any of the years of production.

<u>SILENT KNIGHT</u> Musical TUNE: Silent Night

E-5642

73

Year	Description	Production	Issue Price	Size	Mark	Status	Value
*	Boy Angel & Knight	UPP	$45.00	6.25"	UM	Susp/Sec	$220.00
81		UPP	45.00		TRI	Susp/Sec	225.00
82		UPP	55.00		HRG	Susp/Sec	210.00
83		UPP	55.00		FSH	Susp/Sec	205.00
84		UPP	60.00		CRS	Susp/Sec	200.00
85		UPP	60.00		DVE	Susp/Sec	195.00

* UNMARKED pieces could have been produced in any of the years of production.
Exists in a double mark TRIANGLE/HOURGLASS.

<u>TWO SECTION WALL</u> Figurines Set of 2 Nativity Addition

E-5644

74

Year	Description	Production	Issue Price	Size	Mark	Status	Value
*	Two Section Wall	UPP	$ 60.00	6.00"	UM	Secondary	$145.00
81		UPP	60.00		TRI	Secondary	165.00
82		UPP	80.00		HRG	Secondary	145.00
83		UPP	80.00		FSH	Secondary	138.00
84		UPP	90.00		CRS	Secondary	135.00
85		UPP	90.00		DVE	Secondary	132.00
86		UPP	90.00		OLB	Secondary	130.00
87		UPP	100.00		CED	Secondary	125.00
88		UPP	100.00		FLW	Secondary	125.00
89		UPP	110.00		B&A	Secondary	120.00
90		UPP	120.00		FLM	Secondary	120.00
91		UPP	120.00		VSL	Secondary	120.00
92		UPP	120.00		G/CL	Primary	120.00
93		UPP	120.00		BFY	Primary	120.00
94		OPEN	120.00		TRP	Primary	120.00

* UNMARKED pieces could have been produced in any of the years of production.

<u>REJOICE O EARTH</u> Musical TUNE: Joy To The World

E-5645

67

Year	Description	Production	Issue Price	Size	Mark	Status	Value
81	Angel with Trumpet	UPP	$35.00	6.25"	UM	Ret'd/Sec	$130.00
81		UPP	35.00		TRI	Ret'd/Sec	145.00
82		UPP	40.00		HRG	Ret'd/Sec	120.00
83		UPP	40.00		FSH	Ret'd/Sec	115.00
84		UPP	45.00		CRS	Ret'd/Sec	110.00
85		UPP	45.00		DVE	Ret'd/Sec	105.00
86		UPP	45.00		OLB	Ret'd/Sec	100.00
87		UPP	50.00		CED	Ret'd/Sec	98.00
88		UPP	50.00		FLW	Ret'd/Sec	95.00

<u>COME LET US ADORE HIM</u> Plate First Issue "Christmas Collection" Series
Individually Numbered

E-5646

22

Year	Description	Production	Issue Price	Size	Mark	Status	Value
81	Nativity Scene	15,000	$40.00	8.50"	UM	Secondary	$60.00

BUT LOVE GOES ON FOREVER — Candle Climbers — Set of 2
E-6118
56 57

81	Angels on Clouds	UPP	$14.00	2.50"	UM	Susp/Sec	$90.00
84		UPP	20.00		CRS	Susp/Sec	78.00
85		UPP	20.00		DVE	Susp/Sec	75.00
86		UPP	20.00		OLB	Susp/Sec	70.00
87		UPP	22.50		CED	Susp/Sec	65.00
88		UPP	25.00		FLW	Susp/Sec	62.00

WE HAVE SEEN HIS STAR — Ornament
E-6120
16

81	Boy Holding Lamb	UPP	$ 6.00	3.00"	NM	Ret'd/Sec	$70.00
81		UPP	6.00		TRI	Ret'd/Sec	65.00
82		UPP	6.00		HRG	Ret'd/Sec	60.00
83		UPP	9.00		FSH	Ret'd/Sec	58.00
84		UPP	10.00		CRS	Ret'd/Sec	55.00

MIKEY — Doll
E-6214B
75

81	Mikey	UPP	$150.00	16.50"	UM	Susp/Sec	$230.00
83		UPP	175.00		FSH	Susp/Sec	220.00
84		UPP	200.00		CRS	Susp/Sec	220.00
85		UPP	200.00		DVE	Susp/Sec	220.00

DEBBIE — Doll
E-6214G
76

81	Debbie	UPP	$150.00	16.50"	UM	Susp/Sec	$240.00
83		UPP	175.00		FSH	Susp/Sec	230.00
84		UPP	200.00		CRS	Susp/Sec	230.00
85		UPP	200.00		DVE	Susp/Sec	230.00

GOD SENDS THE GIFT OF HIS LOVE — Figurine
E-6613
204

84	Girl with Present and Kitten	UPP	$22.50	5.75"	FSH	Susp/Sec	$115.00
84		UPP	22.50		CRS	Susp/Sec	68.00
85		UPP	22.50		DVE	Susp/Sec	62.00
86		UPP	22.50		OLB	Susp/Sec	60.00
87		UPP	22.50		CED	Susp/Sec	58.00

COLLECTION PLAQUE — Plaque
E-6901
56

82	Boy Angel on Cloud	UPP	$19.00	3.50"	HRG	Susp/Sec	$110.00
83		UPP	19.00		FSH	Susp/Sec	55.00
84		UPP	20.00		CRS	Susp/Sec	50.00
85		UPP	20.00		DVE	Susp/Sec	42.00
86		UPP	20.00		OLB	Susp/Sec	40.00

Exists in a double mark HOURGLASS/FISH.

GOD IS LOVE, DEAR VALENTINE — Figurine
E-7153
102

82	Boy Holding Heart	UPP	$16.00	5.50"	TRI	Susp/Sec	$55.00
82		UPP	16.00		HRG	Susp/Sec	45.00
83		UPP	16.00		FSH	Susp/Sec	40.00
84		UPP	17.00		CRS	Susp/Sec	35.00
85		UPP	17.00		DVE	Susp/Sec	35.00
86		UPP	17.00		OLB	Susp/Sec	30.00

GOD IS LOVE, DEAR VALENTINE — Figurine
E-7154
103

82	Girl Holding Heart	UPP	$16.00	5.50"	TRI	Susp/Sec	$60.00
82		UPP	16.00		HRG	Susp/Sec	45.00
83		UPP	16.00		FSH	Susp/Sec	40.00
84		UPP	17.00		CRS	Susp/Sec	35.00
85		UPP	17.00		DVE	Susp/Sec	35.00
86		UPP	17.00		OLB	Susp/Sec	35.00

THANKING HIM FOR YOU — Figurine
E-7155
58

82	Girl Praying in Field	UPP	$16.00	5.50"	HRG	Susp/Sec	$68.00
83		UPP	16.00		FSH	Susp/Sec	60.00
84		UPP	17.00		CRS	Susp/Sec	55.00

I BELIEVE IN MIRACLES Figurine

E-7156	82	Boy Holding Chick	UPP	$17.00	4.25"	HRG	S/R/Sec	$115.00
105	83		UPP	17.00		FSH	S/R/Sec	100.00
	84		UPP	19.00		CRS	S/R/Sec	95.00
	85		UPP	19.00		DVE	S/R/Sec	90.00

The above piece, E-7156, was re-introduced in July 1987 as E-7156R (below).
Both pieces were subsequently retired in January 1992.

I BELIEVE IN MIRACLES Figurine

E-7156R	87	Boy Holding Bluebird	UPP	$22.50	4.50"	CED*	Ret'd/Sec	$78.00
374	88		UPP	22.50		FLW	Ret'd/Sec	70.00
	89		UPP	25.00		B&A	Ret'd/Sec	65.00
	90		UPP	27.50		FLM	Ret'd/Sec	62.00
	91		UPP	27.50		VSL	Ret'd/Sec	60.00

First introduced in 1982 as E-7156, the original version of this figurine had the boy holding a yellow chick. E-7156 was suspended in 1985, and in 1987 was re-sculptured and returned to production as E-7156R. Among the changes made was the addition of the incised "Sam B" on the base of the figurine, and a change in the color of the chick - from yellow to blue. The re-sculptured piece is also considerably larger than the original version. * During the early part of production in 1987, the molds from the suspended piece, E-7156, were pulled and used along with the molds for the new re-introduced piece, E-7156R. Shipments of figurines crafted from the old suspended mold but with the new blue painting of the chick were made before the error was discovered. These pieces are the rare version. All rare versions have the CED Symbol. The GREENBOOK TRUMARKET PRICE for the rare version is $225.00. Full color photographs: 4th Ed., pg. 197 or 5th Ed., pg. 206. One color photo: 6th Ed., pg. 226.

THERE IS JOY IN SERVING JESUS Figurine

E-7157	82	Waitress Carrying Food	UPP	$17.00	5.50"	HRG	Ret'd/Sec	$70.00
106	83		UPP	17.00		FSH	Ret'd/Sec	55.00
	84		UPP	19.00		CRS	Ret'd/Sec	52.00
	85		UPP	19.00		DVE	Ret'd/Sec	50.00
	86		UPP	19.00		OLB	Ret'd/Sec	48.00

LOVE BEARETH ALL THINGS Figurine

E-7158	82	Nurse Giving Shot to Bear	UPP	$25.00	5.15"	HRG	Secondary	$75.00
107	83		UPP	25.00		FSH	Secondary	58.00
	84		UPP	27.50		CRS	Secondary	52.00
	85		UPP	27.50		DVE	Secondary	50.00
	86		UPP	27.50		OLB	Secondary	48.00
	87		UPP	30.00		CED	Secondary	45.00
	88		UPP	32.50		FLW	Secondary	42.00
	89		UPP	36.00		B&A	Secondary	42.00
	90		UPP	37.50		FLM	Secondary	40.00
	91		UPP	37.50		VSL	Secondary	40.00
	92		UPP	37.50		G/CL	Secondary	40.00
	93		UPP	37.50		BFY	Primary	40.00
	94		OPEN	40.00		TRP	Primary	40.00

LORD GIVE ME PATIENCE Figurine

E-7159	82	Bandaged Boy by Sign	UPP	$25.00	5.50"	HRG	Susp/Sec	$60.00
108	83		UPP	25.00		FSH	Susp/Sec	55.00
	84		UPP	27.50		CRS	Susp/Sec	50.00
	85		UPP	27.50		DVE	Susp/Sec	45.00

THE PERFECT GRANDPA Figurine

E-7160	82	Grandpa in Rocking Chair	UPP	$25.00	5.00"	HRG	Susp/Sec	$80.00
109	83		UPP	25.00		FSH	Susp/Sec	72.00
	84		UPP	27.50		CRS	Susp/Sec	70.00
	85		UPP	27.50		DVE	Susp/Sec	68.00
	86		UPP	27.50		OLB	Susp/Sec	65.00

HIS SHEEP AM I Figurine
E-7161
110

*	Shepherd Painting Lamb	UPP	$25.00	5.25"	UM	Susp/Sec	$120.00
82		UPP	25.00		HRG	Susp/Sec	72.00
83		UPP	25.00		FSH	Susp/Sec	68.00
84		UPP	27.50		CRS	Susp/Sec	65.00

*UNMARKED pieces could have been produced in any of the years of production.

LOVE IS SHARING Figurine
E-7162
111

82	Girl at School Desk	UPP	$25.00	4.75"	HRG	Susp/Sec	$175.00
83		UPP	25.00		FSH	Susp/Sec	160.00
84		UPP	27.50		CRS	Susp/Sec	155.00

GOD IS WATCHING OVER YOU Figurine
E-7163
112

82	Boy with Ice Bag on Head	UPP	$27.50	5.25"	HRG	Susp/Sec	$100.00
83		UPP	27.50		FSH	Susp/Sec	90.00
84		UPP	30.00		CRS	Susp/Sec	85.00

BLESS THIS HOUSE Figurine
E-7164
113

82	Boy & Girl Painting Dog House	UPP	$45.00	5.50"	HRG	Susp/Sec	$225.00
83		UPP	45.00		FSH	Susp/Sec	200.00
84		UPP	50.00		CRS	Susp/Sec	185.00

LET THE WHOLE WORLD KNOW Figurine
E-7165
114

82	Boy & Girl in Baptism Bucket	UPP	$45.00	6.00"	HRG	Susp/Sec	$125.00
83		UPP	45.00		FSH	Susp/Sec	115.00
84		UPP	50.00		CRS	Susp/Sec	110.00
85		UPP	50.00		DVE	Susp/Sec	105.00
86		UPP	50.00		OLB	Susp/Sec	100.00
87		UPP	50.00		CED	Susp/Sec	95.00

THE LORD BLESS YOU AND KEEP YOU Frame
E-7166
38

82	Bride and Groom	UPP	$22.50	5.50"	HRG	Susp/Sec	$65.00
83		UPP	22.50		FSH	Susp/Sec	62.00
84		UPP	25.00		CRS	Susp/Sec	60.00
85		UPP	25.00		DVE	Susp/Sec	58.00
86		UPP	25.00		OLB	Susp/Sec	55.00
87		UPP	25.00		CED	Susp/Sec	50.00
88		UPP	27.50		FLW	Susp/Sec	45.00
89		UPP	30.00		B&A	Susp/Sec	42.00
90		UPP	32.50		FLM	Susp/Sec	40.00
91		UPP	32.50		VSL	Susp/Sec	38.00
92		UPP	32.50		G/CL	Susp/Sec	35.00
93		UPP	32.50		BFY	Susp/Sec	33.00

THE LORD BLESS YOU AND KEEP YOU Covered Box
E-7167
38

82	Bride and Groom	UPP	$22.50	5.00"	HRG	Susp/Sec	$58.00
83		UPP	22.50		FSH	Susp/Sec	55.00
84		UPP	25.00		CRS	Susp/Sec	52.00
85		UPP	25.00		DVE	Susp/Sec	50.00

MY GUARDIAN ANGEL Frame
E-7168
265

82	Boy Angel	UPP	$18.00	5.50"	HRG	Susp/Sec	$60.00
83		UPP	18.00		FSH	Susp/Sec	55.00
84		UPP	19.00		CRS	Susp/Sec	50.00

MY GUARDIAN ANGEL Frame
E-7169
266

82	Girl Angel	UPP	$18.00	5.50"	HRG	Susp/Sec	$65.00
83		UPP	18.00		FSH	Susp/Sec	60.00
84		UPP	19.00		CRS	Susp/Sec	58.00

JESUS LOVES ME Frame
E-7170
1

82	Boy with Teddy	UPP	$17.00	4.25"	HRG	Susp/Sec	$58.00
83		UPP	17.00		FSH	Susp/Sec	55.00
84		UPP	19.00		CRS	Susp/Sec	52.00
85		UPP	19.00		DVE	Susp/Sec	50.00

JESUS LOVES ME Frame

E-7171 (2)

82	Girl with Bunny	UPP	$17.00	4.25"	HRG	Susp/Sec	$65.00
83		UPP	17.00		FSH	Susp/Sec	62.00
84		UPP	19.00		CRS	Susp/Sec	60.00
85		UPP	19.00		DVE	Susp/Sec	58.00

REJOICING WITH YOU Plate

E-7172 (50)

82	Christening	UPP	$30.00	7.25"	UM	Susp/Sec	$45.00
84		UPP	30.00		CRS	Susp/Sec	40.00
85		UPP	30.00		DVE	Susp/Sec	40.00

THE PURR-FECT GRANDMA Plate Second Issue "Mother's Love" Series
Individually Numbered

E-7173 (33)

82	Grandma in Rocker	15,000	$40.00	8.50"	UM	Secondary	$45.00

MAKE A JOYFUL NOISE Plate Second Issue "Inspired Thoughts" Series
Individually Numbered

E-7174 (5)

82	Girl with Goose	15,000	$40.00	8.50"	UM	Secondary	$45.00
					CRS	Secondary	40.00

THE LORD BLESS YOU AND KEEP YOU Bell

E-7175 (46)

82	Boy Graduate	UPP	$17.00	5.75"	UM	Susp/Sec	$45.00
84		UPP	19.00		CRS	Susp/Sec	42.00
85		UPP	19.00		DVE	Susp/Sec	40.00

THE LORD BLESS YOU AND KEEP YOU Bell

E-7176 (47)

82	Girl Graduate	UPP	$17.00	5.75"	UM	Susp/Sec	$60.00
84		UPP	19.00		CRS	Susp/Sec	52.00
85		UPP	19.00		DVE	Susp/Sec	50.00

THE LORD BLESS YOU AND KEEP YOU Frame

E-7177 (46)

82	Boy Graduate	UPP	$18.00	5.50"	HRG	Susp/Sec	$52.00
83		UPP	18.00		FSH	Susp/Sec	48.00
84		UPP	19.00		CRS	Susp/Sec	46.00
85		UPP	19.00		DVE	Susp/Sec	45.00
86		UPP	19.00		OLB	Susp/Sec	42.00
87		UPP	20.00		CED	Susp/Sec	40.00

THE LORD BLESS YOU AND KEEP YOU Frame

E-7178 (47)

82	Girl Graduate	UPP	$18.00	5.25"	HRG	Susp/Sec	$75.00
83		UPP	18.00		FSH	Susp/Sec	72.00
84		UPP	19.00		CRS	Susp/Sec	70.00
85		UPP	19.00		DVE	Susp/Sec	68.00
86		UPP	19.00		OLB	Susp/Sec	65.00
87		UPP	20.00		CED	Susp/Sec	62.00

THE LORD BLESS YOU AND KEEP YOU Bell

E-7179 (38)

82	Bride and Groom	UPP	$22.50	5.50"	UM	Susp/Sec	$75.00
84		UPP	25.00		CRS	Susp/Sec	72.00
85		UPP	25.00		DVE	Susp/Sec	70.00
86		UPP	25.00		OLB	Susp/Sec	68.00
87		UPP	25.00		CED	Susp/Sec	68.00
88		UPP	30.00		FLW	Susp/Sec	65.00
89		UPP	33.00		B&A	Susp/Sec	62.00
90		UPP	35.00		FLM	Susp/Sec	60.00
91		UPP	35.00		VSL	Susp/Sec	58.00
92		UPP	35.00		G/CL	Susp/Sec	55.00
93		UPP	35.00		BFY	Susp/Sec	50.00

THE LORD BLESS YOU AND KEEP YOU Musical TUNE: Wedding March

E-7180 (38)

Year	Description	Status	Issue Price	Size	Mark	Market	Value
82	Bride and Groom	UPP	$55.00	6.00"	UM	Secondary	$130.00
84	on Cake	UPP	55.00		CRS	Secondary	100.00
85		UPP	60.00		DVE	Secondary	90.00
86		UPP	60.00		OLB	Secondary	85.00
87		UPP	60.00		CED	Secondary	85.00
88		UPP	70.00		FLW	Secondary	85.00
89		UPP	75.00		B&A	Secondary	85.00
90		UPP	80.00		FLM	Secondary	85.00
91		UPP	80.00		VSL	Secondary	85.00
92		UPP	80.00		G/CL	Secondary	85.00
93		UPP	85.00		BFY	Secondary	85.00
94		OPEN	85.00		TRP	Primary	85.00

MOTHER SEW DEAR Bell

E-7181 (30)

Year	Description	Status	Issue Price	Size	Mark	Market	Value
82	Mother Needlepointing	UPP	$17.00	5.50"	UM	Susp/Sec	$52.00
84		UPP	19.00		CRS	Susp/Sec	45.00
85		UPP	19.00		DVE	Susp/Sec	42.00
86		UPP	19.00		OLB	Susp/Sec	40.00
87		UPP	20.00		CED	Susp/Sec	38.00
88		UPP	22.50		FLW	Susp/Sec	37.00

MOTHER SEW DEAR Musical TUNE: You Light Up My Life

E-7182 (30)

Year	Description	Status	Issue Price	Size	Mark	Market	Value
82	Mother Needlepointing	UPP	$35.00	6.25"	UM	Secondary	$95.00
84		UPP	37.50		CRS	Secondary	75.00
85		UPP	37.50		DVE	Secondary	70.00
86		UPP	37.50		OLB	Secondary	68.00
87		UPP	37.50		CED	Secondary	65.00
88		UPP	45.00		FLW	Secondary	62.00
89		UPP	50.00		B&A	Secondary	60.00
90		UPP	55.00		FLM	Secondary	60.00
91		UPP	55.00		VSL	Secondary	60.00
92		UPP	55.00		G/CL	Primary	60.00
93		UPP	60.00		BFY	Primary	60.00
94		OPEN	60.00		TRP	Primary	60.00

THE PURR-FECT GRANDMA Bell

E-7183 (33)

Year	Description	Status	Issue Price	Size	Mark	Market	Value
82	Grandma in Rocker	UPP	$17.00	5.50"	UM	Susp/Sec	$52.00
84		UPP	19.00		CRS	Susp/Sec	50.00
85		UPP	19.00		DVE	Susp/Sec	45.00
86		UPP	19.00		OLB	Susp/Sec	42.00
87		UPP	20.00		CED	Susp/Sec	40.00
88		UPP	22.50		FLW	Susp/Sec	38.00

THE PURR-FECT GRANDMA Musical TUNE: Always In My Heart

E-7184 (33)

Year	Description	Status	Issue Price	Size	Mark	Market	Value
82	Grandma in Rocker	UPP	$35.00	6.00"	UM	Susp/Sec	$110.00
84		UPP	37.50		CRS	Susp/Sec	90.00
85		UPP	37.50		DVE	Susp/Sec	85.00
86		UPP	37.50		OLB	Susp/Sec	82.00
87		UPP	37.50		CED	Susp/Sec	80.00
88		UPP	45.00		FLW	Susp/Sec	80.00
89		UPP	50.00		B&A	Susp/Sec	78.00
90		UPP	55.00		FLM	Susp/Sec	78.00
91		UPP	55.00		VSL	Susp/Sec	75.00
92		UPP	55.00		G/CL	Susp/Sec	72.00
93		UPP	60.00		BFY	Susp/Sec	70.00

LOVE IS SHARING Musical TUNE: School Days

E-7185 (111)

Year	Description	Status	Issue Price	Size	Mark	Market	Value
82	Girl at School Desk	UPP	$40.00	5.75"	HRG	Ret'd/Sec	$185.00
83		UPP	40.00		FSH	Ret'd/Sec	160.00
84		UPP	45.00		CRS	Ret'd/Sec	155.00
85		UPP	45.00		DVE	Ret'd/Sec	150.00

LET THE WHOLE WORLD KNOW — Musical — TUNE: What A Friend We Have In Jesus

E-7186 (114)

Yr	Description		Issue Price	Size	Mark	Status	Value
82	Boy & Girl in Baptism Bucket	UPP	$60.00	6.25"	UM	Susp/Sec	$160.00
82		UPP	60.00		HRG	Susp/Sec	145.00
83		UPP	60.00		FSH	Susp/Sec	130.00
84		UPP	65.00		CRS	Susp/Sec	125.00
85		UPP	65.00		DVE	Susp/Sec	120.00
86		UPP	65.00		OLB	Susp/Sec	115.00

MOTHER SEW DEAR — Frame

E-7241 (30)

Yr	Description		Issue Price	Size	Mark	Status	Value
82	Mother Needlepointing	UPP	$18.00	5.50"	HRG	Susp/Sec	$52.00
83		UPP	18.00		FSH	Susp/Sec	50.00
84		UPP	19.00		CRS	Susp/Sec	48.00
85		UPP	19.00		DVE	Susp/Sec	45.00
86		UPP	19.00		OLB	Susp/Sec	42.00

THE PURR-FECT GRANDMA — Frame

E-7242 (33)

Yr	Description		Issue Price	Size	Mark	Status	Value
82	Grandma in Rocker	UPP	$18.00	5.50"	HRG	Susp/Sec	$55.00
83		UPP	18.00		FSH	Susp/Sec	50.00
84		UPP	19.00		CRS	Susp/Sec	48.00
85		UPP	19.00		DVE	Susp/Sec	46.00
86		UPP	19.00		OLB	Susp/Sec	45.00
87		UPP	20.00		CED	Susp/Sec	42.00
88		UPP	22.50		FLW	Susp/Sec	40.00

CUBBY — Doll — Individually Numbered on Bottom of Foot — Certificate of Authenticity

E-7267B (115)

Yr	Description		Issue Price	Size	Mark	Status	Value
82	Groom Doll	5,000	$200.00	18.00"	UM	Secondary	$450.00

TAMMY — Doll — Individually Numbered on Bottom of Foot — Certificate of Authenticity

E-7267G (116)

Yr	Description		Issue Price	Size	Mark	Status	Value
82	Bride Doll	5,000	$300.00	18.00"	UM	Secondary	$625.00

RETAILER'S DOME — Figurine under Dome — Gift to Centers

E-7350 (411)

Yr	Description		Issue Price	Size	Mark	Status	Value
84	Kids on Cloud under Dome	UPP	GIFT	9.00"	CRS	Secondary	$800.00
						w/o dome	625.00

Full color photograph: 5th Ed., pg. 194.

LOVE IS PATIENT — Figurine

E-9251 (135)

Yr	Description		Issue Price	Size	Mark	Status	Value
83	Boy Holding Blackboard	UPP	$35.00	5.00"	FSH	Susp/Sec	$90.00
84	with Teacher	UPP	35.00		CRS	Susp/Sec	85.00
85		UPP	35.00		DVE	Susp/Sec	82.00

FORGIVING IS FORGETTING — Figurine

E-9252 (136)

Yr	Description		Issue Price	Size	Mark	Status	Value
83	Boy & Girl with Bandage	UPP	$37.50	5.75"	FSH	Susp/Sec	$86.00
84		UPP	37.50		CRS	Susp/Sec	82.00
85		UPP	37.50		DVE	Susp/Sec	75.00
86		UPP	37.50		OLB	Susp/Sec	72.00
87		UPP	37.50		CED	Susp/Sec	70.00
88		UPP	42.50		FLW	Susp/Sec	68.00
89		UPP	47.50		B&A	Susp/Sec	65.00

THE END IS IN SIGHT — Figurine

E-9253 (137)

Yr	Description		Issue Price	Size	Mark	Status	Value
*	Boy with Dog Ripping Pants	UPP	$25.00	5.25"	UM	Susp/Sec	$160.00
83		UPP	25.00		HRG	Susp/Sec	75.00
83		UPP	25.00		FSH	Susp/Sec	65.00
84		UPP	25.00		CRS	Susp/Sec	62.00
85		UPP	25.00		DVE	Susp/Sec	60.00

*UNMARKED pieces could have been produced in any of the years of production, however it is known many were released in the first year of production.

PRAISE THE LORD ANYHOW Figurine

E-9254 (138)	83	Girl at Typewriter	UPP	$35.00	4.75"	HRG	Ret'd/Sec	$120.00
	83		UPP	35.00		FSH*	Ret'd/Sec	95.00
	84		UPP	35.00		CRS	Ret'd/Sec	90.00
	85		UPP	35.00		DVE	Ret'd/Sec	87.00
	86		UPP	35.00		OLB	Ret'd/Sec	85.00
	87		UPP	38.50		CED	Ret'd/Sec	85.00
	88		UPP	40.00		FLW	Ret'd/Sec	82.00
	89		UPP	47.50		B&A	Ret'd/Sec	82.00
	90		UPP	50.00		FLM	Ret'd/Sec	80.00
	91		UPP	50.00		VSL	Ret'd/Sec	80.00
	92		UPP	50.00		G/CL	Ret'd/Sec	75.00
	93		UPP	50.00		BFY	Ret'd/Sec	75.00
	94		UPP	55.00		TRP	Ret'd/Sec	70.00

* *Classic Variation: "Inked Fish."* During 1983, the FISH appeared as part of the understamp decal on many pieces. Pieces were also produced that did not have a FISH at all - incised or decal. When this occurred we can only theorize an attempt was made to correct it by actually drawing the FISH on the bottom of the piece. This inked symbol can be washed off, creating an unmarked piece. The GREENBOOK TRUMARKET PRICE for the "Erasable Inked Fish" is $125.00. Full color photo: 4th Ed., pg. 200 or 5th Ed., pg. 203. One color photo: 6th Ed., pg. 225.

BLESS YOU TWO Figurine

E-9255 (139)	83	Groom Carrying Bride	UPP	$21.00	5.25"	FSH	Secondary	$50.00
	84		UPP	21.00		CRS	Secondary	45.00
	85		UPP	21.00		DVE	Secondary	42.00
	86		UPP	21.00		OLB	Secondary	40.00
	87		UPP	23.00		CED	Secondary	38.00
	88		UPP	25.00		FLW	Secondary	38.00
	89		UPP	30.00		B&A	Secondary	38.00
	90		UPP	32.50		FLM	Secondary	38.00
	91		UPP	32.50		VSL	Secondary	38.00
	92		UPP	32.50		G/CL	Secondary	38.00
	93		UPP	35.00		BFY	Primary	37.50
	94		OPEN	37.50		TRP	Primary	37.50

THE HAND THAT ROCKS THE FUTURE Plate Third Issue "Mother's Love" Series Individually Numbered

E-9256 (32)	83	Girl Rocking Cradle	15,000	$40.00	8.50"	UM	Secondary	$40.00
	84					CRS	Secondary	40.00

I BELIEVE IN MIRACLES Plate Third Issue "Inspired Thoughts" Series Individually Numbered

E-9257 (105)	83	Boy Holding Chick	15,000	$40.00	8.50"	UM	Secondary	$40.00
	84			40.00		CRS	Secondary	40.00

WE ARE GOD'S WORKMANSHIP Figurine

E-9258 (140)	83	Bonnet Girl with Butterfly	UPP	$19.00	5.25"	HRG	Secondary	$55.00
	83		UPP	19.00		FSH	Secondary	40.00
	84		UPP	19.00		CRS	Secondary	38.00
	85		UPP	19.00		DVE	Secondary	32.00
	86		UPP	19.00		OLB	Secondary	30.00
	87		UPP	21.00		CED	Secondary	30.00
	88		UPP	22.50		FLW	Secondary	30.00
	89		UPP	25.00		B&A	Secondary	30.00
	90		UPP	27.50		FLM	Secondary	30.00
	91		UPP	27.50		VSL	Secondary	30.00
	92		UPP	27.50		G/CL	Primary	30.00
	93		UPP	30.00		BFY	Primary	30.00
	94		OPEN	30.00		TRP	Primary	30.00

WE'RE IN IT TOGETHER — Figurine

E-9259 (141)

83	Boy with Piggy	UPP	$24.00	3.75"	HRG	Susp/Sec	$85.00
83		UPP	24.00		FSH	Susp/Sec	65.00
84		UPP	24.00		CRS	Susp/Sec	60.00
85		UPP	24.00		DVE	Susp/Sec	58.00
86		UPP	24.00		OLB	Susp/Sec	55.00
87		UPP	27.00		CED	Susp/Sec	52.00
88		UPP	30.00		FLW	Susp/Sec	50.00
89		UPP	33.00		B&A	Susp/Sec	50.00
90		UPP	35.00		FLM	Susp/Sec	48.00

GOD'S PROMISES ARE SURE — Figurine — "Heavenly Halos" Series

E-9260 (142)

83	Boy Angel Winding Rainbow	UPP	$30.00	5.50"	FSH	Susp/Sec	$80.00
84		UPP	30.00		CRS	Susp/Sec	75.00
85		UPP	30.00		DVE	Susp/Sec	72.00
86		UPP	30.00		OLB	Susp/Sec	70.00
87		UPP	33.50		CED	Susp/Sec	68.00

SEEK YE THE LORD — Figurine

E-9261 (143)

83	Boy Graduate with Scroll	UPP	$21.00	4.75"	FSH*	Susp/Sec	$55.00
84		UPP	21.00		CRS	Susp/Sec	48.00
85		UPP	21.00		DVE	Susp/Sec	45.00
86		UPP	21.00		OLB	Susp/Sec	42.00

* Most figurines with the FISH Annual Production Symbol do not have the "h" in the word "he" in the inscription on the graduate's scroll capitalized. Full color photograph: 4th Ed., pg. 199 or 5th Ed., pg. 198.

SEEK YE THE LORD — Figurine

E-9262 (144)

83	Girl Graduate with Scroll	UPP	$21.00	4.75"	FSH*	Susp/Sec	$75.00
84		UPP	21.00		CRS	Susp/Sec	65.00
85		UPP	21.00		DVE	Susp/Sec	62.00
86		UPP	21.00		OLB	Susp/Sec	60.00

* Most figurines with the FISH Annual Production Symbol do not have the "h" in the word "he" in the inscription on the graduate's scroll capitalized. Full color photograph: 4th Ed., pg. 199 or 5th Ed., pg. 198.

HOW CAN TWO WALK TOGETHER EXCEPT THEY AGREE — Figurine

E-9263 (145)

83	Boy and Girl in Horse	UPP	$35.00	5.25"	HRG	Susp/Sec	$165.00
83	Costume	UPP	35.00		FSH	Susp/Sec	135.00
84		UPP	35.00		CRS	Susp/Sec	125.00
85		UPP	35.00		DVE	Susp/Sec	120.00

PRESS ON — Figurine

E-9265 (146)

83	Girl Ironing Clothes	UPP	$40.00	5.75"	HRG	Secondary	$95.00
83		UPP	40.00		FSH	Secondary	75.00
84		UPP	40.00		CRS	Secondary	70.00
85		UPP	40.00		DVE	Secondary	68.00
86		UPP	40.00		OLB	Secondary	65.00
87		UPP	45.00		CED	Secondary	62.00
88		UPP	45.00		FLW	Secondary	60.00
89		UPP	50.00		B&A	Secondary	60.00
90		UPP	55.00		FLM	Secondary	60.00
91		UPP	55.00		VSL	Secondary	60.00
92		UPP	55.00		G/CL	Secondary	60.00
93		UPP	60.00		BFY	Primary	60.00
94		OPEN	60.00		TRP	Primary	60.00

I'M FALLING FOR SOMEBUNNY Box

E-9266 (308)	Yr	Description		Price	Size	Mark	Status	Value
	83	Lamb and Bunny	UPP	$13.50	3.00"	UM	Susp/Sec	$54.00
	83		UPP	13.50		FSH	Susp/Sec	50.00
	84		UPP	16.00		CRS	Susp/Sec	48.00
	85		UPP	16.00		DVE	Susp/Sec	45.00
	86		UPP	16.00		OLB	Susp/Sec	42.00
	87		UPP	16.00		CED	Susp/Sec	40.00
	88		UPP	18.50		FLW	Susp/Sec	40.00

Some understamp decals have title "Somebunny Cares."

OUR LOVE IS HEAVEN SCENT Box

E-9266 (308)	Yr	Description		Price	Size	Mark	Status	Value
	83	Lamb and Skunk	UPP	$13.50	3.00"	UM	Susp/Sec	$50.00
	83		UPP	13.50		FSH	Susp/Sec	45.00
	84		UPP	16.00		CRS	Susp/Sec	42.00
	85		UPP	16.00		DVE	Susp/Sec	40.00
	86		UPP	16.00		OLB	Susp/Sec	38.00
	87		UPP	16.00		CED	Susp/Sec	38.00
	88		UPP	18.50		FLW	Susp/Sec	35.00

Some understamp decals have title "Somebunny Cares."

ANIMAL COLLECTION Figurines Set of 6 (Divide by 6 for an "each" value)

E-9267 (147)	Yr	Description		Price	Size	Mark	Status	Value
	83	Animals	UPP	$39.00	2.50"	UM	Susp/Sec	$162.00
	83		UPP	39.00		FSH	Susp/Sec	150.00
	84		UPP	45.00		CRS	Susp/Sec	144.00
	85		UPP	45.00		DVE	Susp/Sec	138.00
	86		UPP	45.00		OLB	Susp/Sec	132.00
	87	Some CED have the A - F suffix	UPP	48.00		CED	Susp/Sec	126.00

Please note: The Animal Collection was shipped to retailers in sets of 6, consequently they do not have individual boxes.

In 1988, individual Enesco Item #s were assigned for each figurine in the above set of 6:

Item	Yr	Description		Price	Size	Mark	Status	Value
E-9267/A (414)	88	Teddy Bear	UPP	$ 8.50	2.50"	FLW	Susp/Sec	$21.00
	89		UPP	10.00		B&A	Susp/Sec	20.00
	90		UPP	11.00		FLM	Susp/Sec	20.00
	91		UPP	11.00		VSL	Susp/Sec	19.00
E-9267/B (407)	88	Dog with Slippers	UPP	$ 8.50	3.00"	FLW	Susp/Sec	$20.00
	89		UPP	10.00		B&A	Susp/Sec	19.00
	90		UPP	11.00		FLM	Susp/Sec	19.00
	91		UPP	11.00		VSL	Susp/Sec	18.00
E-9267/C (408)	88	Bunny with Carrot	UPP	$ 8.50	2.60"	FLW	Susp/Sec	$21.00
	89		UPP	10.00		B&A	Susp/Sec	20.00
	90		UPP	11.00		FLM	Susp/Sec	20.00
	91		UPP	11.00		VSL	Susp/Sec	19.00
E-9267/D (413)	88	Cat with Bow Tie	UPP	$ 8.50	2.40"	FLW	Susp/Sec	$21.00
	89		UPP	10.00		B&A	Susp/Sec	20.00
	90		UPP	11.00		FLM	Susp/Sec	20.00
	91		UPP	11.00		VSL	Susp/Sec	19.00
E-9267/E (409)	88	Lamb with Bird on Back	UPP	$ 8.50	2.60"	FLW	Susp/Sec	$21.00
	89		UPP	10.00		B&A	Susp/Sec	20.00
	90		UPP	11.00		FLM	Susp/Sec	20.00
	91		UPP	11.00		VSL	Susp/Sec	19.00
E-9267/F (412)	88	Pig with Patches	UPP	$ 8.50	2.10"	FLW	Susp/Sec	$21.00
	89		UPP	10.00		B&A	Susp/Sec	20.00
	90		UPP	11.00		FLM	Susp/Sec	20.00
	91		UPP	11.00		VSL	Susp/Sec	19.00

NOBODY'S PERFECT! Figurine
E-9268
148

83 Boy with Dunce Cap	UPP	$21.00	7.00"	HRG*	Ret'd/Sec	$90.00
83	UPP	21.00		FSH	Ret'd/Sec	80.00
84	UPP	21.00		CRS	Ret'd/Sec	75.00
85	UPP	21.00		DVE	Ret'd/Sec	72.00
86	UPP	21.00		OLB	Ret'd/Sec	70.00
87	UPP	23.00		CED	Ret'd/Sec	68.00
88	UPP	24.00		FLW	Ret'd/Sec	65.00
89	UPP	27.00		B&A	Ret'd/Sec	62.00
90	UPP	30.00		FLM	Ret'd/Sec	62.00

**Classic Variation: "Smiling Dunce."* The first HRG pieces produced are known as "Smiling Dunces" or "Smiley" and appeared with a smile. The "O" shaped mouth is the normal piece. The GREENBOOK TRUMARKET PRICE for "Smiley" is $550.00. Full color photo: 4th Ed., pg. 193 or 5th Ed., pg. 197. One color photo: 6th Ed., pg. 219.

LET LOVE REIGN Figurine
E-9273
149

83 Girl with Chicks in Umbrella	UPP	$27.50	5.25"	HRG*	Ret'd/Sec	$250.00
83	UPP	27.50		FSH	Ret'd/Sec	80.00
84	UPP	27.50		CRS	Ret'd/Sec	75.00
85	UPP	27.50		DVE	Ret'd/Sec	72.00
86	UPP	27.50		OLB	Ret'd/Sec	70.00
87	UPP	30.00		CED	Ret'd/Sec	68.00

* Extremely rare, consider FISH as first Annual Production Symbol.

TASTE AND SEE THAT THE LORD IS GOOD Figurine "Heavenly Halos" Series
E-9274
150

83 Girl Angel Preparing Food	UPP	$22.50	6.25"	FSH	Ret'd/Sec	$75.00
84	UPP	22.50		CRS	Ret'd/Sec	65.00
85	UPP	22.50		DVE	Ret'd/Sec	55.00
86	UPP	22.50		OLB	Ret'd/Sec	55.00

JESUS LOVES ME Plate
E-9275
1

83 Boy with Teddy	UPP	$30.00	7.25"	UM	Susp/Sec	$50.00
84	UPP	30.00		CRS	Susp/Sec	45.00

JESUS LOVES ME Plate
E-9276
2

83 Girl with Bunny	UPP	$30.00	7.25"	UM	Susp/Sec	$58.00
84	UPP	30.00		CRS	Susp/Sec	55.00

JESUS LOVES ME Figurine
E-9278
1

83 Boy with Teddy	UPP	$ 9.00	3.00"	HRG	Secondary	$35.00
83	UPP	9.00		FSH	Secondary	25.00
84	UPP	10.00		CRS	Secondary	22.00
85	UPP	10.00		DVE	Secondary	22.00
86	UPP	10.00		OLB	Secondary	20.00
87	UPP	10.00		CED	Secondary	20.00
88	UPP	12.50		FLW	Secondary	18.00
89	UPP	13.50		B&A	Secondary	18.00
90	UPP	15.00		FLM	Secondary	16.00
91	UPP	15.00		VSL	Secondary	16.00
92	UPP	15.00		G/CL	Secondary	16.00
93	UPP	15.00		BFY	Primary	16.00
94	OPEN	16.00		TRP	Primary	16.00

JESUS LOVES ME	Figurine						
E-9279	83 Girl with Bunny	UPP	$ 9.00	3.00"	HRG	Secondary	$38.00
2	83	UPP	9.00		FSH	Secondary	28.00
	84	UPP	10.00		CRS	Secondary	25.00
	85	UPP	10.00		DVE	Secondary	25.00
	86	UPP	10.00		OLB	Secondary	20.00
	87	UPP	10.00		CED	Secondary	20.00
	88	UPP	12.50		FLW	Secondary	20.00
	89	UPP	13.50		B&A	Secondary	18.00
	90	UPP	15.00		FLM	Secondary	18.00
	91	UPP	15.00		VSL	Secondary	16.00
	92	UPP	15.00		G/CL	Secondary	16.00
	93	UPP	15.00		BFY	Primary	16.00
	94	OPEN	16.00		TRP	Primary	16.00

JESUS LOVES ME	Box						
E-9280	83 Boy with Teddy	UPP	$17.50	5.00"	HRG	Susp/Sec	$50.00
1	83	UPP	17.50		FSH	Susp/Sec	45.00
	84	UPP	19.00		CRS	Susp/Sec	42.00
	85	UPP	19.00		DVE	Susp/Sec	40.00

JESUS LOVES ME	Box						
E-9281	83 Girl with Bunny	UPP	$17.50	5.00"	HRG	Susp/Sec	$58.00
2	83	UPP	17.50		FSH	Susp/Sec	55.00
	84	UPP	19.00		CRS	Susp/Sec	52.00
	85	UPP	19.00		DVE	Susp/Sec	50.00

TO SOMEBUNNY SPECIAL	Figurine						
E-9282	* Bunny on Heart Base	UPP	$ 8.00	3.00"	UM	Susp/Sec	$42.00
152	83	UPP	8.00		FSH	Susp/Sec	38.00
	84	UPP	9.00		CRS	Susp/Sec	35.00
	85	UPP	9.00		DVE	Susp/Sec	35.00
	86	UPP	9.00		OLB	Susp/Sec	32.00
	87	UPP	10.00		CED	Susp/Sec	32.00
	* UNMARKED pieces could have been produced in any of the years of production.						
E-9282A	88 Bunny on Heart Base	UPP	$10.50	3.00"	FLW	Susp/Sec	$30.00
152	89	UPP	12.00		B&A	Susp/Sec	28.00
	90	UPP	13.50		FLM	Susp/Sec	25.00

YOU'RE WORTH YOUR WEIGHT IN GOLD	Figurine						
E-9282	* Pig with Patches on Base	UPP	$ 8.00	2.50"	UM	Susp/Sec	$42.00
151	83	UPP	8.00		FSH	Susp/Sec	38.00
	84	UPP	9.00		CRS	Susp/Sec	35.00
	85	UPP	9.00		DVE	Susp/Sec	35.00
	86	UPP	9.00		OLB	Susp/Sec	32.00
	87	UPP	10.00		CED	Susp/Sec	32.00
	* UNMARKED pieces could have been produced in any of the years of production.						
E-9282B	88 Pig with Patches on Base	UPP	$10.50	2.50"	FLW	Susp/Sec	$30.00
151	89	UPP	12.00		B&A	Susp/Sec	28.00
	90	UPP	13.50		FLM	Susp/Sec	28.00

ESPECIALLY FOR EWE	Figurine						
E-9282	* Lamb with Bird	UPP	$ 8.00	3.00"	UM	Susp/Sec	$40.00
153	83	UPP	8.00		FSH	Susp/Sec	35.00
	84	UPP	9.00		CRS	Susp/Sec	32.00
	85	UPP	9.00		DVE	Susp/Sec	32.00
	86	UPP	9.00		OLB	Susp/Sec	30.00
	87	UPP	10.00		CED	Susp/Sec	30.00
	* UNMARKED pieces could have been produced in any of the years of production. The original title for this figurine was "Loving Ewe."						
E-9282C	88 Lamb with Bird	UPP	$10.50	3.00"	FLW	Susp/Sec	$28.00
153	89	UPP	12.00		B&A	Susp/Sec	27.00
	90	UPP	13.50		FLM	Susp/Sec	25.00

FORFVER FRIENDS — Box

E-9283/A (309)

Year	Description		Price	Size	Mark	Status	Value
83	Dog	UPP	$15.00	4.25"	HRG	Susp/Sec	$70.00
83		UPP	15.00		FSH	Susp/Sec	65.00
84		UPP	17.00		CRS	Susp/Sec	62.00
*					DVE	Susp/Sec	60.00

* Piece was suspended in 1984 yet exists in a DOVE.

FOREVER FRIENDS — Box

E-9283/B (309)

Year	Description		Price	Size	Mark	Status	Value
83	Cat	UPP	$15.00	4.10"	HRG	Susp/Sec	$100.00
83		UPP	15.00		FSH	Susp/Sec	90.00
84		UPP	17.00		CRS	Susp/Sec	85.00

IF GOD BE FOR US, WHO CAN BE AGAINST US — Figurine

E-9285 (154)

Year	Description		Price	Size	Mark	Status	Value
83	Boy at Pulpit	UPP	$27.50	5.85"	FSH	Susp/Sec	$90.00
84		UPP	27.50		CRS	Susp/Sec	75.00
85		UPP	27.50		DVE	Susp/Sec	70.00

PEACE ON EARTH — Figurine

E-9287 (155)

Year	Description		Price	Size	Mark	Status	Value
83	Girl with Lion & Lamb	UPP	$37.50	5.25"	FSH	Susp/Sec	$125.00
84		UPP	37.50		CRS	Susp/Sec	115.00
85		UPP	37.50		DVE	Susp/Sec	105.00
86		UPP	37.50		OLB	Susp/Sec	100.00

SENDING YOU A RAINBOW — Figurine — "Heavenly Halos" Series

E-9288 (156)

Year	Description		Price	Size	Mark	Status	Value
83	Girl Angel with Sprinkler	UPP	$22.50	5.50"	FSH	Susp/Sec	$100.00
84		UPP	22.50		CRS	Susp/Sec	90.00
85		UPP	22.50		DVE	Susp/Sec	88.00
86		UPP	22.50		OLB	Susp/Sec	85.00

TRUST IN THE LORD — Figurine — "Heavenly Halos" Series

E-9289 (157)

Year	Description		Price	Size	Mark	Status	Value
83	Boy Angel Taking	UPP	$20.00	5.90"	FSH	Susp/Sec	$75.00
84	Flying Lessons	UPP	21.00		CRS	Susp/Sec	70.00
85		UPP	21.00		DVE	Susp/Sec	68.00
86		UPP	21.00		OLB	Susp/Sec	65.00
87		UPP	23.00		CED	Susp/Sec	62.00

LOVE COVERS ALL — Figurine

12009 (225)

Year	Description		Price	Size	Mark	Status	Value
85	Girl Making Heart Quilt	UPP	$27.50	4.50"	CRS	Susp/Sec	$65.00
85		UPP	27.50		DVE	Susp/Sec	60.00
86		UPP	27.50		OLB	Susp/Sec	60.00
87		UPP	30.00		CED	Susp/Sec	55.00
88		UPP	32.50		FLW	Susp/Sec	55.00
89		UPP	35.00		B&A	Susp/Sec	52.00
90		UPP	37.50		FLM	Susp/Sec	52.00
91		UPP	37.50		VSL	Susp/Sec	50.00

LOVING YOU — Frame

12017 (102)

Year	Description		Price	Size	Mark	Status	Value
85	Boy Holding Heart	UPP	$19.00	4.50"	CRS	Susp/Sec	$55.00
85		UPP	19.00		DVE	Susp/Sec	50.00
86		UPP	19.00		OLB	Susp/Sec	48.00
87		UPP	20.00		CED	Susp/Sec	45.00

LOVING YOU — Frame

12025 (103)

Year	Description		Price	Size	Mark	Status	Value
85	Girl Holding Heart	UPP	$19.00	4.50"	CRS	Susp/Sec	$60.00
85		UPP	19.00		DVE	Susp/Sec	55.00
86		UPP	19.00		OLB	Susp/Sec	52.00
87		UPP	20.00		CED	Susp/Sec	50.00

GOD'S PRECIOUS GIFT — Frame

12033 (310)

Year	Description		Price	Size	Mark	Status	Value
85	Baby Boy	UPP	$19.00	4.50"	DVE	Susp/Sec	$100.00
86		UPP	19.00		OLB	Susp/Sec	90.00
87		UPP	20.00		CED	Susp/Sec	85.00

GOD'S PRECIOUS GIFT — Frame

12041 (311)	85	Baby Girl	UPP	$19.00	4.50"	DVE	Susp/Sec	$58.00
	86		UPP	19.00		OLB	Susp/Sec	55.00
	87		UPP	19.00		CED	Susp/Sec	52.00
	88		UPP	22.50		FLW	Susp/Sec	50.00
	89		UPP	25.00		B&A	Susp/Sec	48.00
	90		UPP	27.50		FLM	Susp/Sec	48.00
	91		UPP	27.50		VSL	Susp/Sec	46.00
	92		UPP	27.50		G/CL	Susp/Sec	45.00

THE VOICE OF SPRING — Figurine — First Issue "The Four Seasons" Series

12068 (226)	85	Girl with Bible	Annual	$30.00	6.40"	CRS	Secondary	$300.00
						DVE	Secondary	275.00

SUMMER'S JOY — Figurine — Second Issue "The Four Seasons" Series

12076 (227)	85	Girl with Ducklings	Annual	$30.00	6.40"	CRS	Secondary	$105.00
						DVE	Secondary	95.00

AUTUMN'S PRAISE — Figurine — Third Issue "The Four Seasons" Series

12084 (228)	86	Girl in Field of Flowers	Annual	$30.00	6.40"	DVE	Secondary	$80.00
						OLB	Secondary	60.00

WINTER'S SONG — Figurine — Fourth Issue "The Four Seasons" Series

12092 (229)	86	Girl in Snow with Birds	Annual	$30.00	6.40"	DVE	Secondary	$135.00
						OLB	Secondary	115.00

THE VOICE OF SPRING — Plate — First Issue "The Four Seasons" Series

12106 (226)	85	Girl with Bible	Annual	$40.00	8.50"	CRS	Secondary	$110.00
						DVE	Secondary	100.00

SUMMER'S JOY — Plate — Second Issue "The Four Seasons" Series

12114 (227)	85	Girl with Ducklings	Annual	$40.00	8.50"	CRS	Secondary	$105.00
						DVE	Secondary	95.00

AUTUMN'S PRAISE — Plate — Third Issue "The Four Seasons" Series

12122 (228)	86	Girl in Field of Flowers	Annual	$40.00	8.50"	OLB	Secondary	$55.00

WINTER'S SONG — Plate — Fourth Issue "The Four Seasons" Series

12130 (229)	86	Girl in Snow with Birds	Annual	$40.00	8.50"	DVE	Secondary	$65.00
						OLB	Secondary	60.00

PART OF ME WANTS TO BE GOOD — Figurine

12149 (230)	85	Angel Boy in Devil Suit	UPP	$19.00	5.10"	CRS	Susp/Sec	$75.00
	85		UPP	19.00		DVE	Susp/Sec	70.00
	86		UPP	19.00		OLB	Susp/Sec	68.00
	87		UPP	21.00		CED	Susp/Sec	66.00
	88		UPP	22.50		FLW	Susp/Sec	65.00
	89		UPP	25.00		B&A	Susp/Sec	60.00

THIS IS THE DAY (WHICH) THE LORD HAS MADE — Figurine

12157 (314)	87	Birthday Boy	UPP	$20.00	5.00"	OLB	Susp/Sec	$80.00
	87		UPP	22.50		CED	Susp/Sec	60.00
	88		UPP	24.00		FLW	Susp/Sec	58.00
	89		UPP	27.00		B&A	Susp/Sec	56.00
	90		UPP	30.00		FLM	Susp/Sec	55.00

LORD, KEEP MY LIFE IN TUNE — Musical, Set of 2 — "Rejoice In The Lord" Band Series — TUNE: Amazing Grace

12165 (231)	85	Boy Playing Piano	UPP	$37.50	4.50"	DVE	Susp/Sec	$130.00
	86		UPP	37.50		OLB	Susp/Sec	120.00
	87		UPP	40.00		CED	Susp/Sec	115.00
	88		UPP	45.00		FLW	Susp/Sec	110.00
	89		UPP	50.00		B&A	Susp/Sec	105.00

THERE'S A SONG IN MY HEART Figurine "Rejoice In The Lord" Band Series
12173
232

85 Girl Playing Triangle	UPP	$11.00	3.50"	DVE	Susp/Sec	$50.00
86	UPP	11.00		OLB	Susp/Sec	45.00
87	UPP	12.00		CED	Susp/Sec	42.00
88	UPP	13.00		FLW	Susp/Sec	40.00
89	UPP	15.00		B&A	Susp/Sec	38.00
90	UPP	16.50		FLM	Susp/Sec	36.00

GET INTO THE HABIT OF PRAYER Figurine
12203
233

85 Nun	UPP	$19.00	5.10"	CRS	Susp/Sec	$55.00
85	UPP	19.00		DVE	Susp/Sec	38.00
86	UPP	19.00		OLB	Susp/Sec	38.00

BABY'S FIRST HAIRCUT Figurine Third Issue "Baby's First " Series
12211
234

85 Angel Cutting Baby's Hair	UPP	$32.50	4.50"	DVE	Susp/Sec	$138.00
86	UPP	32.50		OLB	Susp/Sec	130.00
87	UPP	32.50		CED	Susp/Sec	125.00

CLOWN FIGURINES Figurines Set of 4 (Divide by 4 for an "each" value)
12238
235

85 Mini Clowns	UPP	$54.00	4.25"	DVE	Secondary	$128.00
86	UPP	54.00		OLB	Secondary	120.00
87	UPP	54.00		CED	Secondary	104.00

Classic Variation. "CLOWNS" was misspelled "CROWNS" on the understamp decal of some sets. The GREENBOOK TRUMARKET PRICE for the set of four figurines with the "CROWNS" title error is $250.00. Color photograph: 5th Ed., pg. 205.

In 1987, individual Enesco Item #s were assigned for each figurine in the above set of 4:

CLOWN FIGURINE Figurine
12238/A
416

87 Boy Balancing Ball	UPP	$16.00	3.00"	CED	Secondary	$26.00
88	UPP	16.00		FLW	Secondary	24.00
89	UPP	17.50		B&A	Secondary	24.00
90	UPP	19.00		FLM	Secondary	22.00
91	UPP	19.00		VSL	Secondary	22.00
92	UPP	19.00		G/CL	Secondary	20.00
93	UPP	20.00		BFY	Primary	20.00
94	OPEN	20.00		TRP	Primary	20.00

CLOWN FIGURINE Figurine
12238/B
417

87 Girl Holding Balloon	UPP	$16.00	4.40"	CED	Secondary	$28.00
88	UPP	16.00		FLW	Secondary	26.00
89	UPP	17.50		B&A	Secondary	26.00
90	UPP	19.00		FLM	Secondary	24.00
91	UPP	19.00		VSL	Secondary	24.00
92	UPP	19.00		G/CL	Secondary	20.00
93	UPP	20.00		BFY	Primary	20.00
94	OPEN	20.00		TRP	Primary	20.00

CLOWN FIGURINE Figurine
12238/C
418

87 Boy Bending over Ball	UPP	$16.00	3.75"	CED	Secondary	$26.00
88	UPP	16.00		FLW	Secondary	24.00
89	UPP	17.50		B&A	Secondary	24.00
90	UPP	19.00		FLM	Secondary	22.00
91	UPP	19.00		VSL	Secondary	22.00
92	UPP	19.00		G/CL	Secondary	20.00
93	UPP	20.00		BFY	Primary	20.00
94	OPEN	20.00		TRP	Primary	20.00

CLOWN FIGURINE Figurine
12238/D
419

87	Girl with Flower Pot	UPP	$16.00	3.75"	CED	Secondary	$28.00
88		UPP	16.00		FLW	Secondary	26.00
89		UPP	17.50		B&A	Secondary	26.00
90		UPP	19.00		FLM	Secondary	24.00
91		UPP	19.00		VSL	Secondary	24.00
92		UPP	19.00		G/CL	Secondary	20.00
93		UPP	20.00		BFY	Primary	20.00
94		OPEN	20.00		TRP	Primary	20.00

PRECIOUS MOMENTS LAST FOREVER Medallion
12246
365

84	Medallion	UPP	$10.00	3.25"	CRS	Secondary	$135.00

LOVE COVERS ALL Thimble
12254
225

85	Girl Making Heart Quilt	UPP	$ 5.50	2.25"	DVE	Susp/Sec	$20.00
86		UPP	5.50		OLB	Susp/Sec	16.00
87		UPP	6.00		CED	Susp/Sec	15.00
88		UPP	7.00		FLW	Susp/Sec	15.00
89		UPP	8.00		B&A	Susp/Sec	14.00
90		UPP	8.00		FLM	Susp/Sec	12.00

I GET A BANG OUT OF YOU Figurine First Issue "Clown" Series
12262
236

85	Clown Holding Balloons	UPP	$30.00	6.60"	DVE	Secondary	$75.00
86		UPP	30.00		OLB	Secondary	62.00
87		UPP	33.50		CED	Secondary	58.00
88		UPP	35.00		FLW	Secondary	57.00
89		UPP	40.00		B&A	Secondary	55.00
90		UPP	45.00		FLM	Secondary	52.00
91		UPP	45.00		VSL	Secondary	50.00
92		UPP	45.00		G/CL	Secondary	45.00
93		UPP	45.00		BFY	Secondary	45.00
94		OPEN	45.00		TRP	Primary	45.00

LORD KEEP ME ON THE BALL Figurine Fourth Issue "Clown" Series
12270
270

86	Clown Sitting on Ball	UPP	$30.00	7.00"	OLB	Secondary	$70.00
87		UPP	33.50		CED	Secondary	62.00
88		UPP	35.00		FLW	Secondary	58.00
89		UPP	40.00		B&A	Secondary	57.00
90		UPP	45.00		FLM	Secondary	55.00
91		UPP	45.00		VSL	Secondary	52.00
92		UPP	45.00		G/CL	Secondary	45.00
93		UPP	45.00		BFY	Secondary	45.00
94		OPEN	45.00		TRP	Primary	45.00

IT IS BETTER TO GIVE THAN TO RECEIVE Figurine
12297
237

85	Policeman Writing Ticket	UPP	$19.00	5.25"	DVE	Susp/Sec	$125.00
86		UPP	19.00		OLB	Susp/Sec	115.00
87		UPP	21.00		CED	Susp/Sec	110.00

LOVE NEVER FAILS Figurine
12300
238

85	Teacher at Desk with	UPP	$25.00	5.50"	DVE	Secondary	$62.00
86	Report Card	UPP	25.00		OLB	Secondary	48.00
87		UPP	27.50		CED	Secondary	45.00
88		UPP	30.00		FLW	Secondary	45.00
89		UPP	33.00		B&A	Secondary	42.00
90		UPP	35.00		FLM	Secondary	40.00
91		UPP	35.00		VSL	Secondary	40.00
92		UPP	35.00		G/CL	Secondary	38.00
93		UPP	37.50		BFY	Primary	37.50
94		OPEN	37.50		TRP	Primary	37.50

GOD BLESS OUR HOME — Figurine
12319
239

Yr	Description	Status	Price	Size	Mark	Market	Value
85	Boy & Girl Building	UPP	$40.00	4.40"	DVE	Secondary	$78.00
86	Sandcastle	UPP	40.00		OLB	Secondary	68.00
87		UPP	45.00		CED	Secondary	65.00
88		UPP	45.00		FLW	Secondary	65.00
89		UPP	50.00		B&A	Secondary	62.00
90		UPP	55.00		FLM	Secondary	60.00
91		UPP	55.00		VSL	Secondary	60.00
92		UPP	55.00		G/CL	Secondary	60.00
93		UPP	60.00		BFY	Primary	60.00
94		OPEN	60.00		TRP	Primary	60.00

YOU CAN FLY — Figurine
12335
271

Yr	Description	Status	Price	Size	Mark	Market	Value
86	Boy Angel on Cloud	UPP	$25.00	5.50"	OLB	Susp/Sec	$70.00
87		UPP	27.50		CED	Susp/Sec	65.00
88		UPP	30.00		FLW	Susp/Sec	60.00

JESUS IS COMING SOON — Figurine
12343
240

Yr	Description	Status	Price	Size	Mark	Market	Value
85	Mary Knitting Booties	UPP	$22.50	4.75"	DVE	Susp/Sec	$42.00
86		UPP	22.50		OLB	Susp/Sec	38.00

HALO, AND MERRY CHRISTMAS — Figurine
12351
241

Yr	Description	Status	Price	Size	Mark	Market	Value
85	Angels Making Snowman	UPP	$40.00	6.10"	DVE	Susp/Sec	$160.00
86		UPP	40.00		OLB	Susp/Sec	155.00
87		UPP	40.00		CED	Susp/Sec	145.00
88		UPP	45.00		FLW	Susp/Sec	140.00

HAPPINESS IS THE LORD — Figurine — "Rejoice In The Lord" Band Series
12378
242

Yr	Description	Status	Price	Size	Mark	Market	Value
85	Boy Playing Banjo	UPP	$15.00	4.75"	DVE	Susp/Sec	$42.00
86		UPP	15.00		OLB	Susp/Sec	38.00
87		UPP	17.00		CED	Susp/Sec	35.00
88		UPP	18.00		FLW	Susp/Sec	35.00
89		UPP	20.00		B&A	Susp/Sec	32.00
90		UPP	22.50		FLM	Susp/Sec	32.00

LORD GIVE ME A SONG — Figurine — "Rejoice In The Lord" Band Series
12386
243

Yr	Description	Status	Price	Size	Mark	Market	Value
85	Girl Playing Harmonica	UPP	$15.00	4.90"	DVE	Susp/Sec	$46.00
86		UPP	15.00		OLB	Susp/Sec	42.00
87		UPP	17.00		CED	Susp/Sec	42.00
88		UPP	18.00		FLW	Susp/Sec	40.00
89		UPP	20.00		B&A	Susp/Sec	40.00
90		UPP	22.50		FLM	Susp/Sec	38.00

HE IS MY SONG — Figurine — "Rejoice In The Lord" Band Series — Set of 2
12394
244

Yr	Description	Status	Price	Size	Mark	Market	Value
85	Boy Playing Trumpet	UPP	$17.50	4.50"	DVE	Susp/Sec	$50.00
86	with Dog	UPP	17.50		OLB	Susp/Sec	48.00
87		UPP	20.00		CED	Susp/Sec	46.00
88		UPP	22.50		FLW	Susp/Sec	45.00
89		UPP	25.00		B&A	Susp/Sec	42.00
90		UPP	27.50		FLM	Susp/Sec	40.00

WE SAW A STAR — Musical — Set of 3 — TUNE: Joy To The World
12408
245

Yr	Description	Status	Price	Size	Mark	Market	Value
85	Two Angels Sawing Star	UPP	$50.00	4.75"	DVE	Susp/Sec	$105.00
86		UPP	50.00		OLB	Susp/Sec	95.00
87		UPP	55.00		CED	Susp/Sec	90.00

HAVE A HEAVENLY CHRISTMAS Ornament

12416

246

Yr	Description	Ed.	Issue Price	Size	Mark	Status	Value
85	Boy in Airplane	UPP	$12.00	2.60"	DVE	Secondary	$34.00
86		UPP	12.00		OLB	Secondary	28.00
87		UPP	13.50		CED*	Secondary	25.00
88		UPP	14.00		FLW	Secondary	22.00
89		UPP	15.00		B&A	Secondary	20.00
90		UPP	16.00		FLM	Secondary	18.00
91		UPP	16.00		VSL	Secondary	18.00
92		UPP	16.00		G/CL	Secondary	18.00
93		UPP	16.00		BFY	Primary	17.50
94		OPEN	17.50		TRP	Primary	17.50

* There are CEDAR TREE pieces with two hooks from the Retailers Wreath, #111465. For further information, see 6th Ed., pg. 209. There are also some ornaments, again from the Retailer's Wreath, that have the inscription "Heaven Bound" upside-down. Color photo: 5th Ed., pg. 210.

AARON Doll

12424

247

Yr	Description	Ed.	Issue Price	Size	Mark	Status	Value
85	Boy Angel	UPP	$135.00	12.00"	DVE	Susp/Sec	$140.00
86		UPP	135.00		OLB	Susp/Sec	140.00

BETHANY Doll

12432

248

Yr	Description	Ed.	Issue Price	Size	Mark	Status	Value
85	Girl Angel	UPP	$135.00	12.00"	DVE	Susp/Sec	$150.00
86		UPP	135.00		OLB	Susp/Sec	150.00

12440 GOD BLESS OUR YEARS TOGETHER

See The Enesco PM Collectors' Club, Membership Pieces, page 261.

WADDLE I DO WITHOUT YOU Figurine Second Issue "Clown" Series

12459

250

Yr	Description	Ed.	Issue Price	Size	Mark	Status	Value
85	Girl Clown with Basket	UPP	$30.00	5.50"	DVE	Ret'd/Sec	$95.00
86	with Goose	UPP	30.00		OLB	Ret'd/Sec	90.00
87		UPP	30.00		CED	Ret'd/Sec	88.00
88		UPP	30.00		FLW	Ret'd/Sec	85.00
89		UPP	40.00		B&A	Ret'd/Sec	82.00

THE LORD WILL CARRY YOU THROUGH Figurine Third Issue "Clown" Series

12467

251

Yr	Description	Ed.	Issue Price	Size	Mark	Status	Value
86	Clown with Dog in Mud	UPP	$30.00	5.75"	OLB	Ret'd/Sec	$85.00
87		UPP	33.50		CED	Ret'd/Sec	80.00
88		UPP	30.00		FLW	Ret'd/Sec	75.00

P.D. Doll

12475

252

Yr	Description	Ed.	Issue Price	Size	Mark	Status	Value
85	Baby Boy	UPP	$50.00	7.00"	UM	Susp/Sec	$85.00
85		UPP	50.00		DVE	Susp/Sec	80.00
86		UPP	50.00		OLB	Susp/Sec	75.00

TRISH Doll

12483

253

Yr	Description	Ed.	Issue Price	Size	Mark	Status	Value
85	Baby Girl	UPP	$50.00	7.00"	UM	Susp/Sec	$90.00
85		UPP	50.00		DVE	Susp/Sec	85.00
86		UPP	50.00		OLB	Susp/Sec	80.00

ANGIE, THE ANGEL OF MERCY Doll Individually Numbered

12491

339

Yr	Description	Ed.	Issue Price	Size	Mark	Status	Value
87	Nurse	12,500	$160.00	12.00"	CED	Secondary	$275.00

LORD KEEP MY LIFE IN TUNE Musical "Rejoice In The Lord" Band Series Set of 2

TUNE: I'd Like To Teach The World To Sing

12580

315

Yr	Description	Ed.	Issue Price	Size	Mark	Status	Value
87	Girl with Piano	UPP	$37.50	4.00"	OLB	Susp/Sec	$190.00
87		UPP	40.00		CED	Susp/Sec	180.00
88		UPP	45.00		FLW	Susp/Sec	175.00
89		UPP	50.00		B&A	Susp/Sec	170.00
90		UPP	55.00		FLM	Susp/Sec	160.00

MOTHER SEW DEAR — Thimble
13293 (30)

Year	Description	Status	Issue Price	Size	Mark	Market	Value
85	Mother Needlepointing	UPP	$ 5.50	2.25"	DVE	Secondary	$18.00
86		UPP	5.50		OLB	Secondary	15.00
87		UPP	6.00		CED	Secondary	12.00
88		UPP	7.00		FLW	Secondary	10.00
89		UPP	8.00		B&A	Secondary	10.00
90		UPP	8.00		FLM	Secondary	9.00
91		UPP	8.00		VSL	Secondary	8.00
92		UPP	8.00		G/CL	Primary	8.00
93		UPP	8.00		BFY	Primary	8.00
94		OPEN	8.00		TRP	Primary	8.00

THE PURR-FECT GRANDMA — Thimble
13307 (33)

Year	Description	Status	Issue Price	Size	Mark	Market	Value
85	Grandma in Rocker	UPP	$ 5.50	2.25"	DVE	Secondary	$18.00
86		UPP	5.50		OLB	Secondary	15.00
87		UPP	6.00		CED	Secondary	12.00
88		UPP	7.00		FLW	Secondary	12.00
89		UPP	8.00		B&A	Secondary	10.00
90		UPP	8.00		FLM	Secondary	10.00
91		UPP	8.00		VSL	Secondary	8.00
92		UPP	8.00		G/CL	Primary	8.00
93		UPP	8.00		BFY	Primary	8.00
94		OPEN	8.00		TRP	Primary	8.00

TELL ME THE STORY OF JESUS — Plate, Dated — Fourth Issue "Joy Of Christmas" Series
15237 (83)

Year	Description	Status	Issue Price	Size	Mark	Market	Value
85	Girl with Doll Reading Book	Annual	$40.00	8.50"	DVE	Secondary	$115.00

MAY YOUR CHRISTMAS BE DELIGHTFUL — Figurine
15482 (254)

Year	Description	Status	Issue Price	Size	Mark	Market	Value
85	Boy Tangled in	UPP	$25.00	5.00"	DVE	Susp/Sec	$65.00
86	Christmas Lights	UPP	25.00		OLB	Susp/Sec	57.00
87		UPP	27.50		CED	Susp/Sec	55.00
88		UPP	30.00		FLW	Susp/Sec	52.00
89		UPP	33.00		B&A	Susp/Sec	51.00
90		UPP	35.00		FLM	Susp/Sec	50.00
91		UPP	35.00		VSL	Susp/Sec	48.00
92		UPP	35.00		G/CL	Susp/Sec	47.00
93		UPP	35.00		BFY	Susp/Sec	45.00
94		UPP	35.00		TRP	Susp/Sec	42.00

HONK IF YOU LOVE JESUS — Figurine — Set of 2 — Nativity Addition
15490 (255)

Year	Description	Status	Issue Price	Size	Mark	Market	Value
85	Mother Goose in Bonnet	UPP	$13.00	3.25"	DVE	Secondary	$32.00
86	with Babies	UPP	13.00		OLB	Secondary	28.00
87		UPP	15.00		CED	Secondary	25.00
88		UPP	15.00		FLW	Secondary	22.00
89		UPP	17.50		B&A	Secondary	20.00
90		UPP	19.00		FLM	Secondary	20.00
91		UPP	19.00		VSL	Secondary	20.00
92		UPP	19.00		G/CL	Secondary	20.00
93		UPP	19.00		BFY	Primary	20.00
94		OPEN	20.00		TRP	Primary	20.00

GOD SENT YOU JUST IN TIME — Musical — TUNE: We Wish You A Merry Christmas
15504 (256)

Year	Description	Status	Issue Price	Size	Mark	Market	Value
85	Clown Holding a	UPP	$45.00	6.25"	DVE	Ret'd/Sec	$120.00
86	Jack- in- the- Box	UPP	45.00		OLB	Ret'd/Sec	105.00
87		UPP	50.00		CED	Ret'd/Sec	100.00
88		UPP	55.00		FLW	Ret'd/Sec	98.00
89		UPP	60.00		B&A	Ret'd/Sec	95.00

BABY'S FIRST CHRISTMAS — Figurine, Dated
15539 (257)

Year	Description	Status	Issue Price	Size	Mark	Market	Value
85	Baby Boy with Bottle	Annual	$13.00	3.00"	DVE	Secondary	$36.00

BABY'S FIRST CHRISTMAS — Figurine, Dated
15547 (258)

Year	Description	Status	Issue Price	Size	Mark	Market	Value
85	Baby Girl with Bottle	Annual	$13.00	3.00"	DVE	Secondary	$38.00

GOD SENT HIS LOVE — Ornament, Dated

15768 (259)

Year	Description	Production	Issue Price	Size	Mark	Status	Value
85	Boy Holding Heart	Annual	$10.00	3.00"	DVE	Secondary	$38.00

MAY YOU HAVE THE SWEETEST CHRISTMAS — Figurine — "Family Christmas Scene" Series

15776 (260)

Year	Description	Production	Issue Price	Size	Mark	Status	Value
85	Mother with Cookie Sheet	UPP	$17.00	4.90"	DVE	Susp/Sec	$52.00
86		UPP	17.00		OLB	Susp/Sec	48.00
87		UPP	19.00		CED	Susp/Sec	46.00
88		UPP	19.00		FLW	Susp/Sec	45.00
89		UPP	23.00		B&A	Susp/Sec	42.00
90		UPP	25.00		FLM	Susp/Sec	40.00
91		UPP	25.00		VSL	Susp/Sec	38.00
92		UPP	25.00		G/CL	Susp/Sec	35.00

THE STORY OF GOD'S LOVE — Figurine — "Family Christmas Scene" Series

15784 (261)

Year	Description	Production	Issue Price	Size	Mark	Status	Value
85	Father Reading Bible	UPP	$22.50	4.00"	DVE	Susp/Sec	$60.00
86		UPP	22.50		OLB	Susp/Sec	55.00
87		UPP	25.00		CED	Susp/Sec	54.00
88		UPP	25.00		FLW	Susp/Sec	52.00
89		UPP	32.50		B&A	Susp/Sec	50.00
90		UPP	35.00		FLM	Susp/Sec	50.00
91		UPP	35.00		VSL	Susp/Sec	48.00
92		UPP	35.00		G/CL	Susp/Sec	46.00

TELL ME A STORY — Figurine — "Family Christmas Scene" Series

15792 (262)

Year	Description	Production	Issue Price	Size	Mark	Status	Value
85	Boy Sitting Listening to	UPP	$10.00	2.00"	DVE	Susp/Sec	$40.00
86	Story	UPP	10.00		OLB	Susp/Sec	38.00
87		UPP	11.00		CED	Susp/Sec	35.00
88		UPP	11.00		FLW	Susp/Sec	34.00
89		UPP	13.50		B&A	Susp/Sec	33.00
90		UPP	15.00		FLM	Susp/Sec	32.00
91		UPP	15.00		VSL	Susp/Sec	30.00
92		UPP	15.00		G/CL	Susp/Sec	28.00

GOD GAVE HIS BEST — Figurine — "Family Christmas Scene" Series

15806 (263)

Year	Description	Production	Issue Price	Size	Mark	Status	Value
85	Girl with Ornament	UPP	$13.00	3.50"	DVE	Susp/Sec	$45.00
86		UPP	13.00		OLB	Susp/Sec	42.00
87		UPP	15.00		CED	Susp/Sec	40.00
88		UPP	15.00		FLW	Susp/Sec	36.00
89		UPP	17.50		B&A	Susp/Sec	35.00
90		UPP	19.00		FLM	Susp/Sec	34.00
91		UPP	19.00		VSL	Susp/Sec	32.00
92		UPP	19.00		G/CL	Susp/Sec	30.00

SILENT NIGHT — Musical — "Family Christmas Scene" Series — TUNE: Silent Night

15814 (264)

Year	Description	Production	Issue Price	Size	Mark	Status	Value
85	Christmas Tree	UPP	$37.50	5.60"	DVE	Susp/Sec	$95.00
86		UPP	37.50		OLB	Susp/Sec	90.00
87		UPP	40.00		CED	Susp/Sec	85.00
88		UPP	40.00		FLW	Susp/Sec	80.00
89		UPP	50.00		B&A	Susp/Sec	75.00
90		UPP	55.00		FLM	Susp/Sec	75.00
91		UPP	55.00		VSL	Susp/Sec	75.00
92		UPP	55.00		G/CL	Susp/Sec	75.00

MAY YOUR CHRISTMAS BE HAPPY — Ornament

15822 (235)

Year	Description	Production	Issue Price	Size	Mark	Status	Value
85	Girl Clown with Balloon	UPP	$10.00	3.25"	DVE	Susp/Sec	$42.00
86		UPP	10.00		OLB	Susp/Sec	38.00
87		UPP	11.00		CED	Susp/Sec	36.00
88		UPP	12.50		FLW	Susp/Sec	35.00
89		UPP	13.50		B&A	Susp/Sec	32.00

HAPPINESS IS THE LORD		Ornament						
15830	85	Boy Clown with Ball	UPP	$10.00	2.10"	DVE	Susp/Sec	$35.00
235	86		UPP	10.00		OLB	Susp/Sec	30.00
	87		UPP	11.00		CED	Susp/Sec	30.00
	88		UPP	12.50		FLW	Susp/Sec	28.00
	89		UPP	13.50		B&A	Susp/Sec	28.00

MAY YOUR CHRISTMAS BE DELIGHTFUL		Ornament						
15849	85	Boy Tangled in	UPP	$10.00	3.00"	DVE	Susp/Sec	$36.00
254	86	Christmas Lights	UPP	10.00		OLB	Susp/Sec	34.00
	87		UPP	11.00		CED	Susp/Sec	34.00
	88		UPP	12.50		FLW	Susp/Sec	33.00
	89		UPP	13.50		B&A	Susp/Sec	33.00
	90		UPP	15.00		FLM	Susp/Sec	32.00
	91		UPP	15.00		VSL	Susp/Sec	32.00
	92		UPP	15.00		G/CL	Susp/Sec	30.00
	93		UPP	15.00		BFY	Susp/Sec	30.00

HONK IF YOU LOVE JESUS		Ornament						
15857	85	Mother Goose in Bonnet	UPP	$10.00	3.60"	DVE	Susp/Sec	$35.00
255	86		UPP	10.00		OLB	Susp/Sec	33.00
	87		UPP	11.00		CED	Susp/Sec	33.00
	88		UPP	12.50		FLW	Susp/Sec	32.00
	89		UPP	13.50		B&A	Susp/Sec	30.00
	90		UPP	15.00		FLM	Susp/Sec	28.00
	91		UPP	15.00		VSL	Susp/Sec	28.00
	92		UPP	15.00		G/CL	Susp/Sec	26.00
	93		UPP	15.00		BFY	Susp/Sec	25.00

GOD SENT HIS LOVE		Thimble, Dated						
15865	85	Boy Holding Heart	Annual	$5.50	2.20"	DVE	Secondary	$60.00
259								

GOD SENT HIS LOVE		Bell, Dated						
15873	85	Boy Holding Heart	Annual	$19.00	5.40"	DVE	Secondary	$45.00
259								

GOD SENT HIS LOVE		Figurine, Dated						
15881	85	Boy Holding Heart	Annual	$17.00	4.50"	DVE	Secondary	$42.00
259								

BABY'S FIRST CHRISTMAS		Ornament, Dated						
15903	85	Baby Boy with Bottle	Annual	$10.00	2.40"	DVE	Secondary	$40.00
257								

BABY'S FIRST CHRISTMAS		Ornament, Dated						
15911	85	Baby Girl with Bottle	Annual	$10.00	2.40"	DVE	Secondary	$40.00
258								

MAY YOUR BIRTHDAY BE WARM		Figurine	"Birthday Circus Train" Series					
15938	86	Teddy on Caboose -	UPP	$10.00	2.75"	DVE	Secondary	$40.00
296	86	"For Baby"	UPP	10.00		OLB	Secondary	25.00
	87		UPP	11.00		CED	Secondary	22.00
	88		UPP	12.00		FLW	Secondary	20.00
	89		UPP	13.50		B&A	Secondary	18.00
	90		UPP	15.00		FLM	Secondary	15.00
	91		UPP	15.00		VSL	Secondary	15.00
	92		UPP	15.00		G/CL	Primary	15.00
	93		UPP	15.00		BFY	Primary	15.00
	94		OPEN	15.00		TRP	Primary	15.00

HAPPY BIRTHDAY LITTLE LAMB Figurine "Birthday Circus Train" Series
15946 297

86 Lamb - Age 1	UPP	$10.00	3.00"	DVE	Secondary	$40.00
86	UPP	10.00		OLB	Secondary	25.00
87	UPP	11.00		CED	Secondary	22.00
88	UPP	12.00		FLW	Secondary	20.00
89	UPP	13.50		B&A	Secondary	18.00
90	UPP	15.00		FLM	Secondary	16.00
91	UPP	15.00		VSL	Secondary	16.00
92	UPP	15.00		G/CL	Primary	15.00
93	UPP	15.00		BFY	Primary	15.00
94	OPEN	15.00		TRP	Primary	15.00

HEAVEN BLESS YOUR SPECIAL DAY Figurine "Birthday Circus Train" Series
15954 299

86 Pig - Age 3	UPP	$11.00	3.50"	DVE	Secondary	$40.00
86	UPP	11.00		OLB	Secondary	25.00
87	UPP	12.00		CED	Secondary	22.00
88	UPP	13.50		FLW	Secondary	20.00
89	UPP	15.00		B&A	Secondary	20.00
90	UPP	16.50		FLM	Secondary	18.00
91	UPP	16.50		VSL	Secondary	17.00
92	UPP	16.50		G/CL	Primary	16.50
93	UPP	16.50		BFY	Primary	16.50
94	OPEN	16.50		TRP	Primary	16.50

GOD BLESS YOU ON YOUR BIRTHDAY Figurine "Birthday Circus Train" Series
15962 298

86 Seal - Age 2	UPP	$11.00	3.75"	DVE	Secondary	$40.00
86	UPP	11.00		OLB	Secondary	25.00
87	UPP	12.00		CED	Secondary	22.00
88	UPP	13.50		FLW	Secondary	20.00
89	UPP	15.00		B&A	Secondary	18.00
90	UPP	16.50		FLM	Secondary	18.00
91	UPP	16.50		VSL	Secondary	17.00
92	UPP	16.50		G/CL	Primary	16.50
93	UPP	16.50		BFY	Primary	16.50
94	OPEN	16.50		TRP	Primary	16.50

MAY YOUR BIRTHDAY BE GIGANTIC Figurine "Birthday Circus Train" Series
15970 300

86 Elephant - Age 4	UPP	$12.50	3.50"	DVE	Secondary	$40.00
86	UPP	12.50		OLB	Secondary	27.00
87	UPP	14.00		CED	Secondary	25.00
88	UPP	15.00		FLW	Secondary	24.00
89	UPP	17.00		B&A	Secondary	22.00
90	UPP	18.50		FLM	Secondary	20.00
91	UPP	18.50		VSL	Secondary	19.00
92	UPP	18.50		G/CL	Primary	18.50
93	UPP	18.50		BFY	Primary	18.50
94	OPEN	18.50		TRP	Primary	18.50

THIS DAY IS SOMETHING TO ROAR ABOUT Figurine "Birthday Circus Train" Series
15989 301

86 Lion - Age 5	UPP	$13.50	4.00"	DVE	Secondary	$40.00
86	UPP	13.50		OLB	Secondary	30.00
87	UPP	15.00		CED	Secondary	28.00
88	UPP	17.50		FLW	Secondary	25.00
89	UPP	20.00		B&A	Secondary	22.00
90	UPP	20.00		FLM	Secondary	20.00
91	UPP	20.00		VSL	Secondary	20.00
92	UPP	20.00		G/CL	Primary	20.00
93	UPP	20.00		BFY	Primary	20.00
94	OPEN	20.00		TRP	Primary	20.00

KEEP LOOKING UP — Figurine — "Birthday Circus Train" Series
15997
302

Yr	Description	Status	Issue	Size	Mark	Market	Value
86	Giraffe - Age 6	UPP	$13.50	5.50"	DVE	Secondary	$40.00
86		UPP	13.50		OLB	Secondary	30.00
87		UPP	15.00		CED	Secondary	28.00
88		UPP	17.50		FLW	Secondary	25.00
89		UPP	20.00		B&A	Secondary	22.00
90		UPP	20.00		FLM	Secondary	20.00
91		UPP	20.00		VSL	Secondary	20.00
92		UPP	20.00		G/CL	Primary	20.00
93		UPP	20.00		BFY	Primary	20.00
94		OPEN	20.00		TRP	Primary	20.00

BLESS THE DAYS OF OUR YOUTH — Figurine — "Birthday Circus Train" Series
16004
303

Yr	Description	Status	Issue	Size	Mark	Market	Value
86	Clown with Pull Rope	UPP	$15.00	5.25"	DVE	Secondary	$45.00
86		UPP	15.00		OLB	Secondary	33.00
87		UPP	17.00		CED	Secondary	30.00
88		UPP	19.50		FLW	Secondary	28.00
89		UPP	22.50		B&A	Secondary	25.00
90		UPP	22.50		FLM	Secondary	23.00
91		UPP	22.50		VSL	Secondary	23.00
92		UPP	22.50		G/CL	Primary	22.50
93		UPP	22.50		BFY	Primary	22.50
94		OPEN	22.50		TRP	Primary	22.50

BABY'S FIRST TRIP — Figurine — Fourth Issue "Baby's First" Series
16012
267

Yr	Description	Status	Issue	Size	Mark	Market	Value
86	Angel Pushing Buggy	UPP	$32.50	5.00"	OLB	Susp/Sec	$215.00
87		UPP	37.00		CED	Susp/Sec	195.00
88		UPP	40.00		FLW	Susp/Sec	180.00
89		UPP	45.00		B&A	Susp/Sec	175.00

GOD BLESS YOU WITH RAINBOWS — Night Light
16020
199

Yr	Description	Status	Issue	Size	Mark	Market	Value
86	Angel behind Rainbow	UPP	$45.00	5.00"	DVE	Susp/Sec	$115.00
86		UPP	45.00		OLB	Susp/Sec	110.00
87		UPP	50.00		CED	Susp/Sec	100.00
88		UPP	52.50		FLW	Susp/Sec	95.00
89		UPP	57.50		B&A	Susp/Sec	90.00

TO MY FAVORITE PAW — Figurine
100021
211

Yr	Description	Status	Issue	Size	Mark	Market	Value
86	Boy Sitting with Teddy	UPP	$22.50	3.50"	DVE	Susp/Sec	$115.00
86		UPP	22.50		OLB	Susp/Sec	65.00
87		UPP	25.00		CED	Susp/Sec	62.00
88		UPP	27.00		FLW	Susp/Sec	58.00

TO MY DEER FRIEND — Figurine
100048
316

Yr	Description	Status	Issue	Size	Mark	Market	Value
87	Girl with Flowers and Deer	UPP	$33.00	5.75"	OLB	Secondary	$115.00
87		UPP	37.00		CED	Secondary	65.00
88		UPP	40.00		FLW	Secondary	58.00
89		UPP	45.00		B&A	Secondary	55.00
90		UPP	50.00		FLM	Secondary	52.00
91		UPP	50.00		VSL	Secondary	50.00
92		UPP	50.00		G/CL	Primary	50.00
93		UPP	50.00		BFY	Primary	50.00
94		OPEN	50.00		TRP	Primary	50.00

SENDING MY LOVE — Figurine
100056
212

Yr	Description	Status	Issue	Size	Mark	Market	Value
86	Boy with Bow & Arrow	UPP	$22.50	5.75"	DVE	Susp/Sec	$65.00
86	on Cloud	UPP	22.50		OLB	Susp/Sec	58.00
87		UPP	25.00		CED	Susp/Sec	54.00
88		UPP	27.00		FLW	Susp/Sec	52.00
89		UPP	30.00		B&A	Susp/Sec	50.00
90		UPP	32.50		FLM	Susp/Sec	48.00
91		UPP	32.50		VSL	Susp/Sec	45.00

WORSHIP THE LORD Figurine
100064
213

86	Girl Kneeling at	UPP	$24.00	5.25"	DVE	Secondary	$52.00
86	Church Window	UPP	24.00		OLB	Secondary	45.00
87		UPP	24.00		CED	Secondary	42.00
88		UPP	30.00		FLW	Secondary	40.00
89		UPP	33.00		B&A	Secondary	38.00
90		UPP	35.00		FLM	Secondary	35.00
91		UPP	35.00		VSL	Secondary	35.00
92		UPP	35.00		G/CL	Primary	35.00
93		UPP	35.00		BFY	Primary	35.00
94		OPEN	35.00		TRP	Primary	35.00

TO MY FOREVER FRIEND Figurine
100072
214

86	Two Girls with Flowers	UPP	$33.00	5.50"	DVE	Secondary	$132.00
86		UPP	33.00		OLB	Secondary	68.00
87		UPP	33.00		CED	Secondary	62.00
88		UPP	40.00		FLW	Secondary	55.00
89		UPP	45.00		B&A	Secondary	52.00
90		UPP	50.00		FLM	Secondary	52.00
91		UPP	50.00		VSL	Secondary	50.00
92		UPP	50.00		G/CL	Primary	50.00
93		UPP	50.00		BFY	Primary	50.00
94		OPEN	50.00		TRP	Primary	50.00

HE'S THE HEALER OF BROKEN HEARTS Figurine
100080
317

87	Girl & Boy with	UPP	$33.00	5.50"	OLB	Secondary	$65.00
87	Bandaged Heart	UPP	37.00		CED	Secondary	60.00
88		UPP	40.00		FLW	Secondary	55.00
89		UPP	45.00		B&A	Secondary	52.00
90		UPP	50.00		FLM	Secondary	52.00
91		UPP	50.00		VSL	Secondary	50.00
92		UPP	50.00		G/CL	Primary	50.00
93		UPP	50.00		BFY	Primary	50.00
94		OPEN	50.00		TRP	Primary	50.00

MAKE ME A BLESSING Figurine
100102
323

87	Girl with Sick Bear	UPP	$35.00	5.50"	OLB	Ret'd/Sec	$135.00
87		UPP	38.50		CED	Ret'd/Sec	95.00
88		UPP	40.00		FLW	Ret'd/Sec	85.00
89		UPP	45.00		B&A	Ret'd/Sec	80.00
90		UPP	50.00		FLM	Ret'd/Sec	75.00

LORD I'M COMING HOME Figurine
100110
215

86	Baseball Player with Bat	UPP	$22.50	5.00"	DVE	Secondary	$90.00
86		UPP	22.50		OLB	Secondary	53.00
87		UPP	25.00		CED	Secondary	42.00
88		UPP	27.00		FLW	Secondary	40.00
89		UPP	30.00		B&A	Secondary	38.00
90		UPP	32.50		FLM	Secondary	35.00
91		UPP	32.50		VSL	Secondary	35.00
92		UPP	32.50		G/CL	Primary	35.00
93		UPP	35.00		BFY	Primary	35.00
94		OPEN	35.00		TRP	Primary	35.00

LORD KEEP ME ON MY TOES Figurine
100129
216

86	Ballerina	UPP	$22.50	5.75"	DVE	Ret'd/Sec	$105.00
86		UPP	22.50		OLB	Ret'd/Sec	88.00
87		UPP	25.00		CED	Ret'd/Sec	80.00
88		UPP	27.00		FLW	Ret'd/Sec	75.00

THE JOY OF THE LORD IS MY STRENGTH Figurine

100137	86 Mother with Babies	UPP	$35.00	5.40"	DVE	Secondary	$130.00
217	86	UPP	35.00		OLB	Secondary	82.00
	87	UPP	35.00		CED	Secondary	60.00
	88	UPP	40.00		FLW	Secondary	55.00
	89	UPP	47.50		B&A	Secondary	53.00
	90	UPP	50.00		FLM	Secondary	52.00
	91	UPP	50.00		VSL	Secondary	52.00
	92	UPP	50.00		G/CL	Secondary	50.00
	93	UPP	50.00		BFY	Primary	50.00
	94	OPEN	50.00		TRP	Primary	50.00

GOD BLESS THE DAY WE FOUND YOU Figurine

100145	86 Mom & Dad with	UPP	$40.00	5.50"	OLB	Susp/Sec	$130.00
272	87 Adopted Daughter	UPP	40.00		CED	Susp/Sec	125.00
	88	UPP	47.50		FLW	Susp/Sec	120.00
	89	UPP	50.00		B&A	Susp/Sec	115.00
	90	UPP	55.00		FLM	Susp/Sec	110.00

GOD BLESS THE DAY WE FOUND YOU Figurine

100153	86 Mom & Dad with	UPP	$40.00	5.50"	OLB	Susp/Sec	$110.00
273	87 Adopted Son	UPP	40.00		CED	Susp/Sec	100.00
	88	UPP	47.50		FLW	Susp/Sec	95.00
	89	UPP	50.00		B&A	Susp/Sec	90.00
	90	UPP	55.00		FLM	Susp/Sec	88.00

SERVING THE LORD Figurine

100161	86 Tennis Girl	UPP	$19.00	5.00"	DVE	Susp/Sec	$75.00
218	86	UPP	19.00		OLB	Susp/Sec	66.00
	87	UPP	21.00		CED	Susp/Sec	62.00
	88	UPP	22.50		FLW	Susp/Sec	60.00
	89	UPP	25.00		B&A	Susp/Sec	58.00
	90	UPP	27.50		FLM	Susp/Sec	55.00

I'M A POSSIBILITY Figurine

100188	86 Boy with Football	UPP	$22.00	5.25"	OLB	Ret'd/Sec	$80.00
274	87	UPP	25.00		CED	Ret'd/Sec	75.00
	88	UPP	27.00		FLW	Ret'd/Sec	70.00
	89	UPP	30.00		B&A	Ret'd/Sec	68.00
	90	UPP	32.50		FLM	Ret'd/Sec	65.00
	91	UPP	32.50		VSL	Ret'd/Sec	62.00
	92	UPP	32.50		G/CL	Ret'd/Sec	60.00
	93	UPP	35.00		BFY	Ret'd/Sec	58.00

THE SPIRIT IS WILLING BUT THE FLESH IS WEAK Figurine

100196	87 Girl on Scale	UPP	$19.00	5.50"	CED	Ret'd/Sec	$75.00
324	88	UPP	24.00		FLW	Ret'd/Sec	70.00
	89	UPP	27.00		B&A	Ret'd/Sec	65.00
	90	UPP	30.00		FLM	Ret'd/Sec	60.00
	91	UPP	30.00		VSL	Ret'd/Sec	58.00

THE LORD GIVETH AND THE LORD TAKETH AWAY Figurine

100226	87 Girl with Cat & Bird Cage	UPP	$33.50	5.25"	CED	Secondary	$54.00
340	88	UPP	36.00		FLW	Secondary	42.00
	89	UPP	38.50		B&A	Secondary	40.00
	90	UPP	40.00		FLM	Secondary	40.00
	91	UPP	40.00		VSL	Secondary	40.00
	92	UPP	40.00		G/CL	Primary	40.00
	93	UPP	40.00		BFY	Primary	40.00
	94	OPEN	40.00		TRP	Primary	40.00

FRIENDS NEVER DRIFT APART Figurine

100250

219

86	Kids in Boat	UPP	$35.00	4.25"	DVE	Secondary	$80.00
86		UPP	35.00		OLB	Secondary	68.00
87		UPP	38.50		CED	Secondary	62.00
88		UPP	42.50		FLW	Secondary	60.00
89		UPP	47.50		B&A	Secondary	58.00
90		UPP	50.00		FLM	Secondary	55.00
91		UPP	50.00		VSL	Secondary	55.00
92		UPP	50.00		G/CL	Primary	55.00
93		UPP	50.00		BFY	Primary	55.00
94		OPEN	55.00		TRP	Primary	55.00

HELP LORD, I'M IN A SPOT Figurine

100269

275

86	Boy Standing in Ink Spot	UPP	$18.50	5.25"	OLB	Ret'd/Sec	$72.00
87		UPP	21.00		CED	Ret'd/Sec	68.00
88		UPP	22.50		FLW	Ret'd/Sec	62.00
89		UPP	25.00		B&A	Ret'd/Sec	60.00

HE CLEANSED MY SOUL Figurine

100277

220

86	Girl in Old Bath Tub	UPP	$24.00	4.90"	DVE	Secondary	$62.00
86		UPP	24.00		OLB	Secondary	48.00
87		UPP	27.00		CED	Secondary	45.00
88		UPP	30.00		FLW	Secondary	42.00
89		UPP	33.00		B&A	Secondary	40.00
90		UPP	35.00		FLM	Secondary	38.00
91		UPP	35.00		VSL	Secondary	38.00
92		UPP	35.00		G/CL	Primary	38.00
93		UPP	35.00		BFY	Primary	37.50
94		OPEN	37.50		TRP	Primary	37.50

HEAVEN BLESS YOU Musical TUNE: Brahm's Lullaby

100285

221

86	Baby with Bunny & Turtle	UPP	$45.00	5.00"	DVE	Susp/Sec	$115.00
86		UPP	45.00		OLB	Susp/Sec	98.00
87		UPP	50.00		CED	Susp/Sec	95.00
88		UPP	52.50		FLW	Susp/Sec	94.00
89		UPP	57.50		B&A	Susp/Sec	92.00
90		UPP	60.00		FLM	Susp/Sec	90.00
91		UPP	60.00		VSL	Susp/Sec	88.00
92		UPP	60.00		G/CL	Susp/Sec	85.00
93		UPP	60.00		BFY	Susp/Sec	82.00

SERVING THE LORD Figurine

100293

222

86	Tennis Boy	UPP	$19.00	5.25"	DVE	Susp/Sec	$58.00
86		UPP	19.00		OLB	Susp/Sec	48.00
87		UPP	21.00		CED	Susp/Sec	45.00
88		UPP	22.50		FLW	Susp/Sec	42.00
89		UPP	25.00		B&A	Susp/Sec	40.00
90		UPP	27.50		FLM	Susp/Sec	38.00

BONG BONG Doll Individually Numbered on Bottom of Foot Certificate

100455

289

86	Boy Clown	12,000	$150.00	13.00"	OLB	Secondary	$265.00

CANDY Doll Individually Numbered on Bottom of Foot Certificate

100463

290

86	Girl Clown	12,000	$150.00	13.00"	OLB	Secondary	$285.00

GOD BLESS OUR FAMILY Figurine

100498

325

87	Parents of the Groom	UPP	$35.00	5.50"	CED	Secondary	$62.00
88		UPP	40.00		FLW	Secondary	55.00
89		UPP	45.00		B&A	Secondary	52.00
90		UPP	50.00		FLM	Secondary	52.00
91		UPP	50.00		VSL	Secondary	50.00
92		UPP	50.00		G/CL	Primary	50.00
93		UPP	50.00		BFY	Primary	50.00
94		OPEN	50.00		TRP	Primary	50.00

GOD BLESS OUR FAMILY Figurine
100501 (326)

Yr	Description	Mark	Issue Price	Size	Mark	Market	Value
87	Parents of the Bride	UPP	$35.00	5.50"	CED	Secondary	$62.00
88		UPP	40.00		FLW	Secondary	55.00
89		UPP	45.00		B&A	Secondary	52.00
90		UPP	50.00		FLM	Secondary	52.00
91		UPP	50.00		VSL	Secondary	50.00
92		UPP	50.00		G/CL	Primary	50.00
93		UPP	50.00		BFY	Primary	50.00
94		OPEN	50.00		TRP	Primary	50.00

SCENT FROM ABOVE Figurine
100528 (327)

Yr	Description	Mark	Issue Price	Size	Mark	Market	Value
87	Girl with Skunk	UPP	$19.00	5.25"	OLB	Ret'd/Sec	$78.00
87		UPP	21.00		CED	Ret'd/Sec	68.00
88		UPP	23.00		FLW	Ret'd/Sec	65.00
89		UPP	25.00		B&A	Ret'd/Sec	60.00
90		UPP	27.50		FLM	Ret'd/Sec	58.00
91		UPP	27.50		VSL	Ret'd/Sec	55.00

I PICKED A (VERY) SPECIAL MOM Figurine
100536 (328)

Yr	Description	Mark	Issue Price	Size	Mark	Market	Value
87	Boy with His Gardening Mother	Annual	$37.50	5.50"	OLB	Secondary	$75.00
					CED	Secondary	65.00

The original announced title for this figurine was "I Picked A Special Mom" and it appears as though all of these annual figurines were produced with an "I Picked A Special Mom"understamp.

BROTHERLY LOVE Figurine
100544 (276)

Yr	Description	Mark	Issue Price	Size	Mark	Market	Value
86	Pilgrim & Indian with Turkey	UPP	$37.00	4.50"	OLB	Susp/Sec	$90.00
87		UPP	40.00		CED	Susp/Sec	80.00
88		UPP	42.50		FLW	Susp/Sec	78.00
89		UPP	47.50		B&A	Susp/Sec	75.00

GOD IS LOVE, DEAR VALENTINE Thimble
100625 (103)

Yr	Description	Mark	Issue Price	Size	Mark	Market	Value
86	Girl Holding Heart	UPP	$5.50	2.25"	DVE	Susp/Sec	$22.00
86		UPP	5.50		OLB	Susp/Sec	18.00
87		UPP	6.00		CED	Susp/Sec	16.00
88		UPP	7.00		FLW	Susp/Sec	15.00
89		UPP	8.00		B&A	Susp/Sec	14.00

THE LORD BLESS YOU AND KEEP YOU Thimble
100633 (313)

Yr	Description	Mark	Issue Price	Size	Mark	Market	Value
86	Bride	UPP	$5.50	2.25"	DVE	Susp/Sec	$22.00
86		UPP	5.50		OLB	Susp/Sec	19.00
87		UPP	6.00		CED	Susp/Sec	18.00
88		UPP	7.00		FLW	Susp/Sec	16.00
89		UPP	8.00		B&A	Susp/Sec	15.00
90		UPP	8.00		FLM	Susp/Sec	14.00
91		UPP	8.00		VSL	Susp/Sec	12.00

FOUR SEASONS THIMBLES Thimbles Set of 4
100641 (226)-(229)

Yr	Description	Mark	Issue Price	Size	Mark	Market	Value
86	Four Seasons Thimbles	Annual	$20.00	2.00"	OLB	Secondary	$80.00

CLOWN THIMBLES Thimbles Set of 2
100668 (235)

Yr	Description	Mark	Issue Price	Size	Mark	Market	Value
86	Clowns	UPP	$11.00	2.00"	OLB	Susp/Sec	$42.00
87		UPP	12.00		CED	Susp/Sec	38.00
88		UPP	14.00		FLW	Susp/Sec	32.00

OUR FIRST CHRISTMAS TOGETHER Musical TUNE: We Wish You A Merry Christmas
101702 (277)

Yr	Description	Mark	Issue Price	Size	Mark	Market	Value
86	Boy & Girl in Box	UPP	$50.00	5.50"	OLB	Ret'd/Sec	$130.00
87		UPP	55.00		CED	Ret'd/Sec	125.00
88		UPP	55.00		FLW	Ret'd/Sec	120.00
89		UPP	67.50		B&A	Ret'd/Sec	118.00
90		UPP	70.00		FLM	Ret'd/Sec	116.00
91		UPP	70.00		VSL	Ret'd/Sec	115.00
92		UPP	70.00		G/CL	Ret'd/Sec	112.00

NO TEARS PAST THE GATE Figurine
101826
329

87	Girl at Gate to Heaven	UPP	$40.00	6.25"	CED	Secondary	$95.00
88		UPP	47.50		FLW	Secondary	72.00
89		UPP	55.00		B&A	Secondary	68.00
90		UPP	60.00		FLM	Secondary	65.00
91		UPP	60.00		VSL	Secondary	65.00
92		UPP	60.00		G/CL	Primary	65.00
93		UPP	65.00		BFY	Primary	65.00
94		OPEN	65.00		TRP	Primary	65.00

I'M SENDING YOU A WHITE CHRISTMAS Plate, Dated First Issue "Christmas Love" Series
101834
169

86	Girl Mailing Snowball	Annual	$45.00	8.50"	OLB	Secondary	$75.00

SMILE ALONG THE WAY Figurine
101842
330

87	Clown Balancing	UPP	$30.00	6.75"	OLB	Ret'd/Sec	$200.00
87	Upside Down	UPP	33.50		CED	Ret'd/Sec	175.00
88		UPP	35.00		FLW	Ret'd/Sec	160.00
89		UPP	40.00		B&A	Ret'd/Sec	155.00
90		UPP	45.00		FLM	Ret'd/Sec	145.00
91		UPP	45.00		VSL	Ret'd/Sec	140.00

LORD, HELP US KEEP OUR ACT TOGETHER Figurine
101850
331

87	Clowns on Unicycle	UPP	$35.00	7.00"	OLB	Ret'd/Sec	$155.00
87		UPP	38.50		CED	Ret'd/Sec	130.00
88		UPP	40.00		FLW	Ret'd/Sec	125.00
89		UPP	45.00		B&A	Ret'd/Sec	120.00
90		UPP	50.00		FLM	Ret'd/Sec	120.00
91		UPP	50.00		VSL	Ret'd/Sec	115.00

WORSHIP THE LORD Figurine
102229
223

86	Boy Kneeling at	UPP	$24.00	5.50"	DVE	Secondary	$45.00
86	Church Window	UPP	24.00		OLB	Secondary	40.00
87		UPP	27.00		CED	Secondary	35.00
88		UPP	30.00		FLW	Secondary	35.00
89		UPP	33.00		B&A	Secondary	35.00
90		UPP	35.00		FLM	Secondary	35.00
91		UPP	35.00		VSL	Secondary	35.00
92		UPP	35.00		G/CL	Primary	35.00
93		UPP	35.00		BFY	Primary	35.00
94		OPEN	35.00		TRP	Primary	35.00

Some of these figurines have the title, "O Worship The Lord."

CONNIE Doll Individually Numbered
102253
291

86	Doll with Stand	7,500	$160.00	12.00"	OLB	Secondary	$250.00

SHEPHERD OF LOVE Figurine Mini Nativity Addition
102261
278

86	Angel with Black Lamb	UPP	$10.00	3.25"	OLB	Secondary	$27.00
87		UPP	10.00		CED	Secondary	22.00
88		UPP	12.50		FLW	Secondary	20.00
89		UPP	13.50		B&A	Secondary	18.00
90		UPP	15.00		FLM	Secondary	16.00
91		UPP	15.00		VSL	Secondary	16.00
92		UPP	15.00		G/CL	Primary	16.00
93		UPP	15.00		BFY	Primary	16.00
94		OPEN	16.00		TRP	Primary	16.00

SHEPHERD OF LOVE — Ornament
102288
278

Year	Description	Issue	Price	Size	Mark	Status	Value
86	Angel with Black Lamb	UPP	$10.00	3.25"	OLB	Susp/Sec	$38.00
87		UPP	11.00		CED	Susp/Sec	32.00
88		UPP	12.50		FLW	Susp/Sec	32.00
89		UPP	13.50		B&A	Susp/Sec	30.00
90		UPP	15.00		FLM	Susp/Sec	30.00
91		UPP	15.00		VSL	Susp/Sec	28.00
92		UPP	15.00		G/CL	Susp/Sec	28.00
93		UPP	15.00		BFY	Susp/Sec	25.00

MINI ANIMAL FIGURINES — Figurines — Set of 3 — Mini Nativity Addition
102296
279

Year	Description	Issue	Price	Size	Mark	Status	Value
86	Black Sheep, Bunny & Turtle	UPP	$13.50	1.75"	OLB	Susp/Sec	$35.00
87		UPP	15.00		CED	Susp/Sec	32.00
88		UPP	15.00		FLW	Susp/Sec	30.00
89		UPP	17.50		B&A	Susp/Sec	30.00
90		UPP	19.00		FLM	Susp/Sec	28.00
91		UPP	19.00		VSL	Susp/Sec	28.00
92		UPP	19.00		G/CL	Susp/Sec	25.00

WISHING YOU A COZY CHRISTMAS — Bell, Dated
102318
280

Year	Description	Issue	Price	Size	Mark	Status	Value
86	Girl with Muff	Annual	$20.00	5.50"	OLB	Secondary	$42.00

WISHING YOU A COZY CHRISTMAS — Ornament, Dated
102326
280

Year	Description	Issue	Price	Size	Mark	Status	Value
86	Girl with Muff	Annual	$10.00	3.00"	OLB	Secondary	$40.00

WISHING YOU A COZY CHRISTMAS — Thimble, Dated
102334
280

Year	Description	Issue	Price	Size	Mark	Status	Value
86	Girl with Muff	Annual	$ 5.50	2.25"	OLB	Secondary	$22.00

WISHING YOU A COZY CHRISTMAS — Figurine, Dated
102342
280

Year	Description	Issue	Price	Size	Mark	Status	Value
86	Girl with Muff	Annual	$18.00	4.75"	OLB	Secondary	$42.00

OUR FIRST CHRISTMAS TOGETHER — Ornament, Dated
102350
277

Year	Description	Issue	Price	Size	Mark	Status	Value
86	Boy and Girl in Package	Annual	$10.00	2.74"	OLB	Secondary	$30.00

WEDDING ARCH — Figurine
102369
332

Year	Description	Issue	Price	Size	Mark	Status	Value
86	Bridal Arch	UPP	$22.50	7.75"	OLB	Susp/Sec	$52.00
87		UPP	25.00		CED	Susp/Sec	50.00
88		UPP	25.00		FLW	Susp/Sec	48.00
89		UPP	27.50		B&A	Susp/Sec	45.00
90		UPP	30.00		FLM	Susp/Sec	42.00
91		UPP	30.00		VSL	Susp/Sec	40.00
92		UPP	30.00		G/CL	Susp/Sec	40.00

TRUST AND OBEY — Ornament
102377
237

Year	Description	Issue	Price	Size	Mark	Status	Value
86	Policeman Writing Ticket	UPP	$10.00	3.00"	OLB	Secondary	$25.00
87		UPP	11.00		CED	Secondary	22.00
88		UPP	12.50		FLW	Secondary	18.00
89		UPP	13.50		B&A	Secondary	17.00
90		UPP	15.00		FLM	Secondary	16.00
91		UPP	15.00		VSL	Secondary	16.00
92		UPP	15.00		G/CL	Secondary	16.00
93		UPP	15.00		BFY	Secondary	16.00
94		OPEN	16.00		TRP	Primary	16.00

LOVE RESCUED ME Ornament
102385
281

Year	Description	Type	Price	Size	Mark	Status	Value
86	Fireman Holding Puppy	UPP	$10.00	3.00"	OLB	Secondary	$25.00
87		UPP	11.00		CED	Secondary	20.00
88		UPP	12.50		FLW	Secondary	18.00
89		UPP	13.50		B&A	Secondary	16.00
90		UPP	15.00		FLM	Secondary	16.00
91		UPP	15.00		VSL	Secondary	16.00
92		UPP	15.00		G/CL	Secondary	16.00
93		UPP	15.00		BFY	Primary	16.00
94		OPEN	16.00		TRP	Primary	16.00

LOVE RESCUED ME Figurine
102393
281

Year	Description	Type	Price	Size	Mark	Status	Value
86	Fireman Holding Puppy	UPP	$22.50	5.50"	OLB	Secondary	$50.00
87		UPP	25.00		CED	Secondary	45.00
88		UPP	27.00		FLW	Secondary	42.00
89		UPP	30.00		B&A	Secondary	40.00
90		UPP	32.50		FLM	Secondary	38.00
91		UPP	32.50		VSL	Secondary	35.00
92		UPP	32.50		G/CL	Secondary	35.00
93		UPP	35.00		BFY	Primary	35.00
94		OPEN	35.00		TRP	Primary	35.00

ANGEL OF MERCY Ornament
102407
282

Year	Description	Type	Price	Size	Mark	Status	Value
86	Nurse with Potted Plant	UPP	$10.00	3.00"	OLB	Secondary	$27.00
87		UPP	11.00		CED	Secondary	22.00
88		UPP	12.50		FLW	Secondary	20.00
89		UPP	13.50		B&A	Secondary	18.00
90		UPP	15.00		FLM	Secondary	16.00
91		UPP	15.00		VSL	Secondary	16.00
92		UPP	15.00		G/CL	Secondary	16.00
93		UPP	15.00		BFY	Primary	16.00
94		OPEN	16.00		TRP	Primary	16.00

IT'S A PERFECT BOY Ornament
102415
127

Year	Description	Type	Price	Size	Mark	Status	Value
86	Boy Angel with	UPP	$10.00	3.00"	OLB	Susp/Sec	$30.00
87	Red Cross Bag	UPP	11.00		CED	Susp/Sec	28.00
88		UPP	12.50		FLW	Susp/Sec	25.00
89		UPP	13.50		B&A	Susp/Sec	22.00

LORD KEEP ME ON MY TOES Ornament
102423
216

Year	Description	Type	Price	Size	Mark	Status	Value
86	Ballerina	UPP	$10.00	3.50"	OLB	Ret'd/Sec	$50.00
87		UPP	11.00		CED*	Ret'd/Sec	45.00
88		UPP	12.50		FLW	Ret'd/Sec	42.00
89		UPP	13.50		B&A	Ret'd/Sec	40.00
90		UPP	15.00		FLM	Ret'd/Sec	38.00

* There are CEDAR TREE pieces with two hooks from the Retailers Wreath, #111465. For further information, see 6th Ed., pg. 209.

SERVE WITH A SMILE Ornament
102431
222

Year	Description	Type	Price	Size	Mark	Status	Value
86	Tennis Boy	UPP	$10.00	3.25"	OLB	Susp/Sec	$30.00
87		UPP	11.00		CED	Susp/Sec	26.00
88		UPP	12.50		FLW	Susp/Sec	24.00

SERVE WITH A SMILE Ornament
102458
218

Year	Description	Type	Price	Size	Mark	Status	Value
86	Tennis Girl	UPP	$10.00	3.25"	OLB	Susp/Sec	$34.00
87		UPP	11.00		CED	Susp/Sec	30.00
88		UPP	12.50		FLW	Susp/Sec	28.00

REINDEER Ornament, Dated Birthday Collection
102466
306

Year	Description	Type	Price	Size	Mark	Status	Value
86	Reindeer and Teddy Bear	Annual	$11.00	3.25"	OLB	Secondary	$190.00

ROCKING HORSE Ornament
102474
283

86 Rocking Horse	UPP	$10.00	2.50"	OLB	Susp/Sec	$34.00
87	UPP	11.00		CED*	Susp/Sec	28.00
88	UPP	12.50		FLW	Susp/Sec	26.00
89	UPP	13.50		B&A	Susp/Sec	25.00
90	UPP	15.00		FLM	Susp/Sec	22.00
91	UPP	15.00		VSL	Susp/Sec	20.00

* There are CEDAR TREE pieces with two hooks from the Retailers Wreath, #111465. For further information, see 6th Ed., pg. 209.

ANGEL OF MERCY Figurine
102482
282

86 Nurse with Potted Plant	UPP	$20.00	5.50"	OLB	Secondary	$44.00
87	UPP	22.50		CED	Secondary	32.00
88	UPP	24.00		FLW	Secondary	32.00
89	UPP	27.00		B&A	Secondary	30.00
90	UPP	30.00		FLM	Secondary	30.00
91	UPP	30.00		VSL	Secondary	30.00
92	UPP	30.00		G/CL	Secondary	30.00
93	UPP	30.00		BFY	Primary	30.00
94	OPEN	30.00		TRP	Primary	30.00

SHARING OUR CHRISTMAS TOGETHER Figurine
102490
284

86 Husband & Wife with	UPP	$37.00	5.25"	OLB	Susp/Sec	$82.00
87 Cookies & Pup	UPP	40.00		CED	Susp/Sec	80.00
88	UPP	45.00		FLW	Susp/Sec	70.00

BABY'S FIRST CHRISTMAS Ornament, Dated
102504
285

86 Girl with Candy Cane	Annual	$10.00	2.75"	OLB	Secondary	$30.00

BABY'S FIRST CHRISTMAS Ornament, Dated
102512
286

86 Boy with Candy Cane	Annual	$10.00	2.75"	OLB	Secondary	$28.00

LET'S KEEP IN TOUCH Musical TUNE: Be A Clown
102520
287

86 Clown on Elephant	UPP	$65.00	7.00"	OLB	Secondary	$115.00
87	UPP	70.00		CED	Secondary	100.00
88	UPP	75.00		FLW	Secondary	95.00
89	UPP	80.00		B&A	Secondary	92.00
90	UPP	85.00		FLM	Secondary	90.00
91	UPP	85.00		VSL	Secondary	90.00
92	UPP	85.00		G/CL	Primary	90.00
93	UPP	90.00		BFY	Primary	90.00
94	OPEN	90.00		TRP	Primary	90.00

WE ARE ALL PRECIOUS IN HIS SIGHT Figurine
102903
373

87 Girl with Pearl	Annual	$30.00	7.10"	CED	Secondary	$80.00

The announcement that "some" figurines were missing the title on the understamp was made in the Fall 1987 GOODNEWSLETTER. However, to date, figurines with the title appear to be nonexistent. Because of the statement in the GOODNEWSLETTER, all who own the piece without the title, and, again, to our knowledge, that's everyone, are under the mistaken impression they own a variation. For more information, see 6th Ed., pg. 223.

GOD BLESS AMERICA Figurine
102938
292

86 Uncle Sam Holding Bible with Dog	Annual	$30.00	5.50"	OLB	Secondary	$70.00

MY PEACE I GIVE UNTO THEE Plate, Dated Second Issue "Christmas Love" Series
102954
341

87 Children around Lamppost	Annual	$45.00	8.50"	CED	Secondary	$90.00

IT'S THE BIRTHDAY OF A KING — Figurine — Nativity Addition

102962 (288)	Yr	Description		Price	Size	Mark	Market	Value
	86	Boy Angel with	UPP	$19.00	5.50"	OLB	Susp/Sec	$42.00
	87	Birthday Cake	UPP	19.00		CED	Susp/Sec	38.00
	88		UPP	21.00		FLW	Susp/Sec	35.00
	89		UPP	25.00		B&A	Susp/Sec	35.00

I WOULD BE SUNK WITHOUT YOU — Figurine

102970 (342)	Yr	Description		Price	Size	Mark	Market	Value
	87	Baby Boy in Tub	UPP	$15.00	3.25"	CED	Secondary	$28.00
	88		UPP	16.00		FLW	Secondary	22.00
	89		UPP	17.50		B&A	Secondary	20.00
	90		UPP	19.00		FLM	Secondary	20.00
	91		UPP	19.00		VSL	Secondary	19.00
	92		UPP	19.00		G/CL	Primary	19.00
	93		UPP	19.00		BFY	Primary	19.00
	94		OPEN	19.00		TRP	Primary	19.00

WE BELONG TO THE LORD — Figurine — Damien-Dutton Piece

103004 (338)	Yr	Description		Price	Size	Mark	Market	Value
	86	Shepherd & Lambs Figurine w/Leather Bound Bible	UPP	$50.00	4.90"	DIA	Secondary	$225.00
							(w/o Bible)	195.00

Color photograph: 5th Ed., pg. 195.

MY LOVE WILL NEVER LET YOU GO — Figurine

103497 (333)	Yr	Description		Price	Size	Mark	Market	Value
	87	Boy with Hat & Fish	UPP	$25.00	5.50"	CED	Secondary	$47.00
	88		UPP	30.00		FLW	Secondary	42.00
	89		UPP	33.00		B&A	Secondary	40.00
	90		UPP	35.00		FLM	Secondary	38.00
	91		UPP	35.00		VSL	Secondary	36.00
	92		UPP	35.00		G/CL	Secondary	35.00
	93		UPP	35.00		BFY	Primary	35.00
	94		OPEN	35.00		TRP	Primary	35.00

I BELIEVE IN THE OLD RUGGED CROSS — Figurine

103632 (224)	Yr	Description		Price	Size	Mark	Market	Value
	86	Girl Holding Cross	UPP	$25.00	5.25"	DVE	Secondary	$55.00
	86		UPP	25.00		OLB	Secondary	42.00
	87		UPP	27.50		CED	Secondary	40.00
	88		UPP	30.00		FLW	Secondary	38.00
	89		UPP	33.00		B&A	Secondary	36.00
	90		UPP	35.00		FLM	Secondary	35.00
	91		UPP	35.00		VSL	Secondary	35.00
	92		UPP	35.00		G/CL	Primary	35.00
	93		UPP	35.00		BFY	Primary	35.00
	94		OPEN	35.00		TRP	Primary	35.00

COME LET US ADORE HIM — Figurines — Set of 9

104000 (307)	Yr	Description		Price	Size	Mark	Market	Value
	86	Nativity Set with Cassette	UPP	$ 95.00	4.75"	OLB	Secondary	$130.00
	87		UPP	95.00		CED	Secondary	125.00
	88		UPP	100.00		FLW	Secondary	125.00
	89		UPP	110.00		B&A	Secondary	125.00
	90		UPP	110.00		FLM	Secondary	125.00
	91		UPP	110.00		VSL	Secondary	125.00
	92		UPP	110.00		G/CL	Primary	125.00
	93		UPP	120.00		BFY	Primary	125.00
	94		OPEN	125.00		TRP	Primary	125.00

WITH THIS RING I... — Figurine

104019 (343)	Yr	Description		Price	Size	Mark	Market	Value
	87	Boy Giving Girl Ring	UPP	$40.00	5.00"	CED	Secondary	$72.00
	88		UPP	45.00		FLW	Secondary	68.00
	89		UPP	50.00		B&A	Secondary	65.00
	90		UPP	55.00		FLM	Secondary	62.00
	91		UPP	55.00		VSL	Secondary	60.00
	92		UPP	55.00		G/CL	Primary	60.00
	93		UPP	60.00		BFY	Primary	60.00
	94		OPEN	60.00		TRP	Primary	60.00

LOVE IS THE GLUE THAT MENDS Figurine

104027 (344)	Yr	Description	Edition	Issue Price	Size	Mark	Status	Value
	87	Boy Mending Hobby Horse	UPP	$33.50	4.00"	CED	Susp/Sec	$64.00
	88		UPP	36.00		FLW	Susp/Sec	60.00
	89		UPP	38.50		B&A	Susp/Sec	58.00
	90		UPP	40.00		FLM	Susp/Sec	55.00

CHEERS TO THE LEADER Figurine

104035 (345)	Yr	Description	Edition	Issue Price	Size	Mark	Status	Value
	87	Girl Cheerleader	UPP	$22.50	5.25"	CED	Secondary	$45.00
	88		UPP	24.00		FLW	Secondary	38.00
	89		UPP	27.00		B&A	Secondary	35.00
	90		UPP	30.00		FLM	Secondary	32.00
	91		UPP	30.00		VSL	Secondary	30.00
	92		UPP	30.00		G/CL	Primary	30.00
	93		UPP	30.00		BFY	Primary	30.00
	94		OPEN	30.00		TRP	Primary	30.00

HAPPY DAYS ARE HERE AGAIN Figurine

104396 (346)	Yr	Description	Edition	Issue Price	Size	Mark	Status	Value
	87	Girl Clown with Books	UPP	$25.00	5.25"	CED	Susp/Sec	$65.00
	88		UPP	27.00		FLW	Susp/Sec	60.00
	89		UPP	30.00		B&A	Susp/Sec	58.00
	90		UPP	32.50		FLM	Susp/Sec	55.00

FRIENDS TO THE END Figurine Birthday Collection

104418 (420)	Yr	Description	Edition	Issue Price	Size	Mark	Status	Value
	88	Rhino with Bird	UPP	$15.00	2.50"	UM	Susp/Sec	$52.00
	88		UPP	17.00		FLW	Susp/Sec	45.00
	89		UPP	17.00		B&A	Susp/Sec	42.00
	90		UPP	18.50		FLM	Susp/Sec	40.00
	91		UPP	18.50		VSL	Susp/Sec	35.00
	92		UPP	18.50		G/CL	Susp/Sec	32.00
	93		UPP	18.50		BFY	Susp/Sec	30.00

BEAR THE GOOD NEWS OF CHRISTMAS Ornament, Dated Birthday Collection

104515 (347)	Yr	Description	Edition	Issue Price	Size	Mark	Status	Value
	87	Teddy Bear in Cup on Skis	Annual	$11.00	2.10"	CED	Secondary	$25.00

"DEALERS ONLY" NATIVITY Figurines Set of 9

104523 (337)	Yr	Description	Edition	Issue Price	Size	Mark	Status	Value
	86	Nativity with Backdrop and Video	UPP	$400.00	9.00"	OLB	Secondary	$485.00

JESUS LOVES ME Figurine Easter Seal Raffle Piece Individually Numbered

104531 (2)	Yr	Description	Edition	Issue Price	Size	Mark	Status	Value
	88	Girl with Bunny	1,000	$500.00	9.00"	CED	Sec'nd'ry	$1700.00

A TUB FULL OF LOVE Figurine

104817 (348)	Yr	Description	Edition	Issue Price	Size	Mark	Status	Value
	87	Baby Boy in Wood Tub	UPP	$22.50	3.75"	CED	Secondary	$42.00
	88		UPP	24.00		FLW	Secondary	35.00
	89		UPP	27.50		B&A	Secondary	32.00
	90		UPP	30.00		FLM	Secondary	30.00
	91		UPP	30.00		VSL	Secondary	30.00
	92		UPP	30.00		G/CL	Primary	30.00
	93		UPP	30.00		BFY	Primary	30.00
	94		OPEN	30.00		TRP	Primary	30.00

SITTING PRETTY Figurine

104825 (349)	Yr	Description	Edition	Issue Price	Size	Mark	Status	Value
	87	Girl Angel on Stool	UPP	$22.50	5.50"	CED	Susp/Sec	$58.00
	88		UPP	24.00		FLW	Susp/Sec	55.00
	89		UPP	27.00		B&A	Susp/Sec	52.00
	90		UPP	30.00		FLM	Susp/Sec	50.00
	*					VSL	Susp/Sec	48.00

*Piece was suspended in 1990 yet exists in a VESSEL.

HAVE I GOT NEWS FOR YOU Figurine Nativity Addition
105635 (350)

87	Boy Reading Scroll	UPP	$22.50	4.75"	CED	Susp/Sec	$58.00
88		UPP	22.50		FLW	Susp/Sec	54.00
89		UPP	27.50		B&A	Susp/Sec	50.00
90		UPP	30.00		FLM	Susp/Sec	48.00
91		UPP	30.00		VSL	Susp/Sec	46.00

SOMETHING'S MISSING WHEN YOU'RE NOT AROUND Figurine
105643 (421)

88	Girl Holding Doll with Dog	UPP	$32.50	5.50"	FLW	Susp/Sec	$75.00
89		UPP	36.00		B&A	Susp/Sec	70.00
90		UPP	37.50		FLM	Susp/Sec	68.00
91		UPP	37.50		VSL	Susp/Sec	65.00

TO TELL THE TOOTH YOU'RE SPECIAL Figurine
105813 (351)

87	Dentist and Patient with	UPP	$38.50	5.00"	CED	Susp/Sec	$115.00
88	Pulled Tooth	UPP	42.50		FLW	Susp/Sec	105.00
89		UPP	47.50		B&A	Susp/Sec	100.00
90		UPP	50.00		FLM	Susp/Sec	95.00

HALLELUJAH COUNTRY Figurine
105821 (377)

88	Cowboy on Fence with Guitar	UPP	$35.00	5.50"	CED	Secondary	*
88		UPP	35.00		FLW	Secondary	$62.00
89		UPP	40.00		B&A	Secondary	55.00
90		UPP	45.00		FLM	Secondary	52.00
91		UPP	45.00		VSL	Secondary	50.00
92		UPP	45.00		G/CL	Secondary	45.00
93		UPP	45.00		BFY	Secondary	45.00
94		OPEN	45.00		TRP	Primary	45.00

* Extremely rare, consider FLOWER as first Annual Production Symbol.

SHOWERS OF BLESSINGS Figurine Birthday Collection
105945 (352)

87	Elephant Showering	UPP	$16.00	3.25"	CED	Ret'd/Sec	$60.00
88	Mouse	UPP	18.50		FLW	Ret'd/Sec	52.00
89		UPP	20.00		B&A	Ret'd/Sec	50.00
90		UPP	20.00		FLM	Ret'd/Sec	48.00
91		UPP	20.00		VSL	Ret'd/Sec	45.00
92		UPP	20.00		G/CL	Ret'd/Sec	42.00
93		UPP	20.00		BFY	Ret'd/Sec	40.00

BRIGHTEN SOMEONE'S DAY Figurine Birthday Collection
105953 (395)

88	Skunk & Mouse	UPP	$12.50	2.50"	CED	Susp/Sec	$45.00
88		UPP	12.50		FLW	Susp/Sec	40.00
89		UPP	13.50		B&A	Susp/Sec	38.00
90		UPP	15.00		FLM	Susp/Sec	35.00
91		UPP	15.00		VSL	Susp/Sec	32.00
92		UPP	15.00		G/CL	Susp/Sec	30.00
93		UPP	15.00		BFY	Susp/Sec	28.00

WE'RE PULLING FOR YOU Figurine
106151 (353)

87	Boy with Donkey	UPP	$40.00	5.00"	CED	Susp/Sec	$78.00
88		UPP	45.00		FLW	Susp/Sec	75.00
89		UPP	50.00		B&A	Susp/Sec	74.00
90		UPP	55.00		FLM	Susp/Sec	72.00
91		UPP	55.00		VSL	Susp/Sec	65.00

GOD BLESS YOU GRADUATE Figurine
106194 (334)

86	Boy Graduate	UPP	$20.00	5.00"	OLB	Secondary	$45.00
87		UPP	22.50		CED	Secondary	35.00
88		UPP	24.00		FLW	Secondary	32.00
89		UPP	27.00		B&A	Secondary	30.00
90		UPP	30.00		FLM	Secondary	30.00
91		UPP	30.00		VSL	Secondary	30.00
92		UPP	30.00		G/CL	Primary	30.00
93		UPP	30.00		BFY	Primary	30.00
94		OPEN	30.00		TRP	Primary	30.00

CONGRATULATIONS, PRINCESS Figurine

106208 (318)	86	Girl Graduate	UPP	$20.00	5.50"	OLB	Secondary	$50.00
	87		UPP	22.50		CED	Secondary	38.00
	88		UPP	24.00		FLW	Secondary	35.00
	89		UPP	27.00		B&A	Secondary	32.00
	90		UPP	30.00		FLM	Secondary	30.00
	91		UPP	30.00		VSL	Secondary	30.00
	92		UPP	30.00		G/CL	Secondary	30.00
	93		UPP	30.00		BFY	Primary	30.00
	94		OPEN	30.00		TRP	Primary	30.00

LORD HELP ME MAKE THE GRADE Figurine

106216 (354)	87	Schoolboy Clown	UPP	$25.00	5.00"	CED	Susp/Sec	$57.00
	88		UPP	27.00		FLW	Susp/Sec	55.00
	89		UPP	30.00		B&A	Susp/Sec	52.00
	90		UPP	32.50		FLM	Susp/Sec	50.00

HEAVEN BLESS YOUR TOGETHERNESS Figurine

106755 (378)	88	Groom Popping out of	UPP	$65.00	5.50"	CED	Secondary	$110.00
	88	Trunk at Bride	UPP	65.00		FLW	Secondary	95.00
	89		UPP	75.00		B&A	Secondary	92.00
	90		UPP	80.00		FLM	Secondary	90.00
	91		UPP	80.00		VSL	Secondary	90.00
	92		UPP	80.00		G/CL	Primary	90.00
	93		UPP	90.00		BFY	Primary	90.00
	94		OPEN	90.00		TRP	Primary	90.00

PRECIOUS MEMORIES Figurine

106763 (379)	88	Couple on Couch Looking	UPP	$37.50	4.50"	CED	Secondary	$75.00
	88	at Wedding Album	UPP	37.50		FLW	Secondary	55.00
	89		UPP	45.00		B&A	Secondary	52.00
	90		UPP	50.00		FLM	Secondary	50.00
	91		UPP	50.00		VSL	Secondary	50.00
	92		UPP	50.00		G/CL	Primary	50.00
	93		UPP	50.00		BFY	Primary	50.00
	94		OPEN	50.00		TRP	Primary	50.00

PUPPY LOVE IS FROM ABOVE Figurine

106798 (380)	88	Anniversary Couple with Dog	UPP	$45.00	5.50"	CED	Secondary	$68.00
	88		UPP	45.00		FLW	Secondary	58.00
	89		UPP	50.00		B&A	Secondary	57.00
	90		UPP	55.00		FLM	Secondary	55.00
	91		UPP	55.00		VSL	Secondary	55.00
	92		UPP	55.00		G/CL	Primary	55.00
	93		UPP	55.00		BFY	Primary	55.00
	94		OPEN	55.00		TRP	Primary	55.00

HAPPY BIRTHDAY POPPY Figurine

106836 (381)	88	Girl Holding Poppy Plant	UPP	$27.50	5.50"	CED	Susp/Sec	$64.00
	88		UPP	27.50		FLW	Susp/Sec	62.00
	89		UPP	31.50		B&A	Susp/Sec	60.00
	90		UPP	33.50		FLM	Susp/Sec	58.00
	91		UPP	33.50		VSL	Susp/Sec	55.00
	92		UPP	33.50		G/CL	Susp/Sec	54.00
	93		UPP	35.00		BFY	Susp/Sec	52.00

SEW IN LOVE Figurine

106844 (382)	88	Girl Sewing Boy's Pants	UPP	$45.00	5.50"	CED	Secondary	$72.00
	88		UPP	45.00		FLW	Secondary	62.00
	89		UPP	50.00		B&A	Secondary	58.00
	90		UPP	55.00		FLM	Secondary	55.00
	91		UPP	55.00		VSL	Secondary	55.00
	92		UPP	55.00		G/CL	Primary	55.00
	93		UPP	55.00		BFY	Primary	55.00
	94		OPEN	55.00		TRP	Primary	55.00

HE WALKS WITH ME Figurine Special Easter Seal Piece Easter Seal Lily on Decal

107999 319

87	Girl on Crutches	Annual	$25.00	5.50"	CED	Secondary	$42.00

THEY FOLLOWED THE STAR Figurines Set of 3 Mini Nativity Addition

108243 65

87	Kings on Camels	UPP	$75.00	6.50"	CED	Secondary	$125.00
88		UPP	75.00		FLW	Secondary	115.00
89		UPP	95.00		B&A	Secondary	112.00
90		UPP	100.00		FLM	Secondary	110.00
91		UPP	100.00		VSL	Secondary	110.00
92		UPP	100.00		G/CL	Primary	110.00
93		UPP	110.00		BFY	Primary	110.00
94		OPEN	110.00		TRP	Primary	110.00

THE GREATEST GIFT IS A FRIEND Figurine

109231 355

87	Baby Boy Sitting by Dog	UPP	$30.00	4.25"	CED	Secondary	$58.00
88		UPP	32.50		FLW	Secondary	44.00
89		UPP	36.00		B&A	Secondary	42.00
90		UPP	37.50		FLM	Secondary	40.00
91		UPP	37.50		VSL	Secondary	38.00
92		UPP	37.50		G/CL	Primary	37.50
93		UPP	37.50		BFY	Primary	37.50
94		OPEN	37.50		TRP	Primary	37.50

BABY'S FIRST CHRISTMAS Ornament, Dated

109401 356

87	Girl on Rocking Horse	Annual	$12.00	3.25"	CED	Secondary	$46.00

BABY'S FIRST CHRISTMAS Ornament, Dated

109428 357

87	Boy on Rocking Horse	Annual	$12.00	3.25"	CED	Secondary	$44.00

ISN'T EIGHT JUST GREAT Figurine "Birthday Circus Train" Series

109460 394

88	Ostrich - Age 8	UPP	$18.50	4.50"	CED	Secondary	$32.00
88		UPP	18.50		FLW	Secondary	25.00
89		UPP	20.00		B&A	Secondary	23.00
90		UPP	22.50		FLM	Secondary	23.00
91		UPP	22.50		VSL	Secondary	23.00
92		UPP	22.50		G/CL	Secondary	23.00
93		UPP	22.50		BFY	Primary	22.50
94		OPEN	22.50		TRP	Primary	22.50

WISHING YOU GRRR-EATNESS Figurine "Birthday Circus Train" Series

109479 393

88	Leopard - Age 7	UPP	$18.50	4.25"	CED	Secondary	$32.00
88		UPP	18.50		FLW	Secondary	28.00
89		UPP	20.00		B&A	Secondary	25.00
90		UPP	22.50		FLM	Secondary	23.00
91		UPP	22.50		VSL	Secondary	23.00
92		UPP	22.50		G/CL	Secondary	23.00
93		UPP	22.50		BFY	Primary	22.50
94		OPEN	22.50		TRP	Primary	22.50

BELIEVE THE IMPOSSIBLE Figurine

109487 383

88	Boy with Barbells	UPP	$35.00	5.50"	CED	Susp/Sec	$110.00
88		UPP	35.00		FLW	Susp/Sec	70.00
89		UPP	40.00		B&A	Susp/Sec	65.00
90		UPP	45.00		FLM	Susp/Sec	60.00
91		UPP	45.00		VSL	Susp/Sec	55.00

HAPPINESS DIVINE Figurine

109584 384

88	Clown Angel with Flowers	UPP	$25.00	5.50"	FLW	Ret'd/Sec	$80.00
89		UPP	27.50		B&A	Ret'd/Sec	70.00
90		UPP	30.00		FLM	Ret'd/Sec	65.00
91		UPP	30.00		VSL	Ret'd/Sec	62.00
92		UPP	30.00		G/CL	Ret'd/Sec	60.00

PEACE ON EARTH — Musical — TUNE: Hark! The Herald Angels Sing

109746

341

88	Kids with Pup, Kitten,	UPP	$100.00	6.50"	FLW	Susp/Sec	$160.00
89	and Bird	UPP	110.00		B&A	Susp/Sec	150.00
90		UPP	120.00		FLM	Susp/Sec	148 00
91		UPP	120.00		VSL	Susp/Sec	146.00
92		UPP	120.00		G/CL	Susp/Sec	145.00
93		UPP	130.00		BFY	Susp/Sec	142.00

WISHING YOU A YUMMY CHRISTMAS — Figurine

109754

358

87	Girl with Ice Cream	UPP	$35.00	5.00"	CED	Susp/Sec	$70.00
88		UPP	35.00		FLW	Susp/Sec	65.00
89		UPP	42.50		B&A	Susp/Sec	62.00
90		UPP	45.00		FLM	Susp/Sec	62.00
91		UPP	45.00		VSL	Susp/Sec	60.00
92		UPP	45.00		G/CL	Susp/Sec	60.00
93		UPP	50.00		BFY	Susp/Sec	58.00
94		UPP	50.00		TRP	Susp/Sec	55.00

WE GATHER TOGETHER TO ASK THE LORD'S BLESSING — Figurines — Set of 6

109762

359

87	Family Thanksgiving Set	UPP	$130.00	5.00"	CED	Secondary	$190.00
88		UPP	130.00		FLW	Secondary	165.00
89		UPP	145.00		B&A	Secondary	160.00
90		UPP	150.00		FLM	Secondary	155.00
91		UPP	150.00		VSL	Secondary	152.00
92		UPP	150.00		G/CL	Secondary	150.00
93		UPP	150.00		BFY	Secondary	150.00
94		OPEN	150.00		TRP	Primary	150.00

LOVE IS THE BEST GIFT OF ALL — Ornament, Dated

109770

360

87	Girl with Package and Doll	Annual	$11.00	2.75"	CED	Secondary	$40.00

MEOWIE CHRISTMAS — Figurine

109800

423

88	Girl with Kitten	UPP	$30.00	4.50"	FLW	Secondary	$50.00
89		UPP	33.00		B&A	Secondary	40.00
90		UPP	35.00		FLM	Secondary	38.00
91		UPP	35.00		VSL	Secondary	35.00
92		UPP	35.00		G/CL	Primary	35.00
93		UPP	35.00		BFY	Primary	35.00
94		OPEN	35.00		TRP	Primary	35.00

OH WHAT FUN IT IS TO RIDE — Figurine

109819

361

87	Grandma on Sled	UPP	$85.00	6.25"	CED	Secondary	$135.00
88		UPP	85.00		FLW	Secondary	118.00
89		UPP	100.00		B&A	Secondary	115.00
90		UPP	110.00		FLM	Secondary	112.00
91		UPP	110.00		VSL	Secondary	110.00
92		UPP	110.00		G/CL	Secondary	110.00
93		UPP	110.00		BFY	Primary	110.00
94		OPEN	110.00		TRP	Primary	110.00

LOVE IS THE BEST GIFT OF ALL — Bell, Dated

109835

360

87	Girl with Package and Doll	Annual	$22.50	5.75"	CED	Secondary	$42.00

LOVE IS THE BEST GIFT OF ALL — Thimble, Dated

109843

360

87	Girl with Package and Doll	Annual	$6.00	2.25"	CED	Secondary	$30.00

WISHING YOU A HAPPY EASTER — Figurine

109886 (388)	Yr	Description		Price	Size	Mark	Type	Value
	88	Girl Holding Bunny	UPP	$23.00	5.50"	CED	Secondary	$42.00
	88		UPP	23.00		FLW	Secondary	38.00
	89		UPP	25.00		B&A	Secondary	35.00
	90		UPP	27.50		FLM	Secondary	32.00
	91		UPP	27.50		VSL	Secondary	30.00
	92		UPP	27.50		G/CL	Secondary	30.00
	93		UPP	30.00		BFY	Primary	30.00
	94		OPEN	30.00		TRP	Primary	30.00

WISHING YOU A BASKET FULL OF BLESSINGS — Figurine

109924 (385)	Yr	Description		Price	Size	Mark	Type	Value
	88	Boy Holding Basket	UPP	$23.00	5.50"	CED	Secondary	$44.00
	88		UPP	23.00		FLW	Secondary	35.00
	89		UPP	25.00		B&A	Secondary	32.00
	90		UPP	27.50		FLM	Secondary	30.00
	91		UPP	27.50		VSL	Secondary	30.00
	92		UPP	27.50		G/CL	Secondary	30.00
	93		UPP	30.00		BFY	Primary	30.00
	94		OPEN	30.00		TRP	Primary	30.00

SENDING YOU MY LOVE — Figurine

109967 (386)	Yr	Description		Price	Size	Mark	Type	Value
	88	Girl with Hearts in Cloud	UPP	$35.00	5.00"	CED	Secondary	$67.00
	88		UPP	35.00		FLW	Secondary	52.00
	89		UPP	40.00		B&A	Secondary	50.00
	90		UPP	45.00		FLM	Secondary	48.00
	91		UPP	45.00		VSL	Secondary	46.00
	92		UPP	45.00		G/CL	Primary	45.00
	93		UPP	45.00		BFY	Primary	45.00
	94		OPEN	45.00		TRP	Primary	45.00

MOMMY, I LOVE YOU — Figurine

109975 (387)	Yr	Description		Price	Size	Mark	Type	Value
	88	Boy with Flower	UPP	$22.50	5.50"	CED	Secondary	$42.00
	88		UPP	22.50		FLW	Secondary	35.00
	89		UPP	25.00		B&A	Secondary	32.00
	90		UPP	27.50		FLM	Secondary	30.00
	91		UPP	27.50		VSL	Secondary	28.00
	92		UPP	27.50		G/CL	Primary	27.50
	93		UPP	27.50		BFY	Primary	27.50
	94		OPEN	27.50		TRP	Primary	27.50

JANUARY GIRL — Figurine — "Calendar Girl" Series

109983 (367)	Yr	Description		Price	Size	Mark	Type	Value
	88	Girl Pushing Doll in Sleigh	UPP	$37.50	5.50"	CED	Secondary	$62.00
	88		UPP	37.50		FLW	Secondary	52.00
	89		UPP	42.50		B&A	Secondary	50.00
	90		UPP	45.00		FLM	Secondary	48.00
	91		UPP	45.00		VSL	Secondary	45.00
	92		UPP	45.00		G/CL	Primary	45.00
	93		UPP	45.00		BFY	Primary	45.00
	94		OPEN	45.00		TRP	Primary	45.00

FEBRUARY GIRL — Figurine — "Calendar Girl" Series

109991 (368)	Yr	Description		Price	Size	Mark	Type	Value
	88	Girl Looking at Plant	UPP	$27.50	5.25"	CED	Secondary	$55.00
	88	Peeking through Snow	UPP	27.50		FLW	Secondary	42.00
	89		UPP	31.50		B&A	Secondary	40.00
	90		UPP	33.50		FLM	Secondary	38.00
	91		UPP	33.50		VSL	Secondary	35.00
	92		UPP	33.50		G/CL	Primary	35.00
	93		UPP	35.00		BFY	Primary	35.00
	94		OPEN	35.00		TRP	Primary	35.00

MARCH GIRL Figurine "Calendar Girl" Series
110019
369

Year	Description	Status	Issue Price	Size	Mark	Market	Value
88	Girl with Kite	UPP	$27.50	5.00"	CED	Secondary	$60.00
88		UPP	27.50		FLW	Secondary	42.00
89		UPP	31.50		B&A	Secondary	38.00
90		UPP	33.50		FLM	Secondary	35.00
91		UPP	33.50		VSL	Secondary	35.00
92		UPP	33.50		G/CL	Secondary	35.00
93		UPP	35.00		BFY	Primary	35.00
94		OPEN	35.00		TRP	Primary	35.00

APRIL GIRL Figurine "Calendar Girl" Series
110027
370

Year	Description	Status	Issue Price	Size	Mark	Market	Value
88	Girl with Umbrella	UPP	$30.00	6.00"	CED	Secondary	$110.00
88		UPP	30.00		FLW	Secondary	52.00
89		UPP	33.00		B&A	Secondary	42.00
90		UPP	35.00		FLM	Secondary	38.00
91		UPP	35.00		VSL	Secondary	36.00
92		UPP	35.00		G/CL	Secondary	35.00
93		UPP	35.00		BFY	Primary	35.00
94		OPEN	35.00		TRP	Primary	35.00

MAY GIRL Figurine "Calendar Girl" Series
110035
371

Year	Description	Status	Issue Price	Size	Mark	Market	Value
88	Girl with Potted Plant	UPP	$25.00	5.75"	CED	Secondary	$150.00
88		UPP	25.00		FLW	Secondary	45.00
89		UPP	27.50		B&A	Secondary	38.00
90		UPP	30.00		FLM	Secondary	35.00
91		UPP	30.00		VSL	Secondary	35.00
92		UPP	30.00		G/CL	Primary	35.00
93		UPP	35.00		BFY	Primary	35.00
94		OPEN	35.00		TRP	Primary	35.00

JUNE GIRL Figurine "Calendar Girl" Series
110043
372

Year	Description	Status	Issue Price	Size	Mark	Market	Value
88	Girl Dressing Up as Bride	UPP	$40.00	5.50"	CED	Secondary	$120.00
88		UPP	40.00		FLW	Secondary	60.00
89		UPP	45.00		B&A	Secondary	55.00
90		UPP	50.00		FLM	Secondary	52.00
91		UPP	50.00		VSL	Secondary	50.00
92		UPP	50.00		G/CL	Secondary	50.00
93		UPP	50.00		BFY	Primary	50.00
94		OPEN	50.00		TRP	Primary	50.00

JULY GIRL Figurine "Calendar Girl" Series
110051
424

Year	Description	Status	Issue Price	Size	Mark	Market	Value
88	Girl with Puppy in Basket	UPP	$35.00	5.50"	FLW	Secondary	$58.00
89		UPP	40.00		B&A	Secondary	50.00
90		UPP	45.00		FLM	Secondary	48.00
91		UPP	45.00		VSL	Secondary	45.00
92		UPP	45.00		G/CL	Primary	45.00
93		UPP	45.00		BFY	Primary	45.00
94		OPEN	45.00		TRP	Primary	45.00

AUGUST GIRL Figurine "Calendar Girl" Series
110078
425

Year	Description	Status	Issue Price	Size	Mark	Market	Value
88	Girl in Pool	UPP	$40.00	4.00"	FLW	Secondary	$60.00
89		UPP	45.00		B&A	Secondary	52.00
90		UPP	50.00		FLM	Secondary	50.00
91		UPP	50.00		VSL	Secondary	50.00
92		UPP	50.00		G/CL	Primary	50.00
93		UPP	50.00		BFY	Primary	50.00
94		OPEN	50.00		TRP	Primary	50.00

SEPTEMBER GIRL Figurine "Calendar Girl" Series
110086
426

Year	Description	Status	Issue Price	Size	Mark	Market	Value
88	Girl Balancing Books	UPP	$27.50	5.75"	FLW	Secondary	$50.00
89		UPP	31.50		B&A	Secondary	42.00
90		UPP	33.50		FLM	Secondary	38.00
91		UPP	33.50		VSL	Secondary	35.00
92		UPP	33.50		G/CL	Secondary	35.00
93		UPP	35.00		BFY	Primary	35.00
94		OPEN	35.00		TRP	Primary	35.00

OCTOBER GIRL Figurine "Calendar Girl" Series
110094
427

Yr	Description	Status	Price	Size	Mark	Market	Value
88	Girl with Pumpkins	UPP	$35.00	5.50"	FLW	Secondary	$55.00
89		UPP	40.00		B&A	Secondary	48.00
90		UPP	45.00		FLM	Secondary	45.00
91		UPP	45.00		VSL	Secondary	45.00
92		UPP	45.00		G/CL	Primary	45.00
93		UPP	45.00		BFY	Primary	45.00
94		OPEN	45.00		TRP	Primary	45.00

NOVEMBER GIRL Figurine "Calendar Girl" Series
110108
428

Yr	Description	Status	Price	Size	Mark	Market	Value
88	Girl in Pilgrim Suit	UPP	$32.50	5.50"	FLW	Secondary	$55.00
89		UPP	35.00		B&A	Secondary	44.00
90		UPP	37.50		FLM	Secondary	40.00
91		UPP	37.50		VSL	Secondary	42.00
92		UPP	37.50		G/CL	Secondary	38.00
93		UPP	37.50		BFY	Primary	37.50
94		OPEN	37.50		TRP	Primary	37.50

DECEMBER GIRL Figurine "Calendar Girl" Series
110116
429

Yr	Description	Status	Price	Size	Mark	Market	Value
88	Girl with Christmas Candle	UPP	$27.50	5.50"	FLW	Secondary	$52.00
89		UPP	31.50		B&A	Secondary	40.00
90		UPP	33.50		FLM	Secondary	38.00
91		UPP	33.50		VSL	Secondary	35.00
92		UPP	33.50		G/CL	Primary	35.00
93		UPP	35.00		BFY	Primary	35.00
94		OPEN	35.00		TRP	Primary	35.00

LOVE IS THE BEST GIFT OF ALL Figurine, Dated
110930
360

Yr	Description	Status	Price	Size	Mark	Market	Value
87	Girl Holding Package with Doll	Annual	$22.50	5.25"	CED	Secondary	$45.00

I'M A POSSIBILITY Ornament
111120
274

Yr	Description	Status	Price	Size	Mark	Market	Value
87	Football Player	UPP	$11.00	3.25"	CED*	Susp/Sec	$35.00
88		UPP	12.50		FLW	Susp/Sec	32.00
89		UPP	13.50		B&A	Susp/Sec	30.00
90		UPP	15.00		FLM	Susp/Sec	28.00

* There are CED pieces with two hooks from the Retailers Wreath, #111465. For further information, see 6th Ed., pg. 209.

FAITH TAKES THE PLUNGE Figurine
111155
389

Yr	Description	Status	Price	Size	Mark	Market	Value
88	Girl with Plunger	UPP	$27.50	5.50"	CED*	Secondary	$60.00
88		UPP	27.50		FLW*	Secondary	42.00
89		UPP	31.50		B&A	Secondary	40.00
90		UPP	33.50		FLM	Secondary	38.00
91		UPP	33.50		VSL	Secondary	35.00
92		UPP	33.50		G/CL	Primary	35.00
93		UPP	35.00		BFY	Primary	35.00
94		OPEN	35.00		TRP	Primary	35.00

* At some point during the 1988 production, the expression on the face was changed from a smile to a "determined frown." The smiling piece is often referred to as the "Smiling Plunger." GREENBOOK TRUMARKET PRICES are smiling with CEDAR TREE (all CED are smiling) Annual Production Symbol - $60.00 and smiling with the FLOWER Annual Production Symbol - $55.00.

TIS THE SEASON Figurine
111163
430

Yr	Description	Status	Price	Size	Mark	Market	Value
88	Girl Adding Seasoning	UPP	$27.50	5.50"	FLW	Secondary	$45.00
89		UPP	31.50		B&A	Secondary	38.00
90		UPP	33.50		FLM	Secondary	35.00
91		UPP	33.50		VSL	Secondary	35.00
92		UPP	33.50		G/CL	Primary	35.00
93		UPP	35.00		BFY	Primary	35.00
94		OPEN	35.00		TRP	Primary	35.00

O COME LET US ADORE HIM	Figurines	Set of 4					
111333	87 Large Nativity	UPP	$200.00	9.00"	CED	Susp/Sec	$250.00
362	88	UPP	200.00		FLW	Susp/Sec	220.00
	89	UPP	220.00		B&A	Susp/Sec	220.00
	90	UPP	220.00		FLM	Susp/Sec	220.00
	91	UPP	220.00		VSL	Susp/Sec	220.00

RETAILER'S WREATH	Wreath						
111465	87 Christmas Wreath	UPP	$150.00	16.00"	CED	Secondary	$225.00
410							

On some wreaths the *Have A Heavenly Christmas* ornament has the inscription "Heaven Bound" upside-down. The GREENBOOK TRUMARKET PRICE for the wreath with the upside-down "Heaven Bound" ornament is $275.00. Also see 6th Ed., pg. 209.

MOMMY, I LOVE YOU	Figurine						
112143	88 Girl with Flower	UPP	$22.50	5.75"	CED	Secondary	$42.00
390	88	UPP	22.50		FLW	Secondary	33.00
	89	UPP	25.00		B&A	Secondary	30.00
	90	UPP	27.50		FLM	Secondary	30.00
	91	UPP	27.50		VSL	Secondary	28.00
	92	UPP	27.50		G/CL	Secondary	28.00
	93	UPP	27.50		BFY	Primary	27.50
	94	OPEN	27.50		TRP	Primary	27.50

A TUB FULL OF LOVE	Figurine						
112313	87 Baby Girl in Wood Tub	UPP	$22.50	3.50"	CED	Secondary	$38.00
363	88	UPP	22.50		FLW	Secondary	32.00
	89	UPP	27.50		B&A	Secondary	30.00
	90	UPP	30.00		FLM	Secondary	30.00
	91	UPP	30.00		VSL	Secondary	30.00
	92	UPP	30.00		G/CL	Primary	30.00
	93	UPP	30.00		BFY	Primary	30.00
	94	OPEN	30.00		TRP	Primary	30.00

RETAILER'S WREATH BELL	Bell						
112348	87 Retailer's Wreath Bell	UPP	N/A	3.25"	CED	Secondary	$75.00
415							

This is the bell from the Retailer's Wreath, #111465. It has its own Enesco Item #.

YOU HAVE TOUCHED SO MANY HEARTS	Ornament						
112356	87 Girl Holding Hearts	UPP	$11.00	3.25"	CED*	Secondary	$25.00
161	88	UPP	12.50		FLW	Secondary	20.00
	89	UPP	13.50		B&A	Secondary	18.00
	90	UPP	15.00		FLM	Secondary	16.00
	91	UPP	15.00		VSL	Secondary	16.00
	92	UPP	15.00		G/CL	Primary	16.00
	93	UPP	15.00		BFY	Primary	16.00
	94	OPEN	16.00		TRP	Primary	16.00

* There are CEDAR TREE pieces with two hooks from the Retailers Wreath, #111465. For further information, see 6th Ed., pg. 209.

WADDLE I DO WITHOUT YOU	Ornament						
112364	87 Girl Clown with Goose	UPP	$11.00	3.50"	CED	Secondary	$27.00
250	88	UPP	12.50		FLW	Secondary	22.00
	89	UPP	13.50		B&A	Secondary	20.00
	90	UPP	15.00		FLM	Secondary	18.00
	91	UPP	15.00		VSL	Secondary	16.00
	92	UPP	15.00		G/CL	Secondary	16.00
	93	UPP	15.00		BFY	Primary	16.00
	94	OPEN	16.00		TRP	Primary	16.00

I'M SENDING YOU A WHITE CHRISTMAS Ornament

112372 (169)

87 Girl Mailing Snowball	UPP	$11.00	3.00"	CED*	Susp/Sec	$35.00
88	UPP	12.50		FLW	Susp/Sec	32.00
89	UPP	13.50		B&A	Susp/Sec	30.00
90	UPP	15.00		FLM	Susp/Sec	28.00
91	UPP	15.00		VSL	Susp/Sec	25.00
92	UPP	15.00		G/CL	Susp/Sec	25.00

* There are CEDAR TREE pieces with two hooks from the Retailers Wreath, #111465. For further information, see 6th Ed., pg. 209.

HE CLEANSED MY SOUL Ornament

112380 (220)

87 Girl in Old Bathtub	UPP	$12.00	2.75"	CED*	Secondary	$25.00
88	UPP	13.00		FLW	Secondary	22.00
89	UPP	15.00		B&A	Secondary	20.00
90	UPP	15.00		FLM	Secondary	18.00
91	UPP	15.00		VSL	Secondary	16.00
92	UPP	15.00		G/CL	Primary	16.00
93	UPP	15.00		BFY	Primary	16.00
94	OPEN	16.00		TRP	Primary	16.00

* There are CEDAR TREE pieces with two hooks from the Retailers Wreath, #111465. For further information, see 6th Ed., pg. 209.

OUR FIRST CHRISTMAS TOGETHER Ornament, Dated

112399 (277)

87 Boy and Girl in Package	Annual	$11.00	2.75"	CED	Secondary	$32.00

I'M SENDING YOU A WHITE CHRISTMAS Musical TUNE: White Christmas

112402 (169)

87 Girl Mailing Snowball	UPP	$55.00	6.00"	CED	Ret'd/Sec	$140.00
88	UPP	55.00		FLW	Ret'd/Sec	130.00
89	UPP	67.50		B&A	Ret'd/Sec	125.00
90	UPP	70.00		FLM	Ret'd/Sec	122.00
91	UPP	70.00		VSL	Ret'd/Sec	120.00
92	UPP	70.00		G/CL	Ret'd/Sec	118.00
93	UPP	75.00		BFY	Ret'd/Sec	115.00

YOU HAVE TOUCHED SO MANY HEARTS Musical TUNE: Everybody Loves Somebody

112577 (161)

88 Girl with Hearts	UPP	$50.00	6.50"	CED	Secondary	$75.00
88	UPP	50.00		FLW	Secondary	65.00
89	UPP	55.00		B&A	Secondary	62.00
90	UPP	60.00		FLM	Secondary	60.00
91	UPP	60.00		VSL	Secondary	60.00
92	UPP	60.00		G/CL	Secondary	60.00
93	UPP	60.00		BFY	Primary	60.00
94	OPEN	60.00		TRP	Primary	60.00

TO MY FOREVER FRIEND Ornament

113956 (214)

88 Girls with Flower Baskets	UPP	$16.00	3.00"	FLW	Secondary	$42.00
89	UPP	17.50		B&A	Secondary	37.00
90	UPP	17.50		FLM	Secondary	28.00
91	UPP	17.50		VSL	Secondary	25.00
92	UPP	17.50		G/CL	Secondary	20.00
93	UPP	17.50		BFY	Secondary	18.00
94	OPEN	17.50		TRP	Primary	17.50

SMILE ALONG THE WAY Ornament

113964 (330)

88 Clown Doing Handstand	UPP	$15.00	3.50"	FLW	Susp/Sec	$38.00
89	UPP	17.00		B&A	Susp/Sec	35.00
90	UPP	17.50		FLM	Susp/Sec	32.00
91	UPP	17.50		VSL	Susp/Sec	30.00
92	UPP	17.50		G/CL	Susp/Sec	28.00
93	UPP	17.50		BFY	Susp/Sec	25.00

GOD SENT YOU JUST IN TIME Ornament

113972	88 Clown with Jack-in-the-Box	UPP	$13.50	3.00"	FLW	Susp/Sec	$38.00
256	89	UPP	15.00		B&A	Susp/Sec	32.00
	90	UPP	15.00		FLM	Susp/Sec	30.00
	91	UPP	15.00		VSL	Susp/Sec	28.00

REJOICE O EARTH Ornament

113980	88 Angel with Trumpet	UPP	$13.50	3.00"	FLW	Ret'd/Sec	$45.00
67	89	UPP	15.00		B&A	Ret'd/Sec	42.00
	90	UPP	15.00		FLM	Ret'd/Sec	40.00
	91	UPP	15.00		VSL	Ret'd/Sec	38.00

CHEERS TO THE LEADER Ornament

113999	88 Cheerleader	UPP	$13.50	3.00"	FLW	Susp/Sec	$38.00
345	89	UPP	15.00		B&A	Susp/Sec	32.00
	90	UPP	15.00		FLM	Susp/Sec	30.00
	91	UPP	15.00		VSL	Susp/Sec	28.00

MY LOVE WILL NEVER LET YOU GO Ornament

114006	88 Fisherman	UPP	$13.50	3.25"	FLW	Susp/Sec	$35.00
333	89	UPP	15.00		B&A	Susp/Sec	32.00
	90	UPP	15.00		FLM	Susp/Sec	30.00
	91	UPP	15.00		VSL	Susp/Sec	28.00

THIS TOO SHALL PASS Figurine

114014	88 Boy with Broken Heart	UPP	$23.00	5.50"	CED	Secondary	$36.00
391	88	UPP	23.00		FLW	Secondary	35.00
	89	UPP	25.00		B&A	Secondary	32.00
	90	UPP	27.50		FLM	Secondary	32.00
	91	UPP	27.50		VSL	Secondary	30.00
	92	UPP	27.50		G/CL	Primary	30.00
	93	UPP	30.00		BFY	Primary	30.00
	94	OPEN	30.00		TRP	Primary	30.00

THE GOOD LORD HAS BLESSED US TENFOLD Figurine 10th Anniversary Commemorative Edition

114022	88 Couple with Dogs and Puppies	Annual	$90.00	5.75"	CED	Secondary	$175.00
392					FLW	Secondary	165.00

YOU ARE MY MAIN EVENT Figurine Special Events Piece

115231	88 Girl Holding Balloons and Bag	Annual	$30.00	6.50"	CED	Secondary	$60.00
397					FLW	Secondary	55.00

The balloon strings on this piece are metal wires covered with colored paper. The first CEDAR TREE pieces produced had pink strings - the rest of the production (balance of CEDAR TREE and all of FLOWER) had white strings. "Pink Strings" is the coveted piece. The GREENBOOK TRUMARKET PRICE for "Pink Strings" is $90.00. Color photograph: 4th Ed., pg. 196 or 5th Ed., pg. 201.

SOME BUNNY'S SLEEPING Figurines Nativity Addition

115274	88 Bunnies	UPP	$15.00	2.75"	FLW	Secondary	$30.00
431	89	UPP	17.00		B&A	Secondary	22.00
	90	UPP	18.50		FLM	Secondary	20.00
	91	UPP	18.50		VSL	Secondary	19.00
	92	UPP	18.50		G/CL	Secondary	19.00
	93	UPP	18.50		BFY	Primary	18.50
	94	OPEN	18.50		TRP	Primary	18.50

BABY'S FIRST CHRISTMAS Ornament, Dated

115282	88 Boy in Sleigh	Annual	$15.00	2.25"	FLW	Secondary	$25.00
432							

OUR FIRST CHRISTMAS TOGETHER Figurine

115290	88 Couple with Gifts	UPP	$50.00	5.50"	FLW	Susp/Sec	$85.00
433	89	UPP	55.00		B&A	Susp/Sec	82.00
	90	UPP	60.00		FLM	Susp/Sec	78.00
	91	UPP	60.00		VSL	Susp/Sec	75.00

TIME TO WISH YOU A MERRY CHRISTMAS Bell, Dated
115304 88 Girl Holding Clock with Mouse Annual $25.00 6.00" FLW Secondary $45.00
434

TIME TO WISH YOU A MERRY CHRISTMAS Thimble, Dated
115312 88 Girl with Clock and Mouse Annual $ 7.00 2.00" FLW Secondary $42.00
434

TIME TO WISH YOU A MERRY CHRISTMAS Ornament, Dated
115320 88 Girl with Clock and Mouse Annual $13.00 3.00" FLW Secondary $50.00
434

TIME TO WISH YOU A MERRY CHRISTMAS Figurine, Dated
115339 88 Girl Holding Clock with Mouse Annual $24.00 5.00" FLW Secondary $38.00
434

BLESSED ARE THEY THAT OVERCOME Figurine Special Easter Seal Piece
115479 88 Boy on Crutches at Finish Line Annual $27.50 5.50" CED Secondary $36.00
396 FLW Secondary 34.00
Easter Seal Lily missing on all decals.

THE VOICE OF SPRING Musical Jack-in-the-Box "The Four Seasons" Series TUNE: April Love
408735 90 Spring Girl 2yr $200.00 13.00" FLM Primary $200.00
226 91 200.00 VSL Primary 200.00

SUMMER'S JOY Musical Jack-in-the-Box "The Four Seasons" Series TUNE: You Are My Sunshine
408743 90 Summer Girl 2yr $200.00 13.00" FLM Primary $200.00
227 91 200.00 VSL Primary 200.00

AUTUMN'S PRAISE Musical Jack-in-the-Box "The Four Seasons" Series TUNE: Autumn Leaves
408751 90 Autumn Girl 2yr $200.00 13.00" FLM Primary $200.00
228 91 200.00 VSL Primary 200.00

WINTER'S SONG Musical Jack-in-the-Box "The Four Seasons" Series TUNE: Thru The Eyes Of Love
408778 90 Winter Girl 2yr $200.00 13.00" FLM Primary $200.00
229 91 200.00 VSL Primary 200.00

THE VOICE OF SPRING Doll "The Four Seasons" Series
408786 90 Spring Girl 2yr $150.00 15.00" FLM Primary $150.00
226 91 150.00 VSL Primary 150.00

SUMMER'S JOY Doll "The Four Seasons" Series
408794 90 Summer Girl 2yr $150.00 15.00" FLM Primary $150.00
227 91 150.00 VSL Primary 150.00

AUTUMN'S PRAISE Doll "The Four Seasons" Series
408808 90 Autumn Girl 2yr $150.00 15.00" FLM Primary $150.00
228 91 150.00 VSL Primary 150.00

WINTER'S SONG Doll "The Four Seasons" Series
408816 90 Winter Girl 2yr $150.00 15.00" FLM Primary $150.00
229 91 150.00 VSL Primary 150.00

MAY YOU HAVE AN OLD FASHIONED CHRISTMAS Musical Jack-in-the-Box
TUNE: Have Yourself A Merry Little
417777 91 Christmas Girl 2yr $200.00 12.00" VSL Primary $200.00
548 92 in Plaid Dress 200.00 G/CL Primary 200.00

MAY YOU HAVE AN OLD FASHIONED CHRISTMAS Doll
417785 91 Christmas Girl 2yr $150.00 12.00" FLM Primary $150.00
548 92 in Plaid Dress 150.00 VSL Primary 150.00
92 150.00 C/CL Primary 150.00

YOU HAVE TOUCHED SO MANY HEARTS — Musical Jack-in-the-Box — TUNE: Everybody Loves Somebody

422282 (161)

91	Girl with String of Hearts	2yr	$175.00	12.00"	FLM	Secondary	$175.00
91			175.00		VSL	Primary	175.00
92			175.00		G/CL	Primary	175.00

YOU HAVE TOUCHED SO MANY HEARTS — Doll

427527 (161)

91	Girl with String of Hearts	2yr	$90.00	12.00"	FLM	Primary	$90.00
91			90.00		VSL	Primary	90.00
92			90.00		G/CL	Primary	90.00

THE EYES OF THE LORD ARE UPON YOU — Motion Musical Doll — TUNE: Brahm's Lullaby

429570 (522)

91	Baby Boy on Pillow	UPP	$65.00	10.00"	FLM	Susp/Sec	$70.00
91		UPP	65.00		VSL	Susp/Sec	65.00
92		UPP	65.00		G/CL	Susp/Prim	65.00
93		UPP	65.00		BFY	Susp/Prim	65.00
94		OPEN	65.00		TRP	Susp/Prim	65.00

THE EYES OF THE LORD ARE UPON YOU — Motion Musical Doll — TUNE: Brahm's Lullaby

429589 (523)

91	Baby Girl on Pillow	UPP	$65.00	10.00"	FLM	Susp/Sec	$70.00
91		UPP	65.00		VSL	Susp/Sec	65.00
92		UPP	65.00		G/CL	Susp/Prim	65.00
93		UPP	65.00		BFY	Susp/Prim	65.00
94		OPEN	65.00		TRP	Susp/Prim	65.00

OUR FIRST CHRISTMAS TOGETHER — Ornament, Dated

520233 (277)

88	Boy and Girl in Package	Annual	$13.00	2.50"	FLW	Secondary	$20.00

BABY'S FIRST CHRISTMAS — Ornament, Dated

520241 (435)

88	Girl in Sleigh	Annual	$15.00	2.25"	FLW	Secondary	$25.00

REJOICE O EARTH — Figurine — Mini Nativity Addition

520268 (67)

88	Angel with Trumpet	UPP	$13.00	3.00"	FLW	Secondary	$30.00
89		UPP	15.00		B&A	Secondary	20.00
90		UPP	15.00		FLM	Secondary	16.00
91		UPP	15.00		VSL	Secondary	16.00
92		UPP	15.00		G/CL	Secondary	16.00
93		UPP	15.00		BFY	Primary	16.00
94		OPEN	16.00		TRP	Primary	16.00

YOU ARE MY GIFT COME TRUE — Ornament, Dated — 10th Anniversary Commemorative Piece

520276 (436)

88	Puppy in Sock	Annual	$12.50	2.50"	FLW	Secondary	$22.00

MERRY CHRISTMAS, DEER — Plate, Dated — Third Issue "Christmas Love" Series

520284 (438)

88	Girl Decorating Reindeer	Annual	$50.00	8.25"	FLW	Secondary	$75.00

HANG ON FOR THE HOLLY DAYS — Ornament, Dated — Birthday Collection

520292 (400)

88	Kitten Hanging on to Wreath	Annual	$13.00	3.50"	FLW	Secondary	$30.00

MAKE A JOYFUL NOISE — Figurine — Easter Seal Raffle Piece — Individually Numbered

520322 (5)

89	Girl with Goose	1,500	$500.00	9.00"	B&A	Secondary	$950.00

JESUS THE SAVIOR IS BORN — Figurine — Nativity Addition

520357 (437)

88	Angel with Newspaper and Dog	UPP	$25.00	4.50"	FLW	Susp/Sec	$55.00
89		UPP	30.00		B&A	Susp/Sec	52.00
90		UPP	32.50		FLM	Susp/Sec	50.00
91		UPP	32.50		VSL	Susp/Sec	48.00
92		UPP	32.50		G/CL	Susp/Sec	45.00
93		UPP	32.50		BFY	Susp/Sec	42.00

I'M NUTS ABOUT YOU Ornament, Dated Birthday Collection

520411	92	Squirrel Decorating Tree atop Log Filled w/Nuts	Annual	$16.00	2.50"	G/CL	Secondary	$22.00
570								

SNO-BUNNY FALLS FOR YOU LIKE I DO Ornament, Dated Birthday Collection

520438	91	Rabbit on Skates	Annual	$15.00	3.25"	VSL	Secondary	$28.00
549								

CHRISTMAS IS RUFF WITHOUT YOU Ornament, Dated Birthday Collection

520462	89	Puppy Resting on Elbow	Annual	$13.00	2.75"	B&A	Secondary	$40.00
470								

TAKE A BOW 'CUZ YOU'RE MY CHRISTMAS STAR Ornament
Distinguished Service Retailer Open House Weekend

520470	94	Pup/Hat/Scarf Carries Holly Sprig	OPEN	$16.00	2.75"	TRP	Primary	$16.00
690								

SLOW DOWN AND ENJOY THE HOLIDAYS Ornament, Dated Birthday Collection

520489	93	Reindeer Turtle Carrying Gift	Annual	$16.00	2.50"	BFY	Secondary	$24.00
616								

WISHING YOU A PURR-FECT HOLIDAY Ornament, Dated Birthday Collection

520497	90	Kitten with Ornament	Annual	$15.00	2.75"	FLM	Secondary	$32.00
521								

THE LORD TURNED MY LIFE AROUND Figurine

520535	92	Ballerina on Pointe	UPP	$35.00	5.75"	G/CL	Secondary	$40.00
571	93		UPP	35.00		BFY	Primary	35.00
	94		OPEN	35.00		TRP	Primary	35.00

IN THE SPOTLIGHT OF HIS GRACE Figurine

520543	91	Ballerina on Pointe	UPP	$35.00	5.75"	VSL	Secondary	$42.00
524	92		UPP	35.00		G/CL	Secondary	35.00
	93		UPP	35.00		BFY	Primary	35.00
	94		OPEN	35.00		TRP	Primary	35.00

LORD, TURN MY LIFE AROUND Figurine

520551	90	Ballerina	UPP	$35.00	5.75"	B&A	Secondary	$52.00
493	90		UPP	35.00		FLM	Secondary	42.00
	91		UPP	35.00		VSL	Secondary	38.00
	92		UPP	35.00		G/CL	Secondary	35.00
	93		UPP	35.00		BFY	Secondary	35.00
	94		OPEN	35.00		TRP	Primary	35.00

YOU DESERVE AN OVATION Figurine

520578	92	Ballerina on Pointe	UPP	$35.00	5.75"	G/CL	Secondary	$38.00
572	93		UPP	35.00		BFY	Primary	35.00
	94		OPEN	35.00		TRP	Primary	35.00

MY HEART IS EXPOSED WITH LOVE Figurine

520624	89	Nurse X-raying Boy's Heart	UPP	$45.00	5.25"	FLW	Secondary	$62.00
458	89		UPP	45.00		B&A	Secondary	55.00
	90		UPP	50.00		FLM	Secondary	50.00
	91		UPP	50.00		VSL	Secondary	50.00
	92		UPP	50.00		G/CL	Primary	50.00
	93		UPP	50.00		BFY	Primary	50.00
	94		OPEN	50.00		TRP	Primary	50.00

A FRIEND IS SOMEONE WHO CARES Figurine

520632	89	Mouse Wiping Clown's Tears	UPP	$30.00	4.25"	FLW	Secondary	$55.00
449	89		UPP	30.00		B&A	Secondary	40.00
	90		UPP	32.50		FLM	Secondary	35.00
	91		UPP	32.50		VSL	Secondary	35.00
	92		UPP	32.50		G/CL	Secondary	35.00
	93		UPP	32.50		BFY	Primary	35.00
	94		OPEN	35.00		TRP	Primary	35.00

I'M SO GLAD YOU FLUTTERED INTO MY LIFE   Figurine

520640

447

89	Angel with Butterfly Net	UPP	$40.00	5.75"	FLW	Ret'd/Sec	$375.00
89		UPP	40.00		B&A	Ret'd/Sec	350.00
90		UPP	45.00		FLM	Ret'd/Sec	290.00
91		UPP	45.00		VSL	Ret'd/Sec	280.00

EGGSPECIALLY FOR YOU   Figurine

520667

455

89	Girl with Hen & Easter Egg	UPP	$45.00	4.75"	FLW	Secondary	$65.00
89		UPP	45.00		B&A	Secondary	55.00
90		UPP	50.00		FLM	Secondary	52.00
91		UPP	50.00		VSL	Secondary	50.00
92		UPP	50.00		G/CL	Primary	50.00
93		UPP	50.00		BFY	Primary	50.00
94		OPEN	50.00		TRP	Primary	50.00

YOUR LOVE IS SO UPLIFTING   Figurine

520675

454

89	Boy Holding Girl at Fountain	UPP	$60.00	6.50"	FLW	Secondary	$85.00
89		UPP	60.00		B&A	Secondary	80.00
90		UPP	65.00		FLM	Secondary	78.00
91		UPP	65.00		VSL	Secondary	75.00
92		UPP	65.00		G/CL	Primary	75.00
93		UPP	75.00		BFY	Primary	75.00
94		OPEN	75.00		TRP	Primary	75.00

SENDING YOU SHOWERS OF BLESSINGS   Figurine

520683

450

89	Boy with Newspaper	UPP	$32.50	5.50"	FLW	Ret'd/Sec	$68.00
89	over Head	UPP	32.50		B&A	Ret'd/Sec	65.00
90		UPP	35.00		FLM	Ret'd/Sec	62.00
91		UPP	35.00		VSL	Ret'd/Sec	60.00
92		UPP	35.00		G/CL	Ret'd/Sec	55.00

LORD, KEEP MY LIFE IN BALANCE   Musical   TUNE: Music Box Dancer

520691

525

91	Ballerina at Barre	UPP	$60.00	7.00"	VSL	Susp/Sec	$82.00
92		UPP	60.00		G/CL	Susp/Sec	75.00
93		UPP	65.00		BFY	Susp/Sec	68.00

BABY'S FIRST PET   Figurine   Fifth Issue "Baby's First" Series

520705

461

89	Boy with Baby Feeding Dog	UPP	$45.00	5.25"	FLW	Susp/Sec	$80.00
89		UPP	45.00		B&A	Susp/Sec	75.00
90		UPP	50.00		FLM	Susp/Sec	72.00
91		UPP	50.00		VSL	Susp/Sec	72.00
92		UPP	50.00		G/CL	Susp/Sec	70.00
93		UPP	50.00		BFY	Susp/Sec	68.00
94		UPP	50.00		TRP	Susp/Sec	65.00

JUST A LINE TO WISH YOU A HAPPY DAY   Figurine

520721

456

89	Dog Pulling Boy's	UPP	$65.00	6.50"	FLW	Secondary	$85.00
89	Fishing Line	UPP	65.00		B&A	Secondary	80.00
90		UPP	70.00		FLM	Secondary	78.00
91		UPP	70.00		VSL	Secondary	75.00
92		UPP	70.00		G/CL	Primary	75.00
93		UPP	75.00		BFY	Primary	75.00
94		OPEN	75.00		TRP	Primary	75.00

FRIENDSHIP HITS THE SPOT   Figurine

520748

453

89	Two Girls Having Tea	UPP	$55.00	5.25"	FLW	Secondary	$78.00
89		UPP	55.00		B&A	Secondary	70.00
90		UPP	60.00		FLM	Secondary	68.00
91		UPP	60.00		VSL	Secondary	65.00
92		UPP	60.00		G/CL	Secondary	65.00
93		UPP	65.00		BFY	Primary	65.00
94		OPEN	65.00		TRP	Primary	65.00

JESUS IS THE ONLY WAY Figurine
520756
464

89	Boy at Crossroads	UPP	$40.00	6.00"	FLW	Susp/Sec	$68.00
89		UPP	40.00		B&A	Susp/Sec	62.00
90		UPP	45.00		FLM	Susp/Sec	60.00
91		UPP	45.00		VSL	Susp/Sec	60.00
92		UPP	45.00		G/CL	Susp/Sec	58.00
93		UPP	45.00		BFY	Susp/Sec	55.00

PUPPY LOVE Figurine
520764
465

89	Two Puppies	UPP	$12.50	2.10"	FLW	Secondary	$25.00
89		UPP	12.50		B&A	Secondary	20.00
90		UPP	13.50		FLM	Secondary	18.00
91		UPP	13.50		VSL	Secondary	16.00
92		UPP	13.50		G/CL	Primary	16.00
93		UPP	15.00		BFY	Primary	16.00
94		OPEN	16.00		TRP	Primary	16.00

MANY MOONS IN SAME CANOE, BLESSUM YOU Figurine
520772
457

89	Indians in Canoe	UPP	$50.00	5.00"	FLW	Ret'd/Sec	$250.00
89		UPP	50.00		B&A	Ret'd/Sec	230.00
90		UPP	55.00		FLM	Ret'd/Sec	200.00

WISHING YOU ROADS OF HAPPINESS Figurine
520780
460

89	Bride & Groom in Car	UPP	$60.00	4.50"	FLW	Secondary	$85.00
89		UPP	60.00		B&A	Secondary	80.00
90		UPP	65.00		FLM	Secondary	75.00
91		UPP	65.00		VSL	Secondary	75.00
92		UPP	65.00		G/CL	Secondary	75.00
93		UPP	70.00		BFY	Secondary	75.00
94		OPEN	75.00		TRP	Primary	75.00

SOMEDAY MY LOVE Figurine
520799
446

89	Bride with Dress	UPP	$40.00	5.50"	FLW	Ret'd/Sec	$85.00
89		UPP	40.00		B&A	Ret'd/Sec	80.00
90		UPP	45.00		FLM	Ret'd/Sec	75.00
91		UPP	45.00		VSL	Ret'd/Sec	72.00
92		UPP	45.00		G/CL	Ret'd/Sec	70.00

MY DAYS ARE BLUE WITHOUT YOU Figurine
520802
462

89	Girl with Paint & Ladder	UPP	$65.00	7.00"	FLW*	Susp/Sec	$110.00
89		UPP	65.00		B&A*	Susp/Sec	95.00
90		UPP	70.00		FLM	Susp/Sec	90.00
91		UPP	70.00		VSL	Susp/Sec	85.00

* Exists with three variations of the mouth - smiling, frowning, and "O." Smiling is considered the variation - Smiling with FLW @ $115.00 and Smiling with B&A @ $105.00.

WE NEED A GOOD FRIEND THROUGH THE RUFF TIMES Figurine
520810
452

89	Grandpa with Cane & Dog	UPP	$35.00	5.00"	FLW	Susp/Sec	$60.00
89		UPP	35.00		B&A	Susp/Sec	52.00
90		UPP	37.50		FLM	Susp/Sec	50.00
91		UPP	37.50		VSL	Susp/Sec	48.00

YOU ARE MY NUMBER ONE Figurine
520829
448

89	Girl Holding Trophy	UPP	$25.00	6.00"	FLW	Secondary	$40.00
89		UPP	25.00		B&A	Secondary	35.00
90		UPP	27.50		FLM	Secondary	32.00
91		UPP	27.50		VSL	Secondary	30.00
92		UPP	27.50		G/CL	Primary	30.00
93		UPP	30.00		BFY	Primary	30.00
94		OPEN	30.00		TRP	Primary	30.00

THE LORD IS YOUR LIGHT TO HAPPINESS Figurine
520837
466

89	Bridal Couple	UPP	$50.00	4.75"	FLW	Secondary	$70.00
89	Lighting Candle	UPP	50.00		B&A	Secondary	65.00
90		UPP	55.00		FLM	Secondary	62.00
91		UPP	55.00		VSL	Secondary	60.00
92		UPP	55.00		G/CL	Primary	60.00
93		UPP	60.00		BFY	Primary	60.00
94		OPEN	60.00		TRP	Primary	60.00

WISHING YOU A PERFECT CHOICE Figurine
520845
459

89	Boy Proposing to Girl	UPP	$55.00	5.80"	FLW	Secondary	$75.00
89		UPP	55.00		B&A	Secondary	70.00
90		UPP	60.00		FLM	Secondary	68.00
91		UPP	60.00		VSL	Secondary	65.00
92		UPP	60.00		G/CL	Primary	65.00
93		UPP	65.00		BFY	Primary	65.00
94		OPEN	65.00		TRP	Primary	65.00

I BELONG TO THE LORD Figurine
520853
463

89	Orphan Girl	UPP	$25.00	5.10"	FLW	Susp/Sec	$50.00
89		UPP	25.00		B&A	Susp/Sec	44.00
90		UPP	27.50		FLM	Susp/Sec	42.00
91		UPP	27.50		VSL	Susp/Sec	40.00

SHARING BEGINS IN THE HEART Figurine Special Events Piece
520861
467

89	Girl with Chalkboard	Annual	$25.00	5.75"	FLW	Secondary	$82.00
					B&A	Secondary	45.00

HEAVEN BLESS YOU Figurine
520934
221

90	Baby with Bunny and	UPP	$35.00	3.50"	B&A	Secondary	$150.00
90	Turtle	UPP	35.00		FLM	Secondary	45.00
91		UPP	35.00		VSL	Secondary	35.00
92		UPP	35.00		G/CL	Primary	35.00
93		UPP	35.00		BFY	Primary	35.00
94		OPEN	35.00		TRP	Primary	35.00

THERE IS NO GREATER TREASURE THAN TO HAVE A FRIEND LIKE YOU Figurine
521000
617

93	Boy Swimmer Holding	UPP	$30.00	5.50"	G/CL	Secondary	$35.00
93	Oyster with Pearl	UPP	30.00		BFY	Primary	30.00
94		OPEN	30.00		TRP	Primary	30.00

TO MY FAVORITE FAN Figurine
521043
501

90	Gorilla and Parrot	UPP	$16.00	2.50"	B&A	Susp/Sec	$55.00
90		UPP	16.00		FLM	Susp/Sec	40.00
91		UPP	16.00		VSL	Susp/Sec	38.00
92		UPP	16.00		G/CL	Susp/Sec	35.00
93		UPP	16.00		BFY	Susp/Sec	32.00

HELLO WORLD! Figurine Birthday Collection
521175
451

89	Kangaroo with Baby	UPP	$13.50	3.25"	FLW	Secondary	$30.00
89		UPP	13.50		B&A	Secondary	20.00
90		UPP	15.00		FLM	Secondary	18.00
91		UPP	15.00		VSL	Secondary	16.00
92		UPP	15.00		G/CL	Secondary	16.00
93		UPP	15.00		BFY	Primary	16.00
94		OPEN	16.00		TRP	Primary	16.00

THAT'S WHAT FRIENDS ARE FOR Figurine
521183
520

90	Crying Girls Hugging	UPP	$45.00	6.00"	FLM	Secondary	$57.00
91		UPP	45.00		VSL	Secondary	50.00
92		UPP	45.00		G/CL	Primary	45.00
93		UPP	45.00		BFY	Primary	45.00
94		OPEN	45.00		TRP	Primary	45.00

HOPE YOU'RE UP AND ON THE TRAIL AGAIN Figurine
521205
494

90	Girl on Hobby Horse	UPP	$35.00	5.50"	B&A	Susp/Sec	$60.00
90		UPP	35.00		FLM	Susp/Sec	52.00
91		UPP	35.00		VSL	Susp/Sec	50.00
92		UPP	35.00		G/CL	Susp/Sec	48.00
93		UPP	35.00		BFY	Susp/Sec	45.00

THE FRUIT OF THE SPIRIT IS LOVE Figurine
521213
618

93	Girl Holding Bowl	UPP	$30.00	6.00"	BFY	Secondary	$33.00
94	of Fruit	OPEN	30.00		TRP	Primary	30.00

TAKE HEED WHEN YOU STAND Figurine
521272
550

91	Boy on Rocking Horse	UPP	$55.00	6.00"	VSL	Susp/Sec	$75.00
92		UPP	55.00		G/CL	Susp/Sec	70.00
93		UPP	55.00		BFY	Susp/Sec	65.00
94		UPP	55.00		TRP	Susp/Sec	62.00

HAPPY TRIP Figurine
521280
499

90	Girl on Roller Skates	UPP	$35.00	5.75"	B&A	Susp/Sec	$95.00
90		UPP	35.00		FLM	Susp/Sec	55.00
91		UPP	35.00		VSL	Susp/Sec	50.00
92		UPP	35.00		G/CL	Susp/Sec	50.00
93		UPP	35.00		BFY	Susp/Sec	48.00
94		UPP	35.00		TRP	Susp/Sec	45.00

HUG ONE ANOTHER Figurine
521299
526

91	Girl and Boy Hugging	UPP	$45.00	5.50"	FLM	Secondary	$55.00
91		UPP	45.00		VSL	Secondary	50.00
92		UPP	45.00		G/CL	Secondary	50.00
93		UPP	45.00		BFY	Primary	50.00
94		OPEN	50.00		TRP	Primary	50.00

MAY ALL YOUR CHRISTMASES BE WHITE Ornament
521302
477

89	Girl Tying Snowball with	UPP	$13.50	3.25"	B&A	Susp/Sec	$32.00
90	Ribbon	UPP	15.00		FLM	Susp/Sec	28.00
91		UPP	15.00		VSL	Susp/Sec	27.00
92		UPP	15.00		G/CL	Susp/Sec	25.00
93		UPP	15.00		BFY	Susp/Sec	24.00
94		UPP	16.00		TRP	Susp/Sec	22.00

YIELD NOT TO TEMPTATION Figurine
521310
505

90	Girl with Apple	UPP	$27.50	5.50"	B&A	Susp/Sec	$50.00
90		UPP	27.50		FLM	Susp/Sec	48.00
91		UPP	27.50		VSL	Susp/Sec	47.00
92		UPP	27.50		G/CL	Susp/Sec	45.00
93		UPP	30.00		BFY	Susp/Sec	42.00

FAITH IS A VICTORY Figurine
521396
496

90	Girl Wearing Boxing Gloves	UPP	$25.00	5.50"	B&A	Ret'd/Sec	$175.00
90		UPP	25.00		FLM	Ret'd/Sec	160.00
91		UPP	25.00		VSL	Ret'd/Sec	150.00
92		UPP	25.00		G/CL	Ret'd/Sec	135.00
93		UPP	27.50		BFY	Ret'd/Sec	120.00

I'LL NEVER STOP LOVING YOU Figurine
521418
511

90	Girl with Letters Y O U	UPP	$37.50	5.50"	B&A	Secondary	$50.00
90		UPP	37.50		FLM	Secondary	42.00
91		UPP	37.50		VSL	Secondary	40.00
92		UPP	37.50		G/CL	Secondary	38.00
93		UPP	37.50		BFY	Primary	37.50
94		OPEN	37.50		TRP	Primary	37.50

TO A VERY SPECIAL MOM AND DAD Figurine
521434
551

91	Girl Holding Picture Frame	UPP	$35.00	5.75"	VSL	Susp/Sec	$50.00
92		UPP	35.00		G/CL	Susp/Sec	45.00
93		UPP	35.00		BFY	Susp/Sec	42.00

LORD, HELP ME STICK TO MY JOB Figurine
521450 (503)

Year	Description	Status	Price	Size	Mark	Market	Value
90	Girl with Account Books	UPP	$30.00	5.75"	B&A	Secondary	$45.00
90	and Glue	UPP	30.00		FLM	Secondary	40.00
91		UPP	30.00		VSL	Secondary	38.00
92		UPP	30.00		G/CL	Primary	35.00
93		UPP	35.00		BFY	Primary	35.00
94		OPEN	35.00		TRP	Primary	35.00

TELL IT TO JESUS Figurine
521477 (476)

Year	Description	Status	Price	Size	Mark	Market	Value
89	Girl on Telephone	UPP	$35.00	5.25"	B&A	Secondary	$58.00
90		UPP	37.50		FLM	Secondary	42.00
91		UPP	37.50		VSL	Secondary	40.00
92		UPP	37.50		G/CL	Primary	38.00
93		UPP	37.50		BFY	Primary	37.50
94		OPEN	37.50		TRP	Primary	37.50

THERE'S A LIGHT AT THE END OF THE TUNNEL Figurine
521485 (527)

Year	Description	Status	Price	Size	Mark	Market	Value
91	Girl Peeking at Bunny	UPP	$55.00	4.00"	VSL	Secondary	$65.00
92	thru Log	UPP	55.00		G/CL	Secondary	58.00
93		UPP	55.00		BFY	Primary	55.00
94		OPEN	55.00		TRP	Primary	55.00

A SPECIAL DELIVERY Figurine
521493 (552)

Year	Description	Status	Price	Size	Mark	Market	Value
91	Girl with Baby	UPP	$30.00	5.75"	VSL	Secondary	$37.00
92		UPP	30.00		G/CL	Secondary	30.00
93		UPP	30.00		BFY	Primary	30.00
94		OPEN	30.00		TRP	Primary	30.00

THE LIGHT OF THE WORLD IS JESUS Musical TUNE: White Christmas
521507 (475)

Year	Description	Status	Price	Size	Mark	Market	Value
89	Girl by Lamppost	UPP	$60.00	7.00"	B&A	Secondary	$87.00
90		UPP	65.00		FLM	Secondary	75.00
91		UPP	65.00		VSL	Secondaru	72.00
92		UPP	65.00		G/CL	Primary	70.00
93		UPP	70.00		BFY	Primary	70.00
94		OPEN	70.00		TRP	Primary	70.00

OUR FIRST CHRISTMAS TOGETHER Ornament, Dated
521558 (460)

Year	Description	Status	Price	Size	Mark	Market	Value
89	Bride and Groom in Car	Annual	$17.50	2.75"	B&A	Secondary	$35.00

GLIDE THROUGH THE HOLIDAYS Ornament
521566 (499)

Year	Description	Status	Price	Size	Mark	Market	Value
90	Girl on Roller Skates	UPP	$13.50	3.50"	FLM	Retired/Sec	$38.00
91		UPP	13.50		VSL	Retired/Sec	35.00
92		UPP	13.50		G/CL	Retired/Sec	30.00

DASHING THROUGH THE SNOW Ornament
521574 (367)

Year	Description	Status	Price	Size	Mark	Market	Value
90	Girl Pushing Doll in Sled	UPP	$15.00	3.00"	FLM	Susp/Sec	$32.00
91		UPP	15.00		VSL	Susp/Sec	28.00
92		UPP	15.00		G/CL	Susp/Sec	27.00
93		UPP	15.00		BFY	Susp/Sec	25.00
94		UPP	16.00		TRP	Susp/Sec	22.00

DON'T LET THE HOLIDAYS GET YOU DOWN Ornament
521590 (471)

Year	Description	Status	Price	Size	Mark	Market	Value
90	Boy with Christmas Tree	UPP	$15.00	2.25"	FLM	Ret'd/Sec	$40.00
91		UPP	15.00		VSL	Ret'd/Sec	35.00
92		UPP	15.00		G/CL	Ret'd/Sec	32.00
93		UPP	15.00		BFY	Ret'd/Sec	30.00
94		UPP	16.00		TRP	Ret'd/Sec	28.00

HOPE YOU'RE OVER THE HUMP Figurine Birthday Collection
521671 (619)

Year	Description	Status	Price	Size	Mark	Market	Value
93	Monkey Riding on	UPP	$17.50	3.00"	BFY	Secondary	$20.00
94	Camel's Back	OPEN	17.50		TRP	Primary	17.50

THUMB-BODY LOVES YOU — Figurine

521698 (528)

91	Girl Misses Nail,	UPP	$55.00	5.25"	FLM	Secondary	$65.00
91	Hits Boy's Thumb	UPP	55.00		VSL	Secondary	60.00
92		UPP	55.00		G/CL	Primary	60.00
93		UPP	60.00		BFY	Primary	60.00
94		OPEN	60.00		TRP	Primary	60.00

SWEEP ALL YOUR WORRIES AWAY — Figurine

521779 (502)

90	Girl Sweeping Dust under	UPP	$40.00	5.25"	B&A	Secondary	$125.00
90	Rug	UPP	40.00		FLM	Secondary	48.00
91		UPP	40.00		VSL	Secondary	40.00
92		UPP	40.00		G/CL	Primary	40.00
93		UPP	40.00		BFY	Primary	40.00
94		OPEN	40.00		TRP	Primary	40.00

GOOD FRIENDS ARE FOREVER — Figurine

521817 (492)

90	Girls with Flower	UPP	$50.00	5.50"	B&A	Secondary	$62.00
90		UPP	50.00		FLM	Secondary	55.00
91		UPP	50.00		VSL	Secondary	52.00
92		UPP	50.00		G/CL	Secondary	50.00
93		UPP	50.00		BFY	Primary	50.00
94		OPEN	50.00		TRP	Primary	50.00

MAY YOUR BIRTHDAY BE MAMMOTH — Figurine — "Birthday Circus Train" Series

521825 (573)

92	Whale Riding Wave Wearing	UPP	$25.00	4.12"	G/CL	Secondary	$30.00
93	Sailor Hat (10)	UPP	25.00		BFY	Primary	25.00
94		OPEN	25.00		TRP	Primary	25.00

BEING NINE IS JUST DIVINE — Figurine — "Birthday Circus Train" Series

521833 (574)

92	Curly Maned	UPP	$25.00	4.25"	G/CL	Secondary	$30.00
93	Prancing Pony (9)	UPP	25.00		BFY	Primary	25.00
94		OPEN	25.00		TRP	Primary	25.00

LOVE IS FROM ABOVE — Figurine

521841 (510)

90	Boy Whispering to Girl	UPP	$45.00	5.50"	B&A	Secondary	$55.00
90		UPP	45.00		FLM	Secondary	48.00
91		UPP	45.00		VSL	Secondary	45.00
92		UPP	45.00		G/CL	Primary	45.00
93		UPP	45.00		BFY	Primary	45.00
94		OPEN	45.00		TRP	Primary	45.00

THE GREATEST OF THESE IS LOVE — Figurine

521868 (483)

89	Angel Holding	UPP	$27.50	5.25"	B&A	Susp/Sec	$50.00
90	Commandments	UPP	30.00		FLM	Susp/Sec	45.00
91		UPP	30.00		VSL	Susp/Sec	40.00

EASTER'S ON ITS WAY — Figurine

521892 (508)

90	Boy Pulling Girl and Lily	UPP	$60.00	5.25"	B&A	Secondary	$74.00
90	in Wagon	UPP	60.00		FLM	Secondary	65.00
91		UPP	60.00		VSL	Secondary	65.00
92		UPP	60.00		G/CL	Primary	65.00
93		UPP	60.00		BFY	Primary	65.00
94		OPEN	65.00		TRP	Primary	65.00

HOPPY EASTER FRIEND — Figurine

521906 (529)

91	Girl Collecting Eggs	UPP	$40.00	5.25"	FLM	Secondary	$50.00
91	with Frog's Help	UPP	40.00		VSL	Secondary	44.00
92		UPP	40.00		G/CL	Primary	40.00
93		UPP	40.00		BFY	Primary	40.00
94		OPEN	40.00		TRP	Primary	40.00

PERFECT HARMONY — Figurine

521914 (674)

94	Boys & Puppies Caroling	OPEN	$55.00	6.50"	TRP	Primary	$55.00

SAFE IN THE ARMS OF JESUS — Figurine — Second Child Evangelism Fellowship Piece
521922 (620)

93 Baby Asleep on Cloud	UPP	$30.00	3.00"	G/CL	Secondary	$35.00
93 Watched by Angel Bird	UPP	30.00		BFY	Primary	30.00
94	OPEN	30.00		TRP	Primary	30.00

WISHING YOU A COZY SEASON — Figurine
521949 (480)

89 Boy by Stump	UPP	$42.50	5.25"	B&A	Susp/Sec	$62.00
90	UPP	45.00		FLM	Susp/Sec	58.00
91	UPP	45.00		VSL	Susp/Sec	55.00
92	UPP	45.00		G/CL	Susp/Sec	54.00
93	UPP	45.00		BFY	Susp/Sec	52.00

HIGH HOPES — Figurine
521957 (498)

90 Boy with Kite	UPP	$30.00	5.25"	B&A	Susp/Sec	$55.00
90	UPP	30.00		FLM	Susp/Sec	50.00
91	UPP	30.00		VSL	Susp/Sec	45.00
92	UPP	30.00		G/CL	Susp/Sec	42.00
93	UPP	30.00		BFY	Susp/Sec	40.00

TO A SPECIAL MUM — Figurine
521965 (530)

91 Boy Looking at Bee	UPP	$30.00	5.25"	FLM	Secondary	$60.00
91 on Flower Pot for Mom	UPP	30.00		VSL	Secondary	45.00
92	UPP	30.00		G/CL	Primary	37.00
93	UPP	35.00		BFY	Primary	35.00
94	OPEN	35.00		TRP	Primary	35.00

TO THE APPLE OF GOD'S EYE — Figurine
522015 (621)

93 Boy Carrying Apple	UPP	$32.50	5.50"	BFY	Secondary	$35.00
94 & Book	OPEN	32.50		TRP	Primary	32.50

MAY YOUR LIFE BE BLESSED WITH TOUCHDOWNS — Figurine
522023 (473)

89 Boy Playing Football	UPP	$45.00	4.25"	B&A	Secondary	$65.00
90	UPP	50.00		FLM	Secondary	58.00
91	UPP	50.00		VSL	Secondary	52.00
92	UPP	50.00		G/CL	Secondary	50.00
93	UPP	50.00		BFY	Primary	50.00
94	OPEN	50.00		TRP	Primary	50.00

THANK YOU LORD FOR EVERYTHING — Figurine
522031 (472)

89 Boy Having Dinner	UPP	$60.00	5.25"	B&A	Susp/Sec	$85.00
90 with Turkey	UPP	60.00		FLM	Susp/Sec	80.00
91	UPP	60.00		VSL	Susp/Sec	75.00
92	UPP	60.00		G/CL	Susp/Sec	72.00
93	UPP	60.00		BFY	Susp/Sec	70.00

NOW I LAY ME DOWN TO SLEEP — Figurine
522058 (675)

94 Boy Carries Candle & Book to Bed	OPEN	$30.00	5.50"	TRP	Primary	$30.00

MAY YOUR WORLD BE TRIMMED WITH JOY — Figurine
522082 (553)

91 Boy Decorating Globe	UPP	$55.00	5.50"	VSL	Secondary	$65.00
92	UPP	55.00		G/CL	Secondary	55.00
93	UPP	55.00		BFY	Primary	55.00
94	OPEN	55.00		TRP	Primary	55.00

THERE SHALL BE SHOWERS OF BLESSINGS — Figurine
522090 (500)

90 Boy and Girl in Garden	UPP	$60.00	5.50"	B&A	Secondary	$75.00
90	UPP	60.00		FLM	Secondary	70.00
91	UPP	60.00		VSL	Secondary	70.00
92	UPP	60.00		G/CL	Secondary	70.00
93	UPP	65.00		BFY	Primary	70.00
94	OPEN	70.00		TRP	Primary	70.00

IT'S NO YOLK WHEN I SAY I LOVE YOU Figurine

522104

575

92	Hens Laugh Cause Girl Drop'd	UPP	$60.00	5.25"	VSL	Susp/Sec	$100.00
92	Egg on Puppy's Head	UPP	60.00		G/CL	Susp/Sec	80.00
93		UPP	60.00		BFY	Susp/Sec	78.00
94		UPP	65.00		TRP	Susp/Sec	75.00

DON'T LET THE HOLIDAYS GET YOU DOWN Figurine

522112

471

89	Boy with Christmas Tree	UPP	$42.50	4.25"	B&A	Ret'd/Sec	$100.00
90		UPP	45.00		FLM	Ret'd/Sec	95.00
91		UPP	45.00		VSL	Ret'd/Sec	90.00
92		UPP	45.00		G/CL	Ret'd/Sec	85.00
93		UPP	45.00		BFY	Ret'd/Sec	80.00

WISHING YOU A VERY SUCCESSFUL SEASON Figurine

522120

478

89	Boy with Box, Puppy & Bat	UPP	$60.00	6.00"	B&A	Secondary	$80.00
90		UPP	65.00		FLM	Secondary	72.00
91		UPP	65.00		VSL	Secondary	70.00
92		UPP	65.00		G/CL	Primary	70.00
93		UPP	70.00		BFY	Primary	70.00
94		OPEN	70.00		TRP	Primary	70.00

BON VOYAGE! Figurine

522201

474

89	Boy & Girl on Motorcycle	UPP	$75.00	6.50"	B&A	Secondary	$105.00
90		UPP	80.00		FLM	Secondary	92.00
91		UPP	80.00		VSL	Secondary	90.00
92		UPP	80.00		G/CL	Primary	90.00
93		UPP	90.00		BFY	Primary	90.00
94		OPEN	90.00		TRP	Primary	90.00

DO NOT OPEN TILL CHRISTMAS Musical TUNE: Toyland

522244

576

92	Boy Peeking into Opened	UPP	$75.00	6.50"	G/CL	Susp/Sec	$95.00
93	Christmas Present	UPP	75.00		BFY	Susp/Sec	90.00
94		UPP	75.00		TRP	Susp/Sec	85.00

HE IS THE STAR OF THE MORNING Figurine

522252

481

89	Angel on Cloud	UPP	$55.00	6.00"	B&A	Susp/Sec	$82.00
90	with Manger	UPP	60.00		FLM	Susp/Sec	75.00
91		UPP	60.00		VSL	Susp/Sec	72.00
92		UPP	60.00		G/CL	Susp/Sec	70.00
93		UPP	60.00		BFY	Susp/Sec	68.00

TO BE WITH YOU IS UPLIFTING Figurine Birthday Collection

522260

484

89	Giraffe with Baby Bear	UPP	$20.00	4.25"	B&A	Ret'd/Sec	$42.00
90		UPP	22.50		FLM	Ret'd/Sec	40.00
91		UPP	22.50		VSL	Ret'd/Sec	38.00
92		UPP	22.50		G/CL	Ret'd/Sec	35.00
93		UPP	22.50		BFY	Ret'd/Sec	32.00
94		UPP	22.50		TRP	Ret'd/Sec	30.00

A REFLECTION OF HIS LOVE Figurine

522279

531

91	Girl and Bird	UPP	$50.00	5.50"	VSL	Secondary	$60.00
92	at Bird Bath	UPP	50.00		G/CL	Secondary	52.00
93		UPP	50.00		BFY	Primary	50.00
94		OPEN	50.00		TRP	Primary	50.00

Title originally announced as "God Has Sent You My Way."

THINKING OF YOU IS WHAT I REALLY LIKE TO DO Figurine

522287

504

90	Kneeling Girl with Bouquet	UPP	$30.00	4.50"	B&A	Secondary	$40.00
90		UPP	30.00		FLM	Secondary	32.00
91		UPP	30.00		VSL	Secondary	30.00
92		UPP	30.00		G/CL	Primary	30.00
93		UPP	30.00		BFY	Primary	30.00
94		OPEN	30.00		TRP	Primary	30.00

MERRY CHRISTMAS, DEER Figurine
522317 (438)

89 Girl Decorating Reindeer	UPP	$50.00	5.50"	B&A	Secondary	$72.00
90	UPP	55.00		FLM	Secondary	65.00
91	UPP	55.00		VSL	Secondary	62.00
92	UPP	55.00		G/CL	Primary	60.00
93	UPP	60.00		BFY	Primary	60.00
94	OPEN	60.00		TRP	Primary	60.00

HIS LOVE WILL SHINE ON YOU Figurine Special Easter Seal Piece Easter Seal Lily on Decal
522376 (443)

89 Girl Holding Easter Lily	Annual	$30.00	5.75"	FLW	Secondary	$55.00
				B&A	Secondary	50.00

OH HOLY NIGHT Figurine, Dated
522546 (482)

89 Girl Playing Violin	Annual	$25.00	4.75"	B&A	Secondary	$38.00

OH HOLY NIGHT Thimble, Dated
522554 (482)

89 Girl Playing Violin	Annual	$7.50	2.25"	B&A	Secondary	$20.00

OH HOLY NIGHT Bell, Dated
522821 (482)

89 Girl Playing Violin	Annual	$25.00	5.50"	B&A	Secondary	$38.00

OH HOLY NIGHT Ornament, Dated
522848 (482)

89 Girl Playing Violin	Annual	$13.50	3.25"	B&A	Secondary	$32.00

HAVE A BEARY MERRY CHRISTMAS Figurine "Family Christmas Scene" Series
522856 (469)

89 Teddy in Rocker	UPP	$15.00	3.75"	B&A	Susp/Sec	$35.00
90	UPP	16.50		FLM	Susp/Sec	30.00
91	UPP	16.50		VSL	Susp/Sec	28.00
92	UPP	16.50		G/CL	Susp/Sec	25.00

MAKE A JOYFUL NOISE Ornament
522910 (5)

89 Girl with Goose	UPP	$15.00	3.25"	B&A	Secondary	$25.00
90	UPP	15.00		FLM	Secondary	20.00
91	UPP	15.00		VSL	Secondary	18.00
92	UPP	15.00		G/CL	Secondary	16.00
93	UPP	15.00		BFY	Primary	16.00
94	OPEN	16.00		TRP	Primary	16.00

LOVE ONE ANOTHER Ornament
522929 (8)

89 Boy & Girl on Stump	UPP	$17.50	3.50"	B&A	Secondary	$25.00
90	UPP	17.50		FLM	Secondary	22.00
91	UPP	17.50		VSL	Secondary	20.00
92	UPP	17.50		G/CL	Secondary	18.00
93	UPP	17.50		BFY	Primary	17.50
94	OPEN	17.50		TRP	Primary	17.50

FRIENDS NEVER DRIFT APART Ornament
522937 (219)

90 Kids in Boat	UPP	$17.50	2.50"	FLM	Secondary	$24.00
91	UPP	17.50		VSL	Secondary	19.00
92	UPP	17.50		G/CL	Secondary	18.00
93	UPP	17.50		BFY	Primary	17.50
94	OPEN	17.50		TRP	Primary	17.50

OUR FIRST CHRISTMAS TOGETHER Ornament, Dated
522945 (378)

91 Groom Popping out of Trunk/Bride	Annual	$17.50	3.00"	VSL	Secondary	$25.00

I BELIEVE IN THE OLD RUGGED CROSS Ornament

522953 (224)

89 Girl with Cross	UPP	$15.00	3.50"	B&A	Susp/Sec	$35.00
90	UPP	15.00		FLM	Susp/Sec	30.00
91	UPP	15.00		VSL	Susp/Sec	28.00
92	UPP	15.00		G/CL	Susp/Sec	27.00
93	UPP	15.00		BFY	Susp/Sec	26.00
94	UPP	16.00		TRP	Susp/Sec	20.00

ISN'T HE PRECIOUS Figurine Mini Nativity Addition

522988 (189)

89 Girl with Broom	UPP	$15.00	3.75"	B&A	Susp/Sec	$35.00
90	UPP	16.50		FLM	Susp/Sec	30.00
91	UPP	16.50		VSL	Susp/Sec	28.00
92	UPP	16.50		G/CL	Susp/Sec	27.00
93	UPP	16.50		BFY	Susp/Sec	25.00

SOME BUNNIES SLEEPING Figurine Mini Nativity Addition

522996 (431)

90 Bunnies	UPP	$12.00	1.75"	FLM	Susp/Sec	$30.00
91	UPP	12.00		VSL	Susp/Sec	28.00
92	UPP	12.00		G/CL	Susp/Sec	26.00
93	UPP	12.00		BFY	Susp/Sec	25.00

MAY YOUR CHRISTMAS BE A HAPPY HOME Plate, Dated Fourth Issue "Christmas Love" Series

523003 (479)

89 Family Christmas Scene	Annual	$50.00	8.50"	B&A	Secondary	$75.00

THERE'S A CHRISTIAN WELCOME HERE Figurine

523011 (491)

89 Angel outside Chapel	UPP	$45.00	4.00"	UM	Secondary	$95.00
92	UPP	45.00		G/CL	Secondary	45.00

Available exclusively at PRECIOUS MOMENTS Chapel or thru catalog. UNMARKED pieces of this figurine exist with and without an eyebrow on the angel boy (bangs cover where the second eyebrow would be). The GREENBOOK TRUMARKET PRICE for the "Without Eyebrow" piece is $125.00.

HE IS MY INSPIRATION Figurine

523038 (563)

91 Sam Butcher as Artist Painting/Animals	OPEN	$60.00	5.00"	UM	Primary	$60.00

Available exclusively at PRECIOUS MOMENTS Chapel or thru catalog.

PEACE ON EARTH Ornament, Dated First Issue "Masterpiece Ornaments" Series

523062 (341)

89 Kids with Pup, Kitten, and Bird	Annual	$25.00	4.25"	B&A	Secondary	$80.00

JESUS IS THE SWEETEST NAME I KNOW Figurine Nativity Addition

523097 (468)

89 Angel with Baby	UPP	$22.50	4.75"	B&A	Susp/Sec	$45.00
90 Name Book	UPP	25.00		FLM	Susp/Sec	40.00
91	UPP	25.00		VSL	Susp/Sec	38.00
92	UPP	25.00		G/CL	Susp/Sec	35.00
93	UPP	25.00		BFY	Susp/Sec	32.00

JOY ON ARRIVAL Figurine

523178 (532)

91 Stork Delivering Baby	UPP	$50.00	5.50"	VSL	Secondary	$58.00
92 to Mother	UPP	50.00		G/CL	Secondary	50.00
93	UPP	50.00		BFY	Primary	50.00
94	OPEN	50.00		TRP	Primary	50.00

BABY'S FIRST CHRISTMAS Ornament, Dated

523194 (432)

89 Boy in Sleigh	Annual	$15.00	2.50"	B&A	Secondary	$25.00

BABY'S FIRST CHRISTMAS Ornament, Dated

523208 (435)

89 Girl in Sleigh	Annual	$15.00	2.50"	B&A	Secondary	$25.00

HAPPY TRAILS IS TRUSTING JESUS Ornament

523224 (494)

91 Girl on Hobby Horse	UPP	$15.00	3.25"	VSL	Susp/Sec	$32.00
92	UPP	15.00		G/CL	Susp/Sec	30.00
93	UPP	15.00		BFY	Susp/Sec	30.00
94	UPP	16.00		TRP	Susp/Sec	27.00

YOU HAVE TOUCHED SO MANY HEARTS Figurine Easter Seal Raffle Piece Individually Numbered

523283 (161)

90 Girl with Hearts 2,000 $500.00 9.00" B&A Secondary $675.00

BLESSED ARE THE MERCIFUL Wall Hanging
Chapel Window Collection - Fifth Issue "Beatitude" Series

523291 (698)

94 Lady Gives Donation to Handicapped Child Annual $55.00 6.50" TRP Primary $55.00
Available exclusively at PRECIOUS MOMENTS CHAPEL or thru Catalog.

BLESSED ARE THE MEEK Wall Hanging
Chapel Window Collection - Third Issue "Beatitude" Series

523313 (627)

93 Native American with Fawn Annual $55.00 6.50" BFY Secondary $55.00
Available exclusively at PRECIOUS MOMENTS Chapel or thru Catalog.

BLESSED ARE THE ONES WHO HUNGER Wall Hanging
Chapel Window Collection- Fourth Issue "Beatitude" Series

523321 (653)

93 Girl Praying Annual $55.00 6.50" BFY Secondary $60.00
Available exclusively at PRECIOUS MOMENTS Chapel or thru Catalog.

BLESSED ARE THE PEACEMAKERS Wall Hanging
Chapel Window Collection - Sixth Issue "Beatitude" Series

523348 (702)

94 Girl Holds Bird in Hands Annual $55.00 6.50" TRP Primary $55.00
Available exclusively at PRECIOUS MOMENTS Chapel or thru Catalog.

BLESSED ARE THE ONES WHO MOURN Wall Hanging
Chapel Window Collection - Second Issue "Beatitude" Series

523380 (609)

92 Girl Crying over Spilled Milk/Kitten Annual $55.00 6.50" G/CL Secondary $65.00
Available exclusively at PRECIOUS MOMENTS Chapel or thru Catalog.

BLESSED ARE THE PURE IN HEART Wall Hanging
Chapel Window Collection - Seventh & Final Issue "Beatitude" Series

523399 (699)

95 Girl with Butterfly Annual $55.00 6.50" TRP Primary $55.00
Available exclusively at PRECIOUS MOMENTS Chapel or thru Catalog.

BLESSED ARE THE HUMBLE Wall Hanging
Chapel Window Collection - First Issue "Beatitude" Series

523437 (610)

92 Princess Washing Servant's Feet Annual $55.00 6.50" G/CL Secondary $75.00
Available exclusively at PRECIOUS MOMENTS Chapel or thru Catalog.

THE GOOD LORD ALWAYS DELIVERS Figurine

523453 (497)

90 Mother-to-Be with Baby	UPP	$27.50	5.50"	B&A	Secondary	$38.00
90 Book	UPP	27.50		FLM	Secondary	35.00
91	UPP	27.50		VSL	Secondary	32.00
92	UPP	27.50		G/CL	Secondary	30.00
93	UPP	30.00		BFY	Primary	30.00
94	OPEN	30.00		TRP	Primary	30.00

THIS DAY HAS BEEN MADE IN HEAVEN Figurine

523496
506

90	Girl Holding Bible and	UPP	$30.00	5.50"	B&A	Secondary	$40.00
90	Cross	UPP	30.00		FLM	Secondary	35.00
91		UPP	30.00		VSL	Secondary	32.00
92		UPP	30.00		G/CL	Secondary	30.00
93		UPP	30.00		BFY	Primary	30.00
94		OPEN	30.00		TRP	Primary	30.00

GOD IS LOVE DEAR VALENTINE Figurine

523518
509

90	Girl Hiding Valentine behind	UPP	$27.50	5.50"	B&A	Secondary	$40.00
90	Her Back	UPP	27.50		FLM	Secondary	35.00
91		UPP	27.50		VSL	Secondary	32.00
92		UPP	27.50		G/CL	Primary	30.00
93		UPP	30.00		BFY	Primary	30.00
94		OPEN	30.00		TRP	Primary	30.00

I'M A PRECIOUS MOMENTS FAN Figurine Special Events Piece

523526
490

90	Girl with Fan	Annual	$30.00	5.50"	B&A	Secondary	$50.00
					FLM	Secondary	40.00

I WILL CHERISH THE OLD RUGGED CROSS Egg, Dated

523534
224

91	Girl Holding Cross	Annual	$27.50	4.75"	FLM	Secondary	$40.00
					VSL	Secondary	35.00

YOU ARE THE TYPE I LOVE Figurine

523542
577

92	Girl Typing Message	UPP	$40.00	5.40"	VSL	Secondary	$48.00
92	on Typewriter	UPP	40.00		G/CL	Secondary	42.00
93		UPP	40.00		BFY	Primary	40.00
94		OPEN	40.00		TRP	Primary	40.00

THE LORD WILL PROVIDE Figurine

523593
622

93	Girl Carrying Seeds for Flowers and Birds	Annual	$40.00	6.50"	G/CL	Secondary	$50.00
					BFY	Secondary	48.00

GOOD NEWS IS SO UPLIFTING Figurine

523615
554

91	Girl on Ladder	UPP	$60.00	6.50"	VSL	Secondary	$70.00
92	by Mailboxes	UPP	60.00		G/CL	Secondary	65.00
93		UPP	60.00		BFY	Primary	65.00
94		OPEN	65.00		TRP	Primary	65.00

I'M SO GLAD THAT GOD BLESSED ME WITH A FRIEND LIKE YOU Figurine

523623
623

93	Girl Holding Kitten While	UPP	$50.00	5.50"	G/CL	Secondary	$60.00
93	Friend Offers Milk	UPP	50.00		BFY	Primary	50.00
94		OPEN	50.00		TRP	Primary	50.00

I WILL ALWAYS BE THINKING OF YOU Figurine

523631
518

94	Girl Stands by Gate	UPP	$45.00	5.50"	BFY	Secondary	$50.00
94	& Holds Flower	OPEN	45.00		TRP	Primary	45.00

THIS DAY HAS BEEN MADE IN HEAVEN Musical TUNE: Amazing Grace

523682
506

92	Girl Holding Bible & Cross	UPP	$60.00	6.60"	VSL	Secondary	$80.00
92		UPP	60.00		G/CL	Secondary	65.00
93		UPP	60.00		BFY	Primary	60.00
94		OPEN	60.00		TRP	Primary	60.00

MAY YOUR CHRISTMAS BE A HAPPY HOME Ornament, Dated

Second Issue "Masterpiece Ornament" Series

523704
479

90	Family Christmas Scene	Annual	$27.50	4.50"	FLM	Secondary	$45.00

Variation: Sitting boy with yellow (usual color is blue) shirt @ $65.00.

Item	Yr	Description	Status	Price	Size	Mark	Market	Value
TIME HEALS — Figurine								
523739	90	Nurse at Desk with Clock	UPP	$37.50	5.50"	FLM	Secondary	$47.00
518	91		UPP	37.50		VSL	Secondary	40.00
	92		UPP	37.50		G/CL	Secondary	38.00
	93		UPP	37.50		BFY	Primary	37.50
	94		OPEN	37.50		TRP	Primary	37.50
BLESSINGS FROM ABOVE — Figurine								
523747	90	Boy and Girl Kissing under	UPP	$45.00	6.50"	FLM	Ret'd/Sec	$105.00
495	91	Mistletoe	UPP	45.00		VSL	Ret'd/Sec	95.00
	92		UPP	45.00		G/CL	Ret'd/Sec	90.00
	93		UPP	50.00		BFY	Ret'd/Sec	85.00
	94		UPP	50.00		TRP	Ret'd/Sec	82.00
JUST POPPIN' IN TO SAY HALO! — Figurine								
523755	94	Girl Looking at Angel Jack-in-the-Box	OPEN	$45.00	6.25"	TRP	Primary	$45.00
676								
I CAN'T SPELL SUCCESS WITHOUT YOU — Figurine								
523763	91	Boy and Dog Using	UPP	$40.00	5.00"	FLM	Susp/Sec	$125.00
533	91	Blocks to Spell	UPP	40.00		VSL	Susp/Sec	65.00
	92		UPP	40.00		G/CL	Susp/Sec	60.00
	93		UPP	40.00		BFY	Susp/Sec	58.00
	94		UPP	45.00		TRP	Susp/Sec	55.00
BABY'S FIRST CHRISTMAS — Ornament, Dated								
523771	90	Baby Girl with Pie	Annual	$15.00	2.75"	FLM	Secondary	$25.00
516								
BABY'S FIRST CHRISTMAS — Ornament, Dated								
523798	90	Baby Boy with Pie	Annual	$15.00	2.75"	FLM	Secondary	$25.00
517								
WISHING YOU A YUMMY CHRISTMAS — Plate, Dated — First Issue "Christmas Blessings" Series								
523801	90	Boy and Girl at Ice Cream Stand	Annual	$50.00	8.25"	FLM	Secondary	$70.00
358								
ONCE UPON A HOLY NIGHT — Bell, Dated								
523828	90	Girl with Book and Candle	Annual	$25.00	5.75"	FLM	Secondary	$38.00
519								
ONCE UPON A HOLY NIGHT — Figurine, Dated								
523836	90	Girl with Book and Candle	Annual	$25.00	5.50"	FLM	Secondary	$40.00
519								
ONCE UPON A HOLY NIGHT — Thimble, Dated								
523844	90	Girl with Book and Candle	Annual	$ 8.00	1.50"	FLM	Secondary	$20.00
519								
ONCE UPON A HOLY NIGHT — Ornament, Dated								
523852	90	Girl with Book and Candle	Annual	$15.00	3.25"	FLM	Secondary	$30.00
624								
BLESSINGS FROM ME TO THEE — Plate, Dated — Second Issue "Christmas Blessings" Series								
523860	91	Girl at Birdhouse	Annual	$50.00	8.50"	VSL	Secondary	$65.00
120								
WE ARE GOD'S WORKMANSHIP — Figurine — Easter Seal Raffle Piece — Individually Numbered								
523879	91	Bonnet Girl with Butterfly	2,000	$500.00	9.00"	FLM	Secondary	$650.00
140								
BABY'S FIRST BIRTHDAY — Figurine — Eighth & Final Issue in "Baby's First" Series								
524069	93	Baby Holding up One Finger	UPP	$25.00	3.50"	G/CL	Secondary	$30.00
624	93	by Cake w/One Candle	UPP	25.00		BFY	Primary	25.00
	94		OPEN	25.00		TRP	Primary	25.00

BABY'S FIRST MEAL Figurine Sixth Issue in "Baby's First" Series

Item	Year	Description	Status	Price	Size	Mark	Market	Value
524077 (534)	91	Baby in Highchair	UPP	$35.00	5.25"	VSL	Secondary	$47.00
	92	with Cereal Bowl	UPP	35.00		G/CL	Secondary	38.00
	93		UPP	35.00		BFY	Primary	37.50
	94		OPEN	37.50		TRP	Primary	37.50

MY WARMEST THOUGHTS ARE YOU Figurine

Item	Year	Description	Status	Price	Size	Mark	Market	Value
524085 (578)	92	Little Bird Watching Girl	UPP	$55.00	5.75"	VSL	Secondary	$66.00
	92	on Tree Swing	UPP	55.00		G/CL	Secondary	60.00
	93		UPP	55.00		BFY	Primary	60.00
	94		OPEN	60.00		TRP	Primary	60.00

GOOD FRIENDS ARE FOR ALWAYS Figurine

Item	Year	Description	Status	Price	Size	Mark	Market	Value
524123 (555)	91	Girl in Snowsuit	UPP	$27.50	5.50"	VSL	Secondary	$35.00
	92	Holding Bunny	UPP	27.50		G/CL	Secondary	30.00
	93		UPP	30.00		BFY	Primary	30.00
	94		OPEN	30.00		TRP	Primary	30.00

GOOD FRIENDS ARE FOR ALWAYS Ornament

Item	Year	Description	Status	Price	Size	Mark	Market	Value
524131 (555)	92	Girl in Snowsuit	UPP	$15.00	3.50"	G/CL	Secondary	$20.00
	93	Holding Bunny	UPP	15.00		BFY	Primary	16.00
	94		OPEN	16.00		TRP	Primary	16.00

LORD, TEACH US TO PRAY Figurine National Day Of Prayer Figurine

Item	Year	Description	Status	Price	Size	Mark	Market	Value
524158 (663)	94	Girl Kneels in Prayer	OPEN	$35.00	4.75"	TRP	Primary	$35.00

MAY YOUR CHRISTMAS BE MERRY Figurine, Dated

Item	Year	Description	Status	Price	Size	Mark	Market	Value
524166 (556)	91	Girl Holding Bird	Annual	$27.50	5.25"	VSL	Secondary	$35.00

MAY YOUR CHRISTMAS BE MERRY Ornament, Dated

Item	Year	Description	Status	Price	Size	Mark	Market	Value
524174 (556)	91	Girl Holding Bird	Annual	$15.00	3.50"	VSL	Secondary	$25.00

MAY YOUR CHRISTMAS BE MERRY Bell, Dated

Item	Year	Description	Status	Price	Size	Mark	Market	Value
524182 (556)	91	Girl Holding Bird	Annual	$25.00	5.75"	VSL	Secondary	$38.00

MAY YOUR CHRISTMAS BE MERRY Thimble, Dated

Item	Year	Description	Status	Price	Size	Mark	Market	Value
524190 (556)	91	Girl Holding Bird	Annual	$ 8.00	2.25"	VSL	Secondary	$24.00

HE LOVES ME Figurine

Item	Year	Description	Status	Price	Size	Mark	Market	Value
524263 (535)	91	Girl Holding Flower	Annual	$35.00	6.25"	FLM	Secondary	$50.00
						VSL	Secondary	45.00

FRIENDSHIP GROWS WHEN YOU PLANT A SEED Figurine

Item	Year	Description	Status	Price	Size	Mark	Market	Value
524271 (579)	92	Girl in Sunbonnet Watering	UPP	$40.00	4.10"	VSL	Ret'd/Sec	$95.00
	92	a Seedling	UPP	40.00		G/CL	Ret'd/Sec	85.00
	93		UPP	40.00		BFY	Ret'd/Sec	80.00
	94		OPEN	40.00		TRP	Ret'd/Sec	75.00

MAY YOUR EVERY WISH COME TRUE Figurine

Item	Year	Description	Status	Price	Size	Mark	Market	Value
524298 (625)	93	Girl Blowing Cake w/Lit	UPP	$50.00	5.50"	G/CL	Secondary	$55.00
	93	Candles to Edge of Table	UPP	50.00		BFY	Primary	50.00
	94		OPEN	50.00		TRP	Primary	50.00

MAY YOUR BIRTHDAY BE A BLESSING Figurine

Item	Year	Description	Status	Price	Size	Mark	Market	Value
524301 (536)	91	Girl with Cake and Candles	UPP	$30.00	5.75"	FLM	Secondary	$48.00
	91		UPP	30.00		VSL	Secondary	35.00
	92		UPP	30.00		G/CL	Primary	30.00
	93		UPP	30.00		BFY	Primary	30.00
	94		OPEN	30.00		TRP	Primary	30.00

OUR FRIENDSHIP IS SODA-LICIOUS Figurine

524336 (626)							
93	Girl & Boy Sharing an	UPP	$65.00	6.00"	G/CL	Secondary	$70.00
93	Ice Cream Soda	UPP	65.00		BFY	Primary	65.00
94		OPEN	65.00		TRP	Primary	65.00

WHAT THE WORLD NEEDS NOW Figurine

524352 (580)							
92	Girl Gazing at Globe Praying	UPP	$50.00	5.75"	VSL	Secondary	$58.00
92	for Peace & Love	UPP	50.00		G/CL	Secondary	52.00
93		UPP	50.00		BFY	Primary	50.00
94		OPEN	50.00		TRP	Primary	50.00

SO GLAD I PICKED YOU AS A FRIEND Figurine

524379 (689)							
94	Girl Standing	UPP	$40.00		BFY	Primary	$40.00
	by Flowerpot	OPEN	40.00		TRP	Primary	40.00

YOU ARE SUCH A PURR-FECT FRIEND Figurine

524395 (585)							
93	Girl Holding Kitten in	UPP	$35.00	6.00"	G/CL	Secondary	$40.00
93	Her Arms	UPP	35.00		BFY	Primary	35.00
94		OPEN	35.00		TRP	Primary	35.00

MAY ONLY GOOD THINGS COME YOUR WAY Figurine

524425 (537)							
91	Girl Holding Net	UPP	$30.00	5.50"	FLM	Secondary	$60.00
91	for Butterfly	UPP	30.00		VSL	Secondary	45.00
92		UPP	30.00		G/CL	Secondary	40.00
93		UPP	35.00		BFY	Primary	35.00
94		OPEN	35.00		TRP	Primary	35.00

SEALED WITH A KISS Figurine

524441 (628)							
93	Bride & Groom Kissing	UPP	$50.00	5.50"	G/CL	Secondary	$57.00
93	over Mailbox	UPP	50.00		BFY	Primary	50.00
94		OPEN	50.00		TRP	Primary	50.00

A SPECIAL CHIME FOR JESUS Figurine

524468 (629)							
93	Boy in PJ's with Toy Duck,	UPP	$32.50	5.50"	BFY	Secondary	$35.00
94	Ringing Bell	OPEN	32.50		TRP	Primary	32.50

GOD CARED ENOUGH TO SEND HIS BEST Figurine

524476 (673)							
94	Girl Hangs Ornament	TRP	$50.00	7.00"	TRP	Primary	$50.00
	on Tree						

NOT A CREATURE WAS STIRRING Figurine Set of 2 Birthday Collection

524484 (514)							
90	Mouse on Cheese and Kitten	UPP	$17.00	2.75"	FLM	Susp/Sec	$35.00
91		UPP	17.00		VSL	Susp/Sec	32.00
92		UPP	17.00		G/CL	Susp/Sec	30.00
93		UPP	17.00		BFY	Susp/Sec	28.00
94		UPP	17.00		TRP	Susp/Sec	27.00

CAN'T BE WITHOUT YOU Figurine Birthday Collection

524492 (538)							
91	Bird on Cage Door	UPP	$16.00	2.50"	VSL	Secondary	$25.00
92	and Cat	UPP	16.00		G/CL	Secondary	18.00
93		UPP	16.00		BFY	Primary	16.00
94		OPEN	16.00		TRP	Primary	16.00

OINKY BIRTHDAY Figurine Birthday Collection

524506 (657)							
94	Pig Holds	UPP	$13.50	2.50"	BFY	Secondary	$13.50
94	Wrapped Present	OPEN	13.50		TRP	Primary	13.50

ALWAYS IN HIS CARE Figurine Special Easter Seal Piece Easter Seal Lily on Decal

524522 (507)							
90	Girl Looking at Sleeping	Annual	$30.00	5.00"	B&A	Secondary	$45.00
	Chick in Egg				FLM	Secondary	40.00

HAPPY BIRTHDAY DEAR JESUS Figurine Nativity Addition

524875
513

90	Teddy Bear in Package	UPP	$13.50	2.25"	FLM	Susp/Sec	$30.00
91		UPP	13.50		VSL	Susp/Sec	25.00
92		UPP	13.50		G/CL	Susp/Sec	22.00
93		UPP	13.50		BFY	Susp/Sec	20.00

CHRISTMAS FIREPLACE Figurine "Family Christmas Scene" Series

524883
512

90	Fireplace with Stockings	UPP	$37.50	4.50"	FLM	Susp/Sec	$62.00
91		UPP	37.50		VSL	Susp/Sec	55.00
92		UPP	37.50		G/CL	Susp/Sec	50.00

IT'S SO UPLIFTING TO HAVE A FRIEND LIKE YOU Figurine

524905
581

92	Girl on Skis Startled by	UPP	$40.00	6.00"	G/CL	Secondary	$44.00
93	Ski Jump	UPP	40.00		BFY	Primary	40.00
94		OPEN	40.00		TRP	Primary	40.00

WE'RE GOING TO MISS YOU Figurine

524913
515

90	Girl and Melting Snowman	UPP	$50.00	5.50"	FLM	Secondary	$62.00
91		UPP	50.00		VSL	Secondary	52.00
92		UPP	50.00		G/CL	Primary	50.00
93		UPP	50.00		BFY	Primary	50.00
94		OPEN	50.00		TRP	Primary	50.00

ANGELS WE HAVE HEARD ON HIGH Figurine

524921
557

91	Two Angels on Stool	UPP	$60.00	7.25"	VSL	Secondary	$70.00
92	Afraid of Mouse	UPP	60.00		G/CL	Secondary	65.00
93		UPP	65.00		BFY	Primary	65.00
94		OPEN	65.00		TRP	Primary	65.00

Production error: Mismatched painting of hands and feet!

GOOD FRIENDS ARE FOREVER Figurine Special Events Piece Rosebud Decal Understamp

525049
492

90	Girls with Flower	Annual		5.50"	B&A	Secondary	$700.00

Identical to 521817 with exception of Rosebud decal.
One per Center for 1990 Events, see 6th Ed., pg. 213.

BUNDLES OF JOY Ornament Limited to Centers

525057
96

90	Girl with Presents	Annual	$15.00	3.25"	FLM	Secondary	$30.00

TUBBY'S FIRST CHRISTMAS Figurine Mini Nativity Addition

525278
126

92	Rooster Sitting on	UPP	$10.00	1.75"	G/CL	Secondary	$12.00
93	Pig's Back	UPP	10.00		BFY	Primary	10.00
94		OPEN	10.00		TRP	Primary	10.00

IT'S A PERFECT BOY Figurine Mini Nativity Addition

525286
127

91	Boy Angel with	UPP	$16.50	3.50"	VSL	Secondary	$25.00
92	Red Cross Bag	UPP	16.50		G/CL	Secondary	17.00
93		UPP	16.50		BFY	Primary	17.00
94		OPEN	17.00		TRP	Primary	17.00

MAY YOUR FUTURE BE BLESSED Figurine

525316
630

93	Girl at Her First Communion	UPP	$35.00	6.00"	G/CL	Secondary	$42.00
93		UPP	35.00		BFY	Primary	35.00
94		OPEN	35.00		TRP	Primary	35.00

OUR FIRST CHRISTMAS TOGETHER Ornament, Dated

525324
460

90	Bride and Groom in Car	Annual	$17.50	2.50"	FLM	Secondary	$28.00

LORD KEEP ME ON MY TOES Ornament

525332
582

92	Ballerina on Pointe	UPP	$15.00	3.75"	G/CL	Secondary	$20.00
93		UPP	15.00		BFY	Primary	16.00
94		OPEN	16.00		TRP	Primary	16.00

RING THOSE CHRISTMAS BELLS Figurine

Item	Yr	Description	Limit	Issue Price	Size	Mark	Market	Value
525898	92	Angel Ringing Bell, Angel	UPP	$95.00	6.25"	G/CL	Secondary	$100.00
583	93	Pray'g, Bunny Cover'g Ears	UPP	95.00		BFY	Primary	95.00
	94		OPEN	95.00		TRP	Primary	95.00

WE ARE GOD'S WORKMANSHIP Egg, Dated

Item	Yr	Description	Limit	Issue Price	Size	Mark	Market	Value
525960	92	Bonnet Girl with Butterfly	Annual	$27.50	4.10"	VSL	Secondary	$32.00
140						G/CL	Secondary	30.00

GOING HOME Figurine

Item	Yr	Description	Limit	Issue Price	Size	Mark	Market	Value
525979	92	Angel Stopping to Take	UPP	$60.00	4.60"	VSL	Secondary	$70.00
584	92	God's Child to Heaven	UPP	60.00		G/CL	Secondary	62.00
	93		UPP	60.00		BFY	Primary	60.00
	94		OPEN	60.00		TRP	Primary	60.00

YOU ARE SUCH A PURR-FECT FRIEND Figurine Individually Numbered

Item	Yr	Description	Limit	Issue Price	Size	Mark	Market	Value
526010	92	Little Girl Cuddling Kitten	2,000	$500.00	9.00"	VSL	Secondary	$625.00
585		in Arms				G/CL	Secondary	600.00

All are signed by Artist Sam Butcher, Enesco President Eugene Freedman, and Sculptor Fujioka-San. Benefits Easter Seal Society.

I WOULD BE LOST WITHOUT YOU Figurine

Item	Yr	Description	Limit	Issue Price	Size	Mark	Market	Value
526142	92	Girl Checking Roadmap	UPP	$27.50	5.75"	VSL	Secondary	$35.00
586	92		UPP	27.50		G/CL	Secondary	30.00
	93		UPP	30.00		BFY	Primary	30.00
	94		OPEN	30.00		TRP	Primary	30.00

FRIENDS TO THE VERY END Figurine

Item	Yr	Description	Limit	Issue Price	Size	Mark	Market	Value
526150	94	Duck Upset at Boy	UPP	$40.00	4.50"	BFY	Secondary	$40.00
658	94	Plucking Tail Feathers	OPEN	40.00		TRP	Primary	40.00

YOU ARE MY HAPPINESS Figurine

Item	Yr	Description	Limit	Issue Price	Size	Mark	Market	Value
526185	92	Bluebird Sitting on Bouquet	Annual	$37.50	6.75"	VSL	Secondary	$55.00
587		of Roses Held by Girl				G/CL	Secondary	50.00

YOU SUIT ME TO A TEE Figurine

Item	Yr	Description	Limit	Issue Price	Size	Mark	Market	Value
526193	94	Girl Chooses Club for a	OPEN	$35.00	5.50"	TRP	Primary	$35.00
662		Round of Golf						

SHARING SWEET MOMENTS TOGETHER Figurine

Item	Yr	Description	Limit	Issue Price	Size	Mark	Market	Value
526487	94	Boy Eats Candy as	UPP	$45.00	4.00"	BFY	Secondary	$45.00
659	94	Dog Licks his Face	OPEN	45.00		TRP	Primary	45.00

BLESS THOSE WHO SERVE THEIR COUNTRY - NAVY Figurine

Item	Yr	Description	Limit	Issue Price	Size	Mark	Market	Value
526568	91	Boy in Sailor Suit & Hat	UPP	$32.50	5.50"	FLG	Susp/Sec	$60.00
588	92	with Duffel Bag	UPP	32.50		FLG/*	Susp/Sec	60.00

BLESS THOSE WHO SERVE THEIR COUNTRY - ARMY Figurine

Item	Yr	Description	Limit	Issue Price	Size	Mark	Market	Value
526576	91	Boy in Dress Uniform with	UPP	$32.50	5.50"	FLG	Susp/Sec	$45.00
589	92	Duffel, Saluting	UPP	32.50		FLG/*	Susp/Sec	45.00

BLESS THOSE WHO SERVE THEIR COUNTRY - AIR FORCE Figurine

Item	Yr	Description	Limit	Issue Price	Size	Mark	Market	Value
526584	91	Boy in Dress Uniform, Hand	UPP	$32.50	5.50"	FLG	Susp/Sec	$45.00
590	92	Resting on Duffel	UPP	32.50		FLG/*	Susp/Sec	45.00

WISHING YOU WERE HERE Musical TUNE: "When You Wish Upon A Star"

Item	Yr	Description	Limit	Issue Price	Size	Mark	Market	Value
526916	93	Girl Dropping Coin into	UPP	$100.00	7.00"	G/CL	Secondary	$125.00
631	93	Wishing Well	UPP	100.00		BFY	Primary	100.00
	94		OPEN	100.00		TRP	Primary	100.00

HOW CAN I EVER FORGET YOU Figurine Birthday Collection

Item	Yr	Description	Limit	Issue Price	Size	Mark	Market	Value
526924	91	Elephant with Knot	UPP	$15.00	3.00"	VSL	Secondary	$20.00
558	92	in Trunk	UPP	15.00		G/CL	Secondary	16.00
	93		UPP	15.00		BFY	Primary	16.00
	94		OPEN	16.00		TRP	Primary	16.00

MAY YOUR CHRISTMAS BE MERRY — Ornament, Dated — Third Issue "Masterpiece Ornament" Series
526940 — 556

91	Girl Holding Bird	Annual	$30.00	4.25"	VSL	Secondary	$45.00

WE HAVE COME FROM AFAR — Figurine — Nativity Addition
526959 — 559

91	Penguins	UPP	$17.50	2.50"	VSL	Susp/Sec	$30.00
92		UPP	17.50		G/CL	Susp/Sec	24.00
93		UPP	17.50		BFY	Susp/Sec	22.00
94		UPP	17.50		TRP	Susp/Sec	20.00

BABY'S FIRST CHRISTMAS — Ornament, Dated
527084 — 560

91	Boy with Drum	Annual	$15.00	2.50"	VSL	Secondary	$25.00

BABY'S FIRST CHRISTMAS — Ornament, Dated
527092 — 561

91	Girl with Drum	Annual	$15.00	2.50"	VSL	Secondary	$25.00

HE IS NOT HERE FOR HE IS RISEN AS HE SAID — Figurine — Chapel Exclusive
527106 — 693

93	Angel by Cave	UPP	$60.00		UM	Secondary	$78.00
94		OPEN	60.00		TRP	Primary	60.00

SHARING A GIFT OF LOVE — Figurine — Special Easter Seal Piece — Easter Seal Lily on Decal
527114 — 539

91	Girl Helping Bird to Fly	Annual	$30.00	5.75"	FLM	Secondary	$55.00
					VSL	Secondary	42.00

YOU CAN ALWAYS BRING A FRIEND — Figurine — Special Events Piece
527122 — 546

91	Girl Holding Puppy	Annual	$27.50	5.75"	FLM	Secondary	$50.00
					VSL	Secondary	46.00

THE GOOD LORD ALWAYS DELIVERS — Ornament
527165 — 497

91	Expectant Mother	UPP	$15.00	3.50"	VSL	Susp/Sec	$25.00
92		UPP	15.00		G/CL	Susp/Sec	20.00
93		UPP	15.00		BFY	Susp/Sec	18.00

A UNIVERSAL LOVE — Figurine — Special Easter Seal Piece — Easter Seal Lily on Decal
527173 — 591

92	Seated Child Signing Message	Annual	$32.50	5.10"	VSL	Secondary	$50.00
					G/CL	Secondary	45.00

SHARE IN THE WARMTH OF CHRISTMAS — Ornament
527211 — 429

93	Girl with Christmas Candle	UPP	$15.00	3.25"	BFY	Secondary	$18.00
94		OPEN	16.00		TRP	Primary	16.00

BABY'S FIRST WORD — Figurine — Seventh Issue in "Baby's First" Series
527238 — 592

92	Baby/Footed Sleepers Talk'g	UPP	$25.00	4.50"	G/CL	Secondary	$30.00
93	into a Microphone	UPP	25.00		BFY	Primary	25.00
94		OPEN	25.00		TRP	Primary	25.00

LET'S BE FRIENDS — Figurine — Birthday Collection
527270 — 593

92	Pup w/Bow & Pup w/Party	UPP	$15.00	3.00"	VSL	Secondary	$20.00
92	Hat Hugging Each Other	UPP	15.00		G/CL	Secondary	16.00
93		UPP	15.00		BFY	Primary	16.00
94		OPEN	16.00		TRP	Primary	16.00

BLESS THOSE WHO SERVE THEIR COUNTRY - GIRL SOLDIER — Figurine
527289 — 594

91	Girl Soldier in Dress Uniform,	UPP	$32.50	5.50"	FLG	Susp/Sec	$45.00
92	Saluting	UPP	32.50		FLG/*	Susp/Sec	45.00

BLESS THOSE WHO SERVE THEIR COUNTRY - AFRICAN-AMERICAN SOLDIER — Figurine
527297 — 595

91	African-American Soldier in	UPP	$32.50	5.50"	FLG	Susp/Sec	$42.00
92	Dress Uniform w/Duffel	UPP	32.50		FLG/*	Susp/Sec	42.00

AN EVENT WORTH WADING FOR — Figurine — Special Events Piece
527319 — 596

92	Girl Wading to View Mother Duck w/Eggs	Annual	$32.50	5.12"	VSL	Secondary	$48.00
					G/CL	Secondary	40.00

ONWARD CHRISTMAS SOLDIERS   Ornament

527327	680	94	Soldier Boy	OPEN	$16.00	4.75"	TRP	Primary	$16.00

BLESS-UM YOU   Figurine

527335	632	93	Native American Girl Raising	UPP	$35.00	5.50"	G/CL	Secondary	$40.00
		93	Hand in Blessing	UPP	35.00		BFY	Primary	35.00
		94		OPEN	35.00		TRP	Primary	35.00

HAPPY BIRDIE   Figurine   Birthday Collection

527343	597	92	Bird in Party Hat Blowing	UPP	$16.00	3.25"	G/CL	Secondary	$20.00
		93	Lit Candle on B/Day Cake	UPP	16.00		BFY	Primary	16.00
		94		OPEN	16.00		TRP	Primary	16.00

YOU ARE MY FAVORITE STAR   Figurine

527378	598	92	Girl Placing Star on	UPP	$60.00	5.50"	G/CL	Secondary	$65.00
		93	Decorated Boy's Head	UPP	60.00		BFY	Primary	60.00
		94		OPEN	60.00		TRP	Primary	60.00

527386 THIS LAND IS OUR LAND   See The Enesco PRECIOUS MOMENTS Collectors' Club, page 261.

BABY'S FIRST CHRISTMAS - GIRL   Ornament, Dated

527475	600	92	Girl Sitting on Upside-down Candy Cane	Annual	$15.00	3.50"	G/CL	Secondary	$20.00

BABY'S FIRST CHRISTMAS - BOY   Ornament, Dated

527483	601	92	Boy Sitting on Upside-down Candy Cane	Annual	$15.00	3.50"	G/CL	Secondary	$20.00

BLESS THOSE WHO SERVE THEIR COUNTRY - MARINE   Figurine

527521	602	91	Boy Marine in Full Dress	UPP	$32.50	5.50"	FLG	Susp/Sec	$42.00
		92	Stands at Attention	UPP	32.50		FLG/*	Susp/Sec	42.00

BRING THE LITTLE ONES TO JESUS   Figurine   First Child Evangelism Fellowship Piece

527556	603	92	Mom Reading "Wordless	UPP	$90.00	5.00"	VSL	Secondary	$110.00
		92	Book" to Children	UPP	90.00		G/CL	Secondary	100.00
		93		UPP	90.00		BFY	Primary	90.00
		94		OPEN	90.00		TRP	Primary	90.00

GOD BLESS THE USA   Figurine

527564	604	92	Uncle Sam Kneeling	Annual	$32.50	4.75"	VSL	Secondary	$42.00
			in Prayer				G/CL	Secondary	38.00

National Day Of Prayer Figurine. Original 9" accepted by President Bush May 2,1991 during National Day Of Prayer ceremonies.

TIED UP FOR THE HOLIDAYS   Figurine

527580	633	93	Dog Pulling Ribbon Tangling	UPP	$40.00	6.00"	BFY	Secondary	$45.00
		94	Girl with Gift	OPEN	40.00		TRP	Primary	40.00

BRINGING YOU A MERRY CHRISTMAS   Figurine

527599	634	93	Boy on Sled Watching	UPP	$45.00	4.50"	BFY	Secondary	$50.00
		94	Turtle with Gift	OPEN	45.00		TRP	Primary	45.00

WISHING YOU A HO HO HO   Figurine

527629	605	92	Boy in Santa Suit Look'g at	UPP	$40.00	5.75"	G/CL	Secondary	$45.00
		93	Pup Hold'g Santa Whiskers	UPP	40.00		BFY	Primary	40.00
		94		OPEN	40.00		TRP	Primary	40.00

YOU HAVE TOUCHED SO MANY HEARTS   Figurine   Available at Distinguished Service Retailers (DSRs) Only

527661	161	91	Girl with Hearts	UPP	$35.00	5.50"	VSL	Secondary	$35.00
		92		UPP	35.00		G/CL	Secondary	35.00
		93		UPP	35.00		BFY	Primary	35.00
		94		OPEN	35.00		TRP	Primary	35.00

"Especially For You" version w/letter transfer kit so collectors may personalize figurine.

BUT THE GREATEST OF THESE IS LOVE — Figurine, Dated

527688 (606)	92	Girl Holding Her List to Santa Claus	Annual	$27.50	5.50"	G/CL	Secondary	$35.00

BUT THE GREATEST OF THESE IS LOVE — Ornament, Dated

527696 (606)	92	Girl Holding Her List to Santa Claus	Annual	$15.00	4.00"	G/CL	Secondary	$32.00

BUT THE GREATEST OF THESE IS LOVE — Thimble, Dated

527718 (606)	92	Girl Holding Her List to Santa Claus	Annual	$ 8.00	2.50"	G/CL	Secondary	$18.00

BUT THE GREATEST OF THESE IS LOVE — Bell, Dated

527726 (606)	92	Girl Holding Her List to Santa Claus	Annual	$25.00	6.50"	G/CL	Secondary	$35.00

BUT THE GREATEST OF THESE IS LOVE — Ball Ornament, Dated
Fourth Issue, "Masterpiece Ornament" Series

527734 (606)	92	Girl Holding Her List to Santa Claus	Annual	$30.00	4.00"	G/CL	Secondary	$40.00

BUT THE GREATEST OF THESE IS LOVE — Plate, Dated — Third Issue "Christmas Blessings" Series

527742 (606)	92	Girl Holding Her List to Santa Claus	Annual	$50.00	8.50"	G/CL	Secondary	$55.00

WISHING YOU A COMFY CHRISTMAS — Figurine — Nativity Addition

527750 (607)	92	Angel Holding Favorite	UPP	$27.50	5.50"	G/CL	Secondary	$30.00
	93	Patched Blanket	UPP	27.50		BFY	Primary	27.50
	94		OPEN	27.50		TRP	Primary	27.50

I ONLY HAVE ARMS FOR YOU — Figurine — Birthday Collection

527769 (635)	93	Octopus and Fish Hugging	UPP	$15.00	3.00"	G/CL	Secondary	$20.00
	93		UPP	15.00		BFY	Primary	16.00
	94		OPEN	16.00		TRP	Primary	16.00

THIS LAND IS OUR LAND — Figurine

527777 (608)	92	Explorer on One Knee Hold'g Flag & Teddy	Annual	$35.00	4.88"	G/CL	Secondary	$40.00

THERE'S A CHRISTIAN WELCOME HERE — Ornament

528021 (491)	92	Angel outside Chapel	OPEN	$22.50	2.00"	UM	Primary	$22.50

Available exclusively at PRECIOUS MOMENTS Chapel or thru Catalog.

NATIVITY CART — Figurine — Nativity Addition

528072 (683)	94	Chicken in Farm Wagon w/Gift-wrapped Egg	OPEN	$18.50	4.75"	TRP	Primary	$18.50

HAVE I GOT NEWS FOR YOU — Figurine — Mini Nativity Addition

528137 (350)	94	Boy Reading Scroll	OPEN	$16.00	4.25"	TRP	Primary	$16.00

SENDING YOU A WHITE CHRISTMAS — Ornament

528218 (681)	94	Girl Angel w/Basket of Snowflakes	OPEN	$16.00	4.50"	TRP	Primary	$16.00

BRINGING YOU A MERRY CHRISTMAS — Ornament

528226 (679)	94	Boy Dressed as Santa w/Bag of Toys	OPEN	$16.00	4.50"	TRP	Secondary	$16.00

MAKE A JOYFUL NOISE — Egg, Dated

528617 (5)	93	Girl with Goose	Annual	$27.50	4.75"	G/CL	Secondary	$32.00
						BFY	Secondary	30.00

TO A VERY SPECIAL SISTER Figurine
528633 664 | 94 Girls Receive Kittens from Each Other | UPP $60.00 4.75" BFY Secondary $60.00
OPEN 60.00 TRP Primary 60.00

IT'S SO UPLIFTING TO HAVE A FRIEND LIKE YOU Ornament
528846 581 | 93 Girl on Skis Startled by Jump | UPP $16.00 3.25" BFY Secondary $20.00
94 | OPEN 16.00 TRP Primary 16.00

AMERICA, YOU'RE BEAUTIFUL Figurine 1993 National Day Of Prayer Figurine
528862 636 | 93 Girl, as Statue Of Liberty, Celebrates America | Annual $35.00 5.50" G/CL Secondary $48.00
BFY Secondary 40.00

OUR FIRST CHRISTMAS TOGETHER Ornament, Dated
528870 378 | 92 Groom Popping out of Trunk/Bride | Annual $17.50 3.00" G/CL Secondary $20.00

A REFLECTION OF HIS LOVE Egg, Dated Fourth & Final Issue in Annual Eggs Series
529095 531 | 94 Girl & Bird at Bird Bath | Annual $27.50 4.25" BFY Secondary $27.50
TRP Primary 27.50

OUR FIRST CHRISTMAS TOGETHER Ornament, Dated
529206 684 | 94 Boy & Girl Sweethearts on Reindeer | OPEN $18.50 4.00" TRP Primary $18.50

THE MAGIC STARTS WITH YOU Ornament
1992 Ornament for Distinguished Service Retailer Open House Wkend
529648 637 | 92 Bunny Popping out of Top Hat/Girl in Magician's Cape | Annual $16.00 3.00" G/CL Secondary $25.00

GATHER YOUR DREAMS Figurine Easter Seal Raffle Piece, Individually Numbered
529680 638 | 93 Girl Hold'g Bunnies in Apron | 2,000 $500.00 7.75" G/CL Secondary $575.00
BFY Secondary 550.00

HAPPINESS IS AT OUR FINGERTIPS Figurine Spring Catalog Exclusive
529931 649 | 93 Girl Reaching for Butterfly | Annual $35.00 5.50" G/CL Secondary $80.00
BFY Secondary 65.00

RING OUT THE GOOD NEWS Figurine Nativity Addition
529966 639 | 93 Girl Holding Doll and Ringing a Bell | UPP $27.50 2.50" BFY Secondary $32.00
94 | OPEN 27.50 TRP Primary 27.50

AN EVENT FOR ALL SEASONS Ornament
1993 Ornament for Distinguished Service Retailer Open House Weekend
529974 641 | 93 Girl Protecting Puppy inside Slicker | Annual $15.00 3.00" BFY Secondary $22.00

MEMORIES ARE MADE OF THIS Figurine, 1994 Special Event Figurine
529982 688 | 94 Girl Blowing Bubbles | Annual $30.00 5.00" BFY Secondary $30.00
TRP Primary 30.00

YOU'RE MY NUMBER ONE FRIEND Figurine Special Easter Seal Piece Easter Seal Lily on Decal
530026 640 | 93 Girl Wearing First Place Award, Holding Trophy | Annual $30.00 5.50" G/CL Secondary $30.00
BFY Primary 30.00

AN EVENT FOR ALL SEASONS Figurine Special Events Piece
530158 641 | 93 Girl Protecting Puppy inside Slicker | Annual $30.00 5.25" G/CL Secondary $50.00
BFY Secondary 40.00

WISHING YOU THE SWEETEST CHRISTMAS Figurine, Dated
530166 642 | 93 Girl in PJ's Holding Gingerbread Cookie for Santa | Annual $27.50 4.75" BFY Secondary $40.00

WISHING YOU THE SWEETEST CHRISTMAS Bell, Dated
530174 93 Girl in PJ's Holding Annual $25.00 5.75" BFY Secondary $35.00
642 Gingerbread Cookie for Santa

WISHING YOU THE SWEETEST CHRISTMAS Thimble, Dated
530182 93 Girl in PJ's Holding Annual $ 8.00 2.25" BFY Secondary $15.00
642 Gingerbread Cookie for Santa

WISHING YOU THE SWEETEST CHRISTMAS Ball Ornament, Dated
Fifth Issue, "Masterpiece Ornament" Series
530190 93 Girl in PJ's Holding Annual $30.00 4.00" BFY Secondary $35.00
642 Gingerbread Cookie for Santa

WISHING YOU THE SWEETEST CHRISTMAS Plate, Dated
Fourth/Final Issue "Christmas Blessings" Series
530204 93 Girl in PJ's Holding Annual $50.00 8.50" BFY Secondary $60.00
642 Gingerbread Cookie for Santa

WISHING YOU THE SWEETEST CHRISTMAS Ornament, Dated
530212 93 Girl in PJ's Holding Annual $15.00 3.25" BFY Secondary $30.00
642 Gingerbread Cookie for Santa

BABY'S FIRST CHRISTMAS Ornament, Dated
530255 94 Baby Girl w/Doll Rides Annual $16.00 3.00" TRP Primary $16.00
686 Hobby Horse Deer

BABY'S FIRST CHRISTMAS Ornament, Dated
530263 94 Baby Boy w/Teddy Annual $16.00 3.00" TRP Primary $16.00
685 Rides Hobby Horse Deer

YOU'RE AS PRETTY AS A CHRISTMAS TREE Ball Ornament, Dated
Sixth Issue, "Masterpiece Ornament" Series
530387 94 Girls Wear Decorated Tree Annual $30.00 5.25" TRP Primary $30.00
672 Outfit & Holds Star Aloft

YOU'RE AS PRETTY AS A CHRISTMAS TREE Ornament, Dated
530395 94 Girls Wear Decorated Tree Annual $16.00 4.75" TRP Primary $16.00
672 Outfit & Holds Star Aloft

YOU'RE AS PRETTY AS A CHRISTMAS TREE Plate, Dated
530409 94 Girls Wear Decorated Tree Annual $50.00 9.50" TRP Primary $50.00
672 Outfit & Holds Star Aloft

YOU'RE AS PRETTY AS A CHRISTMAS TREE Figurine, Dated
530425 94 Girls Wear Decorated Tree Annual $27.50 6.75" TRP Primary $27.50
672 Outfit & Holds Star Aloft

HAPPY BIRTHDAY JESUS Figurine Mini Nativity Addition
530492 93 Elephant Carrying Gift UPP $20.00 3.50" BFY Secondary $23.00
643 94 OPEN 20.00 TRP Primary 20.00

OUR FIRST CHRISTMAS TOGETHER Ornament, Dated
530506 93 Boy and Girl in Sleigh Annual $17.50 2.50" BFY Secondary $20.00
644

SERENITY PRAYER GIRL Figurine
530697 94 Girl Kneels by Serenity UPP $35.00 4.12" BFY Secondary $35.00
654 94 Prayer Plaque OPEN 35.00 TRP Primary 35.00

SERENITY PRAYER BOY Figurine
530700 94 Boy Kneels by Serenity UPP $35.00 4.12" BFY Secondary $35.00
655 94 Prayer Plaque OPEN 35.00 TRP Primary 35.00

15 HAPPY YEARS TOGETHER, WHAT A TWEET! Figurine 15th Anniversary Commemorative
530786 93 Two Bunnies Listen as Angel Leads Bluebird Choir in Anniversary Song — Annual $100.00 5.25" G/CL Secondary $125.00; BFY Secondary 105.00
645
Error: 14 Bluebirds.
Walnut base Display Dome with brass plate and Cloisonne 15 year logo Medallion, one per retailer, selling @ $150.00.

15 YEARS, TWEET MUSIC TOGETHER Ornament 15th Anniversary Commemorative
530840 93 Angel with Bluebird and Songbook — Annual $15.00 3.50" G/CL Secondary $25.00; BFY Secondary 24.00
646

BABY'S FIRST CHRISTMAS Ornament, Dated
530859 93 Boy in PJ's Wrapped in Ribbon — Annual $15.00 3.25" BFY Secondary $20.00
647

BABY'S FIRST CHRISTMAS Ornament, Dated
530867 93 Girl in PJ's Wrapped in Ribbon — Annual $15.00 3.25" BFY Secondary $22.00
648

YOU ARE ALWAYS IN MY HEART Ornament, Dated
530972 94 Teddy Bear Rests on Heart — OPEN $16.00 4.00" TRP Primary $16.00
682

I STILL DO Figurine
530999 94 Girl Points to Finger w/Wedding Ring
94 — UPP $30.00 5.75" BFY Secondary $30.00
94 — OPEN 30.00 TRP Primary 30.00
667

I STILL DO Figurine
531006 94 Boy Points to Finger w/Wedding Ring
94 — UPP $30.00 5.25" BFY Secondary $30.00
94 — OPEN 30.00 TRP Primary 30.00
668

MONEY'S NOT THE ONLY GREEN THING WORTH SAVING Figurine, Retailer Catalog Program
531073 94 Boy Sitting on Piggy Bank Bandaging Tree — OPEN $50.00 5.50" TRP Primary $50.00
692

IT IS NO SECRET WHAT GOD CAN DO Figurine Special Easter Seal Piece Easter Seal Lily on Decal
531111 94 Girl Holds Open Oyster to Reveal Pearl Inside — Annual $30.00 4.62" BFY Primary $30.00; 30.00 TRP Primary 30.00
660

YOU ARE THE ROSE OF HIS CREATION Figurine Easter Seal Raffle Piece, Individually Numbered
531243 94 Girl in Bonnet & Long Dress, Holds Basket/Roses — 2,000 $500.00 9.00" BFY Primary $500.00; 500.00 TRP Primary 500.00
661

BRING THE LITTLE ONES TO JESUS Plate, Child Evengelism Fellowship Piece
531359 94 Mother Reads "Wordless Book"/Children — UPP $50.00 8.50" BFY Primary $50.00; 50.00 TRP Primay 50.00
603

SURROUNDED WITH JOY Figurine Chapel Exclusive
531677 94 Girl with Wreath — OPEN $30.00 5.00" UM Secondary $30.00; TRP Primary 30.00
694

SURROUNDED WITH JOY Ornament Chapel Exclusive
531685 94 Girl with Wreath — OPEN $17.50 3.25" UM Secondary $17.50; TRP Primary 17.50
694

THE LORD IS COUNTING ON YOU Figurine
531707 94 Girl Embroiders Phrase — OPEN $32.50 5.50" TRP Primary $32.50
666

THINKING OF YOU IS WHAT I REALLY LIKE TO DO Plate First Issue "Mother's Day" Series
531766 504 94 Kneeling Girl with Bouquet UPP $50.00 8.50" BFY Primary $50.00
OPEN 50.00 TRP Primary 50.00

DEATH CAN'T KEEP HIM IN THE GROUND Figurine Chapel Exclusive
531928 695 94 Angel Looking Over a Lily OPEN $30.00 UM Primary $30.00

DROPPING IN FOR THE HOLIDAYS Figurine
531952 678 94 Angel Takes Rest in Egg Nog Cup OPEN $40.00 6.00" TRP Primary $40.00

A KING IS BORN Ornament Chapel Exclusive
532088 696 94 Baby Jesus in Manger OPEN $17.50 UM Primary $17.50

THE LORD BLESS YOU AND KEEP YOU Figurine
532118 669 94 African American UPP $40.00 5.25" BFY Secondary $40.00
94 Bride & Groom OPEN 40.00 TRP Primary 40.00

THE LORD BLESS YOU AND KEEP YOU Figurine
532126 670 94 African American UPP $30.00 5.25" BFY Secondary $30.00
94 Girl Graduate OPEN 30.00 TRP Primary 30.00

THE LORD BLESS YOU AND KEEP YOU Figurine
532134 671 94 African American UPP $30.00 BFY Secondary $30.00
94 Boy Graduate OPEN 30.00 TRP Primary 30.00

LUKE 2:10 - 11 Figurine
532916 677 94 Shepherd/Lamb Kneels by Creche-shaped Manger OPEN $35.00 4.50" TRP Primary $35.00

BISQUE ORNAMENT HOLDER Ornament Holder
603171 691 94 Angel Perches atop Open, Framed Window OPEN $30.00 6.00" TRP Primary $30.00

ON THE HILL OVERLOOKING THE QUIET BLUE STREAM ... Figurine
603503 697 94 Two Angels Standing Guard over Poem OPEN $45.00 UM Primary $45.00

NOTHING CAN DAMPEN THE SPIRIT OF CARING Figurine First Issue "Good Samaritan" Series
603864 687 94 Boy Fills Sandbag as Pup Holds Sack Open UPP $35.00 5.12" BFY Secondary $35.00
OPEN 35.00 TRP Primary 35.00

A KING IS BORN Figurine Chapel Exclusive
604151 696 94 Baby Jesus in Manger OPEN $25.00 UM Primary $25.00

A POPPY FOR YOU Figurine
604208 665 94 Girl Holds Poppy Honoring Those Who Died in War OPEN $35.00 5.75" TRP Primary $35.00

YOU'RE AS PRETTY AS A CHRISTMAS TREE Bell
604216 672 94 Girl Wears Decorated Tree & Holds Star Aloft OPEN $27.50 5.75" TRP Primary $27.50

REJOICE, O EARTH	Musical Tree Topper	TUNE: Hark! The Herald Angels Sing
617334	90 Angel	Annual $125.00 14.00" FLM Secondary $125.00
545

THE ENESCO PRECIOUS MOMENTS COLLECTORS' CLUB
SYMBOLS OF CHARTER MEMBERSHIP

Title	Type	Item	Ref	No.	Description	Availability	Issue Price	Size	Mark	Market	Value
BUT LOVE GOES ON FOREVER	Figurine	E-0001	39	81	Boy & Girl Angels on Cloud	MemOnly	$15.00	5.00"	NM	Secondary	$190.00
									TRI	Secondary	170.00
									HRG	Secondary	165.00
BUT LOVE GOES ON FOREVER*	Plaque	E-0102	39	82	Boy & Girl Angels on Cloud	MemOnly	$15.00	5.00"	NM	Secondary	$140.00
									TRI	Secondary	82.00
									HRG	Secondary	70.00
					*Note: "Precious Moments Last Forever" inscription on front of plaque confuses many because the Inspirational Title of this piece is "But Love Goes On Forever."						
LET US CALL THE CLUB TO ORDER	Figurine	E-0103	158	83	Club Meeting	MemOnly	$15.00	5.75"	HRG	Secondary	$65.00
									FSH	Secondary	60.00
JOIN IN ON THE BLESSINGS	Figurine	E-0104	205	84	Girl with Dues Bank	MemOnly	$17.50	4.50"	FSH	Secondary	$65.00
									CRS	Secondary	55.00
SEEK AND YE SHALL FIND	Figurine	E-0105	104	85	Girl with Shopping Bag	MemOnly	$17.50	5.25"	CRS	Secondary	$55.00
									DVE	Secondary	50.00
					Variation: 1985 Charter Member Inscription.						
BIRDS OF A FEATHER COLLECT TOGETHER	Figurine	E-0106	295	86	Girl with Embroidery Hoop and Bird	MemOnly	$17.50	5.75"	DVE	Secondary	$50.00
									OLB	Secondary	48.00
SHARING IS UNIVERSAL	Figurine	E-0107	336	87	Girl Sending Package to Friend	MemOnly	$17.50	5.00"	OLB	Secondary	$50.00
									CED	Secondary	45.00
A GROWING LOVE	Figurine	E-0108	399	88	Girl with Flowerpot and Sunflower	MemOnly	$18.50	4.50"	CED	Secondary	$48.00
									FLW	Secondary	42.00
ALWAYS ROOM FOR ONE MORE	Figurine	C-0109	444	89	Girl with Puppies in Box	MemOnly	$19.50	4.50"	FLW	Secondary	$50.00
									B&A	Secondary	40.00
MY HAPPINESS	Figurine	C-0110	489	90	Girl at Table w/Figurine	MemOnly	$21.00	4.50"	B&A	Secondary	$48.00
									FLM	Secondary	42.00
SHARING THE GOOD NEWS TOGETHER	Figurine	C-0111	562	91	Girl at Mailbox with Club Newsletter	MemOnly	$22.50	5.25"	FLM	Secondary	$45.00
									VSL	Secondary	42.00
THE CLUB THAT'S OUT OF THIS WORLD	Figurine	C-0112	569	92	Girl in Spacesuit Holding Space Helmet	MemOnly	$25.00	5.00"	VSL	Secondary	$42.00
									G/CL	Secondary	40.00
LOVING, CARING AND SHARING ALONG THE WAY	Figurine	C-0113	650	93	Girl at Crossroads	MemOnly	$25.00	5.00"	G/CL	Secondary	$45.00
									BFY	Secondary	40.00
YOU ARE THE END OF MY RAINBOW	Figurine	C-0114	706	94	Girl in Pot of Gold	MemOnly	$26.00	5.00"	BFY	Secondary	$40.00
									TRP	Primary	40.00

SYMBOLS OF MEMBERSHIP

Title / Item No.	Type / Description	Availability	Issue Price	Size	Mark	Market	Price
BUT LOVE GOES ON FOREVER*	Plaque						
E-0202	82 Boy & Girl Angels on Cloud	MemOnly	$15.00	5.00"	UM	Secondary	$115.00
39					TRI	Secondary	80.00
					HRG	Secondary	65.00

*NOTE: "Precious Moments Last Forever" inscription on front of plaque confuses many because the Inspirational Title of this piece is "But Love Goes On Forever."
- Termed the "Canadian Plaque Error," approximately 750 pieces of this 1982 Symbol Of Membership piece were produced in 1985 and shipped to Canada. These pieces are stamped "TAIWAN" and have a DOVE Annual Production Symbol. The GREENBOOK TRUMARKET Price for the "Canadian Plaque Error" is $125.00. Photograph: 6th Ed., pg. 225.

Title / Item No.	Type / Description	Availability	Issue Price	Size	Mark	Market	Price
LET US CALL THE CLUB TO ORDER	Figurine						
E-0303	83 Club Meeting	MemOnly	$15.00	5.75"	HRG	Secondary	$60.00
158					FSH	Secondary	55.00
					CRS	Secondary	55.00
JOIN IN ON THE BLESSINGS	Figurine						
E-0404	84 Girl with Dues Bank	MemOnly	$17.50	4.50"	HRG	Secondary	$120.00
205					FSH	Secondary	70.00
					CRS	Secondary	50.00
SEEK AND YE SHALL FIND	Figurine						
E-0005	85 Girl with Shopping Bag	MemOnly	$17.50	5.25"	CRS	Secondary	$50.00
104					DVE	Secondary	45.00
BIRDS OF A FEATHER COLLECT TOGETHER	Figurine						
E-0006	86 Girl with Embroidery Hoop and Bird	MemOnly	$17.50	5.75"	DVE	Secondary	$42.00
295					OLB	Secondary	38.00
SHARING IS UNIVERSAL	Figurine						
E-0007	87 Girl Sending Package to Friend	MemOnly	$17.50	5.00"	OLB	Secondary	$45.00
336					CED	Secondary	40.00
A GROWING LOVE	Figurine						
E-0008	88 Girl with Flowerpot and Sunflower	MemOnly	$18.50	4.50"	CED	Secondary	$42.00
399					FLW	Secondary	35.00
ALWAYS ROOM FOR ONE MORE	Figurine						
C-0009	89 Girl with Puppies in Box	MemOnly	$19.50	4.50"	FLW	Secondary	$45.00
444					B&A	Secondary	38.00
					FLM	Secondary	35.00
MY HAPPINESS	Figurine						
C-0010	90 Girl at Table w/Figurine	MemOnly	$21.00	4.50"	B&A	Secondary	$40.00
489					FLM	Secondary	35.00
SHARING THE GOOD NEWS TOGETHER	Figurine						
C-0011	91 Girl at Mailbox with Club Newsletter	MemOnly	$22.50	5.25"	FLM	Secondary	$42.00
562					VSL	Secondary	30.00
THE CLUB THAT'S OUT OF THIS WORLD	Figurine						
C-0012	92 Girl in Spacesuit Holding Space Helmet	MemOnly	$25.00	5.00"	VSL	Secondary	$40.00
569					G/CL	Secondary	40.00
LOVING, CARING AND SHARING ALONG THE WAY	Figurine						
C-0013	93 Girl at Crossroads	MemOnly	$25.00	5.00"	G/CL	Secondary	$40.00
650					BFY	Secondary	40.00
YOU ARE THE END OF MY RAINBOW	Figurine						
C-0014	94 Girl in Pot of Gold	MemOnly	$26.00	5.00"	BFY	Secondary	$40.00
706					TRP	Primary	40.00

MEMBERSHIP PIECES

Title / Item	Description	Type	Issue Price	Size	Mark	Market	Value
HELLO LORD, IT'S ME AGAIN — Figurine PM-811 (78)	81 Boy on Telephone	MemOnly	$25.00	4.75"	TRI	Secondary	$450.00
					HRG	Secondary	425.00
SMILE, GOD LOVES YOU — Figurine PM-821 (117)	82 Girl with Curlers	MemOnly	$25.00	5.25"	HRG	Secondary	$230.00
					FSH	Secondary	215.00
PUT ON A HAPPY FACE — Figurine PM-822 (159)	83 Boy Clown Holding Mask	MemOnly	$25.00	5.50"	HRG	Secondary	$215.00
					FSH	Secondary	195.00
					CRS	Secondary	190.00
DAWN'S EARLY LIGHT — Figurine PM-831 (160)	83 Girl Covering Kitten	MemOnly	$25.00	4.50"	FSH	Secondary	$90.00
					CRS	Secondary	85.00
GOD'S RAY OF MERCY — Figurine PM-841 (206)	84 Boy Angel with Flashlight	MemOnly	$25.00	4.75"	FSH	Secondary	$85.00
					CRS	Secondary	60.00
					DVE	Secondary	55.00
TRUST IN THE LORD TO THE FINISH — Figurine PM-842 (207)	84 Boy with Racing Cup	MemOnly	$25.00	5.50"	CRS	Secondary	$70.00
THE LORD IS MY SHEPHERD — Figurine PM-851 (293)	85 Girl Holding Lamb	MemOnly	$25.00	5.50"	DVE	Secondary	$80.00
I LOVE TO TELL THE STORY — Figurine PM-852 (294)	85 Boy with Lamb and Book	MemOnly	$27.50	3.50"	DVE	Secondary	$65.00
GRANDMA'S PRAYER — Figurine PM-861 (305)	86 Praying Grandma	MemOnly	$25.00	4.50"	DVE	Secondary	$85.00
					OLB	Secondary	78.00
					CED	Secondary	75.00
I'M FOLLOWING JESUS — Figurine PM-862 (320)	86 Boy in Car	MemOnly	$25.00	4.25"	OLB	Secondary	$85.00
FEED MY SHEEP — Figurine PM-871 (366)	87 Girl Feeding Lamb	MemOnly	$25.00	4.75"	CED	Secondary	$60.00
					FLW	Secondary	57.00
IN HIS TIME — Figurine PM-872 (375)	87 Boy Waiting for Seed to Grow	MemOnly	$25.00	4.10"	CED	Secondary	$55.00
					FLW	Secondary	50.00
LOVING YOU DEAR VALENTINE — Figurine PM-873 (321)	87 Boy Painting Valentine	MemOnly	$25.00	5.50"	OLB	Secondary	$45.00
					FLW	Secondary	40.00
LOVING YOU DEAR VALENTINE — Figurine PM-874 (322)	87 Girl Drawing Valentine	MemOnly	$25.00	5.25"	OLB	Secondary	$50.00
					FLW	Secondary	45.00
GOD BLESS YOU FOR TOUCHING MY LIFE — Figurine PM-881 (439)	88 Girl Painting Butterfly	MemOnly	$27.50	4.75"	CED	Secondary	$65.00
					FLW	Secondary	55.00
					B&A	Secondary	48.00

YOU JUST CANNOT CHUCK A GOOD FRIENDSHIP Figurine
PM-882 88 Boy Rescuing Puppy from Trash Can MemOnly $27.50 5.00" FLW Secondary $50.00
442 B&A Secondary 42.00

BEAUTITUDE ORNAMENT SERIES Ornaments Set of 7*
PM-890 90 Chapel Stained Glass Window Replicas MemOnly $105.00 5.50" UM Secondary $105.00
542
*Set of 7 also individually numbered PM-190 through PM-790. For individual titles see the QUIKREFERENCE SECTION pg. 135.

YOU WILL ALWAYS BE MY CHOICE Figurine
PM-891 89 Girl with Ballot Box MemOnly $27.50 4.75" B&A Secondary $45.00
485 FLM Secondary 40.00

MOW POWER TO YA Figurine
PM-892 89 Boy Pushing Lawn Mower MemOnly $27.50 4.75" B&A Secondary $48.00
486 FLM Secondary 42.00

TEN YEARS AND STILL GOING STRONG Figurine
PM-901 90 Girl in Race Car MemOnly $30.00 3.75" FLM Secondary $50.00
540 VSL Secondary 45.00

YOU ARE A BLESSING TO ME Figurine
PM-902 90 Girl Sewing Patch on Teddy Bear MemOnly $27.50 5.00" FLM Secondary $50.00
541 VSL Secondary 45.00

ONE STEP AT A TIME Figurine
PM-911 91 Child Hold'g Mom's Hands Tak'g First Steps MemOnly $33.00 5.25" VSL Secondary $45.00
564 G/CL Secondary 40.00

LORD, KEEP ME IN TEEPEE TOP SHAPE Figurine
PM-912 91 Indian Boy Holding Can of Spinach MemOnly $27.50 4.50" VSL Secondary $48.00
565 G/CL Secondary 45.00

ONLY LOVE CAN MAKE A HOME Figurine
PM-921 92 Mr. Webb Building Bird Home MemOnly $30.00 4.25" G/CL Secondary $48.00
613 BFY Secondary 45.00

SOWING THE SEEDS OF LOVE Figurine
PM-922 92 Girl Kneeling & Praying by New Growing Flower MemOnly $30.00 4.50" G/CL Secondary $40.00
614 BFY Secondary 35.00

HIS LITTLE TREASURE Figurine
PM-931 93 Girl Pointing to Sand Dollar MemOnly $30.00 4.25" BFY Secondary $35.00
652 TRP Secondary 30.00

LOVING Figurine
PM-932 93 Girl Hugs Teddy Bear MemOnly $30.00 5.50" BFY Secondary $00.00
700 TRP Primary 00.00

CARING Figurine
PM-941 94 Girl Gives First Aid to Teddy MemOnly $35.00 TRP Primary $00.00
707

COMMEMORATIVE MEMBERSHIP PIECES

GOD BLESS OUR YEARS TOGETHER Figurine 5th Anniversary Club Commemorative Piece
12440 85 Mom, Dad, Kids, and Cake w/5 Candles MemOnly $175.00 5.50" DVE Secondary $285.00
249

THIS LAND IS OUR LAND Figurine
Commemorates 500th Anniversary Christopher Columbus' Voyage
527386 92 Explorer & Animal Crew Sailing the High Seas in a Sail Boat MemOnly $350.00 9.50" G/CL Secondary $385.00
599

SHARING SEASON ORNAMENTS

Gift to Club Members for signing up new members.
For additional information, see WE JUST WANTED YOU TO KNOW, 7th Ed., pg. 228.

BIRDS OF A FEATHER COLLECT TOGETHER Ornament
PM-864 86 Girl with Embroidery Hoop and Bird MemOnly $12.50 2.25" OLB Secondary $190.00
295

SHARING SEASON ORNAMENT Ornament
PM-008 87 Brass Filagree - Kids on Cloud MemOnly $ 3.50 2.75" UM Secondary $45.00
376

A GROWING LOVE Ornament
520349 88 Girl with Flowerpot and Sunflower MemOnly $15.00 2.80" FLW Secondary $80.00
399

ALWAYS ROOM FOR ONE MORE Ornament
522961 89 Girl with Puppies in Box MemOnly $15.00 2.80" B&A Secondary $105.00
444

MY HAPPINESS Ornament
PM-904 90 Girl at Table w/Figurine MemOnly $15.00 3.00" FLM Secondary $85.00
489

SHARING THE GOOD NEWS TOGETHER Ornament
PM-037 91 Girl at Mailbox with Club Newsletter MemOnly $17.50 3.25" VSL Secondary $75.00
562

THE CLUB THAT'S OUT OF THIS WORLD Ornament
PM-038 92 Girl in Spacesuit Holding Space Helmet MemOnly $17.50 3.00" G/CL Secondary $60.00
569

MEMBERS ONLY ORNAMENTS

LOVING, CARING AND SHARING Ornament
PM-040 93 Girl at Crossroads MemOnly $15.00 3.25" BFY Secondary $25.00
650

NOTES

THE ENESCO PRECIOUS MOMENTS BIRTHDAY CLUB
SYMBOLS OF CHARTER MEMBERSHIP

Title / Item	Ref.	Description	Availability	Issue Price	Size	Mark	Market	Price
<u>OUR CLUB CAN'T BE BEAT</u> Figurine								
B-0001	304	86 Clown with Drum	MemOnly	$10.00	3.50"	DVE	Secondary	$80.00
						OLB	Secondary	75.00
						CED	Secondary	72.00
<u>A SMILE'S THE CYMBAL OF JOY</u> Figurine								
B-0102	364	87 Clown with Cymbals	MemOnly	$10.00	4.50"	OLB	Secondary	$72.00
						CED	Secondary	68.00
		The first of these were shipped with a title error on the understamp decal - "A Smile's The <u>Symbol</u> Of Joy." The GREENBOOK TRUMARKET Price for the "Symbol Error" is $95.00. Color photograph: 5th Ed., pg. 208.						
<u>THE SWEETEST CLUB AROUND</u> Figurine								
B-0103	440	88 Pippin Popping out of Cake	MemOnly	$11.00	4.50"	FLW	Secondary	$50.00
						B&A	Secondary	45.00
<u>HAVE A BEARY SPECIAL BIRTHDAY</u> Figurine								
B-0104	487	89 Teddy Bear with Balloon	MemOnly	$11.50	4.50"	FLW	Secondary	$48.00
						B&A	Secondary	35.00
						FLM	Secondary	32.00
<u>OUR CLUB IS A TOUGH ACT TO FOLLOW</u> Figurine								
B-0105	543	90 Clown with Puppy Leaping thru Drum	MemOnly	$13.50	4.00"	FLM	Secondary	$36.00
						VSL	Secondary	32.00
<u>JEST TO LET YOU KNOW YOU'RE TOPS</u> Figurine								
B-0106	568	91 Jester Clown Popping out of Box	MemOnly	$15.00	4.25"	VSL	Secondary	$35.00
						G/CL	Secondary	30.00
<u>ALL ABOARD FOR BIRTHDAY CLUB FUN</u> Figurine								
B-0107	612	92 Engineer Riding Locomotive	MemOnly	$16.00	4.50"	G/CL	Secondary	$32.00
						BFY	Secondary	28.00
<u>HAPPINESS IS BELONGING</u> Figurine								
B-0108	705	93 Clown Carries Balloon	MemOnly	$17.50	4.75"	BFY	Secondary	$25.00
						TRP	Secondary	$20.00

SYMBOLS OF MEMBERSHIP

Title / Item	Ref.	Description	Availability	Issue Price	Size	Mark	Market	Price
<u>A SMILE'S THE CYMBAL OF JOY</u> Figurine								
B-0002	364	87 Clown with Cymbals	MemOnly	$10.00	4.50"	OLB	Secondary	$65.00
						CED	Secondary	60.00
						FLW	Secondary	55.00
<u>THE SWEETEST CLUB AROUND</u> Figurine								
B-0003	440	88 Pippin Popping out of Cake	MemOnly	$11.00	4.50"	FLW	Secondary	$45.00
						B&A	Secondary	40.00
<u>HAVE A BEARY SPECIAL BIRTHDAY</u> Figurine								
B-0004	487	89 Teddy Bear with Balloon	MemOnly	$11.50	4.50"	B&A	Secondary	$32.00
						FLM	Secondary	28.00
<u>OUR CLUB IS A TOUGH ACT TO FOLLOW</u> Figurine								
B-0005	543	90 Clown with Puppy Leaping thru Drum	MemOnly	$13.50	4.00"	FLM	Secondary	$32.00
						VSL	Secondary	28.00
<u>JEST TO LET YOU KNOW YOU'RE TOPS</u> Figurine								
B-0006	568	91 Jester Clown Popping out of Box	MemOnly	$15.00	4.25"	VSL	Secondary	$30.00
						G/CL	Secondary	25.00

Title	Item No.	No.	Year / Description	Availability	Issue Price	Size	Mark	Market	Value
ALL ABOARD FOR BIRTHDAY CLUB FUN (Figurine)	B-0007	612	92 Engineer Riding Locomotive	MemOnly	$25.00	4.50"	G/CL	Secondary	$25.00
							BFY	Secondary	25.00
HAPPINESS IS BELONGING (Figurine)	B-0008	705	93 Clown Carries Balloon	MemOnly	$17.50	4.75"	BFY	Secondary	$22.00
							TRP	Secondary	$18.00

MEMBERSHIP PIECES

Title	Item No.	No.	Year / Description	Availability	Issue Price	Size	Mark	Market	Value
FISHING FOR FRIENDS (Figurine)	BC-861	335	86 Raccoon Holding Fish	MemOnly	$10.00	2.50"	OLB	Secondary	$130.00
							CED	Secondary	125.00
HI SUGAR! (Figurine)	BC-871	398	87 Mouse in Sugar Bowl	MemOnly	$11.00	2.60"	CED	Secondary	$100.00
							FLW	Secondary	95.00
							B&A	Secondary	92.00
SOMEBUNNY CARES (Figurine)	BC-881	441	88 Bunny with Carrot	MemOnly	$13.50	3.00"	FLW	Secondary	$60.00
							B&A	Secondary	55.00
CAN'T BEE HIVE MYSELF WITHOUT YOU (Figurine)	BC-891	488	89 Teddy Bear with Bee and Bee Hive	MemOnly	$13.50	2.50"	B&A	Secondary	$55.00
							FLM	Secondary	50.00
							VSL	Secondary	48.00
COLLECTING MAKES GOOD SCENTS (Figurine)	BC-901	544	90 Skunk with Flowers	MemOnly	$15.00	2.50"	FLM	Secondary	$40.00
							VSL	Secondary	35.00
I'M NUTS OVER MY COLLECTION (Figurine)	BC-902	547	90 Squirrel with Nuts/ Mesh Bag	MemOnly	$15.00	2.50"	FLM	Secondary	$40.00
							VSL	Secondary	35.00
LOVE PACIFIES (Figurine)	BC-911	566	91 Baby Monkey in Bonnet with Pacifer	MemOnly	$16.00	3.00	VSL	Secondary	$35.00
							G/CL	Secondary	32.00
TRUE BLUE FRIENDS (Figurine)	BC-912	567	91 Puppy & Kitten Sharing Paint & Brush	MemOnly	$15.00	2.50"	VSL	Secondary	$38.00
							G/CL	Secondary	32.00
EVERY MAN'S HOUSE IS HIS CASTLE (Figurine)	BC-921	615	92 Beaver Building Home	MemOnly	$16.50	2.50"	G/CL	Secondary	$32.00
							BFY	Secondary	30.00
I GOT YOU UNDER MY SKIN (Figurine)	BC-922	651	92 Pup Wearing Fleece	MemOnly	$16.00	2.50"	G/CL	Secondary	$30.00
							BFY	Secondary	28.00
PUT A LITTLE PUNCH IN YOUR BIRTHDAY (Figurine)	BC-931	704	93 Kangaroo Boxer	MemOnly	$15.00	3.50"	BFY	Secondary	$20.00
							TRP	Primary	15.00
OWL ALWAYS BE YOUR FRIEND (Figurine)	BC-932	703	93 Two Owls Share Tree Branch	MemOnly	$16.00	3.00"	BFY	Secondary	$18.00
							TRP	Primary	16.00
GOD BLESS OUR HOME (Figurine)	BC-941	701	94 Mouse Naps on Turtle Shell	MemOnly	$16.00	3.50"	TRP	Primary	$16.00

GLOSSARY continued

Sharing Season Ornaments -

The "Sharing Season" program was begun in 1983 and appears to have been discontinued in 1993. The objective of the program was to recruit new members to the Enesco Precious Moments Collectors' Club. Although the requirements changed occasionally, as did the rewards, the basic program was that if a member of the Enesco Precious Moments Collectors' Club recruited two new members to the Club, he/she would receive a gift. The gifts varied, but the ones most noted and sought after by collectors are known as the "Sharing Season Ornaments."

Symbol Of Charter Membership -

Charter Members to the Enesco Precious Moments Collectors' Club were those who joined the Club during the first -- or Charter -- year of its existence -- 1981. The Charter Members of the Club receive the same figurine as a renewal gift each year as do other members of the Club -- with two exceptions. First of all, the number assigned to the figurine is different -- and secondly, the decal on the figurine reads "Charter Member." Several years ago, Enesco decided that Charter memberships could no longer be transferred from one collector to another, so in time, "Charter Memberships" in the Club may no longer exist.

Symbol Of Membership -

Members in the Enesco Precious Moments Collectors' Club receive a special figurine -- commemorating a club activity -- as part of their annual membership dues. Each piece has the Club logo on it, and is identical to the pieces produced for Charter Members, other than the fact that the product number is different, and the decal does not read "Charter Member."

Rosebud Decal -

In 1990, a special promotion was held at Precious Moments Collectors' Centers (DSR's) in an effort to encourage collectors to bring a friend to an event, and get them involved in the Precious Moments Collection. At that event, each participating store was given a "Good Friends Are Forever" figurine with a special product number (525049) and a rosebud included as part of the decal. In order to have a chance to win the figurine, a collector had to attend the event and bring a friend. Both the collector and guest had their name entered into a drawing for the "Rosebud" figurine, which was given away at the end of the event. This piece (estimated at less than 1,000 released) is of some interest to collectors who enjoy owning unusual pieces. However, it is important to realize that this piece is identical to the 521817 "Good Friends Are Forever" figurine -- with the exception of the different product number and rosebud on the decal.

... continued on page 302

GIFT GIVER'S GUIDE™

The GIFT GIVER'S GUIDE contains *currently available* pieces that are appropriate as gifts for special people and special occasions. It does not include retired, suspended, limited editions etc. which may not be readily available. Categories are:

- Valentine's Day / Love
- Easter
- Graduation / School Days
- Communion / Christening
- Mother's Day
- Father's Day
- Friendship
- Engagement / Wedding / Anniversary
- Birthday
- Missing You
- Grief / Bereavement
- Baby / Adoption
- Thanksgiving
- Inspirational
- Christmas Nativity
- Christmas General

Itemized for each piece are the Enesco Item Number, GREENBOOK ARTCHART Number, Inspirational Title, Type of Product, and the current Suggested Retail Price. Items in bold are 1994 annuals and historically have only been readily available at issue price for the calendar year.

VALENTINE'S DAY/LOVE

E-1376	(8)	Love One Another	FIG	$ 37.50
522929			ORN	17.50
E-3110G	(35)	Loving Is Sharing	FIG	30.00
E-3113	(37)	Thou Art Mine	FIG	37.50
E-3115	(39)	But Love Goes On Forever	FIG	35.00
103497	(333)	My Love Will Never Let You Go	FIG	35.00
106844	(382)	Sew In Love	FIG	55.00
109967	(386)	Sending You My Love	FIG	45.00
520624	(458)	My Heart Is Exposed With Love	FIG	50.00
520675	(454)	Your Love Is So Uplifting	FIG	75.00
520764	(465)	Puppy Love	FIG	16.00
521418	(511)	I'll Never Stop Loving You	FIG	37.50
521698	(528)	Thumb-body Loves You	FIG	60.00
521841	(510)	Love Is From Above	FIG	45.00
523518	(509)	God Is Love Dear Valentine	FIG	30.00
523542	(577)	You Are The Type I Love	FIG	40.00
524492	(538)	Can't Be Without You	FIG	16.00
526193	(662)	You Suit Me To A Tee	FIG	35.00
526487	(659)	Sharing Sweet Moments Together	FIG	45.00
527769	(635)	I Only Have Arms For You	FIG	15.00

EASTER

103632	(224)	I Believe In The Old Rugged Cross	FIG	$ 35.00
109886	(388)	Wishing You A Happy Easter	FIG	30.00
109924	(385)	Wishing You A Basket Full Of Blessings	FIG	30.00
520667	(455)	Eggspecially For You	FIG	50.00
521892	(508)	Easter's On Its Way	FIG	65.00
521906	(529)	Hoppy Easter Friend	FIG	40.00
529095	**(531)**	**A Reflection Of His Love**	**EGG**	**27.50**

GRADUATION/SCHOOL DAYS

E-4721	(47)	The Lord Bless You And Keep You (Girl)	FIG	$ 30.00
12300	(238)	Love Never Fails	FIG	37.50
106194	(334)	God Bless You Graduate	FIG	30.00
106208	(318)	Congratulations, Princess	FIG	30.00
110086	(426)	September Calendar Girl	FIG	33.50
532126	(670)	The Lord Bless You And Keep You (Girl)	FIG	30.00
532134	(671)	The Lord Bless You And Keep You (Boy)	FIG	30.00

COMMUNION/CHRISTENING

E-4724	(50)	Rejoicing With You	FIG	$ 50.00
100064	(213)	Worship The Lord (Girl)	FIG	35.00
100277	(220)	He Cleansed My Soul	FIG	37.50
102229	(223)	Worship The Lord (Boy)	FIG	35.00
523496	(506)	This Day Has Been Made In Heaven	FIG	30.00
523682			MUS	60.00
525316	(630)	May Your Future Be Blessed	FIG	35.00

MOTHER'S DAY

E-0514	(30)	Mother Sew Dear	ORN	$ 16.00
E-3106			FIG	30.00
E-7182			MUS	60.00
13293			THMBL	8.00
E-0516	(33)	The Purr-fect Grandma	ORN	16.00
E-3109			FIG	30.00
13307			THMBL	8.00
E-2824	(164)	To A Very Special Mom	FIG	37.50
100137	(217)	The Joy Of The Lord Is My Strength	FIG	50.00
109975	(387)	Mommy, I Love You (Boy)	FIG	27.50
112143	(390)	Mommy, I Love You (Girl)	FIG	27.50
521965	(530)	To A Special Mum	FIG	35.00
522287	(504)	Thinking Of You Is What I Really Like To Do	FIG	30.00
531766			**PLT**	**50.00**
523453	(497)	The Good Lord Always Delivers	FIG	30.00

FATHER'S DAY

E-5212	(59)	To A Special Dad	FIG	$ 35.00

FRIENDSHIP

12262	(236)	I Get A Bang Out Of You	FIG	$ 45.00
100048	(316)	To My Deer Friend	FIG	50.00
100072	(214)	To My Forever Friend	FIG	50.00
113956			ORN	17.50
100250	(219)	Friends Never Drift Apart	FIG	55.00
522937			ORN	17.50
109231	(355)	The Greatest Gift Is A Friend	FIG	37.50
520632	(449)	A Friend Is Someone Who Cares	FIG	35.00
520748	(453)	Friendship Hits The Spot	FIG	65.00
521000	(617)	There Is No Greater Treasure Than To Have A Friend Like You	FIG	30.00
521183	(520)	That's What Friends Are For	FIG	45.00
521299	(526)	Hug One Another	FIG	50.00
521817	(492)	Good Friends Are Forever	FIG	50.00
523623	(623)	I'm So Glad That God Blessed Me With A Friend Like You	FIG	50.00
523631	(656)	I Will Always Be Thinking Of You	FIG	45.00
524085	(578)	My Warmest Thoughts Are You	FIG	60.00
524123	(555)	Good Friends Are For Always	FIG	30.00
524336	(626)	Our Friendship Is Soda-Licious	FIG	65.00
524395	(585)	You Are Such A Purr-fect Friend	FIG	35.00
524905	(581)	It's So Uplifting To Have A Friend Like You	FIG	40.00
528846			ORN	16.00
526142	(586)	I Would Be Lost Without You	FIG	30.00
526150	(658)	Friends To The Very End	FIG	40.00
526924	(558)	How Can I Ever Forget You	FIG	16.00
527270	(593)	Let's Be Friends	FIG	16.00

ENGAGEMENT/WEDDING/ANNIVERSARY

E-2828	(168)	Precious Memories	FIG	$ 65.00
E-2831	(170)	Bridesmaid	FIG	22.50
E-2832	(171)	God Bless The Bride	FIG	50.00
E-2833	(208)	Ringbearer	FIG	17.00
E-2835	(209)	Flower Girl	FIG	17.00
E-2836	(172)	Groomsman	FIG	22.50
E-2837	(269)	Groom	FIG	25.00
E-2845	(210)	Junior Bridesmaid	FIG	20.00
E-2846	(313)	Bride	FIG	25.00
E-2853	(179)	God Blessed Our Years Together With So Much Love & Happiness (Happy Anniversary)	FIG	50.00
E-2854	(180)	God Blessed Our Year Together With So Much Love & Happiness (1st Anniversary)	FIG	50.00
E-2855	(181)	God Blessed Our Years Together With So Much Love & Happiness (5th Anniversary)	FIG	50.00
E-2856	(182)	God Blessed Our Years Together With So Much Love & Happiness (10th Anniversary)	FIG	50.00
E-2857	(183)	God Blessed Our Years Together With So Much Love & Happiness (25th Anniversary)	FIG	50.00
E-2859	(184)	God Blessed Our Years Together With So Much Love & Happiness (40th Anniversary)	FIG	50.00
E-2860	(185)	God Blessed Our Years Together With So Much Love & Happiness (50th Anniversary)	FIG	50.00
E-3114	(38)	The Lord Bless You And Keep You	FIG	40.00
E-7180			MUS	85.00
E-9255	(139)	Bless You Two	FIG	37.50
100498	(325)	God Bless Our Family (Groom)	FIG	50.00
100501	(326)	God Bless Our Family (Bride)	FIG	50.00
104019	(343)	With This Ring I ...	FIG	60.00
106755	(378)	Heaven Bless Your Togetherness	FIG	90.00
106763	(379)	Precious Memories	FIG	50.00
106798	(380)	Puppy Love Is From Above	FIG	55.00
110043	(372)	June Calendar Girl	FIG	50.00
520780	(460)	Wishing You Roads Of Happiness	FIG	75.00
520837	(466)	The Lord Is Your Light To Happiness	FIG	60.00
520845	(459)	Wishing You A Perfect Choice	FIG	65.00
524441	(628)	Sealed With A Kiss	FIG	50.00
530999	(667)	I Still Do (Girl)	FIG	30.00
531006	(668)	I Still Do (Boy)	FIG	30.00
532118	(669)	The Lord Bless You And Keep You	FIG	40.00

BIRTHDAY

BIRTHDAY CIRCUS TRAIN:

15938	(296)	May Your Birthday Be Warm (Baby)	FIG	$ 15.00
15946	(297)	Happy Birthday Little Lamb (Age 1)	FIG	15.00
15962	(298)	God Bless You On Your Birthday (Age 2)	FIG	16.50
15954	(299)	Heaven Bless Your Special Day (Age 3)	FIG	16.50
15970	(300)	May Your Birthday Be Gigantic (Age 4)	FIG	18.50
15989	(301)	This Day Is Something To Roar About (Age 5)	FIG	20.00
15997	(302)	Keep Looking Up (Age 6)	FIG	20.00
109479	(393)	Wishing You Grrr-eatness (Age 7)	FIG	22.50
109460	(394)	Isn't Eight Just Great (Age 8)	FIG	22.50
521833	(574)	Being Nine Is Just Divine (Age 9)	FIG	25.00
521825	(573)	May Your Birthday Be Mammoth (Age 10)	FIG	25.00
16004	(303)	Bless The Days Of Our Youth	FIG	22.50

CALENDAR GIRLS:

109983	(367)	January Calendar Girl	FIG	$ 45.00
109991	(368)	February Calendar Girl	FIG	35.00
110019	(369)	March Calendar Girl	FIG	35.00
110027	(370)	April Calendar Girl	FIG	35.00
110035	(371)	May Calendar Girl	FIG	35.00
110043	(372)	June Calendar Girl	FIG	50.00
110051	(424)	July Calendar Girl	FIG	45.00
110078	(425)	August Calendar Girl	FIG	50.00
110086	(426)	September Calendar Girl	FIG	35.00
110094	(427)	October Calendar Girl	FIG	45.00
110108	(428)	November Calendar Girl	FIG	37.50
110116	(429)	December Calendar Girl	FIG	35.00

BIRTHDAY GENERAL:

524069	(624)	Baby's First Birthday	FIG	$ 25.00
524298	(625)	May Your Every Wish Come True	FIG	50.00
524301	(536)	May Your Birthday Be A Blessing	FIG	30.00
524506	(657)	Oinky Birthday	FIG	13.50
527343	(597)	Happy Birdie	FIG	16.00

MISSING YOU

102520	(287)	Let's Keep In Touch	MUS	$ 90.00
112364	(250)	Waddle I Do Without You	ORN	16.00
522201	(474)	Bon Voyage!	FIG	90.00
524492	(538)	Can't Be Without You	FIG	16.00
524913	(515)	We're Going To Miss You	FIG	50.00
526916	(631)	Wishing You Were Here	MUS	100.00

GRIEF/BEREAVEMENT

101826	(329)	No Tears Past The Gate	FIG	$ 65.00
103632	(224)	I Believe In The Old Rugged Cross	FIG	35.00
521485	(527)	There's A Light At The End Of The Tunnel	FIG	55.00
521922	(620)	Safe In The Arms Of Jesus	FIG	30.00
523739	(518)	Time Heals	FIG	37.50
525979	(584)	Going Home	FIG	60.00

BABY/ADOPTION

E-1372B	(1)	Jesus Loves Me (Boy)	FIG	$ 25.00
E-9278			FIG	16.00
E-1372G	(2)	Jesus Loves Me (Girl)	FIG	25.00
E-9279			FIG	16.00
E-2852A	(401)	Baby Figurine - Boy Standing	FIG	17.50
E-2852B	(402)	Baby Figurine - Girl w/Bow Standing	FIG	17.50
E-2852C	(403)	Baby Figurine - Boy Sitting	FIG	17.50
E-2852D	(404)	Baby Figurine - Girl Clapping	FIG	17.50
E-2852E	(405)	Baby Figurine - Boy Crawling	FIG	17.50
E-2852F	(406)	Baby Figurine - Girl Lying Down	FIG	17.50
520934	(221)	Heaven Bless You	FIG	35.00
521175	(451)	Hello World!	FIG	16.00
521493	(552)	A Special Delivery	FIG	30.00
523178	(532)	Joy On Arrival	FIG	50.00
523453	(497)	The Good Lord Always Delivers	FIG	30.00
524077	(534)	Baby's First Meal	FIG	37.50
527238	(592)	Baby's First Word	FIG	25.00

THANKSGIVING

109762	(359)	We Gather Together To Ask The Lord's Blessing	FIGS	$150.00
110108	(428)	November Calendar Girl	FIG	37.50

INSPIRATIONAL

E-0523	(128)	Onward Christian Soldiers	FIG	$ 35.00
E-3117	(41)	Walking By Faith	FIG	75.00
E-7158	(107)	Love Beareth All Things	FIG	40.00
E-9258	(140)	We Are God's Workmanship	FIG	30.00
E-9265	(146)	Press On	FIG	60.00
100137	(217)	The Joy Of The Lord Is My Strength	FIG	50.00
100226	(340)	The Lord Giveth And The Lord Taketh Away	FIG	40.00
100277	(220)	He Cleansed My Soul	FIG	37.50
112380			ORN	16.00
101826	(329)	No Tears Past The Gate	FIG	65.00
103632	(224)	I Believe In The Old Rugged Cross	FIG	35.00
522953			ORN	16.00
111155	(389)	Faith Takes The Plunge	FIG	35.00
114014	(391)	This Too Shall Pass	FIG	30.00
520535	(571)	The Lord Turned My Life Around	FIG	35.00
520551	(493)	Lord, Turn My Life Around	FIG	35.00
521450	(503)	Lord, Help Me Stick To My Job	FIG	35.00
521477	(476)	Tell It To Jesus	FIG	37.50
521485	(527)	There's A Light At The End Of The Tunnel	FIG	55.00
521671	(619)	Hope You're Over The Hump	FIG	17.50
521779	(502)	Sweep All Your Worries Away	FIG	40.00
522090	(500)	There Shall Be Showers Of Blessings	FIG	70.00
530697	(654)	Serenity Prayer Girl	FIG	35.00
530700	(655)	Serenity Prayer Boy	FIG	35.00
531707	(666)	The Lord Is Counting On You	FIG	32.50

CHRISTMAS

NATIVITY:

104000	(307)	Come Let Us Adore Him	FIGS	$125.00

NATIVITY ADDITIONS:

E-2360	(87)	I'll Play My Drum For Him	FIG	$ 25.00
E-2363	(90)	Camel	FIG	32.50
E-5379	(189)	Isn't He Precious	FIG	30.00
E-5621	(63)	Donkey	FIG	15.00
E-5624	(65)	They Followed The Star	FIGS	225.00
E-5635	(66)	Wee Three Kings	FIGS	75.00
E-5636	(67)	Rejoice O Earth	FIG	30.00
E-5637	(68)	The Heavenly Light	FIG	27.50
E-5638	(69)	Cow	FIG	32.50
E-5644	(74)	Two Section Wall	FIGS	120.00
15490	(255)	Honk If You Love Jesus	FIGS	20.00
115274	(431)	Some Bunny's Sleeping	FIGS	18.50
527750	(607)	Wishing You A Comfy Christmas	FIG	27.50
528072	(683)	Nativity Cart	FIG	18.50
529966	(639)	Ring Out The Good News	FIG	27.50

MINI NATIVITY:

E-2395	(22)	Come Let Us Adore Him	FIGS	$125.00

MINI NATIVITY ADDITIONS:

E-2387	(101)	House Set And Palm Tree	FIGS	$ 75.00
E-5384	(87)	I'll Play My Drum For Him	FIG	16.00
102261	(278)	Shepherd Of Love	FIG	16.00
108243	(65)	They Followed The Star	FIGS	110.00
520268	(67)	Rejoice O Earth	FIG	16.00
525278	(126)	Tubby's First Christmas	FIG	10.00
525286	(127)	It's A Perfect Boy	FIG	17.00
528137	(350)	Have I Got News For You	FIG	16.00
530492	(643)	Happy Birthday Jesus	FIG	20.00

CHRISTMAS GENERAL:

E-0514	(30)	Mother Sew Dear	ORN	$ 16.00
E-0516	(33)	The Purr-fect Grandma	ORN	16.00
E-2829	(169)	I'm Sending You A White Christmas	FIG	50.00
12416	(246)	Have A Heavenly Christmas	ORN	17.50
102377	(237)	Trust And Obey	ORN	16.00
102385	(281)	Love Rescued Me	ORN	16.00
102407	(282)	Angel Of Mercy	ORN	16.00
109231	(355)	The Greatest Gift Is A Friend	FIG	37.50
109800	(423)	Meowie Christmas	FIG	35.00
109819	(361)	Oh What Fun It Is To Ride	FIG	110.00
110116	(429)	December Calendar Girl	FIG	35.00
111163	(430)	'Tis The Season	FIG	35.00
112356	(161)	You Have Touched So Many Hearts	ORN	16.00
112364	(250)	Waddle I Do Without You	ORN	16.00
112380	(220)	He Cleansed My Soul	ORN	16.00
113956	(214)	To My Forever Friend	ORN	17.50
521507	(475)	The Light Of The World Is Jesus	MUS	70.00
521914	(674)	Perfect Harmony	FIG	55.00
522058	(675)	Now I Lay Me Down To Sleep	FIG	30.00
522082	(553)	May Your World Be Trimmed With Joy	FIG	55.00
522120	(478)	Wishing You A Very Successful Season	FIG	70.00

TRIMMING

CHRISTMAS GENERAL continued:

522317	(438)	Merry Christmas, Deer	FIG	$ 60.00
522910	(5)	Make A Joyful Noise	ORN	16.00
522929	(8)	Love One Another	ORN	17.50
522937	(219)	Friends Never Drift Apart	ORN	17.50
524131	(555)	Good Friends Are For Always	ORN	16.00
524476	(673)	God Cared Enough To Send His Best	FIG	50.00
524913	(515)	We're Going To Miss You	FIG	50.00
524921	(557)	Angels We Have Heard On High	FIG	65.00
525332	(582)	Lord Keep Me On My Toes	ORN	16.00
525898	(583)	Ring Those Christmas Bells	FIG	95.00
527211	(429)	Share In The Warmth Of Christmas	ORN	16.00
527327	(680)	Onward Christmas Soldiers	ORN	16.00
527378	(598)	You Are My Favorite Star	FIG	60.00
527580	(633)	Tied Up For The Holidays	FIG	40.00
527599	(634)	Bringing You A Merry Christmas	FIG	45.00
527629	(605)	Wishing You A Ho Ho Ho	FIG	40.00
528218	(681)	Sending You A White Christmas	ORN	16.00
528226	(679)	Bringing You A Merry Christmas	ORN	16.00
528846	(581)	It's So Uplifting To Have A Friend Like You	ORN	16.00
529206	**(684)**	**Our First Christmas Together**	**ORN**	**18.50**
530255	**(686)**	**Baby's First Christmas**	**ORN**	**16.00**
530263	**(685)**	**Baby's First Christmas**	**ORN**	**16.00**
530387	**(672)**	**You're As Pretty As A Christmas Tree**	**ORN**	**30.00**
530395			**ORN**	**16.00**
530409			**PLT**	**50.00**
530425			**FIG**	**27.50**
604216			**BELL**	**27.50**
530972	**(682)**	**You Are Always In My Heart**	**ORN**	**16.00**
531952	(678)	Dropping In For The Holidays	FIG	40.00

DIAGRAMMING THE BIRTHDAY COLLECTION

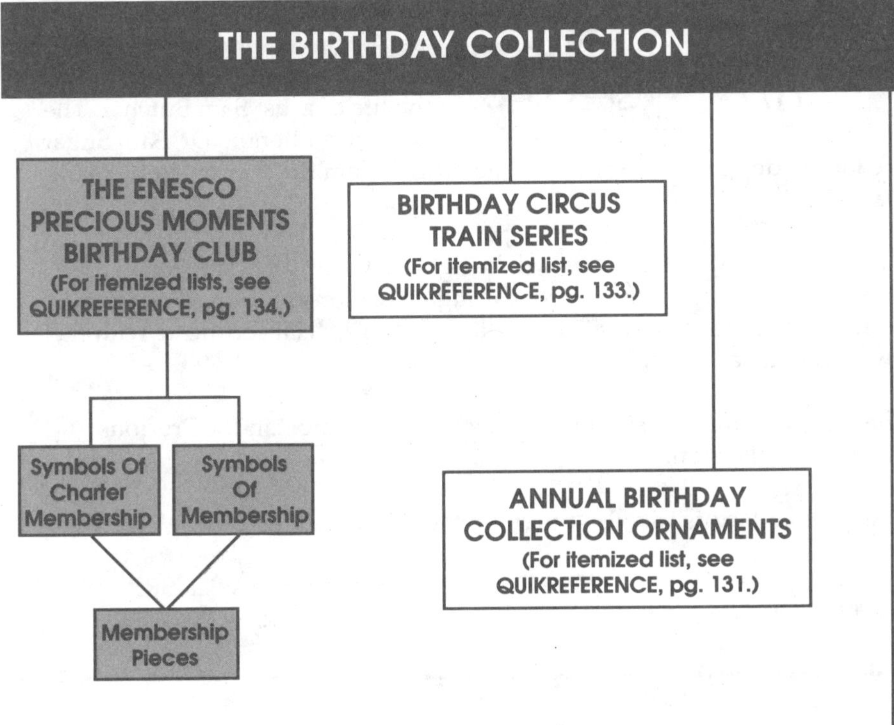

NOTE:
Only pieces in shaded areas require Birthday Club Membership!

ADDITIONAL PIECES

104418	Friends To The End
105945	Showers Of Blessings
105953	Brighten Someone's Day
521175	Hello World!
521671	Hope You're Over The Hump
522260	To Be With You Is Uplifting
524484	Not A Creature Was Stirring
524492	Can't Be Without You
524506	Oinky Birthday
526924	How Can I Ever Forget You
527270	Let's Be Friends
527343	Happy Birdie
527769	I Only Have Arms For You

In SUGAR TOWN every building, person, accessory, and ornament will have, or be part of, a story related to the life of artist Sam Butcher. The name itself honors Dr. Sam Sugar, the family doctor who assisted in the birth of Sam Butcher on New Year's Day 1939.

All SUGAR TOWN buildings will be lighted. Collectors can become honorary citizens of Sugar Town through a response card packed with each building. Honorary citizens will receive a special certificate with their own personal address.

The figurines are on a slightly smaller scale than most in the Precious Moments Collection.

This year collectors can also purchase the following packages:

- #529281, 1994 Scene,7-Piece Doctor's Office Collector's Set, SRP $189.00.
- #770272, Accessory Enhancements, 7-Piece Prepack, SRP $70.00.

SUGAR TOWN QUIKREFERENCE

ANNUALS

529567	1992	Sam Butcher with Sign Figurine
529842	1993	Sam Butcher with Sign Figurine
530484	1993	Sugar Town Chapel Ornament
529788	1994	Stork with Baby Sam Figurine
530468	1994	Sam's House Ornament

SUGAR TOWN ALPHABETICAL INDEX

BUILDINGS

PEOPLE

ACCESSORIES

ORNAMENTS

SUGAR TOWN BUILDINGS

STB-1

CHAPEL NIGHT LIGHT
Country church with bow trimmed garlands. Belltower with heart shaped windows. Snow on roof. The Chapel represents Sam Butcher's faith and commitment.

STB-2

HOUSE NIGHT LIGHT
L-Shaped house with snow-filled flower boxes, welcome mat, and half circle window with heart. The scene shares the joy of celebrating Christmas at home.

STB-3

DOCTOR'S OFFICE NIGHT LIGHT
Office for Dr. Sugar.

STB-4

SUGAR TOWN SQUARE CLOCK
Toy and candy stores with clock, figure of a caroler.

ART CHART #	INTRO DATE & NAME	ITEM #	SIZE	SET?	!	MARKET STATUS	ORIG SRP	CURRENT SRP
	NOTES							
STB-1	1992 **CHAPEL NIGHT LIGHT**	529621	8.00"	No	✓	Open	$ 85.00	$ 85.00
	'92 G Clef @ $100.00; '93 Butterfly; '94 Trumpet. Response card to receive personalized "Honorary Citizenship Certificate."							
STB-2	1993 **HOUSE NIGHT LIGHT**	529605	5.00"	No	✓	Open	80.00	80.00
	'93 Butterfly @ $90.00; '94 Trumpet. Response card to receive personalized "Honorary Citizenship Certificate."							
STB-3	1994 **DOCTOR'S OFFICE N'LIGHT**	529869	7.00"	No	✓	Open	80.00	80.00
	'94 Trumpet. Response card to receive personalized "Honorary Citizenship Certificate."							
STB-4	1994 **SUGAR TOWN SQUARE CLOCK**	532908	7.50"	No		Open	80.00	80.00
	'94 Trumpet. Not dimensional like buildings, works as stand-alone piece as well.							

SUGAR TOWN PEOPLE . . .

STP-1 **AUNT RUTH & AUNT DOROTHY** Two little girls singing carols from songbook.	STP-2 **PHILIP** Little boy caroller snug in hat, earmuffs, and scarf singing from upside-down songbook.	STP-3 **GRANDFATHER** Preacher kneels and prays.	STP-4 **SAM BUTCHER** Sam, as young man, painting Village Welcome Sign.
STP-5 **SAMMY** Boy ready to throw snowballs.	STP-6 **DUSTY** Boy carrying house and tree decorations.	STP-7 **KATYLYNNE** Girl with snowman.	STP-8 **SAM BUTCHER** Sam, as young man, holding candy cane standing by town sign.

ART CHART #	INTRO DATE & NAME	ITEM #	SIZE	SET?	(symbol)	MARKET STATUS	ORIG SRP	CURRENT SRP
	NOTES							
STP-1	1992 **AUNT RUTH & AUNT DOROTHY**	529486	3.00"	No		Open	$ 20.00	$ 20.00
	'92 G Clef @ $27.00; '93 Butterfly; '94 Trumpet.							
STP-2	1992 **PHILIP**	529494	3.00"	No		Open	17.00	17.00
	'92 G Clef @ $25.00; '93 Butterfly; '94 Trumpet.							
STP-3	1992 **GRANDFATHER**	529516	2.50"	No		Open	15.00	15.00
	'92 G Clef @ $22.00; '93 Butterfly; '94 Trumpet.							
STP-4	1992 **SAM BUTCHER**	529567	3.25"	No		Annual	22.50	-----
	'92 G Clef @ $55.00. Sign reads: "Established 1992. Population 5 and Growing."							
STP-5	1993 **SAMMY**	528668	3.00"	No		Open	17.00	17.00
	'93 Butterfly @ $22.00; '94 Trumpet.							
STP-6	1993 **DUSTY**	529435	3.25"	No		Open	17.00	17.00
	'93 Butterfly @ $22.00; '94 Trumpet.							
STP-7	1993 **KATY LYNNE**	529524	3.50"	No		Open	20.00	20.00
	'93 Butterfly @ $25.00; '94 Trumpet.							
STP-8	1993 **SAM BUTCHER**	529842	3.25"	No		Annual	22.50	-----
	'93 Butterfly @ $40.00. Sign reads: "This Way to Sugar Town. Population 9 and Growing."							

. . . SUGAR TOWN PEOPLE

STP-9	STP-10	STP-11	STP-12
STORK WITH BABY SAM Stork holds Sam and birth announcement town sign.	**MR. & MRS. BUTCHER** Sam's father and mother just before his birth.	**JAN** Girl nurse.	**DR. SAM SUGAR** Dr. Sugar raises hand in greeting.

ART CHART #	INTRO DATE & NAME	ITEM #	SIZE	SET?	!	MARKET STATUS	ORIG SRP	CURRENT SRP
	NOTES							
STP-9	1994 **STORK WITH BABY SAM**	529788	4.50"	No		Annual	$ 22.50	$ 22.50
	'94 Trumpet. Sign reads, "It's a Boy. Population 13 + 1 and Growing."							
STP-10	1994 **MR. & MRS. BUTCHER**	529818	4.75"	No		Open	20.00	20.00
	'94 Trumpet.							
STP-11	1994 **JAN**	529826	4.75"	No		Open	17.00	17.00
	'94 Trumpet.							
STP-12	1994 **DR. SAM SUGAR**	529850	4.50"	No		Open	17.00	17.00
	'94 Trumpet.							

SUGAR TOWN ACCESSORIES . . .

STA-1

EVERGREEN TREE
Evergreen tree decorated with garlands, ornaments, and large star as tree topper.

STA-2

NATIVITY
Creche depicts Holy Family - Joseph, Mary, and Baby Jesus in manger.

STA-3

CAR
Tree tied to roof of car, pup peeking out of window.

STA-4

FENCE
Post on board fence section makes perch for bluebird.

STA-5

Christmas Puppies FREE

FREE CHRISTMAS PUPPIES
Pups in a basket.

STA-6

LAMP POST
Lamp post decorated with bow.

STA-7

MAILBOX
House curbside mailbox.

STA-8

CURVED ROAD
Curved roadway for cars.

ART CHART #	INTRO DATE & NAME	ITEM #	SIZE	SET?	!	MARKET STATUS	ORIG SRP	CURRENT SRP
	NOTES							
STA-1	1992 **EVERGREEN TREE**	528684	4.25"	No		Open	$ 15.00	$ 15.00
	'92 G Clef @ $22.00; '93 Butterfly; '94 Trumpet.							
STA-2	1992 **NATIVITY**	529508	2.00"	No		Open	20.00	20.00
	'92 G Clef @ $25.00; '93 Butterfly; '94 Trumpet.							
STA-3	1993 **CAR**	529443	3.50"	No		Open	22.50	22.50
	'93 Butterfly @ $27.00; '94 Trumpet.							
STA-4	1993 **FENCE**	529796	2.00"	No		Open	10.00	10.00
	'93 Butterfly @ $15.00; '94 Trumpet.							
STA-5	1994 **FREE CHRISTMAS PUPPIES**	528064	2.50"	No		Open	12.50	12.50
	'94 Trumpet.							
STA-6	1994 **LAMP POST**	529559	5.25"	No		Open	8.00	8.00
	'94 Trumpet.							
STA-7	1994 **MAILBOX**	531847	3.00"	No		Open	5.00	5.00
	'94 Trumpet.							
STA-8	1994 **CURVED ROAD**	533149	7.25"	No		Open	10.00	10.00
	'94 Trumpet.							

. . . SUGAR TOWN ACCESSORIES

STA-9	STA-10	STA-11	STA-12
STRAIGHT SIDEWALK People walkway.	**SUGAR AND HER DOG HOUSE** Mother dog, Sugar, with her dog house.	**SINGLE TREE** Decorated evergreen tree.	**DOUBLE TREE** Double trees decorated for holidays.
STA-13 **COBBLE STONE BRIDGE** Bunny peeks from cobble stone bridge.			

ART CHART #	INTRO DATE & NAME	ITEM #	SIZE	SET?	!	MARKET STATUS	ORIG SRP	CURRENT SRP
	NOTES							
STA-9	1994 **STRAIGHT SIDEWALK**	533157	7.25"	No		Open	$ 10.00	$ 10.00
	'94 Trumpet.							
STA-10	1994 **SUGAR AND HER DOG HOUSE**	533165	3.00"	Set of 2		Open	20.00	20.00
	'94 Trumpet.							
STA-11	1994 **SINGLE TREE**	533173	4.25"	No		Open	10.00	10.00
	'94 Trumpet.							
STA-12	1994 **DOUBLE TREE**	533181	4.00"	No		Open	10.00	10.00
	'94 Trumpet.							
STA-13	1994 **COBBLE STONE BRIDGE**	533203	3.25"	No		Open	17.00	17.00
	'94 Trumpet.							

SUGAR TOWN ORNAMENTS

STO-1

CHAPEL ORNAMENT
Sam waving outside Chapel.

STO-2

SAM'S HOUSE ORNAMENT
Sam stands outside his house.

ART CHART #	NAME	ITEM #	SIZE	SET?	💡	MARKET STATUS	ORIG SRP	CURRENT SRP
	NOTES							
STO-1	1993 **CHAPEL ORNAMENT**	530484	2.75"	No		Annual	$17.50	-----
	'93 Butterfly @ $35.00.							
STO-2	1994 **SAM'S HOUSE ORNAMENT**	530468	3.00"	No	✓	Annual	17.50	$17.50
	'94 Trumpet. May be lighted by placing a miniature Christmas light into opening on bottom.							

ASK THE PRECIOUS MOMENTS HISTORIAN

"What about saving boxes and paperwork?"

In the early days of the Precious Moments Collection, many retailers did not keep the old cardboard and black and white boxes for the pieces, but sent figurines home packed in their own gift boxes. It is not unusual for "No Mark" figurines to be missing their boxes. Now most collectors save the boxes for their figurines, and as a general rule, pieces without their boxes sell for less.

If you're running out of storage space for the boxes, you can easily collapse the boxes by popping out the bottoms. You'll find you can store your boxes in a lot less space. Recycle the bubble wrap and styrofoam.

When the Collection was first introduced, figurines were shipped with a gold foil hang tag, and in 1981, with the introduction of the Precious Moments Collectors Club, boxes were shipped with the tag and with a club promotional sheet with membership application. In 1983, the tent tag with the line art and title of the figurine was added. Some collectors are very insistent on having all the paperwork with the piece, but you must understand the sequence in which the various forms of paperwork appeared -- there were no tent tags shipped with No Mark, Triangle, Hourglass and some Fish marked pieces.

Some of the collectibles also have a Certificate of Authenticity included with them, and I feel that if any piece of paper were considered to be important, it would be this one.

However, there is no secondary market value associated with the paperwork included in the boxes. I personally don't keep any of the paperwork other than the Certificate Of Authenticity for my collection. In my opinion, the Club applications expire each year, the hang tags are very dangerous to leave on your figurines. I've seen figurines wearing these tags get tangled up, fall, and break -- more than a time or two -- and I have never displayed the tent tags. I've been hoping that someday, Enesco will release a complete set of tent tags for the Collection on a nice paper -- and without the line art. I would use these, so those who look at my collection can see the title of the piece and have a greater appreciation of the figurine by reading its inspirational message. One interesting note regarding boxes and paperwork is the fact that during the floods of the summer of 1993 in the Midwest, many collectors lost the boxes for their figurines, although the porcelain was unharmed. They found that when they submitted insurance claims for the boxes and paperwork, the insurance companies refused to pay for the boxes, stating that the paper was a perishable product and that it was not considered insurable by the company -- in essence, the insurance company did not include the cardboard box and tags in assessing the value of the collectible.

An additional comment regarding paperwork and boxes ... in over 16 years of collecting, and making many purchases on the secondary market, I have NEVER passed up a figurine I really wanted because it was missing the box. Although I prefer to have the boxes for my pieces, I collect Precious Moments porcelains, not cardboard boxes!

Bunnies	#530123	TT-5
Elephants	#530131	TT-6
Giraffes	#530115	TT-4
Llamas	#531375	TT-7
Noah, His Wife & Ark	#530042	TT-1
Pigs	#530085	TT-3
Sheep	#230077	TT-2

Also available:
#530948, 8 Piece Collector's Set, SRP $190.00
(includes all but the Llamas)

TWO BY TWO

TT-1
NOAH, HIS WIFE & ARK
Noah & wife welcome animals to ark.

TT-2
SHEEP
Girl & boy sheep.

TT-3
PIGS
Girl and boy pigs.

TT-4
GIRAFFES
Girl and boy giraffes.

TT-5
BUNNIES
Girl and boy bunnies with carrot.

TT-6
ELEPHANTS
Girl and boy elephants with entwined trunks.

TT-7
LLAMAS
Girl and boy llamas.

ART CHART #	INTRO DATE & NAME	ITEM #	SIZE	SET?	!	MARKET STATUS	ORIG SRP	CURRENT SRP
	NOTES							
TT-1	**1993 NOAH, HIS WIFE AND ARK**	530042	1.68 - 5.00"	Set of 3	✓	Open	$125.00	$125.00
	'93 Butterfly; '94 Trumpet. Ark animals include two chickens, two dogs, and one bird.							
TT-2	**1993 SHEEP**	230077	1.68"	No		Open	10.00	10.00
	'93 Butterfly; '94 Trumpet.							
TT-3	**1993 PIGS**	530085	3.25"	No		Open	12.00	12.00
	'93 Butterfly; '94 Trumpet.							
TT-4	**1993 GIRAFFES**	530115	3.00"	No		Open	16.00	16.00
	'93 Butterfly; '94 Trumpet.							
TT-5	**1993 BUNNIES**	530123	1.38"	No		Open	9.00	9.00
	'93 Butterfly; '94 Trumpet.							
TT-6	**1993 ELEPHANTS**	530131	2.00"	No		Open	18.00	18.00
	'93 Butterfly; '94 Trumpet.							
TT-7	**1994 LLAMAS**	531375	2.50"	No		Open	15.00	15.00
	'94 Trumpet.							

ASK THE PRECIOUS MOMENT HISTORIAN

"What about cleaning my Precious Moments?"

First of all, I would suggest keeping your collectibles in curio cabinets, which will help immensely in keeping them clean. Personally, I have been collecting for sixteen years, and only once have I ever given the entire Collection a bath. Because I keep them all in curios, I've had very little trouble with the figurines becoming dirty.

If you do feel that you want to clean your porcelains, you must be very careful when doing so. What I have done, which works very well for me, is to prepare a container of warm water with a little bit of dish detergent -- preferably a biodegradable product and a second container is filled with warm, clear water. (Make sure your plastic is a soft plastic -- I use two large Tupperware containers -- the size that holds about 10 pounds of flour.) Dip your figurines, upside down, into the soapy water, and gently swish them back and forth, making certain that you don't bump little birds and butterflies against the sides. Then rinse them in clear water, and set them out on a soft towel to air dry. You will want to leave them out for a while because it is nearly impossible to keep water out of the figurines -- and you don't want little puddles on your nice clean curio shelves!

Plan your cleaning project over several days, depending on how much space you have to air dry your pieces. One cabinet at a time , one shelf at a time, over several days, will help prevent accidents from happening to your collectibles when they're out of their cabinets.

And NEVER, NEVER put them in the dishwasher! You wouldn't believe how many people have asked if it's okay! Ouch!

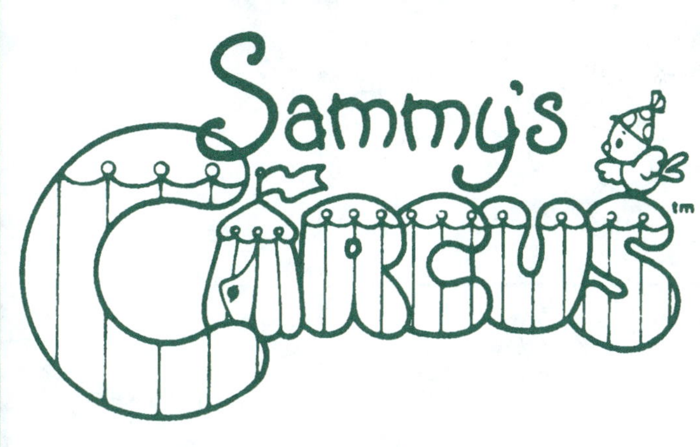

A backyard circus hosted by Sam Butcher's grandchildren and friends.

QUIKREFERENCE

DATED ANNUAL

529222 1994 Sammy

SAMMY'S CIRCUS

SC-1 **MARKIE** Girl acrobat on balance beam.	SC-2 U M **CIRCUS TENT** Monkey holds balloons at entrance to tent.	SC-3 **DUSTY** Clown prepares to shoot teddy from cannon.	SC-4 **KATIE** Girl clown juggles hearts.
SC-5 **TIPPY** Pup balances mouse on a ball with his paws.	SC-6 **COLLIN** Boy ringmaster announces acts with drum roll.	SC-7 **SAMMY** Sam hangs circus ad on fence.	

ART CHART #	INTRO DATE & NAME	ITEM #	SIZE	SET?	!	MARKET STATUS	ORIG SRP	CURRENT SRP
	NOTES							
SC-1	1994 **MARKIE**	528099	4.75"	No		Open	$ 18.50	$ 18.50
	'94 Butterfly & Trumpet.							
SC-2	1994 **CIRCUS TENT NIGHTLIGHT**	528196	6.50"	No	✓	Open	90.00	90.00
	'94 Unmarked, Butterfly, & Trumpet.							
SC-3	1994 **DUSTY**	529176	3.50"	No		Open	22.50	22.50
	'94 Butterfly & Trumpet.							
SC-4	1994 **KATIE**	529184	3.50"	No		Open	17.00	17.00
	'94 Butterfly & Trumpet.							
SC-5	1994 **TIPPY**	529192	3.00"	No		Open	12.00	12.00
	'94 Butterfly & Trumpet.							
SC-6	1994 **COLLIN**	529214	4.00"	No		Open	20.00	20.00
	'94 Butterfly & Trumpet.							
SC-7	1994 **SAMMY**	529222	3.00"	No		Annual	20.00	20.00
	Dated. '94 Butterfly & Trumpet.							

INSURANCE PREPARATION IS WORTH YOUR TIME

*What to do **before** you suffer a loss*

THE BASICS

- Maintain a complete up-to-date inventory listing of your PRECIOUS MOMENTS collectibles including the title of each piece, the Enesco Item Number, a brief description, the Annual Production Symbol, what you paid, and the current value (GREENBOOK TRUMARKET PRICE). Keep the original bill of sale, or, if it was a gift, record the name of the person who gave it to you as well as the occasion or date. If you have a one-of-a-kind piece and need a value, write to us - being sure to include a photo of the piece.

- Take photos (video or still) of your collection in its normal setting to document ownership.

- Keep copies of the inventory listing and photos in a safe deposit box or another location outside the home.

WHAT NEXT?

For an answer to this question we turned to a specialist in the field. He writes:

"The following is an attempt to answer the question of insurance for the PRECIOUS MOMENTS collector. This is meant to be an overview of the coverage forms available. Collectors should consult their agent or brokers for more detail.

A Personal Article Floater or a Fine Art Floater can be attached to a Homeowner's Policy or separately written. These forms provide protection for those items you feel warrant specific coverage.

The forms are written on an All Risk basis and customarily are not subject to a deductible. The actual underwriting can be done three different ways: Blanket, Itemized, or a combination of the two.

The Blanket form is a one limit form that covers the entire collection. In the event of a loss, the limit would apply to either the entire collection or a portion of the collection. Normally this form has a sub-limit per item, i.e. if you have a $10,000 blanket limit the maximum paid for any one item might be $2,500. In other words, the company would only pay up to $2,500 per piece, if only one piece is damaged. With the Blanket form, you should be certain the amount insured contemplates a total loss. Obviously, this form eliminated the need to list each piece specifically, but requires you to establish the value at the time of loss.

The Itemized form is more specific. A value per item is determined through appraisals, bill of sale, or for our purposes, the GREENBOOK Guide to The Enesco PRECIOUS MOMENTS Collection. Each item is then described and insured for the determined amount. Itemized lists should be updated periodically to make sure there is adequate coverage. In the event of a loss the itemized piece would be settled for the limit it is insured for. No other substantiation of value is required.

The combination of the Blanket form and the Itemized form separate out the high value pieces of the collection and losses are settled per an itemized list, with a Blanket up to $2,500 per piece for the balance.

With floaters your insurance company may consider the item to be insured as "fragile." If so, "Breakage" coverage should be included. Your insurance representative will be able to advise you - be sure to raise the question.

It is very important to insure your Fine Arts and/or Personal Articles to current value. This will ensure satisfaction at the time of loss as insurance companies pay up to the value insured and no more.

Without the above referred to coverage forms, your existing insurance policy may automatically provide protection for personal property. Generally it would be subject to a deductible with settlement on either an actual cash value basis or replacement cost basis and subject to a breakage exclusion. You should consult your agent or broker as to these details.

Please be advised that the above is an extremely broad explanation of coverage and it would be advisable to consult your agent or broker to define the coverage to your complete satisfaction."

SNEAK PEEK at *Spring 1995 Introductions ...*

RE-INTRODUCED SUSPENDED FIGURINES

100145R (Girl)
God Bless The Day We Found You
Mom, Dad & Girl Adoption
SRP...$60.00
Size...5 1/2"

100153R (Boy)
God Bless The Day We Found You
Mom, Dad & Girl Adoption
SRP...$60.00
Size...5 1/2"

127019
Love Blooms Eternal
Girl Kneeling by Cross
1995 Dated Figurine with Base
SRP...$35.00
Size...6"

128309
Dreams Really Do Come True
Girl on Rainbow Figurine
SRP...$37.50
Size...4 3/4"

520659
Wishing You A Happy Bear Hug
Bear Carries Cake with
Mouse Popping out
Birthday Series Addition
SRP...$27.50
Size...5 "

524387
Take Time To Smell The Flowers
Girl Holds Basket of Flowers Figurine
1995 Easter Seal Commemorative
SRP...$30.00
Size...6"

531065
What The World Needs Is Love
Angel with World Filled with Hearts
Figurine
SRP...$45.00
Size...5 1/2"

531146
Vaya Con Dios (To Go With God)
Hispanic Girl in Party Gown Figurine
SRP...$32.50
Size...5 1/2"

532010
Sending You Oceans Of Love
Boy by Ocean with Note in Bottle
Figurine
SRP...$35.00
Size...4 3/4"

532002
Hallelujah For The Cross
Boy with Lily & Cross Figurine
SRP...$35.00
Size...5 1/2"

532037
I Can't Bear To Let You Go
Cowgirl Lassos Bear with Rope
Figurine
SRP...$50.00
Size...5 1/4"

GLOSSARY continued

Child Evangelism Pieces -

One of Sam Butcher's first places of employment was Child Evangelism Fellowship, an organization which is dedicated to teaching children Christian principles by means of summertime programs held in the back yards of sponsoring families. The sessions include Bible stories and songs, and materials are provided by CEF for these activities. In an effort to help provide funding for CEF, Sam created two pieces of artwork which Enesco translated into porcelain, "Bring The Little Ones To Jesus" (both a plate and a figurine) and "Safe In The Arms Of Jesus." A portion of the proceeds of the sale of the figurines and plate are given to CEF to support their ministry.

Precious Moments Chapel -

Ten years ago, on a trip from a trade show in California to his home in Michigan, Sam Butcher made a stop in Joplin, Missouri -- a stop that would change his life, and the direction of his ministry through Precious Moments forever.

Sam had, for many years, harbored a dream of building a little Chapel, and adorning its walls with favorite stories and lessons from the Bible -- all illustrated with his world-famous Precious Moments children. In his travels, Sam had visited the Sistine Chapel in Rome, and had come away with the feeling that, although beautiful, it depicted God as an angry and wrathful God. Sam wanted to portray God in a different manner -- as a kind and loving Heavenly Father.

In June of 1989, the Precious Moments Chapel, located on the outskirts of Carthage, Missouri (about 12 miles from Joplin -- southwest corner of the state), opened its doors to welcome the first visitors. Now, five years later, the Chapel -- where Sam had originally planned for a parking lot to hold about 20 cars -- has welcomed nearly 2 million collectors and tourists from around the world.

The Chapel, nestled in the beautiful Ozark region of Missouri, houses over 54 huge murals, including a ceiling featuring 75 Precious Moments angels. The sanctuary contains stories from the Old and New Testaments, and the most touching mural ever created by the artist graces the front of the sanctuary. Entitled "Hallelujah Square," the mural - some 35 feet high - depicts heaven - through the eyes of a child. Galleries of stained glass windows, reputed to be among the most beautiful works in stained glass in the entire country, feature the Beatitudes and the 23rd Psalm. Many other works of art by Sam Butcher grace the walls and the surrounding property while many other ideas and plans still wait in the artist's mind for him to find the time to make them a reality.

The Precious Moments Chapel is Sam Butcher's gift to God -- a gift of thanksgiving for what the Lord has allowed him to do through Precious Moments. Admission is free, and the Chapel is open from March 1 through December 31 each year.

Precious Insights Magazine -

In honor of the 5th Anniversary of the opening of the Precious Moments Chapel, a special edition of Precious Insights Magazine was produced. It features a 40 page tour of the Chapel, complete with approximately 130 color photos of the Chapel murals. This special edition is available only by special order from Precious Insights Magazine at $12 per copy (postage included).

In order to keep up on the Enesco Precious Moments Collection, secondary market activity, events at and new additions to the Precious Moments Chapel, and to learn much more about collecting Precious Moments, a subscription to Precious Insights Magazine is a must. The magazine has been published since 1988. It is published six times per year -- approximately 64 pages per issue in full color -- at a subscription rate of $23.50 per year. (Other rates apply for Canadian and overseas subscriptions -- first class postage options also available.) Currently, the magazine is available by subscription or at the Precious Moments Chapel Gift Shop. To place your order, call 218-746-3108 with your Mastercard or Visa number, or Fax your order to 218-746-3109. Mail orders with your personal check or money order can be sent to:

Precious Insights Magazine
Sheryl J. Williams, Editor
P.O. Box 249
Pillager, MN 56473-0249

OTHER GUIDES FROM GREENBOOK

May 1994

Enesco Collectibles

(Includes Cherished Teddies, Memories Of Yesterday,
The Enesco Treasury Of Christmas Ornaments, Laura's Attic,
North Pole Village, Maud Humphrey Bogart and Lucy & Me)
1st Edition
ISBN 0-923628-18-5

July 1994

Department 56 Collectibles

4th Edition
ISBN 0-923628-20-7

August 1994

Hallmark Collectibles

2nd Edition
ISBN 0-923628-21-5

September 1994

Walt Disney Classics Collection

Premiere Edition
ISBN 0-923628-22-3